The Birth of the Modern NBA

The Birth of the Modern NBA
Pro Basketball in the Year of the Merger, 1949-1950

JOSH ELIAS

McFarland & Company, Inc., Publishers
Jefferson, North Carolina

All photographs are publicity shots issued by the NBA, BAA, AAU, NCAA, or Harlem Globetrotters teams except when otherwise credited.

Library of Congress Cataloguing-in-Publication Data

Names: Elias, Josh, 2000– author.
Title: The birth of the modern NBA : pro basketball in the year of the merger, 1949–1950 / Josh Elias.
Description: Jefferson, North Carolina : McFarland & Company, Inc., Publishers, 2024 | Includes bibliographical references and index.
Identifiers: LCCN 2024020120 | ISBN 9781476694177 (paperback : acid free paper) ♾
ISBN 9781476652429 (ebook)
Subjects: LCSH: National Basketball Association—History. | Basketball—United States—History.
Classification: LCC GV885.515.N38 E56 2024 | DDC 796.323/6406—dc23/eng/20240502
LC record available at https://lccn.loc.gov/2024020120

British Library cataloguing data are available

ISBN (print) 978-1-4766-9417-7
ISBN (ebook) 978-1-4766-5242-9

© 2024 Josh Elias. All rights reserved

*No part of this book may be reproduced or transmitted in any form
or by any means, electronic or mechanical, including photocopying
or recording, or by any information storage and retrieval system,
without permission in writing from the publisher.*

Front cover image: Minneapolis Lakers point guard Slater Martin (TSN Archives)

Printed in the United States of America

McFarland & Company, Inc., Publishers
Box 611, Jefferson, North Carolina 28640
www.mcfarlandpub.com

Table of Contents

Preface   1

1. The First Game, the Merger, and No Possible Chance Agreement   3
2. Origins, Naismith, and a Childhood Game Called Duck on a Rock   23
3. Ferris, Duffey, and the Undertaker for the Underworld   40
4. Black Basketball, the New York Renaissance, and Sidat-Singh Is Not a Hindu   61
5. Trade Season, the BAA, and Three-and-a-Half-Million Dollars   82
6. The Celtics, the New Year, and You Just Can't Play Basketball with Glasses On   101
7. The Minor League Debate, the Future of the League, and Is President Podoloff Doing a Good Job?   118
8. Sales and Trades, the Playoff Picture Takes Shape, and Are Coaches People?   130
9. Baltimore vs. Boston vs. Philadelphia, a Crowd of Just 700, and King Fulks   142
10. The Playoffs   156
11. The Finals   172
12. Expulsion and Integration   185

Chapter Notes   211
Bibliography   223
Index   233

Preface

It's only natural for the allure of the present to stand above all else. Certainly, the way human memory works plays a significant role in that phenomenon. I can recall, with great ease, what I ate for breakfast this morning, who the most recent person I spoke with was and what we discussed, and whether or not yesterday it rained or the sun shone—whereas far less mundane things that took place weeks, months or years ago are called forth only with great effort, and then with details grown hazy or even misremembered. Similarly, past generations of the NBA are recalled either nostalgically or not at all the further back one goes. That's especially the case with the very beginning. As of this writing, less than one-tenth of the world's current population was alive in 1949, at the start of the NBA's first season. Add to that fact pro basketball's then-narrow appeal and the result is that vanishingly few people remember the people and events of the time.

My aim for this book, then, is to bring those early days back to life—to provide in-depth analysis of key games, players, and the cultural backdrop of the 1949–50 season. I will range chronologically from the merger that brought together the dueling elements of the East Coast's BAA and the Midwest's NBL the prior summer to the reckoning that would result in professional basketball's permanent integration following the season. Along the way, the reader will encounter a whole host of characters, such as the owner who used to be a mafioso and the player who only agreed to join the Celtics because he was allowed to play the accordion at halftime.

1

The First Game, the Merger, and No Possible Chance Agreement

The National Basketball Association (NBA) came into existence on August 3, 1949, when the large-market, East Coast–based Basketball Association of America (BAA) and the small-market but better established, primarily Midwestern-based National Basketball League (NBL) officially signed papers to merge the two leagues into one.[1] Maurice Podoloff, a Russian-born Jewish lawyer who had been president of the BAA for all three years of its existence, was named the inaugural NBA president. Ten of the BAA's 12 teams—the Baltimore Bullets, Boston Celtics, Chicago Stags, Fort Wayne Pistons, Minneapolis Lakers, New York Knicks, Philadelphia Warriors, Rochester Royals, St. Louis Bombers, and Washington Capitols—made the transition over to the NBA. They were joined by six of the nine NBL teams: the Anderson Packers, Denver Nuggets, Sheboygan Redskins, Syracuse Nationals, Tri-Cities Blackhawks, and Waterloo Hawks, as well as one previously NBL-bound expansion team, the Indianapolis Olympians.

A ticket to the first-ever NBA game cost $1.25 plus tax. It was played on October 29, 1949, in Moline, Illinois, between the Tri-Cities Blackhawks and the Denver Nuggets. The Blackhawks' Wharton Field House was just over half full, with approximately 3,450 fans attending to witness history as the Blackhawks beat Denver 93–85 in the 6,000-seat arena. The Nuggets had trailed by only a point at 83–82 with four minutes and 31 seconds left, but consecutive baskets from guards Whitey Von Nieda, Dee Gibson, Dike Eddleman, and Gene Berce without response put Tri-Cities in position to win comfortably.[2]

The NBA doesn't recognize this as the date of the first NBA game, though. According to the league itself, the first NBA game happened three years prior, on November 1, 1946, when the New York Knicks won 66–64 against the Toronto Huskies to open the first season of the BAA in front of 7,090 fans—more than twice as many as the first game post-merger. As a publicity stunt, the Huskies offered free admission to anyone taller than 6'8" center George Nostrand. Ossie Schectman of the Knicks, highly regarded ever since he had led Long Island University to an undefeated season and two national championships between 1939 and 1941, scored the first basket with a fast-break layup. Schectman, then, is officially recognized as the scorer of the first points in NBA history.

The NBA's official claim that the BAA is part of its history, rather than preceding it, is factually questionable. The NBA was advertised as a "newly-formed" league in 1949, and media guides for the 1949–50 and 1950–51 seasons refer to it as entering its first and second seasons.³ A new organizational constitution was drawn up and new rules sent out to each organization and each referee.⁴ Each of these facts point toward the BAA and NBL both having been precursors to the NBA, as opposed to the BAA having already been the NBA, as league authorities allege.

The first step the NBA explicitly took toward establishing the three years of BAA basketball as the first three of NBA history wasn't until a year later, when news reports began to refer to Joe Fulks' 63-point BAA record as an NBA record. The league did more explicitly at the 1952 NBA All-Star Game.⁵ During halftime, there was a ceremony during which Podoloff recognized all of the players who had been in the league every year since 1946–47, the year the BAA had been founded.⁶ The players recognized in the ceremony included former BAA players Joe Fulks, Max Zaslofsky, and Fred Scolari, but did not include George Mikan, Bob Davies, or Arnie Risen, all of whom had been playing in the NBL during the BAA's first season.

The NBA today recognizes the BAA as the same entity as itself while refusing to acknowledge the NBL as a direct part of its history, officially referring to the BAA–NBL merger as an expansion of the BAA accompanied by a name change. From how the league was marketed in the lead-up to and during the 1949–50 NBA season, all signs point to that being incorrect. It could feasibly be argued, given that only two of the former NBL teams lasted in the NBA longer than a single season, that it was a failed merger, but it is the case that it was, in fact, a merger.

With that established, it follows that Ossie Schectman did not score the first points in NBA history. At the same time, it makes him no less consequential than if he had. After all, Schectman still scored the first points in BAA history for the Knicks, and it is the case that the NBA wouldn't be what it is today without the BAA there to precede it alongside the latter seasons of the NBL. We also have no historical record as to who among the Nuggets' or Blackhawks' rosters was the first scorer post-merger, while there is video of Schectman's famous bucket, which makes it even easier to perpetuate the idea that Schectman is the correct answer to this particular piece of sports trivia.

Schectman continued to play a significant role for the New York Knicks team throughout the rest of the 1946–47 season. It's no small matter that the Knicks were a heavily Jewish team upon their organization, particularly so soon after the end of World War II, or that Schectman and his New York costar, Sonny Hertzberg, were both Jews with at least one Russian-born parent who had come to the United States from Russia to escape rampant and systemic anti–Semitism in their home country. It quickly became glaringly clear, though, that this was less of an intentional decision by Knicks founder Ned Irish than it was geographical coincidence, purely a reflection of the demographics of mid–twentieth-century New York itself.

Schectman had played for the all–Jewish Philadelphia Sphas for five seasons before joining the BAA. The Sphas were named after the South Philadelphia Hebrew Association and spent much of their early days without a stadium of their own, leading to the self-coined nickname of the Wandering Jews, and going so far as to often include Hebrew script or the Star of David on their jerseys.

The Knicks' upper management in 1947 did not handle things quite as well. In the wake of constant anti–Semitic heckling, Irish and Knicks coach Neil Cohalan made the decision to quickly disband the Knicks' original cultural core. By the BAA's second season, only Hertzberg, Stan Stutz, and Leo Gottlieb remained on the roster of the original eight Jewish players. None of them would last past that year.⁷

While the Knicks' shared Jewish roots provided a basis for camaraderie prior to their dismantling, incidents of racism directed toward Jews were not uncommon in the league. The most notable such incident revolved around the league-worst Pittsburgh Ironmen.

The Ironmen were coached by Paul Birch, who had just reached the tail end of a very successful playing career as a defensive specialist with a capable long-range shot, in which he was an All-NBL player, a two-time NBL champion with the Fort Wayne Zollners, and the first Duquesne University basketball player ever to be named to a National Collegiate Athletic Association (NCAA) All-American team.

It was that last accomplishment that earned him the job, as he was regarded in a very high light in Pittsburgh, having been the first true star of a golden generation of Duquesne players that would include five more All-Americans over the next six years. Having just finished his first season in coaching as player-coach for the NBL's Youngstown Bears, he was the natural choice for the team based so close to where his career began.

Paul Birch faced a unique challenge in assembling his inaugural Pittsburgh Ironmen team: while most charter teams had some sort of pipeline of top college talent to choose from, Birch had to rely on his own recruiting skills due to Duquesne's absence from college basketball during the war. He centered his team around players with one of three general backgrounds: experienced players who'd carved out successful professional careers for themselves after playing for Duquesne in the 1930s or early 1940s, teammates from the 1945–46 Youngstown Bears, and returning World War II veterans whose college careers had been cut short by their military service.

Moe Becker was the one player on the roster who was all three. A star for Duquesne around the turn of the previous decade, Becker had his college career cut short a year early, right after an All-American First Team season in his own right, by the first of four years serving in the U.S. Army. In the first year after his service ended, he joined Birch's team in Youngstown and quickly established himself as one of the better players on the team. By the end of the year, Becker averaged 9.0 points, the third most on the Bears. Coming into the summer, he was already set to join a BAA team—the Chicago Stags—but Birch made him one of his top targets and eventually convinced him to make the move east with him to Pittsburgh instead.

Birch had a reputation in his playing days as a dirty player, foulmouthed, and an obsessive perfectionist. As a coach, and particularly coaching a losing team in Pittsburgh, he devolved into a tyrant who was infamous for screaming at his players after every missed shot; throwing basketballs at their heads in practice; launching chairs at them in the locker rooms at halftime; wandering onto the court in the middle of games trying to trip fast-breaking opponents who were close enough to the sideline; and punching his players, opposing players, opposing coaches, and referees in repeated instances.

He took even the smallest mistake as a personal insult. In one early-season away game against the Cleveland Rebels, 5'11" shooting guard Mel Riebe was hitting shot after shot against Pittsburgh to inspire a Cleveland comeback. Riebe ended up with 20 points in a two-point win for the Rebels, but not before Birch ran onto the court and socked him upside the head. The Cleveland crowd, naturally, was not happy and many fans attempted to storm the court to attack him. Birch went back over to his players begging for backup, which he got from precisely zero of them.

A week later, Pittsburgh faced off against the Washington Capitols, who were off to a thrilling start to the season. With the best defense in the league and a 17-game winning streak, Washington had a reputation for slowing down games and playing with extreme physicality, led by point guard Fred Scolari and power forward Bones McKinney. All of those things combined to make Washington the perfect team to ignite a firestorm of anger from Birch.

This particular firestorm wasn't directed at either his players or at Scolari or McKinney, both of whom had relatively bad games that day. It was directed at Irv Torgoff, Washington's slinky sixth man who was losing defenders left and right and drawing fouls all game long en route to 10 points off the bench.

Torgoff was also a Jew from New York who had spent most of his playing career up until that year as a costar of Ossie Schectman on the Philadelphia Sphas. He was a son of immigrants who had fled to America to avoid persecution in Russia after a series of pogroms throughout the country had left thousands of Russian Jews dead. His older brother Leo was killed in battle in 1937 by the fascist Spanish Nationalist forces during the Battle of Jarama.

As the game came to a close and it became apparent that Washington was going to walk away with the win, Birch had some choice words for Torgoff.

Particularly, the word "kike."

Torgoff, outraged, yelled back at him and they came to blows. Birch was kicked out of the game and had to wait in the Ironmen's locker room until after the final whistle before he could learn that Washington had finished the job and ended with a 49–40 win.

Once the Ironmen got back to the locker room, Pittsburgh's starting shooting guard, Moe Becker, was prepared to unleash his own fit of rage at his coach for the anti–Semitic slur. Becker was one of Birch's biggest targets of abuse as he struggled with his performance on the court during the early season. He also, like Torgoff, was a second-generation Russo-Jewish immigrant born and raised in New York City, so he took offense at the language not just on moral terms, but also personally. He found himself furious enough that he had to be restrained by two of his teammates from physically confronting Birch. When teammate Stan Noszka tried to calm him down by saying that the coach didn't mean it in an anti–Semitic way, Becker took it as a sign that Noszka was siding with the coach and started throwing punches at him. As teammates begged Birch to break the two up, the coach instead sat back in his chair and remarked, "Let the Jew take care of himself."[8]

Coming into the 1949–50 season, the new league planned to model its structure after Major League Baseball (MLB)'s setup of two separate leagues within a parent competition. Similar to baseball's National League and American League, the NBA would consist of a National Division made up of former NBL teams and an American Division made up of former BAA teams, each division comprising a West and East section. Every American Division team was scheduled to play every other team six times in addition to two matchups against every National Division team, for a grand total of 70 games, while National Division teams were all to play against each other seven times in addition to the two-game home-and-home series against their American Division rivals for a sum total of 69 games played.[9]

The American Division East included the Baltimore Bullets, Boston Celtics, New York Knicks, Philadelphia Warriors, and Washington Capitols.

The American Division West included the Chicago Stags, Fort Wayne Pistons, Minneapolis Lakers, Rochester Royals, and St. Louis Bombers.

The National Division East included the Anderson Packers, Indianapolis Olympians, Sheboygan Redskins, and Syracuse Nationals.

The National Division West included the Denver Nuggets, Milwaukee All-Stars, Tri-Cities Blackhawks, and Waterloo Hawks.

The Milwaukee All-Stars never played a game in the NBA. They also never played a game in Milwaukee.

One of the oldest and best-established teams involved in the merger, the All-Stars' story began 20 years earlier, in 1929, when a seed distributor named Lon Darling, desperate to find something to do during the offseason of seed work, founded a barnstorming basketball team based out of his hometown of Oshkosh, Wisconsin, at the suggestion of a friend. The Oshkosh All-Stars, as they came to be known, traveled throughout Wisconsin and gained a passionate following over the next few years.

In 1937, Oshkosh faced off against the New York Renaissance, an all-black basketball team widely considered the best in the world, in a five-game series dubbed the "World Series of Basketball." The Renaissance, featuring star players Tarzan Cooper and Willie Smith, won three out of five games, but the series was so successful that it was extended to seven games. The All-Stars won the final two and with them, the unofficial title of world champions.

Two years after their first meeting, the All-Stars and the Renaissance met up again in the final series of the newly created World Professional Basketball Tournament (WPBT), a tournament in Chicago which had been created to host the best basketball teams in the country regardless of whether they were in an organized league or not. The WPBT's creation was directly inspired by the success of the series between the All-Stars and the Renaissance.

After the two quickly disposed of opposing teams such as the Harlem Globe Trotters, Sheboygan Redskins, and Original Celtics, they faced off in their second battle for the title of world champions, and the New York Renaissance defeated Oshkosh, 34–25. After the game ended and the Renaissance were proclaimed champions, rookie guard John Isaacs took a razor blade to his championship jacket that proclaimed New York the "Colored World Champions" and cut off the word "Colored," leaving behind, simply "World Champions." That was, after all, the title they had earned.[10]

In the two years between the two matchups between Oshkosh and New York, the Oshkosh All-Stars found themselves a home in the NBL as a part of a reorganization of the former Midwest Basketball Conference (MBC) alongside 10 MBC teams and two other new teams, and they excelled in the new league right out of the gate.

Oshkosh made the championship in each of the NBL's first five seasons, and won the NBL Finals in 1940–41 and 1941–42 with Leroy Edwards leading the way, but fell to the middle of the league quickly after losing three important players to the military and a fourth to professional football. By the time of the merger, things were starting to turn around again, but the team was losing money and a group of investors from Milwaukee was willing to buy the team for $80,000, a record amount for a professional basketball team.

As such, arrangements were made and the All-Stars were set to move to Milwaukee. The new investors were discouraged, though, after the team had trouble securing an arena for the team to play at, and eventually reneged on the deal, selling full ownership of the team back to Darling and moving the All-Stars back to Oshkosh. With Darling unable to pay the $7,200 fee to enter the NBA without the additional investment, the

NBA canceled Oshkosh's membership in the league on September 10, 1949, a month and a half before the start of the season.[11]

Without the All-Stars, the NBA was faced with a major scheduling problem to resolve on very short notice, with an odd number of teams in the National Division and only three in the National Division West.

The decision that the league came to in order to remedy that was to start over entirely, reluctantly abolishing the divisional setup that partially separated the former BAA and NBL teams while still attempting to disproportionately match teams up against opponents they had consistently faced off against before the merger, and creating a brand-new schedule along with it.[12]

The result was a disheveled mess of a season in which three teams played 62 games, four teams played 64 games, and the other 10 played 68 games. The league was organized into three divisions: the Eastern Division, Central Division, and Western Division. In order to keep teams from each of the former leagues scheduled mainly against other teams from the same league, the Western Division was composed entirely of the remaining former NBL teams, minus Syracuse, who was shifted over to the Eastern Division for geographical reasons.

Despite their place in the Eastern Division, though, Syracuse's schedule involved 44 games against Western Division teams compared to just 20 games against teams from the Central Division and Eastern Division combined. They received the same scheduling treatment as the teams in the Western Division in order to avoid giving them a competitive disadvantage in comparison to the other former NBL teams.

This stringent approach to keeping the leagues at least partially separated led to what was, on face value, one of the weirdest possible geographical distributions of teams between the divisions. The Minneapolis Lakers were placed in the Central Division despite being the second-westernmost team in the league and well over 250 miles west of three of the six teams placed in the Western Division. The Anderson Packers and Indianapolis Olympians were both allocated to the Western Division to play against the Denver Nuggets seven times each, while only playing twice against their intrastate adversary, the Fort Wayne Pistons of the Central Division. The Rochester Royals had four more clashes with Minneapolis, 800 miles away, than they did against Syracuse, just over 70 miles away.

The Nuggets, by far the furthest removed team from any other in the league, had the toughest schedule of all. They began with 14 consecutive away games and had additional stretches of 10 and nine straight games away from home.

Logistical nightmares notwithstanding, there was now a set schedule that accommodated a 17-team league and didn't stray too far from the general vision of the original merger details despite having one less team than was originally expected.

Seventeen franchises, split into three divisions, would play a total 557 regular season games between the dates of October 29, 1949, and March 19, 1950. The top four teams from each division would qualify for the playoffs, creating a 12-team postseason competition. Each division would host divisional semifinals and finals until only three teams were left, one from each division. The team with the best regular-season record among the remaining three teams would receive a bye and directly qualify for the NBA Finals, while the other two teams would compete in the NBA Semifinals to earn the second championship spot. All series leading up to the NBA Finals would be best-of-three, while the Finals would be best-of-seven. The winner out of the final two teams would become the first-ever NBA champion.

There's no lack of irony in the fact that the first NBA game was won by Tri-Cities, considering they just one year prior had nearly brought the merger negotiations between the BAA and NBL to a halt altogether.

The roots of turmoil between the two leagues sprung up in the summer of 1947, when the Chicago Gears left the NBL for the upstart Professional Basketball League of America (PBLA). At the start of the previous year, Chicago had acquired the services of George Mikan, a rookie center out of DePaul who had been a three-time All-American and two-time National Player of the Year during his college career.

Chicago, despite being located in the biggest market in the NBL, had been struggling to stand out in comparison to the leading teams of the mid–1940s NBL—the Sheboygan Redskins and Fort Wayne Zollners. The NBL had tried time and again to conquer the Chicago market, but hadn't managed to establish a successful team in the city.

The first attempt to set up a team in Chicago had proven successful in the short term, although not without controversy. Before the NBL had been established out of the reorganization of the MBC, the MBC included the Duffy Florals of Chicago. The MBC had nine teams in its first season and required each to play at least eight games against other MBC teams to qualify for the playoffs. The Duffy Florals only played five, with a 3–2 record, but were admitted into the playoffs anyways, taking the second spot in the MBC Western Division that the Detroit Hed-Aids rightfully earned. Chicago then defeated the Akron Firestones and the Indianapolis Kautskys in close games to win the league title.

The Duffy Florals left during the restructuring into the NBL, but major league basketball would return to Chicago in 1939, when George Halas, longtime coach and owner of the National Football League's (NFL) Chicago Bears, decided to revive the basketball team he had run in the 1920s and enter them into the NBL. For the Chicago Bruins, Halas recruited a team full of former DePaul University standouts, a pair of Second Team All-Americans in Loyola University stars Mike Novak and Wibs Kautz, and even some of his football players joined the team, but all but three of their players were gone within two years and they never retained a coach longer than one season. They never had a winning season. The team disbanded during World War II due to a lack of personnel, with Halas and most of the players leaving to serve in the military.

They were replaced by the Chicago Studebakers, who were only able to retain star center Mike Novak from the Bruins. In order to fill out the roster, the decision was made to integrate the team, and the Studebakers became the joint-first integrated NBL team alongside the Toledo White Chevrolets. They finished the season 8–15, the worst record in the condensed league, and shut down operations upon the threat of further financial and political instability as the war raged on.

The Chicago Gears were attempt number four for the NBL to establish a team in Chicago as the league began to rebuild coming into the 1944–45 season with the Allied Forces' imminent victory in the war becoming increasingly inevitable. Founded by Maurice White, owner of the American Gear Company, the Gears' first two seasons were a mixed bag, ending with 14–16 and 17–17 records, respectively.

The addition of George Mikan, who had dominated the college game at DePaul, was expected to turn around the fortunes of the Chicago Gears for the 1946–47 season. At 6'10", Mikan was three inches taller than the average NBL starting center that season and the second-tallest player in the league. Mikan was a revolutionary archetype of player in a sport that had just begun to truly recognize extraordinary height as a tactical advantage over the course of the wartime period of the sport.

However, Mikan retired seven games into his rookie season and sued White for failing to live up to their contractual agreement after White requested Mikan take a pay cut of nearly half his salary. Halfway through the season, with the team limping to a 9–12 record and firmly outside of playoff contention without him, Mikan finally rejoined the team after settling out of court with White, signing a five-year, $60,000 deal that made him the highest-paid player in professional basketball.[13]

Mikan wasn't the only major midseason acquisition for the Gears, though. The Gears also acquired Bobby McDermott, a four-time MVP for the Fort Wayne Zollners who had been waived after drunkenly assaulting teammate Milo Komenich, mere months after having been named the NBL's greatest player ever in a poll of NBL coaches.

Mikan and McDermott immediately clicked with the rest of the team, and the Gears went 17–6 in the back end of the season, securing a 26–18 record overall and sneaking into the playoffs. During the Gears' first-round playoff series against the Indianapolis Kautskys, which was marred by an incident in which Bobby McDermott lost his cool in the deciding game five after what he believed to be an incorrect foul call, slapping referee Norris Ward and subsequently punching him in the eye, resulting in a three-day suspension and $100 fine. Without McDermott, the game came down almost entirely to post battles between Mikan and Arnie Risen, and fortunately for Chicago, Mikan won that battle handily, outscoring Risen 26–9 in a win. Following that, Chicago quickly disposed of the Oshkosh All-Stars and Rochester Royals in the NBL Semifinals and Finals en route to the championship.

The Gears were never awarded a trophy for their title. Other owners throughout the league didn't like Maurice White, finding him unpredictable and hard to work with at the best of times, and instead gifted the trophy to the regular season champions, the Finals-losing Royals.[14]

Frustrated by the blatant disrespect from his colleagues, White ran for the role of NBL president that summer. The influential Indianapolis owner Frank Kautsky, particularly wary of putting White in control of league operations, nominated Fort Wayne Zollners coach and general manager Carl Bennett as an alternative and Bennett won.

Believing that the rest of the league was working against him and that, with both the biggest market and the best player in the NBL, he didn't need the other teams, White announced later that summer that he was pulling his team out of the NBL.

He would start his own league.

The PBLA was the result, a league with every team owned by White himself. The league was divided into Northern and Southern Divisions rather than the standard West/East division and recruited notable coaches and former players to serve as general managers who would run each team for him. One such general manager was Gerald Ford, who would later become the 38th President of the United States. White aimed to rival the NBL with Midwestern cities such as Omaha, St. Paul, and Grand Rapids, while also including teams from the Deep South with cities such as Atlanta, Birmingham, and Houston.

The PBLA lasted just 18 days into the season before disbanding. Profoundly high travel costs between interdivisional teams and attendance that rarely topped 1,000 made the cost of operations vastly outweigh White's profits, and he lost over $600,000 during the league's short existence. He petitioned the NBL to allow the Gears to rejoin the league, but the owners unanimously refused to take them back. In order to determine where PBLA players would play next, the NBL held a dispersal draft.[15]

Mikan ended up in Minneapolis. McDermott was sent to Sheboygan. The rest of the team was spread out across the rest of the NBL.

The BAA, which would end up losing half a million dollars in its first year of operations, opted against competing with the NBL over the players, but the situation made executives in both leagues remarkably aware that it was a future possibility.

In an effort to avoid a player war in the upcoming offseason, NBL commissioner Ward Lambert and BAA president Maurice Podoloff negotiated an agreement between the two leagues to stop players from jumping between them.

One week after the agreement was announced, the Boston Celtics were found to be courting NBL stars Bob Davies and Don Otten, which led to other teams trying to convince players to join the BAA for bigger markets and competitive contracts as well.[16] Although not many players made the move due to the NBL's larger crowds and the BAA's financial instability, those who did threatened to drain the BAA's coffers, prompting the need for a strategic reassessment.

Podoloff proposed to absorb some of the top NBL teams, so as to get the top talents and the top markets competing within the same league and establish the BAA as the premier professional basketball league. He first approached Carl Bennett of the Fort Wayne Zollners, outlining his plan: the Zollners, Minneapolis Lakers, Indianapolis Kautskys, and Rochester Royals would all join the BAA. The Lakers were in the process of transforming into the biggest and best team in basketball with the addition of Mikan, and, as such, were the crux of the deal.

Fort Wayne agreed to switch leagues. Soon after, so did Indianapolis. Next came the big fish, Minneapolis. Not wanting to be left behind in a league that was set to be a shadow of its former self, Rochester begrudgingly switched sides too. Lon Darling of the Oshkosh All-Stars applied to make the move as well, as did Toledo Jeeps owner Virgil Gladieux. They were both denied.[17]

As part of the deal struck between the two leagues' commissioners the previous offseason to prevent the leagues from warring over players, the 1948 draft would be a joint draft held by the BAA and NBL congruently with each drafting team being granted exclusive rights to sign a player. This meant if a player was drafted by an NBL team, BAA teams could not bid for his rights, and vice versa. One day before the joint draft, the Tri-Cities Blackhawks signed Murray Wier, a 5'9" red-headed All-American from the University of Iowa and a master of unorthodox, running one-handed jump shots, to a contract without alerting any other teams.

The day of the draft, May 10, 1948, both leagues held their annual meetings. In the NBL meeting, Commissioner Ward Lambert announced he was stepping down due to health reasons. That news was quickly overshadowed, though, by the announcement that Minneapolis, Rochester, Fort Wayne, and Indianapolis were resigning from the NBL to jump ship to the BAA.

With Lambert out and the NBL reeling from the loss of four of its top teams, Anderson Packers owner Ike Duffey and Tri-Cities Blackhawks co-owner Leo Ferris took over interim operations of the league, immediately pulling out of the joint draft and conducting their own separate draft, as well as ending preliminary merger negotiations that had been happening without the knowledge of the ulterior motive of the four departed teams.

Later that day, Fort Wayne drafted Wier in the 1948 BAA draft, at which point the Blackhawks publicly announced that they had already signed Wier. This angered Podoloff, having been a breach of the terms of the leagues' prior agreement. The Blackhawks argued that the BAA's prior secret negotiations with the four teams breached the good faith of the agreement, and the NBL deserved reparations for losing top players. This dispute threatened to escalate into a player war.

The two leagues held a meeting that June in an attempt to settle their differences. Podoloff hosted Duffey to once again attempt to resolve the threat of teams battling over players.

They emerged from the meeting with an agreement that players who had jumped between the leagues would be returned to their previous league, except for those on the four teams who had just switched leagues. Teams could not approach players on the reserve list of a team from the rival league until the team explicitly released the player. Additionally, neither league could expand into the other league's markets.

After Duffey walked out of the room with the two having shook hands to unofficially seal the deal, Podoloff noticed a note Duffey had written was left behind. The note—an intended telegram to be sent to the other NBL owners—stated, "Members of the Executive Board, National Basketball League: No possible chance agreement with the BAA—stop—Consider yourself free to operate as you see fit in contacting and signing any of their players—stop—Ike W. Duffey, President, NBL."

The BAA and NBL were back to out-and-out war.

Duffey declared the leagues to be at "open warfare," while Podoloff dismissed the NBL as a minor league. Despite this, the number of players moving between the leagues remained insignificant, a fact both league presidents seemed to overlook. Either way, the possibility of the two leagues merging seemed less likely than ever before.[18]

Sixteen months later, Murray Wier would come off the bench for the Blackhawks in the first post-merger NBA game.

Billy Hassett, who Wier backed up at point guard, led the Blackhawks to victory in that game over Denver 93–85 with a 15-point effort. Hassett had spent his entire professional career with Tri-Cities, except for a couple of weeks with Chicago in the ill-fated PBLA. Leading both teams in scoring was Denver's Bob Brown, entering his first full professional season after having his college career interrupted by the war and a three-year stint in the U.S. Marine Corps. Brown joined the BAA's Providence Steamrollers midway through his final collegiate season with an exemption from Maurice Podoloff and was free to sign with Denver after the Steamrollers folded.

November 1, 1949, was the second day of NBA action. The New York Knicks beat the Chicago Stags in Chicago 89–87 after overtime. The Rochester Royals outclassed the Sheboygan Redskins 108–75 in the first game between a former BAA and a former NBL team. Both Tri-Cities and Denver lost their second games of the season, as Tri-Cities fell 72–51 to a St. Louis Bombers team that flourished on the back of 21 points from point guard Johnny Logan while the Nuggets lost a relatively close game, 71–64, against the Indianapolis Olympians.

The Knicks were led to their close victory by a combined 50 points from their dynamic trio of Dick McGuire, Carl Braun, and Harry Gallatin. Braun hit three long-range shots in the final minutes of regulation, while McGuire drew a crucial foul when the Knicks were still two points down. Gallatin then tapped in McGuire's intentionally missed free throw to tie the game 78–78 with just one second left. In overtime,

McGuire got things going and the Knicks jumped to a quick five-point lead that the Stags could not overcome.[19]

Rookie point guard Dick McGuire, a product of the playgrounds of 1940s New York City, played a crucial role in his first professional game for the Knicks. Known for his flair for passing and no-look passes that often left defenders confounded, McGuire was synonymous with Rockaway Beach street ball.[20] His reputation in college was built on his ability to control the tempo of the game, and after six seasons split between St. John's, Dartmouth, and the U.S. Navy, he was drafted seventh overall by the Knicks in the 1949 BAA draft.

One of the players who had traveled to play against McGuire during the height of his street ball fame was Carl Braun, then the star of Garden City High School in Garden City, New York, and his eventual teammate on the Knicks. While Braun left Colgate University early to pursue professional baseball in the New York Yankees' farm system, his career in the two sports went in vastly different directions, with his baseball career ending due to a shoulder injury just as his basketball career was taking off. He was an immediate starter at small forward for the Knicks despite his youth, and in just his tenth professional game, Braun scored 47 points in a blowout win over a dismal Providence Steamrollers team, breaking what was then the BAA's single-game scoring record of 41. Braun would solely hold the record for just shy of a year, at which point George Mikan tied it. Mikan would then break the record in dominant fashion by surpassing that 47-point mark four separate times in the next 86 days, with the highest being 53. Braun was named All-BAA Second Team as a rookie and became the Knicks' main scoring threat for the foreseeable future.

Harry Gallatin, who hailed from the small industrial village of Roxana, Illinois, was perhaps a less natural cultural fit for the bright lights of the Knicks, but that didn't make him any less of a fan favorite than the born-and-breds. Gallatin was selected in the second round of the 1948 BAA draft following two superb years at Northeast Missouri State Teachers College. Having graduated in two years, his eligibility wasn't standard as per BAA rules, and New York had to agree with the league office to forfeit the following year's second-round pick in order to sign him, something that could've put a damper on their ongoing attempt to build a contender if it weren't for the fact that Knicks owner Ned Irish was a master of manipulating the league into letting him do whatever he wanted.

In New York, Gallatin quickly carved out a role as a sixth man, earning significant playing time due to his durability and strength as a backup center with occasional minutes at power forward and gaining the nickname "Horse," short for workhorse. In the 1949 BAA playoffs, as a rookie, he had proved himself an important player in the Eastern Division Finals against Washington despite being plagued by significant foul trouble, averaging 13.3 points and emerging as the heart of the team.

Meanwhile, the Olympians' debut win over Denver was not only a victory in their NBA introduction but also a successful start to their franchise's first-ever competitive game. Indianapolis stood out from the bunch during the merger as the lone franchise who hadn't been part of the 1948–49 lineup of either the BAA or NBL, instead set up by the NBL league office specifically with the goal of forcing the merger, as well as to replace the Indianapolis Kautskys, who had been immensely influential throughout the past decade-plus of professional basketball.

Frank Kautsky founded his basketball team within days of watching the sport for the first time in 1931. Owner of the Kautsky grocery chain, Kautsky sponsored his team with his eponymous store name, and they gained modest success in the first year with a roster of former Indiana Central College players. The dire financial conditions of the Great Depression cleverly allowed Kautsky to recruit players he might not have had the means to attract otherwise. This included a large number of former Purdue University and Butler University standouts, chief among them Purdue star Johnny Wooden.

Wooden was the most highly regarded basketball player in the world by the time he graduated from Purdue. Fresh off of becoming the tenth player ever and one of only four since 1909–10 to be named a consensus All-American three times in a row, earning National Player of the Year accolades in 1931–32 as a senior, and leading his school to a national championship, Wooden was fielding offers from the likes of the Original Celtics, who offered him $5,000 per year to join. Wooden turned them down to teach high school English at Dayton High School in Dayton, Kentucky, for $1,500.

However, Wooden lost his life savings during the financial crash and agreed to make the weekly 115-mile drive to join the Kautskys part-time on weekends to supplement his income. Led by Wooden, the Kautskys quickly ascended through the ranks of professional basketball and competed against some of the top teams in the country. In 1935, the New York Renaissance, Original Celtics, and Akron Goodyears were all victims of Indianapolis during a 15-game winning streak, and the team began to gain acclaim during a 46-game period in which Wooden made a record-breaking 138 consecutive free throws—something that's still never been done in professional basketball since.[21]

In 1935, Kautsky teamed up with Paul Sheeks, the longtime recreational director of the Firestone Tire and Rubber Company, to form the Midwest Basketball Conference (MBC), a league composed of industrial, company-sponsored teams. Sheeks served as the general manager and coach for all professional sports teams sponsored by Firestone, including basketball's Akron Firestones. The objective was to create a formal league for the existing company-sponsored teams that made up the best basketball teams in the Midwest, featuring some of the world's most talented players, many of whom worked for the companies they represented but were compensated extra for their basketball services. The Kautskys finished the first MBC season with the best record in the league at 9–3 but lost the championship, with Wooden leaving the team after only playing four games the following year.

While Kautsky partnered with Firestone, Goodyear, and General Electric to successfully refound the MBC as the NBL, establishing a professional league with mandatory salaries for players and the foundation of an increasingly nationalized audience, the Kautskys struggled without Wooden and made only one playoff appearance between 1936–37 and 1941–42. Kautsky disbanded the team for three seasons during World War II, but they returned to the NBL in the 1945–46 season with three returning players and plenty of new faces. One of those new faces was 6'9" center Arnie Risen.

Risen, who had grown up on a small, struggling tobacco farm in rural northern Kentucky, rose to prominence over a two-year term playing for Harold Olsen at Ohio State. Risen had been offered a scholarship to play for world-renowned coach Adolph Rupp at the University of Kentucky, but instead opted to stay closer to home and attend Eastern Kentucky State Teachers College before transferring to Ohio State when Eastern Kentucky shut down all of its sports programs during the escalation of the war; when he was drafted to join the war effort, Risen was told by the U.S. Army that he was too tall to serve.[22]

He led Ohio State to a Big Ten title and two consecutive Final Four appearances, but after catching pneumonia early in his senior year, he flunked out of school. Frank Kautsky offered Risen $15 per game to play for the team once he recovered, and he turned Indianapolis around from second worst in the league at 10–22 to 27–17 and the toughest playoff opponents of the Mikan-led eventual champion Chicago Gears within a single season.

However, following the tournament win, financial struggles plagued the Kautskys, leading to the sale of 49 percent ownership to Indianapolis hotelier and radio advertising executive Paul Walk. Despite the emergence of Risen as a star center, Walk struggled to keep player salaries affordable and the team continued to lose money. They got off to a rough start and, after a January loss to the Rochester Royals continued to push them toward the bottom of the league, Rochester owner Les Harrison walked up to Risen and informed him, "You're with us now." Walk had sold his star to the Royals, mid-game, for a fee of $25,000.[23] The Kautskys snuck into the playoffs without Risen. Risen and the Royals made the NBL Finals.

The summer during which the Kautskys joined the BAA included the biggest change yet for the franchise, as Frank Kautsky sold his remaining 51 percent of the team to Walk, citing Walk's "extravagant" management of the team as a chief reason for his departure.[24]

The team now known as the Indianapolis Jets struggled to adapt to the new league and their financial woes played out on the court, as the team played 25 different players and was involved in 20 different transactions over the course of the season. They finished rock bottom of the Western Division with a dismal 18–42 record and remained unprofitable.

Shortly after season's end in mid–March, two players—George Glamack, who had been the team's replacement at center for Arnie Risen a year prior, and midseason acquisition Leo Mogus—sued Walk and the Jets organization for combined damages of $54,662.51 in unpaid wages. Walk was unable to pay the money demanded in the lawsuit, leading to the team's liquidation and dissolution just 11 days before negotiations on the merger that would create the NBA began.[25]

First-year NBL commissioner Doxie Moore was well aware of the Jets' financial struggles, having gained access to their accounts during their time in the league as the Kautskys. When Walk approached Anderson Packers owner Ike Duffey to sell the team in an attempt to avoid bankruptcy, Moore saw an opportunity to reclaim the Indianapolis market for the NBL. He granted the city a new expansion franchise and secured the playing rights for the University of Kentucky's Fabulous Five, a popular college basketball team at the time. Together with Duffey and NBL vice president Leo Ferris, and in collaboration with the City of Indianapolis, Moore offered the Wildcats' five starters a $30,000 loan and majority ownership of the team.[26]

The Fabulous Five from Kentucky, consisting of Alex Groza, Ralph Beard, Kenny Rollins, Cliff Barker, and Wah Wah Jones, had risen to national prominence during the 1947–48 college season, ending with a national championship and a record of 36–3, with an average winning margin of 24.6 points. Their popularity soared even further when all five were named to the U.S. national team for the 1948 Summer Olympic Games in London, the first Olympics in over a decade because of World War II.

The Kentucky stars, alongside the starting lineup of the Amateur Athletic Union's (AAU) Phillips Oilers, easily led the U.S. to a gold medal, with an average winning margin of 33.5 points, including a 65–21 victory over France in the gold medal game. Groza led the United States in scoring and Jones was also instrumental in their run to gold.

Rollins graduated a year earlier than the other four and was already a member of the BAA's Chicago Stags, so he couldn't take part in the ownership group and was replaced by another fellow Kentucky player in Joe Holland.

Holland had been an All-SEC forward in the 1946–47 season, but was relegated to the bench early in his senior year. Despite only averaging 3.7 points per game as a senior, Holland's physicality and willingness to do the dirty work made him an invaluable asset to his team. Chicago selected him with the 18th pick overall in the BAA draft, but he declined to play for the team and instead took a job as an automobile salesperson because the Stags' location and salary offer weren't suitable, issues that were both resolved in the part-ownership deal for the new Indianapolis team.

The star of the team was Alex Groza, a rare breed of a center with a combination of size, athleticism, and skill that made him one of the most revered players in basketball. His repertoire of post moves and pump fakes, along with his elite rebounding and innate feel for the game, made him a formidable force on the court. He came from an athletic family, with his brother Lou Groza's football career with the Cleveland Browns hard to live up to. Lou, an MVP, nine-time Pro Bowler, and eight-time champion, is now a Pro Football Hall of Famer.

Alex Groza wanted to attend Ohio State University, where Lou had played football, but Ohio State coaches weren't interested in him, so he ended up at Kentucky, where he quickly became a team leader and a standout player. After a stint in the military, he was immediately an NCAA All-American, and by his senior year in 1948–49, he was the National Player of the Year.

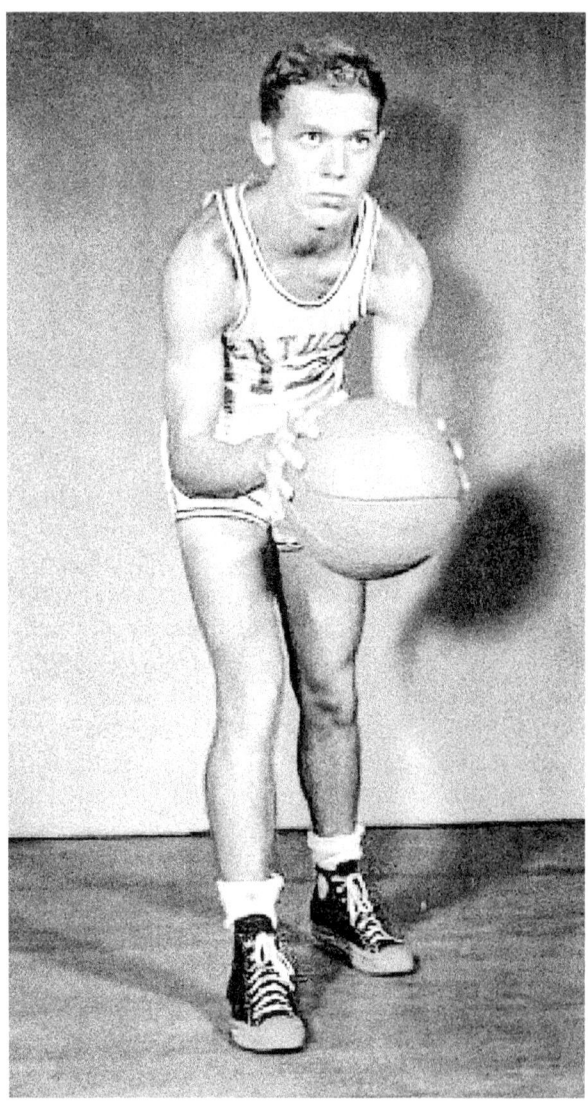

Ralph Beard (1948) was in the top ten in the NBA in both points per game and assists per game, making a splash as a rookie and setting a cultural tone for the Indianapolis Olympians as a team desperate to win.

Wah Wah Jones, like Groza's brother, was initially a football star. He was at Kentucky on a scholarship for his abilities as a defensive end, but he also started at power forward for their basketball team and pitched during baseball season. One of the few players to have played both basketball under Adolph Rupp and football under Bear Bryant (and one of even fewer to be well liked by both), he was twice All-SEC in football and three times All-American in basketball. At the time the national scoring record holder at the high school level, Jones was indeed a very competent scorer, but the strongest part of his game came on second-chance points with his signature high-release shot. His aggressive playing style, honed on the football field, made him a commanding presence in the paint and a formidable opponent for any defender.

Ralph Beard grew up poor in the Great Depression. His father abandoned his family when Beard was a young child and his mother cleaned houses in Louisville for a living, a job that wasn't the most reliable source of income for a single mother of two kids. Beard's upbringing shaped him in life and in basketball. He was remarkably frugal, known for always making his own sandwiches for away trips and refusing to splurge on so much as a McDonald's hamburger even after making the NBA. He also had an insatiable competitive streak that gave him the irresistible compulsion to win. Despite his small stature of only 5'10", Beard was a masterful initiator of fast breaks, a terror on defense, and a force to be reckoned with on the court, but what made him truly stand out was his focus and intensity—the very same attributes that caused him to once wake up in the middle of the night before a game dreaming about choking out his defensive assignment after coach Rupp told him to "strangle the guy."[27]

Beard was larger than life on the basketball court. He was the soul of every single trip down the floor and back, and he not just controlled but manipulated the tempo of the game to his own design. He was the puppet master, both the impresario and the maestro of the opera that is the game of basketball.

Cliff Barker was the one member of Kentucky's core who wasn't an outstanding scorer, but he was a great primary defender who could drive to the rack with ease and had extraordinary skills at handling and passing the basketball for a wing.

The origin of both his outstanding skills with the basketball in his hands and his unreliable jump shot comes down to the time he spent in the military. While many athletes who were drafted into the military didn't see any combat and many could even still participate in sports for service teams, Barker was involved directly with aerial warfare against Nazi Germany during World War II, serving for five years as a heavy bomber gunner for the U.S. Army Air Corps.

He served as a left waist gunner in a Boeing B-17 Flying Fortress, flying perilous missions over enemy territory. On his fifth mission, while en route to Braunschweig, the aircraft he was in was shot down and crashed near the German village of Beienrode. Five of the 10 men on board lost their lives in the wreckage, while Barker and the other survivors were taken captive by Nazi German forces. Barker was held as a prisoner of war in the Stalag Luft IV camp for 16 months.[28]

During those months imprisoned within enemy territory, there was a volleyball on the premises that he often used to pass the time that ultimately helped him to refine his ballhandling skills. As soon as he was released, he went back home, re-enrolled at Kentucky, and started playing again for the Wildcats.

As four of the five former Kentucky stars who co-owned the new Indianapolis-based team were members of the U.S. Olympic team that won gold in 1948, the name to be chosen for the rookie organization was obvious from a marketing standpoint: the Indianapolis Olympians. The team opted to select Babe Kimbrough, a fellow Kentuckian and a recently retired writer for the *Lexington Herald*, as team president.

Groza was the not-so-unlikely hero in their franchise debut win over Denver, with a game-high 19 points, while backup small forward Marshall Hawkins, acquired from the ashes of the Oshkosh All-Stars, contributed 11 points as the only other teammate in double figures.

The first 30-point outing from an individual player in NBA history came with the third slate of games for the new league, on November 2, when the Philadelphia Warriors hosted the Minneapolis Lakers for the first game of their respective seasons.

It was a heavily anticipated matchup that featured two of the previous three BAA champions and superstar players George Mikan and Joe Fulks, who were the league's two leading scorers in the previous season, but both underperformed in this game as Mikan scored just 17 points on 6-of-16 shooting and Fulks shot a dismal 7-of-27 en route to 20 points, while forward Jim Pollard led the Lakers to an 81–69 victory with Philadelphia shooting poorly as a unit.[29]

Pollard was a remarkable athlete with a reputation for exceptional offensive skills dating back to his high school days in Oakland; while rumors of his ability to dunk from the free throw line and to touch the top of the backboard cannot be officially confirmed, he did once injure his elbow hitting the rim late in his career with the Lakers after his athleticism had already waned noticeably, so it's not out of the realm of possibility.[30]

Stanford University coach Everett Dean, who had just recently arrived at the program following a successful 14 years at Indiana University, was so smitten with Pollard's game that he enlisted former Stanford standout Hank Luisetti with the role of recruiting him to the program.

During much of the 1930s and all decades prior, the status quo at all levels of basketball offensively was to attempt to score using a variety of a two-handed set shot. The popular overhand method of this shot involved a player flicking the ball toward the hoop with their hands equally spaced behind the ball and their thumbs facing each other. It relied on a combination of wrist strength, the natural balance provided by keeping your feet close to the ground pointed toward the hoop, a leading motion with your primary foot in the setup of the shot acting as a catalyst for shot strength, and the use of both hands allowing for a high level of shot control.

Luisetti was the first major catalyst in the sport moving away from the set shot, as he relied primarily on a form referred to as the one-handed push shot. The push shot, as Luisetti performed it, involved shooting off the dribble with your dominant hand while using your non-dominant foot as a launching point for a jump. Luisetti rode his innovative shooting technique to the top of the college basketball world at Stanford, earning consensus All-American First Team honors in all three seasons and National Player of the Year in both 1936–37 and 1937–38, leading the NCAA in scoring both years too. Many newspaper articles about Luisetti referred to him as "the greatest basketball player ever to roam the floor" or something similar.

Luisetti succeeded in helping to recruit Jim Pollard to his alma mater two years removed from his own time playing there, and Pollard quickly made an impact. By his sophomore season, he was a first-team All-American and the high scorer for a Stanford team that finished the year 28–4 with both a conference championship and a national championship under its belt, although Pollard missed the championship game with a sinus infection and fever. That summer, Pollard was drafted into the military. Luisetti was too.

Pollard served in the U.S. Coast Guard in Alameda, California, just five miles away from the neighborhood he grew up in. He got to play basketball in the service leagues with the Coast Guard Sealions.

Luisetti served in the U.S. Navy as a physical education director for Navy cadets in Moraga, California. His team, the St. Mary's Pre-Flight, played against Pollard's Sealions three times.

In their first encounter, the game was a nail-biting affair with the Sealions leading 34–32 with 27 seconds to go. Luisetti suddenly launched a running one-hander from nearly 40 feet out when he noticed Pollard out of position defensively, hoping one of his teammates would grab the rebound. None did, and it was Luisetti himself who ran in and gained control of the ball as it hurtled down from the backboard before dishing out the assist to George Ziegenfuss, an ex–University of Washington player, for the game-tying shot. After another of Luisetti's teammates, Bob Ulm, went one for two at the free throw line on the next possession, the Pre-Flight came away with the 35–34 win.

Their second game against each other wasn't quite so close. Luisetti dominated with 32 points in a 48–43 win and no one, not even Pollard, was able to stop his sensational offensive showcase.

Just over a week after that, the two teams met again for a regional service league championship and the Sealions put up a strong defensive front and held Luisetti to just four points with seven minutes left in the game. However, after receiving a barrage of insults from the opposing bench, Luisetti roared back and scored 15 points in the final minutes, leading the Pre-Flight to a come-from-behind 41–38 victory, capping off an undefeated season for St. Mary's.

Little did anyone know that would be Luisetti's final game. Soon after, Luisetti was shipped off to Norfolk, Virginia, while awaiting orders for assignment to an aircraft carrier where he would serve as an onboard physical education director.

While in Norfolk, he suddenly fell ill and was hospitalized on October 24, 1944. Luisetti was diagnosed with cerebrospinal meningitis and fell into a coma for a week. He was treated with sulfathiazole and slowly regained his health, eventually being discharged after four months of hospitalization, his weight having dropped by 40 lbs. in the meantime.

After being released from the hospital, he took a job as an assistant coach at the college level for the U.S. Naval Academy basketball team. In 1946, upon the establishment of the BAA, the owners of both the Knicks and Stags offered Luisetti a contract, but his doctors cautioned against it, revealing that the medication he had been treated with weakened his heart and the scar tissue from his illness could result in debilitating headaches during games, so he had to turn both teams down.[31]

Upon his return from the military, Pollard decided to continue playing basketball as an amateur in the AAU instead of joining the NBL or BAA, allowing him to stay in his home state. He spent one season playing for the San Diego Dons and another for his hometown Oakland Bittners. In both seasons, he was an AAU All-American and led the AAU in scoring, and in both seasons, his team made but lost the championship game.

In 1947–48, the Minneapolis Lakers came into existence when sportswriter Sid Hartman convinced a pair of Minneapolis businessmen, Ben Berger and Morris Chalfen, that they would be guaranteed to acquire George Mikan in the event of the PBLA's

Hank Luisetti (left, shooting over 6'8" center John Freiberger, 1941) was the highest-profile college player ever during his late 1930s career with Stanford, later starring in the AAU and military leagues and playing an early role in the trajectory of fellow Bay Area players such as Jim Pollard and Fred Scolari.

dissolution if they purchased the franchise rights of the last-place Detroit Gems due to an inverse allocation rule regarding players who are considered league property. Pollard joined the team expecting to be the franchise centerpiece, a designation that lasted for four games.

When the PBLA did, in fact, disband after a short existence and the NBL held a dispersal draft, the Detroit Gems having held the worst record in the league the year before and the Lakers' owners having bought the Gems' franchise rights instead of applying for expansion caused Minneapolis to have the first choice in the draft and the opportunity to select the best player in the world, George Mikan, as Hartman promised.[32]

Mikan and Pollard struggled to adjust to each other's games at first, though, with both of them trying to dominate possession of the ball offensively. After following up a 3–1 Pollard-led start by losing five of their first six games with Mikan, Lakers coach John Kundla convinced Pollard, a more useful off-ball player than Mikan, to take a more supporting role on offense, allowing Mikan to be the first option.[33] The strategy worked perfectly, and the Lakers ended up with a league-best 43–17 record and won the championship. The next year, they repeated their success in the BAA, securing a title once again.

While the Lakers' introduction to NBA basketball ended in a positive result, the Boston Celtics came out of their first NBA game on the wrong side of an upset that showcased a lot of flaws in exactly the things they were built to succeed at.

Second-year head coach Doggie Julian, who had led the College of the Holy Cross to consecutive Final Fours and won the 1946–47 NCAA championship, had failed to bring the success that he had at the college level in his first year in charge of the Celtics, but one of the few bright spots in the season came in the form of Boston's February acquisition of George Kaftan, the star of Julian's national championship–winning team. Boston's plan to build around Kaftan centered around bringing a backcourt of Sonny Hertzberg and Howie Shannon to the team.

Hertzberg had played a significant role as a core member of the Washington Capitols, having previously been the scoring leader of the New York Knicks during their historic first BAA win, and was only attainable by the Boston Celtics due to the Capitols' new general manager and coach's desire to revamp the team after the acrimonious departure of former coach Red Auerbach following the Capitols' defeat in the Finals to the Lakers.

Shannon, a Celtic by way of the Steamrollers' dissolution, had just completed an excellent rookie campaign after a tumultuous collegiate career that spanned eight years, three schools, included military service, and ended in ineligibility. The unofficial 1948–49 BAA Rookie of the Year, Shannon was technically the first pick overall in the 1949 BAA draft as a result of Providence having signed him before he was draft eligible.[34] Shannon's first game in Boston didn't go well, as he shot 1-of-5 and finished with just two points, all the more accentuated by second pick Alex Groza and third pick Bob Harris both playing major roles in wins during their debuts. Ball movement was an issue and, especially troubling as a team filled out with defensive-minded role players, they conceded nearly 100 points in a 15-point loss to a Sheboygan team that had lost by 33 points two days before. Power forward Bob Brannum and point guard Bobby Cook led the Redskins in scoring with 16 points each.

For Denver, a humiliating 84–51 loss to Syracuse left them with an 0–4 start. They only scored 18 points in the entire second half and only three Nuggets—Bobby Royer, Bob Brown, and Jack Toomay—scored more than six points. Former Providence standout Kenny Sailors had an unsteady start to the season despite being their only recognizable contributor, and his only points in this game were a pair of free throws.[35]

Meanwhile, Joe Fulks' shot wasn't going in and it hurt the Philadelphia Warriors badly to start off the season. Fulks had the rags-to-riches story familiar to a lot of Kentuckians of his era, having grown up virtually penniless in a working-class family in one of the most Great Depression–ravaged spots in the country.

Fulks was a shy, introverted country kid whose father, a correctional officer at a prison, suffered from alcoholism and frequently vented his frustration on his wife and children. In coping with his dysfunctional family and personal challenges, Fulks found solace in basketball, practicing shooting with makeshift objects like tin cans and bricks, since his family was much too poor to afford a ball. He honed his dribbling skills by stuffing socks with rags, toilet paper, or sawdust. Eventually, he caught his high school coach's attention enough to be given one of only two basketballs owned by his school.

What made his game so unique almost certainly came down to him having learned to play without an actual basketball. With how heavy the bricks were that he often used while practicing, he had to get more force behind his shots than players who grew up using real basketballs did. His solution for that was to bend his knees and jump while shooting, exerting force from his entire body into the movement of the brick—and eventually the movement of the basketball.

Fulks wasn't the first player to shoot a jump shot—it was likely invented by Snake Deal in Philadelphia at the turn of the 20th century, and it truly entered the sport's lexicon via John Miller Cooper of the University of Missouri and Glenn Roberts of Emory & Henry College in the early 1930s—but he was, along with Kenny Sailors, instrumental in popularizing it.

As a high school student, Fulks attracted the attention of Adolph Rupp, the coach of the University of Kentucky basketball team, but he opted for Millsaps College in Jackson, Mississippi, before transferring to Murray State Teachers College, where he emerged as a dominant player, utilizing his athleticism and a reliable jump shot. Fulks also had the ability to jump while facing away from the basket and contort his body midair into a position he could shoot the ball from—an early form of the turnaround jumper.

After two years at Murray State, he, like most young, athletic men in 1943, left to join the military. He served in Guam and the Japanese island of Iwo Jima, but during the portion of his time not deployed overseas, he continued to play basketball at a high level for the Fleet Marine Force Leathernecks.

Eddie Gottlieb, the coach and manager of the newly founded Warriors in 1946, was impressed by his play for the Leathernecks and offered him $5,000 to play for the team after he was discharged that May.[36]

Fulks immediately became a star player for Philadelphia in the BAA's inaugural season, leading the Warriors to win the championship after averaging 23.2 points, and putting up 34 points in the decisive game five victory. In his second and third years as a professional, he was just as dominant individually, although Philadelphia failed to make another championship series.

The great shooting innovator couldn't make his shot fall in the early days of the new league, though, exemplified by his forgettable 14-point performance in a home game against Washington in which Dick O'Keefe held Fulks scoreless in the first half. Fulks shot just 4-of-17 from the field, 6-of-10 on free throws, and fouled out to cap it off.[37] Before long, Philadelphia, a perennial playoff contender in the BAA, sat at just 1–5.

2

Origins, Naismith, and a Childhood Game Called Duck on a Rock

The Blackhawks, despite their triumphant victory in the inaugural game following the merger, plummeted into a streak of four consecutive losses, prompting owner Ben Kerner to abruptly dismiss Roger Potter, the Tri-Cities head coach. Potter, formerly the coach at nearby Moline High School, had been summoned midseason the previous year as a successor for outgoing player-coach Bobby McDermott. Despite a convincing job in the latter part of 1948–49, Potter was ousted early in the season by an impatient Kerner, who swiftly arranged for Potter's replacement. Red Auerbach, previously associated with the Washington Capitols, now assumed the helm.[1]

Auerbach, unlike many of his colleagues, didn't have a wealth of playing experience before getting his first coaching gig. Primarily playing at the grassroots level while kickstarting his coaching career, the former George Washington University defensive ace made a solitary appearance for the Harrisburg Senators in the American Basketball League (ABL), scoring one point.

His coaching journey began at the high school level, at St. Alban's School and Theodore Roosevelt High School in Washington, D.C., before World War II intervened. He enlisted in the U.S. Navy and found himself working at the Norfolk Naval Training Station in Norfolk, Virginia, as an assistant coach under the tutelage of Gary Bodie, helping mold a Norfolk NTS Bluejackets team led by Bob Feerick, Red Holzman, and John Norlander into one of the most successful service league teams in the nation.[2]

When offered the head coaching position for the Washington Capitols in 1946–47, Auerbach's appointment was founded upon the recognition he had garnered during his time in Norfolk. Assembling a formidable roster, he enlisted the services of Feerick and Norlander on the wings, alongside onetime Bluejacket opponent Bones McKinney of the Cherry Point Leathernecks and the scoring-oriented Californian guard Fred Scolari.

The Capitols were soon off and running with Auerbach at the helm, finishing the first BAA season with a record of 49–11 that featured two separate 15-game winning streaks and was 10 and a half games better than that of the second-best team. Feerick's bona fide skills as their shooting guard, displaying remarkable efficiency and ranking second in scoring despite fewer shot attempts than his teammates, made him a standout player. Only power forward Joe Fulks of the Warriors had any sort of realistic claim toward being his equal.

Washington's playoff matchup in the BAA Semifinals, after bypassing the Quarterfinals automatically with a bye due to their regular season record, was the Chicago Stags.

The guard-heavy Stags showcased a fast break–centered offense led by Max Zaslofsky, but also benefited from the creative skills of center Chuck Halbert in half-court sets.

For the series against the Capitols, Chicago embraced the half-court offense out of necessity and strategically inserted 6'4", 250 lb. backup center Chuck Gilmur into the starting lineup as a more imposing presence at power forward, tasked with the explicit goal of aggressively fouling Washington's key players to disrupt their game.

Gilmur did precisely that, racking up almost as many fouls as he did points, simultaneously stifling McKinney and limiting him to just three field goals in the first three games, which ultimately led to Chicago's triumphant victories. Wins in games four and five were not enough to overcome a 3–0 series deficit and they were knocked out in the first round by the Stags after six games.[3]

Auerbach's second season at the helm in Washington was a step backward, as a string of injuries resulted in a late-season slump of eight losses in nine games which led them to a three-way tie for two playoff berths. They had to defeat the Stags in a tiebreaker in order to secure a playoff spot, but crumbled under pressure and suffered a 74–70 defeat to their injury-plagued opponents, who fielded just six players, despite holding a lead until halfway through the fourth quarter, with Max Zaslofsky leading Chicago with 24 points.

As a result, Auerbach found himself on the precipice of unemployment, but Mike Uline couldn't convince his top choice for a replacement, Navy head coach Ben Carnevale, to join the team.[4] Reluctantly, Auerbach was welcomed back for a third season, which started with a remarkable streak of 15 consecutive victories that would remain unmatched as an opening stretch until 1993–94.

Bolstered by the acquisitions of young big men Jack Nichols and Kleggie Hermsen, the Capitols were a more balanced team overall and maintained a high level of play despite an aging Feerick's decline and season-ending injury, ultimately winning their division and finally experiencing playoff success, but falling short against the Lakers in the BAA Finals, where George Mikan's scoring dominance led to a more lopsided matchup than the 4–2 series record indicates.

After the season, Auerbach, having previously signed one-year contracts, insisted on a multiyear deal from Uline and advised him that the best course of action would be to rebuild the aging team with the league merger on the horizon. Uline wasn't ready to rebuild and refused to give him a multiyear deal. Auerbach was out.[5]

He joined Duke University as an assistant coach with the expectation of becoming the next coach after Gerry Gerard, who was battling terminal cancer, died, but he quickly left to coach the Blackhawks, in no small part due to being uncomfortable with the arrangement he had with Duke. He later wrote that "waiting for [Gerard] to die … was no way to get a job."[6]

A significant factor in Auerbach's decision to join Tri-Cities was the willingness of Blackhawks owner Ben Kerner, in stark contrast to Uline, to grant him and business manager Mike Fitzgerald the authority to go ahead with a comprehensive roster rebuild. Tri-Cities would go on to trade, sell, sign, or waive 12 players over the course of the seven weeks after his arrival.

While it was clearly too early to tell much from the first five or so games of each team, Auerbach's old team was among the five—Anderson, Fort Wayne, Minneapolis, Syracuse, and Washington—who were beginning to stand out as he settled into his new job. Anderson, Fort Wayne, and Minneapolis, the league's last three undefeated teams, all fell for the first time on November 12, 1949.[7]

The Lakers and Packers, as the reigning champions of the BAA and NBL, respectively, came into the season expecting to get off and running, but the early success of Fort Wayne was much less predictable.

The story of the Pistons began in 1912, when Ted Zollner of Duluth, Minnesota, invented a machine that could automatically weigh bulk shipments of sugar and grain. He quit his job as the superintendent of a local shipbuilding company and founded the Zollner Manufacturing Company, later Zollner Machine Works, to sell his new machine.

Joined by his son Fred, the company expanded its focus beyond the original invention and ventured into the automotive industry, specializing in engine rebuilding and manufacturing parts for iron mines. The regional reputation of Zollner Machine Works grew in the 1920s for its pneumatic tools and aluminum pistons. In 1928, Zollner sold the pneumatic tool parts division to focus on pistons. The company's pistons, largely considered superior to the automakers' original equipment, became highly sought after by engine manufacturers, necessitating a relocation to Fort Wayne, Indiana, for improved accessibility.

In the run-up to America's involvement in World War II, Zollner Machine Works became a crucial supplier to the U.S. military for the engines of bomber and fighter planes. The workforce behind Zollner pistons grew from just 12 people upon moving to Fort Wayne in 1929 to approximately 18,000 employees during the war. They were presented the Army-Navy "E" Award for their efforts.

By the 1940s, Fred Zollner and his sister Janet had become integral to the company alongside their father. While Ted preferred to oversee the plant itself, Fred ran the front office and Janet managed the financial records. The Zollners fostered a friendly, first-name basis atmosphere within their company, and encouraged recreational activities, with a culture influenced by Ted's outdoor sports background and Fred's passion for spectating professional sports, especially baseball.

Fred Zollner started sports operations at the company in the 1930s with a company-sponsored softball team that quickly achieved local success after he began poaching top players from opposing teams by offering them jobs. One such player was Carl Bennett, who received a job offer from Zollner after Bennett was named MVP of the local industrial softball league. Bennett quickly rose to the role of personnel director at Zollner Machine Works and got the go-ahead from Zollner to start a company-sponsored basketball team as well.

After an undefeated first season, the Zollners qualified for the 1941 WPBT by defeating the Fort Wayne Harvesters, and although they lost to the reigning NBL champions, the Oshkosh All-Stars, they put up a commendable fight and only lost by six points.

Encouraged by the good showing in their first time on the world stage, Fred Zollner went to Leo Fischer, WPBT founder and second-year NBL president, with a proposal to host exhibition games against NBL teams. Fischer suggested that the Zollners turn professional and join the NBL instead. By the start of the 1941–42 season, the Fort Wayne Zollners were an NBL team.

Fort Wayne had a history of involvement in professional basketball leagues, starting with the Fort Wayne Caseys (later known as the Hoosiers) in the American Basketball League (ABL) in the 1920s. The Hoosiers reached consecutive championships, but the team was doomed when the league as a whole folded in 1931, unable to keep up with expenses in the wake of the Great Depression.

Fort Wayne had also been a founding member of the NBL just a few years before the Zollners joined, with the Fort Wayne General Electrics playing a major part in encouraging the restructuring of the MBC into the NBL in 1937, but the team left after one season. It was one of their former players, Jim Hilgemann, who inspired Zollner and Bennett to sponsor a basketball team.[8]

The Fort Wayne Zollners achieved immediate success, boasting the joint–second best regular season record in the league as a first-year league member in 1941–42.

National worries about the country's impending entry into war then gave Fort Wayne an advantage over the established teams in the league: stability. As Zollner Machine Works was ramping up production and distribution of military aircraft pistons, Fred Zollner could promise potential players that they would not be conscripted into military service by virtue of qualifying for a Class II-B deferment as long as they took a job within his company rather than directly signing for the team—the same trick that had been used in the MBC and not too dissimilar from a tactic employed in certain AAU circles as well. A person who received a Class II-B deferment did not have to serve in the military by virtue of necessity to national defense as a war production laborer. Whether the player was actually expected to do any work for the company outside of basketball was strictly optional in the Zollners' case.[9]

The first major signing the Zollners pulled off was that of Fort Wayne native Herman Schaefer, a masterful strategist and deft passer who had electrified the hardwood for the victorious Indiana University team in the 1939–40 NCAA tournament. Schaefer assumed the dual role of player-coach, while Curly Armstrong, his backcourt partner at Indiana, Central High School in Fort Wayne, and every other basketball team he had been on since fourth grade, soon followed, as did Carlisle Towery, a formidable Western Kentucky player at 6'4", 210 lbs. who excelled as a rebounder and narrowly came second in the NCAA in scoring as a senior. Schaefer recruited him to the team as they were both finishing up their degrees, and Towery hitchhiked nearly 200 miles from Bowling Green to Bloomington after graduation, catching a ride with Schaefer the rest of the way to Fort Wayne.

Three games into their first season, Carl Bennett secured the signature of Bobby McDermott, and in doing so, added the best basketball player in the world to his young team.

McDermott's game was a combination of pure grit and unprecedented mastery of the most audacious long-range shots. Well before the advent of the three-point line, McDermott astonished spectators with his ability to sink baskets from well beyond 20 feet, ranging as far back as, at times, beyond half-court.

His shot was a high-arcing set shot full of backspin launched from chest height, and his proficiency at it allowed his teams to do things no other basketball team had done before. Traditionally, the game of basketball, in its half-court setting, was largely played horizontally. A guard would advance the ball up the court before pitching it to the center, and from there, play initiation primarily revolved around off-ball movement along the baseline. McDermott's play style opened up an unexplored realm of offensive creativity, permanently transforming the sport's strategies.

A high school dropout, he first began his career semiprofessionally, earning a meager $5 per game and making more wagering on one-on-one street ball games. Midway through 1934–35, McDermott signed his first full-time professional contract with the Brooklyn Visitation of the ABL. He quickly established himself as one of the league's top players, but many of his older teammates were skeptical of what the way he played meant for basketball, and as a rookie he was sometimes frozen out of the offense to such an extent that, on occasion, he had to actively steal the ball from his teammates to get possession.

After picking up a championship and two scoring titles in three years for the Visitation, McDermott spent four of the next five seasons with the Original Celtics, playing over 100 games a year and traveling across the country. At a time when the average team scored between 30 and 35 points in a game, he would sometimes score 30 or 40 points on his own. In a blowout win over an amateur team from Matewan, West Virginia, he scored 56.[10]

Upon arriving in Fort Wayne, McDermott emerged as the focal point of the team and a firm, long-term favorite for NBL MVP. In their first year, the team made it to the NBL Finals but fell short to Oshkosh in the deciding game three by six points, with Armstrong's 23 points keeping them in the game until the final moments.

On the back of another championship loss the following year in 1942–43 in the form of a Sheboygan Redskins last-second bucket, the Zollners took full advantage of a short-handed league during World War II that only featured four teams and finished the season with an 18–4 record and swept the playoffs, with McDermott now serving as player-coach after Schaefer went off to war. The next year was much the same: even without the army-bound Towery they again claimed the league's top spot with a 25–5 record and secured another championship by defeating Sheboygan. McDermott became the joint-first player to average upwards of 20 points per game that year along with the Cleveland Transfers' Mel Riebe.

With the NBL back to eight teams in 1945–46, the Zollners were still the team to beat, their 26–8 record was a league-best again, and McDermott won NBL MVP for the fifth time in a row. However, in the playoffs, Fort Wayne faced a formidable challenge from the Rochester Royals, and McDermott underperformed in the face of the exceptional defense of Rochester's Al Cervi. Rochester won the series 3–1.

Thirteen games into the next season, the Zollners stood at a disappointing 7–6. Morale plummeted after a demoralizing loss to Syracuse, marking their sixth loss in the last seven games. Schaefer departed for the rival Indianapolis Kautskys at the start of the year; McDermott struggled defensively against quicker guards; and the loss of Buddy Jeannette and aging of the team's core led to a more conservative style of play. Center was also an impending issue, with Jake Pelkington nearing retirement and his intended replacement, Ed Sadowski, having jumped to the BAA. A potential replacement was found in Milo Komenich, an offensively adept left-handed center fresh out of college, where he had been an All-American and an NCAA champion at Wyoming alongside Kenny Sailors.

On the train ride home from Syracuse, McDermott, Komenich, and veteran guard Charley Shipp got into a fight over a craps game that ended with Carl Bennett having to intervene and break up McDermott and Shipp, after McDermott knocked Komenich unconscious.[11]

All three were suspended indefinitely. Before the suspensions were complete, Shipp had been sold to Anderson and McDermott had been waived, free to sign with the Chicago Gears.

Without McDermott, the Pistons remained competitive but not in contention, finishing their last two NBL seasons with winning records but never returning to the NBL Finals.

After moving to the BAA, the team struggled to regain their former success, resulting in the removal of Bennett from coaching duties after a 0–6 start and a lackluster overall performance. While they retained significance throughout the merger talks, with Fred Zollner's kitchen table serving as the site for the initial agreement for the two leagues to consolidate, a 22–38 record was the worst of all the BAA teams that survived the merger.

It was for that reason, with only Curly Armstrong remaining from their championships by the time the merger took place, that the Pistons' strong start to time in the NBA was such a surprise, kicking the season off with 87–72, 87–70, and 89–59 wins. The main catalysts for the strong start were Armstrong, Charlie Black, and Fred Schaus.

At 30 years old, Armstrong's role on the team shifted to primarily relying on his spot-up shooting and satisfactory facilitation skills, while his value became centered on his aggressive defensive presence and ability to disrupt opponents' scoring and passing.

Schaus, a rookie small forward who'd slipped to 27th in the draft, showcased his exceptional scoring ability and displayed promising all-around skills, exhibiting the capacity to generate his own offense, great composure, and few discernible weaknesses in the early days of his career.

Black, a two-time first-team All-American from the University of Kansas and a P-38 reconnaissance pilot who flew 51 missions over war-torn Europe, entered his third year in the professional ranks of basketball having been a late-season acquisition in 1948–49. Black's natural feel for the game often drew him into exterior scoring positions, but he didn't possess the foot speed to thrive outside of the post when he got himself into these situations. In the first three games, Black's shooting masked his limitations, but against Baltimore, ex–Zollner Carlisle Towery frequently pushed him to the perimeter, leading to an 82–75 Bullets win behind the strength of Paul Hoffman's 24 points.

Anderson, meanwhile, suffered a thorough defeat against Syracuse, with Al Cervi's scoring outburst proving to be too much for the Packers to deal with. Minneapolis' loss that same day was in spite of George Mikan scoring 30 points as he lacked help from his teammates. Mikan's previous game had been a much happier occasion, with 37 points in a win over Boston, his highest-scoring performance since the previous year's Finals. It was rookie Alex Groza of Indianapolis, though, who achieved the distinction of becoming the NBA's first post-merger 40-point scorer, recording 41 points in a win against the Knicks in Madison Square Garden.

Not content to stop there when it came to NBA firsts, the Indianapolis Olympians matched up with the Sheboygan Redskins on November 13 for what would be the first NBA game in which both teams exceeded 100 points. Both the Redskins and Olympians had a very free-flowing attitude to the game of basketball, and it certainly helped that they each had very offensively adept centers leading the way.

Groza scored 30 points, accompanied by 24 from Ralph Beard and 19 from Wah Wah Jones, but it was Sheboygan who pulled off the 104–101 win to get off to a 4–1 start that they would soon extend to 6–1. Six Sheboygan players scored in double figures, led by Noble Jorgensen's 17 points.

Jorgensen had joined the pros three years prior by following his brother Roger to the Pittsburgh Ironmen after he was declared academically ineligible midway through his senior year. He left school and signed with Pittsburgh in the fledgling BAA to join his brother, and after a rough start, he earned a spot in the rotation toward the end of the season, proving to be a fluid athlete but desperately in need of refinement on both offense and defense. Following the season, Jorgensen suffered severe injuries in a car crash that resulted in the death of a passenger and injuries to six other people, and by the time Jorgensen recovered from his injuries, the Pittsburgh Ironmen had folded.[12] He signed with the Waterloo Pro-Hawks of the PBLA, and after the league collapsed early in the season, he briefly played minor league ball until Sheboygan came calling, where he helped the Redskins to a playoff spot and became an ideal center for the team's up-tempo play. The close win over Indianapolis was the fifth of what ended up being 12 straight games Jorgensen scored in double figures to kick off Sheboygan's time in the NBA. It was also part of a two-week stretch in which he scored an average of 25.8 points over six games.

While four of the Central Division teams all started the season encouragingly, the St. Louis Bombers found themselves alone within the division as a team with an early losing record. Not only did they follow up wins in their first two games with six losses in the next seven, four of them were by upwards of 20 points.

Owned by C. D. P. Hamilton, Jr., of the Hamilton, Scheu, & Walsh Shoe Company, and managed by Emory Jones, the Bombers never missed out on the playoffs but also never once won a playoff series during their time in the BAA. Known for their strong defense, the Bombers pressed ball handlers and trapped them to force turnovers, with Bob Doll putting forth his best effort to front the center and deny him the ball entirely.

With the departure of Doll, the St. Louis Bombers' prospects dimmed, but their fortune changed when the league established territorial rights and gave them first claim toward Ed Macauley, who had been National Player of the Year and the star of the 1948 National Invitational Tournament (NIT) winners at Saint Louis University. After drafting Macauley, the expectation was definitely not for the Bombers to get markedly worse.

The BAA introduced territorial picks as a solution to the lack of popularity in professional basketball compared to other major professional sports, aiming to make it more locally relevant like college basketball. Starting from the 1949 BAA draft, teams had the option to bypass the regular selection order and choose a local star with a territorial pick. Teams could forfeit their first-round pick to jump the line and select a player who attended college within 50 miles of their home arena.[13] Macauley for the Bombers and Vern Mikkelsen for the Lakers were the first two players selected using this method.

Macauley, a homegrown sensation, rejected offers from top schools nationwide to attend Saint Louis University after his mother told him he could attend any university he wanted as long as it was "Catholic and in St. Louis."[14]

At Saint Louis, he established himself as the premier offensive big man in college basketball, dazzling scouts with his exceptional perimeter shooting, nimble footwork, and effortless low-block skills. He was truly unique as a 6'8", 185 lb. center and had plenty of critics who questioned his translatability to the professional level given his dearth of body strength and a perceived lack of urgency in the way he played. Nonetheless, the potential for stardom as a Bomber was palpable. His start in the NBA wasn't as striking as Groza's, but after scoring just five points in his debut, Macauley had 14 or more in each of the next six games. One thing that stood out right away was just how easily he was getting to the free throw line, debunking any doubts about his urgency and determination.

While he made an immediate impact with the Bombers, quickly surpassing Johnny Logan as their offensive linchpin, their addition of Macauley meant they had to accommodate two natural centers in their starting lineup, alongside Red Rocha. Despite both Macauley and Rocha being quick for the position, this slowed the offense even further and clogged up the lane, making it exceptionally hard for an aging starting backcourt duo of Logan and Belus Smawley to effectively drive to the paint, a near-death blow for an already stagnant offense.

The defending champion Lakers, who beat St. Louis to send the Bombers spiraling to a 3–6 record at a time when no other Central Division team had more than two losses to their name, were the other team to trigger the territorial pick clause that year in order to select Hamline University's Vern Mikkelsen.

After emerging as a basketball talent in the small town of Askov, Minnesota, Mikkelsen had the option of basketball scholarships from either Minnesota or Hamline after graduating high school at 16 years old.[15]

Hamline and Minnesota, 62 years prior, had faced off in the first-ever collegiate basketball game. Hamline's then-athletic director, Raymond Kaighn, was among the 18 men who participated in the inaugural game of basketball on December 21, 1891, which bore little resemblance to the game Vern Mikkelsen played, featuring nine players on each team, a soccer ball, two peach baskets, and no dribbling.

The inventor of basketball and director of the athletic program that led to the first game was James Naismith. Naismith had a colorful upbringing in a small Scottish and Irish immigrant settlement called Bennie's Corners. Orphaned on his ninth birthday, Naismith worked on his uncle's farm in the summer and chopped lumber for the mill in the winter, developing into a rugged individualist known for his initiative and self-reliance and eventually pursuing a degree in philosophy and Hebrew at McGill University, where he became a star athlete in Canadian football, rugby, lacrosse, soccer, and gymnastics.

After graduation, Naismith pursued a theological education at The Presbyterian College, while also acting as a physical education instructor at McGill. He graduated with honors, receiving a master's of divinity and finishing second in his class, but prevailing sentiments within the highly religious community during the late 1800s regarded athletics as a tool of the devil.

Naismith was of a very different opinion and decided to switch career paths after graduating, as he wanted to impact young men's lives through a combination of spirituality and athletics, moving to Springfield, Massachusetts, to study physical education at the International YMCA Training School. Following his two years of enrollment there, he was appointed a physical education instructor at the school after two other instructors resigned, a position he would hold for five years.

At a time when team sports were gaining prominence in college athletics, programs affiliated with the YMCA like Naismith's were some of the cultural leaders in that regard. Many of the best athletes in the country played sports such as football, baseball, and lacrosse in college—oftentimes all three.

With indoor sports still a fledgling concept in the United States at the time of Naismith's first year in the role, Dr. Luther Gulick, Naismith's boss, gave Naismith and his colleagues each an assignment to invent a new game within two weeks to provide an outlet for the students' energy during the winter months.

Gulick's instructions to "make [the sport] fair for all players, and free of rough play" played a significant role in shaping Naismith's original concept. A quick evaluation of America's most popular sports at the time lent Naismith a belief that sports with larger balls were less skill-based and that contact and roughhousing were more prevalent in games that allowed physical defense or ball-carrying. As such, he used a soccer ball as the method of scoring, mounted two goals to the lower railing of a balcony in order to prevent full-contact play, and prohibited carrying the ball while moving.

The first basketball game occurred in December 1891 inside the School for Christian Workers Building. Naismith wrote 13 rules for the game and a secretary typed them up as Naismith went to ask head of maintenance James Stebbins for a pair of eighteen-inch-square wooden boxes to use for the goals. Stebbins couldn't find any boxes and instead brought back two peach baskets: the origin of the name of the sport. The document was posted to the gymnasium bulletin board and the 18 players read from the written rules to learn the basics of the game before Naismith taught them some rudimentary fundamentals.

One of the unwritten rules he taught them was how to shoot the basketball. All major sports at the time that involved throwing did so with either a pitch, bullet pass or lateral pass, and none of those are viable ways to throw a ball into a hoop 10 feet off the ground. Drawing inspiration from his childhood experience playing the medieval English game of duck on a rock, a game blending elements of tag and marksmanship wherein a rock was strategically hurled to dislodge a larger rock, Naismith showed his players how to shoot in an arcing motion, a technique he had devised as a kid that made it harder, in duck on a rock, for the guard to defend the throw.[16]

Naismith's original 13 rules for the game of basketball were as follows:

1. The ball may be thrown in any direction with one or both hands.
2. The ball may be batted in any direction with one or both hands (never with the fist).
3. A player cannot run with the ball, the player must throw it from the spot on which he catches it, allowance to be made for a man who catches the ball when remaining at a good speed.
4. The ball must be held in or between the hands, the arms or body must not be used for holding it.
5. No shouldering, holding, pushing, tripping or striking, in any way the person of an opponent shall be allowed. The first infringement of this rule by any person shall count as a foul, the second shall disqualify him until the next goal is made, or if there was evident intent to injure the person, for the whole of the game, no substitute allowed.
6. A foul is striking at the ball with the fist, violation of rules 3 and 4, and such as described in rule 5.
7. If either side makes three consecutive fouls it shall count a goal for the opponents (consecutive means without the opponents in the meantime making a foul).
8. A goal shall be made when the ball is thrown or batted from the grounds into the basket and stays there, providing those defending the goal do not touch or disturbe *[sp]* the goal. If the ball rests on the edge and the opponent moves the basket it shall count as a goal.
9. When the ball goes out of bounds it shall be thrown into the field, and played by the person first touching it. In case of a dispute the umpire shall throw it straight into the field. The thrower in is allowed five seconds, if he holds it longer it shall go to the opponent. If any side presists *[sp]* in delaying the game, the umpire shall call a foul on them.
10. The umpire shall be judge of the men, and shall note the fouls, and notify the referee when three consecutive fouls have been made. He shall have power to disqualify men according to Rule 5.

11. The referee shall be judge of the ball and shall decide when the ball is in play, in bounds, and to which side it belongs, and shall keep the time. He shall decide when a goal has been made, and keep account of the goals with any other duties that are usually performed by a referee.

12. The time shall be two fifteen minute halves, with five minutes rest between.

13. The side making the most goals in that time shall be declared the winners. In case of a draw the game may, by agreement of the captains, be continued until another goal is made.[17]

The first game ended with a score of 1–0. The sole basket was made in the final minute of action by William Chase, who would go on to work in real estate in New Bedford, Massachusetts. Raymond Kaighn, the man who would soon after host the first intercollegiate basketball game, dislocated his shoulder in the midst of what unintentionally turned into a very physical game, earning the designation of becoming the first man to ever be injured in a basketball game.[18]

A little under a month after the first game was played, Naismith's 13 Rules were printed in the school's newspaper and it quickly caught on with YMCAs and universities around the country. By 1898, just seven years after Naismith's invention of the sport, professional basketball existed.

Kaighn invited students from the Minnesota State School of Agriculture to play against his team at Hamline in 1894. Minnesota State, which merged into the University of Minnesota shortly after, won 9–3.[19]

When faced with the decision between Hamline University—one of the best teams at the National Association of Intercollegiate Basketball (NAIB) level and recent small-school national champions—and Minnesota—an established NCAA team that had experienced two consecutive losing seasons and had a commitment from 6'10" center Jim McIntyre that would potentially relegate Mikkelsen to a bench role—he chose Hamline.

Mikkelsen's baptism of fire came during a challenging invitational tournament against formidable opponents DePaul, Oklahoma A&M, and Bowling Green, led by renowned centers George Mikan, Bob Kurland, and Don Otten, respectively.[20]

He was thoroughly outclassed, as was his team, but his tenacity and rebounding skills soon propelled him to college basketball prominence. He led Hamline to the NAIB Final Four and a further championship title, as his athleticism and speed provided an advantage over taller center matchups. His achievements earned him recognition as an honorable mention All-American and the distinction of being the first NAIB player invited to the College All-Star Game. Soon after graduation, he was also pursued by both the best team in professional basketball and the best team in amateur basketball.

In the early years of the NBA, professional basketball lacked particular allure, with limited financial prospects, scarce endorsement deals, and the absence of a union or league-mandated pension. Many players had second jobs during the summer. A few did during the season as well. George Mikan had the NBA's highest salary in 1949–50, making $15,000 per year.[21] Most of the rest of the league made less than half that.

AAU teams for many players, provided an equally or more appealing option, offering stable jobs and career paths that could secure long-term success beyond their athletic primes. About 20 percent of the players remained with the company they played for long-term. Some became key executives.

An additional perk the AAU could offer was that, since it was an amateur organization, AAU players could represent the United States in the Olympic Games alongside college stars, while NBA players could not. This was exemplified by the 1948 Olympic team, whose gold medal triumph showcased the valuable contributions from both Kentucky's Fabulous Five and the full starting lineup of the Phillips Oilers, AAU champions five times running.

Established in 1919 by Phillips Petroleum Company employees who had served in World War I, the Oilers took their first steps toward building a basketball dynasty in 1936. Phillips Petroleum cofounder and chairman Frank Phillips, after a four-year basketball hiatus due to Great Depression financial constraints, gave the go-ahead to spare no effort this time around in forming a successful and profitable team. Ex–Kansas star Boots Adams, Phillips' eventual successor as chairman, took on the responsibility of organizing the team alongside former National Player of the Year Paul Endacott.[22]

The 1930s Oilers revolved around Joe Fortenberry, a 6'8" Texan center, on the back of his triumphant performance starring for the gold medal–winning United States national team in the 1936 Olympic Games, held in the heart of soon-to-be enemy territory—Berlin, Germany.

Fortenberry's impact on the Oilers led them to immediate results, reaching the championship game in their first year after reorganizing. The acquisitions of Grady Lewis and Bill Martin from the defunct Oklahoma City Parks in 1939 then spurred Phillips to its first AAU championship.

Following a series of consecutive titles between 1943 and 1946 due in part to their players qualifying for Class II-B war production deferments similar to Fort Wayne at the professional level, they received their biggest and best reinforcement yet.

Bob Kurland, both the tallest man and the biggest name in college basketball circa 1945–46, declined BAA and NBL offers ranging as high as $15,000 per year, a salary that would've made him the highest-paid professional basketball player in the world as a rookie, in order to remain in-state, join the Oilers, and work for Phillips Petroleum.

Despite not receiving scholarship offers from his intended choices of Saint Louis University or the University of Missouri, Bob Kurland had seized the opportunity to be the first person in his family to go to college, where sweeping gymnasium floors in exchange for a free education at Oklahoma A&M enabled him to pursue a civil engineering career that would have been otherwise inaccessible to him. He hadn't been an exceptional player in high school, but his towering height made him an intriguing prospect and a friendship with one of coach Hank Iba's former players granted him the tryout that eventually earned him a full scholarship.[23]

He played sparingly as a freshman and averaged only 2.5 points, but Iba's deployment of him as a starter in the final game of the season against the University of Oklahoma showcased his defensive prowess. Placed directly under the basket, Kurland utilized his jumping ability to swat away shots, employing the emerging tactic of goaltending, a technique that was also adopted by fellow freshman centers George Mikan, Don Otten, and Harry Boykoff during the same season. This approach proved effective as Oklahoma A&M emerged victorious with a 40–28 win.

Goaltending propelled Kurland into basketball relevance, but drew both criticism from Oklahoma players and the amusing protest of opposing center Gerald Tucker, who warmed up on stilts in their subsequent matchup. While Kurland achieved notable block numbers during the goaltending era, once recording 17 in a game, he disliked the strategy, considering it a hindrance to a true test of ability. However, he made significant improvements in his post offense and mobility, becoming an All-American as a sophomore and innovating the sport by popularizing dunking when open near the basket. In the following year, he led Oklahoma A&M to their first national championship.

After winning the championship, Oklahoma A&M faced NIT champion DePaul in a highly anticipated Red Cross Benefit game at Madison Square Garden, marketed as a showdown between the two best players in basketball, Kurland and Mikan, and their names, rather than those of their respective teams, featured on the promotional billboard. They had met twice before, with Mikan's DePaul coming out on top in close games both times, including a 41–38 win to knock Oklahoma A&M out of the previous year's NIT.

Despite the way the game was billed, neither center managed to take over the game. Kurland held Mikan to a mere nine points and Mikan fouled out four minutes into the second half. Kurland scored just 14, attempting only two shots in the second half before also fouling out. Oklahoma A&M won 52–44 in an otherwise uneventful game.[24]

Kurland followed that up by staking his claim as the better of the two players as a senior with a National Player of the Year award, a second national championship, and a remarkable 58-point outing in his last home game against Saint Louis University while matched up against a freshman Ed Macauley.

When Kurland chose to join Phillips instead of turning professional, he teamed up with AAU standout Gordon Carpenter and high-scoring Cab Renick, who had primarily played in service leagues for the Navy Zoomers. The trio was seemingly unstoppable together and compiled a 114–5 record over a two-year period. At the end of the 1947–48 season, the Phillips Oilers participated in the Olympic Trials and emerged victorious every game, including a 53–49 victory over

Joe Fortenberry (second from right, 1939) was a key piece for multiple top-level AAU teams in the 1930s and was the first piece of the puzzle toward the Phillips Oilers' sustained period of amateur dominance. He was the star of the 1936 U.S. National team that won Olympic Gold.

the University of Kentucky in the final, securing their spot as the primary starting lineup for the national team.[25]

Kurland was second in scoring, trailing only Alex Groza. Renick captained the team and, with one-quarter Chickasaw and one-quarter Choctaw ancestry, became the second Native American ever to win a gold medal, after Jim Thorpe. Carpenter led the comeback in the one close game they had, a 59–57 squeaker over Argentina.

By the time Vern Mikkelsen was weighing his options between them and the Lakers a year later, Carpenter had left for the Denver Chevrolets and Renick had retired and was now coaching. In his first year, Renick coached the Oilers to a 50–4 record, but they lost the final of the AAU Tournament 55–51 to the Oakland Bittners, an integrated team full of former Pacific Coast Conference standouts. It was the first time in seven years they weren't champions of amateur basketball.

Mikkelsen wasn't a natural fit for either team battling over him, though. Kurland was the focal point

Bob Kurland (shooting, 1951) was the backbone of the mid-1940s Oklahoma A&M teams that won two national championships and, alongside DePaul's George Mikan, the face of wartime basketball. He was one of four primary players responsible for the implementation of the goaltending violation and the first player to popularize dunking as a common method of scoring. He would retain importance as the star of the Phillips Oilers for six years. Also shown (from left): Cliff Crandall, Don Henriksen, and George Yardley, all of the San Francisco Stewart Chevrolets.

of the Oilers and Mikan the star of the Lakers. For a rookie who had played center his entire college career, significant adjustments were necessary in both potential situations.

Max Winter, minority owner and general manager for the Lakers, attempted to reassure him that Mikan was going to retire after the season and he would be the starting center going forward after that, but that seemed unlikely. Although skeptical, Mikkelsen signed with Minneapolis.

It was apparent when he first entered the league that he didn't have the same foot speed advantage that he had in college and that he lacked great shooting touch, but Mikkelsen quickly established himself as a valuable backup to Mikan with his relentless hustle, strong rebounding, and fearless play. Lakers coach John Kundla recognized his worth and decided to implement a dual-center lineup early in the season, similar to the St. Louis Bombers.

The experiment was an immediate and monumental failure, as the two centers frequently obstructed each other and disrupted offensive drives.

Minneapolis lost three games out of four after having won their first four straight, Mikan scored less than 20 points in back-to-back games for the first time in over two years, and he followed up those two games by shooting 7-of-36 as the Lakers lost 83–80 to the Anderson Packers despite two of Anderson's top three scorers, Frank Brian and John Hargis, combining for just two points.

Kundla swiftly adjusted his strategy after that game and began to retrain Mikkelsen to adopt a more forward-like role while still maintaining his post player responsibilities. He was expected to block shots, rebound, and generally be a nuisance to opposing players, but on offense, he became more of a supporting asset to Mikan, utilizing face-up moves and crashing the boards from the corner for second-chance points, particularly through tip-ins.[26] While Mikkelsen took somewhat of a learning curve in transitioning to his new role, the Lakers immediately turned their fortunes around and won their next three games by an average of 19.7 points.

As the Lakers began to rebound from their slump, the Pistons and Stags found themselves atop the Central Division while the other expected championship contender from the division, the Rochester Royals, experienced setbacks of their own.

Arnie Risen, Mikan's rival harkening back to his days on the Kautskys, had never gotten a chance to redeem himself by facing him in a championship series following his defensive breakdown in the 1947 NBL Semifinals, despite being traded to the contending Rochester team midway through the next season.

In their first year with their new teams, Risen's Royals and Mikan's Lakers faced off in the NBL Finals, but Risen missed the series due to a broken jaw, and when both teams joined the BAA the following season, they were placed in the same division and had to settle for a best-of-three divisional finals, which the Lakers won 2–0.

Following the merger, they found themselves once again in the same division despite being nearly a thousand miles apart from each other, ensuring they again would not have a chance for a Finals rematch. Despite having not yet gotten a chance at revenge, Risen had established himself as a prominent center, trailing only Mikan and perhaps now Alex Groza in terms of stature and skill.

A long and lanky player who rarely faced off against an opposing center fewer than 20 pounds heavier than him, Risen excelled in securing advantageous positioning in the post despite not being as effective in standard post-up situations as the other top centers. With plenty of teammates who possessed scoring abilities, he was often tasked with attacking the offensive glass, becoming one of the league's top rebounders and earning numerous high-percentage shots near the rim on second chances. In 1948–49, he led the BAA in field goal percentage and scored the fifth-most points in order to make the All-BAA Second Team.

The heartbeat of this Rochester Royals team, though, was point guard Bob Davies, one of the most exciting players in the league and quite possibly, although advocates of Jim Pollard would beg to differ, the best non-center in the NBA.

Davies first rose to prominence in basketball during his time at Seton Hall University in the early 1940s. Despite initially focusing on baseball, having been scouted by the Boston Red Sox, he dazzled on the basketball court with his mesmerizing ballhandling skills and flamboyant passes. He had a rare combination of creativity and balance and was one of the first players to incorporate behind-the-back dribbles on the fast break.

Leading a formidable Seton Hall team, he spearheaded an exhilarating run of 43 consecutive wins spanning two seasons, just one off of the then-record 44 that the University of Texas set between 1913 and 1917. In the 43rd game, a staggering crowd of 18,403 spectators gathered to watch them dispatch Rhode Island State College with 19 points from Davies leading the way; it was the largest attendance of any basketball game at the time. Three days later, they lost to Long Island University by 23 points.

After graduation, Davies joined the U.S. Navy for three years, playing service league basketball while stationed stateside and later commanding a submarine chaser in the Pacific theater before being discharged and returning to resume his basketball career.[27]

He signed with the Royals, who were in the midst of their first month of NBL action early in 1945–46, when they offered him more money than the Sheboygan Redskins. Prior to this, Rochester had operated as an independent team, at first semiprofessionally, with sponsorship from alcoholic beverage companies like Eber Brothers Wine & Liquor and the Seagram Company since Rochester's Eber Brothers team was established in 1928.

In the early 1943–44 season, the Rochester team responded to local newspaper pressure by dropping their liquor sponsorship and changing their name from the Rochester Seagrams to the Rochester Pros, eventually settling on the Royals when they joined the NBL, referencing their former sponsor by borrowing the name from Crown Royal, Seagram's Canadian whisky.

Les Harrison, a former player for the team who had served as player-coach for the last five years of that stint, became the majority owner after the rebrand. Eddie Malanowicz, their star center from 1932–33 to 1944–45, took over as the team's coach.

In the midst of the post–World War II reconstruction of the NBL, Les Harrison seized the opportunity, having been approached by league executives, to purchase a spot in the league for $25,000, transforming his team into an NBL franchise.[28]

With point guard Al Cervi returning from military service, Harrison quickly assembled a professional-grade roster featuring former New York college stars, players who had been stationed in or off the coast of New York, and John Mahnken and Al Negratti of the Wright Kittyhawks service league team from Dayton, Ohio. Most of the best colleges in the state had great reputations for developing star guards, and as such, the Rochester backcourt was particularly formidable, namely Cervi and former City College of New York star Red Holzman. Bob Davies, who had a penchant for taking too many unnecessary risks on defense, adapted by playing out of position at small forward.

Davies seamlessly converted to his new role and played a vital role in the team's championship win in their inaugural year, followed by an NBL MVP the next season. Upon the departure of Al Cervi and the transition to the BAA, Davies thrived, returning to point guard. In 1948–49, the Royals boasted the best regular season record in the league as Davies topped the BAA in assists and earned a spot on the All-BAA First Team. He was one of the most dynamic and trickiest players in the league, and as the playmaker for an otherwise gritty, methodical team, he made Rochester a very hard opponent to game-plan against.

As their first NBA season commenced, though, the Royals' normally rock-solid

Bob Davies (1950) was a champion in 1945–46, the MVP of the NBL the following season, and the star of the Rochester Royals, as well as the most flamboyant creative force in the NBA. He led the Royals in both scoring and assists and finished the season All-NBA First Team with the third-most votes in the league for the honor, behind just George Mikan and Alex Groza.

defense faltered. The only lineup alteration was the promotion of third-year wing Bobby Wanzer to the starting lineup, which sent Holzman, who had struggled to find his rhythm offensively since the departure of Al Cervi, to a sixth-man role. While it was indeed a defensive downgrade, Wanzer, who was a solid on-ball defender in his own right, was not the primary cause of the team's defensive struggles, and his promotion to the starting lineup allowed Holzman to spend at least half of his minutes at point guard for the first time since he joined the team, while also capitalizing on Wanzer's prowess as a shooter and transition player.

Arnie Risen's lateral quickness was declining and his offensive game was suddenly somewhat stiff and predictable, issues that were exposed by Noble Jorgensen in Rochester's early-season matchups with Sheboygan. This, compounded with the arrival to the professional ranks of Alex Groza and Ed Macauley, the addition of ex–NBL centers Jorgensen and Harry Boykoff, and the stand-out offensive play of Washington's second-year center Jack Nichols, confirmed that Risen's value was starting to become a bit of a question mark.

When a 21-point defeat to St. Louis was compounded by a narrow loss to the Indianapolis Olympians in which Risen gave up 43 points to Alex Groza, a new scoring record surpassing the 41 Groza scored against the Knicks 12 days earlier, Rochester found themselves only one game away from the bottom of the division, with the feeling that their season was spiraling out of control.[29]

3

Ferris, Duffey, and the Undertaker for the Underworld

With a victory over the still-winless Nuggets, the Syracuse Nationals became the first NBA team to reach 10 wins in order to secure a 10–1 start to the year. The most wins any other team had at that same time was Chicago's seven. Having been one of the better NBL teams the previous year, success for Syracuse was expected, but league supremacy, in the form of eight double-digit victories in their first 11 games and consecutive triumphs over the in-state rival Knicks, was not.

The architect of the Nationals team was Leo Ferris, who had also been instrumental in the history of the Tri-Cities Blackhawks, Indianapolis Olympians, and the NBA as a whole.

Ferris and Ben Kerner, business partners at an eponymous advertising firm, cofounded the Buffalo Bisons in the summer of 1946 and registered them in the NBL, becoming the third NBL team in upstate New York, alongside Rochester and Syracuse.

Despite Ferris' efforts to assemble a competitive team, including signing standout player Don Otten, Buffalo struggled to fill even a quarter of their arena's capacity and faced major financial losses. Just 38 days into their first season, Kerner and Ferris relocated the team to Moline, Illinois, rebranding them the Tri-Cities Blackhawks.[1]

Despite the midseason move forcing them to play in the NBL Eastern Division despite being the league's westernmost team, the Blackhawks had a commendable season, only missing the playoffs by two games.

Before the next season got underway, Ferris identified the backcourt as a major need for improvement and promptly pursued the signings of two top-notch shooters.

Whitey Von Nieda, a multi-positional 6'1" player who could effectively play point guard, shooting guard, and small forward, drew the attention of top teams during his rookie season with the Lancaster Red Roses in the minor leagues following his service as a paratrooper in the U.S. Army during the war. Averaging an impressive 22.7 points per game, over five points more than the next-highest scorer, Von Nieda caught the eye of Ferris with his quickness, comfort both on and off the ball, and smooth midrange shot.

Ferris pulled Von Nieda aside to offer him a chance to join the Blackhawks. Von Nieda wasn't interested, given the instability of high-level professional basketball, as he was already making $12,000 per year between basketball and his day job. Ferris offered to match it. He still wasn't fully convinced, until Ferris pulled $2,000 cash from his pocket, saying it would be a signing bonus. Caught off guard and needing to catch a bus in 10 minutes, Von Nieda took the money with him, intending to return it later, figuring Ferris could claim he took it if he just left it there and someone else grabbed it.

He caught his bus and went to a frat party at his alma mater of Penn State that night. By the morning, he no longer had most of the money. No longer able to pay back Ferris in full, he signed the contract and headed to the Tri-Cities area.[2]

Ferris further bolstered the team's roster by acquiring Bobby McDermott in December. McDermott's rights had been acquired by Sheboygan after the Chicago Gears disbanded, and several teams, including Tri-Cities, had passed on adding him due to concerns about his character.

McDermott's stint with Sheboygan was short-lived, as the team compiled a middling record and he clashed with management. Recognizing an opportunity, Ferris orchestrated a trade to bring the aging star, now 34 and past his athletic prime, to the Blackhawks too.

That summer, Ferris had also been elected to the position of NBL vice president. One of his notable contributions was devising much of the idea of replacing the Indianapolis Jets with the player-owned Olympians, securing exclusive arena rights in Indianapolis for the NBL and forcing the BAA out of the market.[3] This move acted as a catalyst for merger discussions, leading the BAA to accept additional teams from Denver Waterloo, Sheboygan, Anderson, and Tri-Cities despite initially only seeking the inclusion of the Syracuse and Indianapolis franchises.

In the summer of 1948, a year before pulling off the coup that was organizing the Indianapolis Olympians franchise, Ferris was tasked with transforming the struggling Syracuse Nationals into a contender while still acting as team president and general manager for an opposing team in Tri-Cities.

Both the BAA and NBL were filled to the brink with teams riddled with financial woes, with owners in both leagues resorting to clandestine arrangements to prevent bankruptcy and grant their respective league an upper hand.

Amid the exodus of the NBL's top franchises, Syracuse's market stood as the league's sole bargaining chip before the Olympians existed, but in their first two years of existence, the Nationals had managed two losing records and were losing money.

Ferris carried the responsibility of increasing attendance enough to make Syracuse a profitable team, or else the franchise would have to consider relocation, a prospect that would have jeopardized any chance of a merger between the two leagues and potentially spelled doom for the NBL's very existence.

Danny Biasone, an Italian restaurateur who had achieved significant success in the past decade operating a Syracuse bowling alley called the Eastwood Sports Center, established the team in 1946, but a veteran team that featured Mike Novak and a mishmash of largely unheralded transplants from around the country was mired in mediocrity from the beginning. Before Ferris could fill stadiums with promotional advertising techniques, he first had to assemble a new roster, which Biasone was entirely on board with funding.

His first move in Syracuse was to sign Al Cervi, whose Rochester Royals had just left for the BAA. Tensions between Cervi and the Royals' management were already high, with Les Harrison misleading Cervi about his teammates' salaries, touting Bob Davies over him for the 1946–47 MVP award, and publicly accusing Cervi of feigning a knee injury.

Cervi, as well as being arguably the most intense, hard-nosed perimeter defender of his day, was a respected leader and team captain, and as part of his deal to move to Syracuse, Ferris appointed him player-coach. He didn't stop his warring with BAA teams after Cervi either; he was intimately involved in the signing of Billy Gabor, Syracuse University's all-time leading scorer at the time, and outbid Rochester to do so.[4]

Adolph Schayes, a standout player from New York University, made history by becoming the first center in a decade to receive the prestigious Haggerty Award for being the top college player in the New York metropolitan area, an award that typically went to guards.

A highly sought-after prospect, Schayes was drafted that summer by his hometown New York Knicks of the BAA and the Ferris-owned Tri-Cities Blackhawks of the NBL. As a Jewish native of the Bronx and the son of Romanian immigrants, Schayes hesitated to leave his home and play for a team based as far away as Moline, Illinois, while the alternative was to become a hometown hero for the Knicks at Madison Square Garden.

New York owner Ned Irish, though, operated the Knicks under a self-imposed salary cap. Ferris, recognizing the opportunity, sold Schayes' draft rights from Tri-Cities to Syracuse and offered him a contract on behalf of the Nationals instead. Syracuse would pay him $7,500 per year, 50 percent more than the Knicks were willing to offer any rookie. Although the Knicks proposed a summer job to potentially increase his earnings, they couldn't guarantee the nature of the job and refused to negotiate his base salary. Schayes joined Cervi and Gabor in Syracuse.[5]

With Ferris' reinforcements and some additional signings by Biasone, the Nationals entered the 1948–49 season with an entirely new starting lineup and four of the previous year's starters available on the bench.

Schayes and Cervi emerged as the top players on the team, and after Cervi made an adjustment to play Schayes, an agile player with a more than capable set shot who didn't like to get unnecessarily physical, at power forward rather than center, they improved from 24–36 to 40–23 in just one season. Additionally, Biasone and Ferris had hit it off so well that Ferris sold his shares in the Blackhawks and joined Syracuse full-time as executive director.

As the Nationals' early-season run established them as the Eastern Division favorites, most of their fellow former NBL teams over in the Western Division struggled, with the exceptions being the Sheboygan Redskins at 7–2 and the Anderson Packers at 6–3.

Sheboygan was proving to be an especially difficult matchup because of their breakneck pace. Right after a season in which the average team, between the BAA and NBL combined, scored 72.2 points, Sheboygan's average score to start off the season was 95–94. Their style of play emphasized quick shots and encouraged their opponents to do the same.

With four of their five starters adept at handling the ball and a center in Noble Jorgensen who possessed both speed and strength, Sheboygan posed a significant offensive threat. Jorgensen displayed exceptional performances against notable centers such as Arnie Risen, Harry Boykoff, and Alex Groza, culminating in a 35-point outburst against the Bullets prior to the Redskins' Thanksgiving matchup against Tri-Cities.

There was some bad blood between Sheboygan and Tri-Cities, as the Blackhawks had eliminated Sheboygan from playoff contention the prior year.

In an attempt to embarrass the Blackhawks and eliminate their key players from the game, second-year coach Kenny Suesens directed his Redskins to relentlessly attack the heart of the defense, specifically targeting Don Otten, the NBL's final MVP, who heavily relied on drawing fouls against Jorgensen and Bob Brannum in the previous playoffs.

Jorgensen himself had become quite proficient at getting to the free throw line in his recent stretch, and that would be a tool to use to his advantage. Otten quickly found himself in serious foul trouble and on the bench, but Sheboygan continued to drive to the rack with the express purpose of drawing as many fouls as possible.

When all was said and done, Jorgensen attempted 13 free throws, Danny Wagner made 14 off the bench, and all but one of Sheboygan's players attempted at least five. Sheboygan ended the game with 71 free throw attempts, compared to 65 shots from the field. Tri-Cities ran out of players.[6]

The Blackhawks started the game with 10 players available, but, one by one, Mac Otten, Billy Hassett, Jim Owens, Warren Perkins, and Don Otten all fouled out. Soon after, Dike Eddleman fouled out as well, but with no one left on the bench, the referees applied a seldom-used rule that permitted him to continue playing but resulted in a technical foul being assessed to the team alongside the regular foul penalty. With three minutes left in the game, Whitey Von Nieda suffered a severe eye contusion and lacerated eyelid during a rough scrap under the basket for a rebound and had to be taken out of the game. As the last player to foul out before Eddleman, Don Otten returned to the game in Von Nieda's stead. Otten fouled Sheboygan shooting guard Jack Burmaster twice in the closing minutes of the game, ending with eight personal fouls, a record that remains unbeaten.

Adolph "Dolph" Schayes (1960) led the Nationals in scoring, placed second in assists, and, while unofficial, certainly led them in rebounds as well. It is estimated that he placed second in the league in rebounds behind George Mikan.

Sheboygan emerged victorious with a 120–113 score, setting a new high-scoring record, propelled by 27 points from Jorgensen and 26 from Wagner.

Later that same day came a rematch of another pair of NBL playoff foes from the previous year: the Anderson Packers and Syracuse Nationals, with Anderson having won a 3–1 series as part of their path to a championship.

Anderson, like Sheboygan known for their fast and gritty style of play, initially appeared poised for a comfortable victory against Syracuse, holding an 11-point lead at halftime; however, the Nationals' backup guards, Ray Corley and Johnny Macknowski, led a remarkable comeback, with Corley tying the game with 28 seconds left with a pair of free throws to send the game into overtime.

In the first overtime, Corley was again Syracuse's savior, sinking a free throw with 32 seconds left after a double foul was called. The second and third overtimes were each similarly tied up by late free throws from unlikely heroes, provided by a pair of Anderson backups in Ed Stanczak and Walt Kirk. Ultimately, it was the Nationals' Fuzzy Levane, formerly Rochester's sixth man, who emerged as the hero, sinking a long-range set shot with two seconds remaining in the fourth overtime to extend the contest to a fifth and final overtime, and later securing victory by stealing the ball from the Packers with a two-point lead and 23 seconds remaining.

The final score was 125–123, breaking many of the records that had been set that same day. Five overtimes also made it the longest game the NBA had seen so far. Syracuse's 125 points were the most points ever scored; Anderson's 123 were the most ever scored by either a road team or a losing team. Two hundred forty-eight points combined broke the record that had been set earlier that day by 15 points.

On top of that, they even managed to break the foul record that Sheboygan and Tri-Cities had just set, as the two teams combined for 122 fouls over the course of the 73 minutes of action. From beginning to end, the game took three hours and 55 minutes.

Syracuse had six players foul out and just five left by the end of the game. Anderson had every player but one foul out, and John Hargis and Rollie Seltz both picked up their seventh foul. No game since has ever come close to 122 fouls. One hundred sixty free throws were attempted; no game since has surpassed 136. Anderson had eight technical fouls called against them, also still a record. The Nationals' Paul Seymour played the entirety of the game until he fouled out with two minutes left in the fifth and final overtime, ending the game with 71 minutes played, a number that has also never been surpassed.[7]

The Denver Nuggets' 101–81 loss to the Minneapolis Lakers, pushing Minneapolis atop the Central Division, was the last of 15 straight losses to start the Nuggets' time in the NBA. It would take 21 years for that number to be matched and an additional 18 for it to be beaten.

Denver's star player, Kenny Sailors, had recently found his form with four consecutive games of 20 or more points, but even 29 against the Lakers couldn't make the game anywhere near close.[8]

The team they were finally able to beat in the next game to end their embarrassing run of defeats, something the Nuggets managed to do despite starting the game by falling behind 21–4, was the Baltimore Bullets, a team that had won a BAA championship just two years earlier but had quickly fallen into a rut that was proving hard to climb out of. Sailors contributed 20 points and Dillard Crocker led Denver in scoring with 24.[9]

The Bullets were the one contribution to the NBA from the ABL, which had been the closest thing the NBL had to a major league competitor before the arrival of the BAA.

They were founded in 1944 to replace a short-lived Baltimore Clippers team that had gone belly-up three years prior. Named after the Old Baltimore Shot Tower, the Bullets defied expectations in their inaugural year, taking advantage of weakened competition due to military commitments to reach the ABL championship series despite a losing record.[10]

In the following season, the microwave scorer Stan Stutz and midseason addition Mike Bloom propelled the Bullets to the 1945–46 ABL championship. That summer, the ABL faced talent depletion as many players were signed by the new BAA. Baltimore was lucky; Stutz was signed by the Knicks but the Bullets replaced him by bringing in Buddy Jeannette from the Zollners as player-coach. Every other ABL playoff team lost three or more starters.

One of the most notable figures in professional basketball, Jeannette had an impressive career that included three NBL championships in the past four seasons, making it especially odd that he would drop down to a league that was in the process of falling into minor league status.

Initially signing with the NBL's Warren Penns to avoid going broke after a teaching job fell through, he found success when they relocated to Detroit and rebranded as the Eagles, only leaving for Rochester once the Eagles ceased operations at the start of World War II.[11] Jeannette joined Sheboygan four games before the 1942–43 playoffs, leading them to the Finals against the favored Fort Wayne Zollners, where he played a pivotal role, leading a winning effort in game one before the Zollners equalized the series with an overtime win.

In game three, neither team wanted to let the game get away from them and it reverted to a plodding slugfest that featured both teams holding on to the ball without attempting a shot for minutes at a time during the second half.

Sheboygan had possession, trailing by one point, after Jeannette grabbed a crucial rebound in the game's closing moments. Jeannette swiftly advanced down the court, hoping to orchestrate the winning play, and passed the ball to dependable defense-first center Ed Dancker in the post. Jeannette made a cut, looking to get the ball back for the last shot, but Dancker opted to back down Fort Wayne's Jake Pelkington and waited till the last second of the game to drain a title-winning close-range hook shot with Pelkington in his face. Sheboygan won the series 2–1 in the first and only time an NBL championship result was decided at the buzzer of the decisive game.[12]

That summer, Jeannette joined the team he had just beaten, teaming up with Bobby McDermott to establish quite possibly the greatest offensive backcourt pairing in professional basketball thus far. With Fort Wayne, he won two more championships in 1943–44 and 1944–45, both over Sheboygan, but the season after that they suffered a stunning series of three straight losses to Rochester in 1945–46, thwarting Fort Wayne's chances of becoming the first team in major league professional basketball to achieve a three-peat within a league.

Baltimore enticed Jeannette to leave Fort Wayne with a five-figure salary to join their team as a player-coach after that, and he didn't disappoint. Dominating the league, the Bullets secured 31 victories out of 34 games. For the final stretch of regular season games, Jeannette added 6'9" center Kleggie Hermsen, a defensive-minded journeyman who had begun to develop a bit of a scoring touch from the right block with the woeful Toronto Huskies earlier in the year, to the roster. Signing with Baltimore was a breach of his contract with Toronto, and Maurice Podoloff responded to the news by banning Hermsen from the BAA for life, the first such punishment doled out by the league.[13] Prior to the 1947 ABL Finals, the Bullets controversially withdrew from the league, declaring themselves league champions and embarking on an exhibition tour instead. While the ABL recognized Trenton as the official champions, the Bullets remained champions in all but name.[14]

With major financial losses in the first BAA season, four teams folded and Maurice Podoloff was stuck desperately scrambling for replacement teams, ultimately adding only the Bullets. As part of their agreement to join the league, they successfully appealed for Hermsen's ban to be lifted.

Baltimore general manager Bill Dyer, most known for his work as an MLB play-by-play announcer, recognized the talent disparity between the leagues and worked on revamping the roster with additions such as Chick Reiser and Dick Schulz, Jeannette's former NBL teammates.

Paul Hoffman, a rookie out of Purdue who had played both basketball and football in college, was also brought in as an enforcer at the small forward position. Jeannette deployed him as a ruthless defender assigned to each opponent's top perimeter scoring threat, but he dealt with knee issues throughout the year, limiting his effectiveness at the start of the season and causing him to miss 11 games. Nonetheless, he held tight to his starting spot, always working hard and steadily developing as an offensive contributor in the latter part of the season.

Baltimore's transformation into a competitive BAA team was completed with the addition of Connie Simmons, acquired in a mid-season trade with the Boston Celtics. Simmons, similar to Jeannette years earlier, stumbled into professional basketball by chance.

After military service and a period dominating New York street ball, Simmons initially planned to enroll at NYU, but changed his decision when his brother joined the New York Yankees' farm system instead of returning to school. Instead, he committed to the College of the Holy Cross, coincidentally driving his brother to the Celtics' training camp in Boston.

When they arrived, Connie stuck around for a little bit and played a pickup game against some of the players. As it turned out, the Celtics were one of the least talented teams the BAA would host that year, and he stood out in comparison to most of the players signed to the team.[15] Celtics coach Honey Russell asked him to stay, and not only did he make the team, he led them in scoring as a rookie.

He also proved to be the final piece of the puzzle for Baltimore, helping them to win nine times in the last 13 games of 1947–48 to sneak into the playoffs by tying the Chicago Stags' and Washington Capitols' records on the last day of the season. In the first round against the Knicks, Simmons played the best basketball of his career, averaging 26.3 points over three games. Both of the Bullets' wins were single-digit games and Simmons scored over a third of Baltimore's points that series.

Hoffman caused a stir by briefly leaving the Bullets prior to their second round series against the Stags, citing his wife's disapproval that he made his living by "running around in public in short pants." Threatened by Podoloff with league blackballing, Hoffman returned for the series against the Chicago Stags, leading Baltimore in scoring as they advanced to the BAA Finals without much trouble.[16]

In the Finals, the heavily favored Philadelphia Warriors took an early lead, winning the first game with a strong defensive effort and taking a 41–20 lead by halftime of game two. However, Buddy Jeannette's playmaking and Connie Simmons' scoring prowess helped the Bullets turn the tide in the second half as they came back to win game two 66–63 despite shooting a dreadful 19 percent from the field.[17]

The Bullets also hung on for two very close wins at home to take a 3–1 series lead despite Fulks' best efforts, and after the Warriors showed a semblance of life back in Philadelphia for game five, Baltimore finished them off in game six with a commanding 88–73 win.

They achieved the unthinkable in their inaugural BAA season, defying limited funding, meager salaries, a glorified roller rink of an arena, and scarce support staff, but their triumph bore unforeseen consequences as players sought better contracts and opportunities with other teams. Kleggie Hermsen and Dick Schulz both left that summer to join the Washington Capitols. Hoffman, who only made $4,000 that year, hinted that he would hold out for an improved contract.

After months of lingering uncertainty surrounding Hoffman's future with the Bullets, it was a bit of a surprise when Hoffman declared he would be showing up for training camp after all, and a massive blow a week into camp when he showed up with a doctor's note stating he had a heart condition that rendered him unfit to play.

He didn't actually have a heart condition at all, and this bizarre spectacle transformed into a farce when he announced he had gotten a second opinion that showed no heart problem after all and was ready to play, requested and was wired money to travel back to Baltimore but never showed up, and asked for more traveling money and was instead sent plane tickets back to Baltimore courtesy of the team and still failed to arrive, although the season had already started. Ultimately, Hoffman came clean, confessing through a letter that the heart ailment was entirely fictitious and his reason for not playing was because of an ultimatum from his wife. He was moving to Atlanta.[18]

Astonishingly, none of that was true either. He didn't move to Atlanta, instead returning to Indiana to work as a Montgomery Ward salesman, and while his wife certainly played a role in the decision, the primary reason he quit remained financial. He believed his play as a rookie warranted a pay rise to $7,500 and the Bullets simply couldn't afford to pay him that much without shedding salary elsewhere. He hated not playing basketball, though, and announced his intention to return to the Bullets shortly after his season away from the sport ended.[19]

When Hoffman returned for 1949–50, he secured the improved contract he desired, but his teammates Reiser and Simmons departed for the Capitols and Knicks, respectively, leaving Hoffman and an aging Jeannette as the sole remnants of the championship-winning core as the Bullets transitioned to the NBA.

Jeannette, affected by age-related decline in athleticism, struggled with scoring and faced a crisis of confidence, resulting in poor shooting performance even for a guard not known for his shooting. With Jeannette forced back into a starting role due to the retirement of his replacement, Sid Tanenbaum, after benching himself the previous year, rookie Joe Dolhon's emergence as a confident and unselfish player with an explosive first step prompted Jeannette to pass the starting position to him early in the season, a decision that proved beneficial as Jeannette battled a niggling knee injury that kept him sidelined for most back-to-back games.

At that same time, the Lakers and Stags met to battle for control of the Central Division. With Minneapolis having surpassed Fort Wayne by winning their last three games while the Pistons lost two straight, the two teams came into the game tied for the top spot of what was proving to be the NBA's most competitive division.

The Stags were a team with a culture of success who consistently delivered winning seasons in the BAA. They exemplified the league's ambition to be the first professional basketball league treated with the same institutional respect as the NCAA by securing the services of renowned college coach Harold Olsen.

Olsen brought his coaching prowess to the professional realm after initiating a period of sustained success as the longtime coach at Ohio State, which he transformed from an overlooked program into a formidable force during his 24-year tenure. Olsen's role within the realm of basketball expanded significantly when he assumed the presidency of the National Association of Basketball Coaches, leading to notable contributions to the sport. In 1932, he introduced the concept of the half-court line and the accompanying time limit rule, which penalized the offensive team for failing to advance into the frontcourt within 10 seconds.[20]

Six years later, Olsen developed a concept for a national tournament that would determine the NCAA champions. His idea came from the success of the NIT and the National College Basketball Tournament (NCBT) in the previous year.

The NIT had just concluded its first-ever tournament in the spring of 1938 at Madison Square Garden. It featured six teams, including four conference champions—Colorado, New York University, Oklahoma A&M, and Temple—with Temple emerging as the victors.

The NCBT, a small-school national championship, was the brainchild of the Rev. Dr. James Naismith, who had a long association with the sport after inventing it and later serving as a physical education director and basketball coach at the University of Kansas.

Despite a modest 55–60 coaching record, Naismith continued as the university's athletic director, briefly interrupted by military chaplaincy during World War I and a YMCA secretary role in Paris.

Recognizing his contributions, the National Association of Basketball Coaches, upon Olsen's suggestion, established a fund to send Naismith to the 1936 Berlin Olympics, where basketball debuted as a competitive Olympic sport. As a ceremonial tribute to his invention of the game, he performed the opening tip-off of the first game, a 34–29 win for Estonia over France, and presented the medals for basketball.[21]

After participating in the Olympics, Naismith collaborated with Baker University coach Emil Liston and Frank Cramer of Cramer Chemical Company to establish a postseason tournament for small colleges, providing recognition to programs overshadowed by larger universities. This was his last contribution to the game of basketball, as he retired days after the conclusion of the first edition of the NCBT following the death of his wife, Maude.

Olsen's invitational tournament, officially run by the NCAA, aimed to determine a national champion among the top eight college basketball teams in the country.

One of the eight teams chosen to participate in the first NCAA basketball tournament would be Olsen's Ohio State, as an alternate when Bradley University declined their invitation and opted for the NIT instead. Ohio State overcame the stigma of not having originally been invited by advancing to the NCAA championship game, ultimately losing 46–33 to the University of Oregon with the Rev. Dr. Naismith in the crowd.

Olsen's team's success didn't parallel the tournament as a whole: while the NIT games attracted large crowds at Madison Square Garden with over 18,000 capacity, the NCAA tournament had difficulties filling up Northwestern University's Patten Gymnasium, with reports of attendance ranging from 4,400 to 5,500. An estimated 400 of them were opposing college coaches, as part of a National Association of Basketball Coaches convention event, and many tickets were given away for free in an unsuccessful attempt to increase attendance.[22]

Despite financial losses initially threatening to doom the tournament, Harold Olsen struck a deal with the NCAA to secure an underwriter for it, ensuring its continuation. The tournament found success in the following years, hosting events in Kansas City and later Madison Square Garden, competing alongside the NIT.

The dynamic between the NIT and NCAA tournaments began to shift in the early to mid–1940s, with the NCAA gaining prominence due to a Red Cross War Benefit Fund Game arranged by Ned Irish, then a basketball promoter at Madison Square Garden.

The idea of basketball for charity arose a year prior when a fan's letter to the *New York Times* led to a game between Long Island University and City College of New York, raising over $7,000 for the U.S. Army. Irish conceptualized and took charge of promoting the Red Cross War Benefit Fund Game, which featured the NIT champion against the NCAA champion in a battle for the title of "Champion of Champions." The NCAA champion emerged victorious in all three editions of the game, raising over $117,000 for the Red Cross.[23]

The rise of Harold Olsen's tournament, on its way to becoming the premier college basketball tournament, coincided with the success of Ohio State, who, led in part by Arnie Risen, made the Final Four three straight years and won the Big Ten twice. After this stretch, Olsen departed for the Stags.

Despite their standing as a prime example of the BAA's aims, though, the Stags already ignited controversy even before their professional debut.

When initially selected as a founding team of the BAA, Chicago's franchise was named the Chicago Atomics, a tribute to the University of Chicago's hosting of the world's first artificial nuclear reactor, Chicago Pile-1, in 1942.[24] Led by physicist Enrico Fermi, CP-1 marked a significant milestone in the Manhattan Project, demonstrating the viability of nuclear chain reactions and the use of synthetic graphite as a neutron moderator.

After just two preseason games, the Atomics name was scrapped. Between the atomic bombings of Hiroshima and Nagasaki, Japan, in the final days of World War II and the increasing international tensions between the United States and the Soviet Union, an ever-present reminder to the general public of the potential of instantaneous annihilation was determined to not be the best possible branding.

Nine days later, the new name and logo were unveiled and the team became the Chicago Stags.

The choice of the Stags name for the Chicago franchise, while also being a clever nod to the abundant deer population in Illinois, primarily paid tribute to Amos Alonzo Stagg, a prominent figure in basketball and football who served as the University of Chicago's athletic director and football coach for over four decades.

In the same fashion as the Rev. Dr. James Naismith, Stagg found his passion for coaching sports after excelling as an athlete himself. He played football and baseball at Yale and even received offers from multiple Major League Baseball teams as a pitcher following his football career as a lineman, during which he contributed to three national championships and a 53–2 record, earning him a spot on the inaugural College Football All-America Team in 1889.

It was at the International YMCA Training School where he and Naismith crossed paths, as Stagg was given his first full-time job as a football coach while studying there, allowing him to showcase his innovative sports thinking.

He devised the ends-back formation as a strategic response to his team's significant disadvantage in size and personnel, which further led to the creation of a sequence of plays he named the "criss cross," now recognized in contemporary football parlance as the reverse.

Under his leadership, the International YMCA Training School admirably achieved a 5–3 record, including a commendable 28–0 loss to Yale, a particularly respectable showing for a school with an enrollment of 42 students against the undefeated national champions, given the fact that it was a narrower deficit than seven of Yale's other opponents had managed that year.

Toward the end of Stagg's second year coaching in Springfield, Naismith, who had played center for Stagg's football team, recruited him to play for the faculty basketball team in the first game open to the public. He scored the faculty team's only point in a 5–1 loss.

In 1892, Stagg was appointed football coach and athletic director at the University of Chicago, where he became football's greatest-ever innovator: he invented the huddle, the lateral pass, the man-in-motion, the quarterback keeper, the seven-man line defense, the direct pass from center, the backfield shift, the short punt, the Statue of Liberty play, the linebacker position, the tackling dummy, wind sprints, football helmets, uniform numbers, and awarding varsity letters; he was a contributor to the center snap, the forward pass, the T formation, and the onside kick; he was the first national sports figure to promote vegetarianism in athletics; and he made the game of football accessible to fans by cowriting (along with University of Minnesota coach Henry Williams) the first book on football that included diagrams of plays.

Stagg won seven Big Ten conference championships and two national championships at Chicago. Thirteen of his assistant coaches became head coaches at the college level. So did 52 of his players.[25]

Stagg also coached baseball at Chicago for 18 years, during which he helped promote the sport in Japan by arranging for the baseball team to tour Japan.

He brought basketball to Chicago and scheduled an experimental exhibition game against the University of Iowa in which both teams agreed to shorten the lineups from then-typical nine or seven players per team to five players a side. Chicago won, 15–12, and five-on-five basketball was born.

By the time the Chicago Stags were chosen to be his namesake in 1946, the University of Chicago no longer had a football team. Stagg was still coaching, heading into his 57th and final season as a collegiate head coach. He remained involved in football, serving as an associate head coach to his son at Susquehanna University and as a special teams coordinator at Stockton Junior College, only retiring from the sport at the remarkable age of 96.

The Chicago Pile-1 nuclear reactor that the Stags had originally been named in honor of was built in a temporary laboratory underneath the west stand of the University of Chicago's Stagg Field, named in his honor decades earlier. As such, the new name honoring Stagg maintained the civic pride in Chicago as the birthplace of nuclear reactions that had been the intention behind the original name, marking the deep understanding of the team's founding owner, John Sbarbaro, regarding the city's history and culture.

Sbarbaro, a prominent figure in Chicago's courtrooms during the early 20th century, earned his legal reputation as part of the prosecution team in the notorious 1924 murder trial of Nathan Leopold and Richard Loeb, and after serving as a municipal and criminal circuit court judge he rose to the position of chief justice of the Cook County Superior Court, where he preferred to preside over family court cases, reflecting his deep commitment to the nuclear family.

He also was a known associate of Chicago crime syndicates in and after Prohibition.

Throughout much of his professional life, he made a practice of bailing out gangsters from prison, and it's commonly speculated that he was responsible for laundering money and whiskey for top Chicago gangsters such as Al Capone.

Sbarbaro gained his notoriety through his family business, Sbarbaro's Funeral Home, which became intertwined with Chicago's criminal outfits. In running that funeral parlor, John Sbarbaro attained his reputation as "The Undertaker for the Underworld."

When Mike Merlo, the influential head of Unione Siciliana, passed away in 1924, Capone financed Merlo's extravagant funeral through Sbarbaro's Funeral Home, solidifying Sbarbaro's reputation and making his lavish services a staple for gangsters' funerals. Sbarbaro planned the funerals of rival gang leaders, such as Dean O'Banion, Hymie Weiss, and Vincent Drucci, with handcrafted caskets made of precious metals and elaborate floral arrangements.

At Weiss' funeral, since Sbarbaro was running for municipal court at the time, he designed gaudy placards displaying the message "John Sbarbaro for Municipal Judge," which he placed on all sides of the hearse carrying Weiss' body, as he figured the spectacle would draw in enough people that the message could influence election results. Six months later, he won the election.[26]

Sbarbaro's politico judicial ambitions, mixed with his public association with organized crime, brought with them an unmistakable target on his back. In spring of 1928, Capone hired a notorious extortionist and contract killer named James Belcastro to attack political opponents of the Capone-backed Chicago mayor William Hale Thompson in the 1928 Republican primary election. Belcastro had worked for Capone before, using hand grenades against saloons that refused to buy Capone's alcohol and causing an estimated 100+ deaths in the process.

The resulting chaos took place in the form of the Pineapple Primary, a series of 62 targeted bombings throughout the city masterminded by Belcastro that resulted in 15 deaths, including the assassinations of two local politicians. One of the first of these bombings was of Sbarbaro's Funeral Home's backroom garage, which Sbarbaro allegedly used as a storage facility for bootleg whiskey.[27]

Following Capone's imprisonment in 1932 and the subsequent leadership of Frank Nitti, who aimed to reduce attention on the gang and cut down on the tradition of extravagant funerals, Sbarbaro severed ties with organized crime and shifted his focus to charitable endeavors in Chicago's Italian-American community. Years later, he had distanced himself enough from criminal circles that no red flags were raised when he applied to own Chicago's BAA team.

The core component Sbarbaro secured for the inaugural roster for the Stags was Chuck Halbert, a 6'10" AAU center christened "the tallest basketball player in America" a decade prior when he began his college career.[28]

After three years at West Texas State College, Halbert attempted to enlist in the U.S. Army to take part in the war effort, but the height limit barred him from joining. He instead spent two years working at the Boeing Airplane Company building heavy bombers for the military and short stints playing for the Phillips Oilers and the Lee Tires before signing with the Stags.

Renowned for his rebounding skills and aggressive playing style, Halbert's court vision and ability to dunk added a unique dimension to his game, combining elements of both old-school and new-school center play and opening up an opportunity for the rest of the roster

Max Zaslofsky (shooting, January 2, 1949) of the Chicago Stags, having been a constant presence in the All-BAA First Team, was the scoring half, along with Andy Phillip, of the most dynamic backcourt in the NBA. He was top five in the league for points in 1949–50 and made the All-NBA First Team, controversially beating out Adolph Schayes for the honor. Also shown (from left): Paul Noel, Irv Rothenberg, and Goebel Ritter, all of the New York Knicks.

composition to be selected on a best-player-available determination.

The best player available that Chicago was able to sign was Max Zaslofsky, a Jewish shooting guard from Brooklyn prized for his exceptional set shot during his lone collegiate year at St. John's.

Between the respect that his deadly shooting stroke commanded from defenders and the bursts of acceleration that made him nearly an equally adept penetrator, Zaslofsky quickly established himself as a dangerous scorer in the BAA, but he was also a player whose impact was overly defined by his ability on any given day to put the ball in the basket.

Under Harold Olsen's guidance, the Stags implemented a high-tempo offense to capitalize on the agility of players like Zaslofsky and exploit the disadvantage of slower-paced veteran teams. Although the season started with average results, a remarkable 10-week period from late January to mid–March saw the Stags' offense thrive, winning 15 out of 17 games and surpassing the 100-point mark in four games (a feat unmatched by any other team that season). They finished the year with the second-best record in the league, and Zaslofsky made All-BAA First Team while Halbert made All-BAA Second Team.

After Olsen outcoached Red Auerbach in an upset over the Washington Capitols, Chicago was positioned as favorites in the first BAA Finals against the Philadelphia Warriors, whom they had beaten five out of six times in the regular season. However, the Warriors presented a unique challenge, having effectively neutralized Chicago's fast-paced style and consistently kept the games close, with both Zaslofsky and Halbert underperforming against them.

The addition of Chuck Gilmur to the starting lineup, a godsend against Washington, backfired against the high-scoring Joe Fulks, who exploded for 37 points in the series opener, with 29 in the second half alone. Despite Fulks' subpar performance in the second game, the Stags' abysmal shooting, worst of all Zaslofsky's 1-of-19 from the field, handed the Warriors a commanding 2–0 series lead.[29]

From there, Chicago's chances dwindled as Zaslofsky was only capable of regaining his scoring touch in one of the remaining games, the Stags as a whole struggled at the line in crucial moments, and Fulks largely controlled the tempo of the series. Philadelphia finished off Chicago in five games with a late comeback sealed by Ralph Kaplowitz, a midseason acquisition from the Knicks.

Early in the following season, the departure of Halbert to the Philadelphia Warriors weakened the Chicago Stags, but they also had a replacement in Stan Miasek via a dispersal draft after the Detroit Falcons disbanded. Miasek had been a first-team All-NBA player the year before, and was in fact the only player on a losing team to make the All-NBA First Team.

Miasek was cut from high school basketball and baseball teams on each attempt before joining the U.S. Navy and excelling in the service leagues, where his size and coordination helped him to become one of the top centers among the military teams for the Bunker Hill Sailors and the Iowa Pre-Flight Seahawks.

Upon his discharge, Miasek garnered significant attention from professional teams, signing with the MLB's Detroit Tigers and ultimately choosing the Detroit Falcons over the Knicks in a BAA bidding war, as they were based in the same city as his MLB team and offered a higher salary.

The Falcons disbanded with a 20–40 record and the second-lowest home attendance in the league and Miasek ended up in Chicago. With the ability to fill the void left by Halbert as an occasional interior playmaker and his impressive agility for a center, Miasek quickly became a valuable asset for the Stags, also excelling as a rim runner during fast breaks.

The addition of Miasek, along with high-profile rookie Andy Phillip, gave Chicago a solid foundation for success with two of the league's top scorers and a facilitator to set them up.

Phillip, leader of the University of Illinois' Whiz Kids in the early 1940s, spearheaded a high-octane team that boasted four future NBA players in its starting lineup and ruled college basketball in the Midwest in 1941–42 and 1942–43. Their near-perfect 1942–43 season included a lone loss when coach Douglas Mills opted to field reserves against the Camp Grant Warriors service league team.

Despite an undefeated conference season, capped off with an outlandish 92–25 win over the University of Chicago at the end of the season, their championship hopes were dashed as three starters were drafted into the war effort. Mills and the remaining players elected not to participate in a postseason tournament with many of their core pieces unavailable.[30]

Four months later, Phillip himself joined the U.S. Marine Corps. He was stationed at Parris Island, Iwo Jima, and Honolulu. After the war, four of the five Whiz Kids starters returned to Illinois, but their reunion effort fell short, and they finished with a modest 14–6 record.

The addition of Phillip to the Stags' lineup sparked a dynamic offensive duo with Zaslofsky, as they averaged a combined 31.8 points in their initial four games, but Phillip strained a knee ligament the next game, sidelining him for over a month, causing the team to lose momentum.

In December 1947, Harold Olsen fell critically ill, putting Phil Brownstein—a Stags' scout, assistant coach during home games, and head coach of nearby Kelvyn Park High School—in charge for a nine-game stretch.[31]

Miasek and Zaslofsky stepped up during this period, but Brownstein eventually had to step down when his high school's winter break ended after leading the Stags to a 7–2 record. That was followed by a 2–6 stretch under the tutelage of former Northwestern University star Saul Farber, with Phillip struggling to get back to top condition upon his return to action, and Chicago's fortunes quickly turned from leading the league to last place in a competitive Western Division in under three weeks.

Olsen's return provided a boost to the team, and Phillip showed signs of his usual form before another knee injury sidelined him for most of the remaining season. Despite his return for the final two games, Chicago fell short, narrowly missing the division title. In the playoffs, Zaslofsky, who narrowly beat Joe Fulks to the scoring title, carried the Stags past Boston, but they couldn't overcome the physicality of the Bullets, who exploited Phillip's injury and forced Miasek into foul trouble, resulting in a quick series sweep.

In the following season, the Stags made minimal roster changes, although John Sbarbaro emphasized the future with the signings of Joe Graboski and Jimmy Browne, both 18-year-old centers fresh out of high school and the league's only players without prior professional, military league, or collegiate experience.

Zaslofsky remained a top scoring threat in the BAA, while Phillip excelled as Chicago's pass-first playmaker, missing out on the league lead in assists by just two. However, Miasek's performance declined, struggling with shooting and foul trouble. In the playoffs, facing the dominant Lakers led by Mikan, the Stags were outmatched and swept.

The roster once again remained largely the same after the merger, but Olsen's health concerns caused him to resign and opened the door for Brownstein to assume the head coaching position. Despite a disappointing overtime loss in their NBA debut, Chicago rebounded with six consecutive wins, including a notable 86–79 victory over the very Lakers team that had consigned them to such a disappointing end to Harold Olsen's time in charge.

Second-year player Odie Spears, renowned for his collegiate success at Western Kentucky University, emerged as a capable third option offensively in addition to being their primary defensive weapon. After an adjustment period during his rookie year, Spears showcased improved scoring abilities, benefiting from the presence of center Kleggie Hermsen and starting the season with renewed confidence in his scoring prowess.

After a pair of blowout wins gave them the opportunity, Chicago capitalized on a chance to surpass the Lakers in the division standings, delivering a convincing 96–82 victory over Minneapolis. Zaslofsky led the way with 23 points, but five additional Stags players scored in double figures, including Spears, Phillip, and Miasek. Mikan scored 34 of his own, but aside from Jim Pollard, he was lacking in help, enabling the Stags to dictate the game's pace and secure a decisive outcome.[32]

While the race for the top team in the Eastern Division was seemingly already wrapped up in Syracuse's favor and the Central Division remained highly competitive, the Western Division turned into a two-team race. Denver and Waterloo both wallowed at the bottom of the league and Tri-Cities and Indianapolis failed to get any real consistency in order to make a run at a winning record. This set the stage for a battle between Sheboygan and Anderson for Western Division supremacy.

Anderson, despite being the reigning champions of the last NBL season, faced significant challenges as the second-smallest market in professional basketball, only ahead of Moline's Tri-Cities Blackhawks.

Packers owner Ike Duffey, though, was a gregarious, self-made millionaire who had built a strong team and played a pivotal role in the league merger, tirelessly championing the NBL's interests.

His initial foray into basketball came when Howard Cronk, the public relations director of Duffey's meatpacking company, proposed sponsoring a barnstorming team hailing from Anderson. Dubbed the Anderson Chiefs after Duffey's Chief Anderson meat brand, they surpassed all expectations. He adopted a standard of employing talented athletes on a full-time basis with bonuses reaching as high as $100 per game for top performers.

His aggressive recruitment tactics rubbed off on the players and fostered a reputation for a rough, fast-paced style predicated on chaos. Within just their first year of existence, they faced renowned barnstorming squads like the Harlem Globetrotters and New York Renaissance, as well as established NBL teams such as the Fort Wayne Zollners and Indianapolis Kautskys, even boasting a winning record against professional teams. Their accomplishments earned them an invitation to the WPBT, where they secured a victory before falling by just two points to the Baltimore Bullets.

Fueled by this taste of success, Duffey invested further by acquiring the NBL's struggling Pittsburgh Raiders' franchise slot and replacing them in the league with Anderson, who he renamed from the Chiefs to the Packers after solidifying his meatpacking monopoly by purchasing the Hughes-Curry Packing Co.[33]

Now a guaranteed participant in organized professional basketball, Duffey assembled a formidable team under the guidance of Murray Mendenhall, a respected high school coach with an impressive track record and the admiration of NBL players, having played an instrumental part in developing Curly Armstrong and Herman Schaefer from high schoolers into NBL champions.

In their pre–NBL year, Ed Stanczak emerged as Anderson's standout player, excelling offensively and providing energy in bounds. Stanczak maintained a prominent role in the Packers' starting lineup through the transition to the NBL.

Aside from Stanczak, the team underwent significant changes, with the arrival of key signings Howie Schultz and Rollie Seltz, college teammates from Hamline University whose simultaneous involvement in professional baseball and college basketball had sparked controversy.

Schultz's sophomore year at Hamline University showcased his leadership as he led the basketball team to a NAIB championship, its first on a national scale. At the same time, he spent his summers playing first base for the Double-A St. Paul Saints, for whom his father was on the board of directors.

During the 1943 baseball season, his exceptional fielding attracted the attention of the major leagues, leading to a trade to the Brooklyn Dodgers and an immediate call-up to replace former MVP Dolph Camilli. Despite his inconsistent hitting, Schultz's flourishing baseball career prompted him to leave Hamline before his senior year, relying on his exceptional defensive skills at first base to contribute as a reliable asset for his team.

After an impressive 1944 season, Schultz returned to Hamline for one final basketball season. He led them to a successful 20–4 record, but his returning presence on the roster brought to attention the fact that Seltz, another of Hamline's starters, had also spent part of the summer playing professional baseball for a Class D affiliate of the St. Louis Cardinals. While NCAA rules didn't expressly forbid either player from participating for Hamline, with amateurism rules having been laxed in wake of the war, the AAU condemned the program for allowing them to participate and blacklisted Hamline and all of their opponents that year.

Prior to the 1946–47 season, Duffey signed both players, with Schultz continuing to split his time between the Packers and the Dodgers, while Seltz's baseball career stagnated when his defensive liabilities stopped him from earning call-ups above the Class B level.

Mendenhall's run-and-gun offense, designed for his relatively undersized team, incorporated tactical elements he borrowed from rubber bridge, emphasizing anticipation and reading opponents. He was also an excellent and passionate motivator who easily got his team to believe in his approach to the sport. They won five of their first six NBL games, but a hypercompetitive Western Division ensured that their 24–20 record wasn't enough to qualify for the playoffs in their first year in the league.

Following the season, Mendenhall capitalized on the absence of a natural professional basketball pathway for college players in the South Central United States. The BAA, NBL, and ABL all avoided expanding into the southern half of the country, and the PBLA went into financial ruin before it could be determined whether the South could support professional basketball. As such, most of the best players from the area ended up in the AAU.

Mendenhall's son, Murray, Jr., began his college career at Rice University in Houston, Texas, so Mendenhall had a better reference point for the talent levels of players in the South than most professional coaches. His top target was Frank Brian of Louisiana State University, reputed to be the most explosively quick player in all of basketball. Over the next year, Brian was joined by John Hargis of the University of Texas, Charlie Black of the University of Kansas, Bill Closs of Rice University, and Frank Gates of Sam Houston State Teachers College.

The southern boys adapted well to rural Indiana's Hoosier culture and Mendenhall's fast-paced way of playing basketball. The 1947–48 season marked Anderson's ascent in the NBL, finishing just two games behind Rochester and reaching the Western Division Finals after sweeping Syracuse, while the following season saw them steamroll the league, winning nine more games than any other team in the regular season and undergoing no real playoff threats as they swept Oshkosh for the title of champions.

Duffey's influence in the basketball world extended beyond Anderson's success in the NBL. His ambitions reached a peak during the 1948–49 season, when he set his sights on acquiring the Indianapolis Jets, a move that would consolidate his power by putting him in control of three of Indiana's four professional teams. He would almost certainly come out of the deal with more power than any other individual in professional basketball, including Maurice Podoloff.

Podoloff, more aware of that than anyone, intervened and pledged that the BAA would not allow a sale but would instead protect the Jets until the season's end, regardless of mounting debts.

Duffey had already handpicked NBL commissioner Doxie Moore. He'd also facilitated the admission of several new teams, including the Waterloo Hawks and Denver Nuggets, both of which would go on to join the NBA. In addition to that, he paid the expenses of both the Sheboygan Redskins and Oshkosh All-Stars. By the end of the 1948–49 season, Duffey had effectively monopolized the entire NBL, with the exception of the Syracuse Nationals and Tri-Cities Blackhawks, which were both operated by Leo Ferris. Duffey had, out of necessity, pulled off the monopolization of an entire basketball league that Maurice White had attempted two years prior with the PBLA.

Duffey's ingenuity materialized in the creation of the Calumet Buccaneers. Duffey acquired the financially strained Toledo Jeeps and tasked Hammond, Indiana-based insurance agent Walter Thornton with organizing a group of local businessmen to form a corporation, Calumet Fans, Inc., that would buy the team from Duffey and, in turn, go public and sell shares to basketball fans around the city, bringing the Buccaneers into existence as a fan-owned team.

Unforeseen challenges then emerged when the Detroit Kings abandoned the NBL midseason with a dismal 2–17 record, throwing the league's schedule into disarray. The preferred solution to that was to convince a team to join the league to replace them immediately and take on both their record and their remaining schedule.

Finding a taker for what seemed to be a rough deal—joining a league in the middle of a season without any real chance at making the playoffs, thanks to the requirement that they add the nearly winless record of another team to their own—wouldn't be easy, especially with teams already locked into their prearranged schedules.

Drawing from his experiences running Anderson as an independent team before joining the NBL, Duffey turned to the world of barnstorming basketball, where relationships with top-tier management proved pivotal in navigating this tumultuous situation.

He contacted Bob Douglas of the New York Renaissance, and was able to convince Douglas to enter the Renaissance in the NBL, although, with as far east as they were compared to the rest of the NBL teams, they would have to relocate to an arena in the Midwest. Duffey financed an arena for the team in Dayton, Ohio, and they became the Dayton Rens, officially adopting the hypocoristic nickname they had informally used for years.

Just two days after Detroit's exit, the Rens became the first and only all–black, black-owned team in a professional league, in stark contrast to the segregationist policies of the rival BAA.[34]

During the scarcity of players in the 1942–43 season, the Toledo White Chevrolets and Chicago Studebakers of the NBL had pioneered integration by signing 10 black players, all former members of the Harlem Globe Trotters.

Toledo owner Sid Goldberg initiated the integration concept to compensate for the limited player pool, and it was the Studebakers who made history on November 25, 1942, as the first team in a major professional sports league to integrate since the NFL's unofficial ban on black players in 1934.[35] The Studebakers fielded seven black players—Bernie Price, Duke Cumberland, Hillery Brown, Roosie Hudson, Sonny Boswell, Ted Strong, and Tony Peyton—on a roster of 11, and four of them were starters.

Neither of the teams that integrated were particularly successful on the court. Toledo played just four games that season, losing all four, before ceasing operation. Chicago completed the entire season but finished with the worst record among the remaining teams and folded at season's end. None of the ten players who broke the color barrier in the NBL during the 1942–43 season went on to play another game in the league. Willie Smith, longtime center for the New York Renaissance, signed with his hometown Cleveland Chase Brass the next year but only played four games before leaving and entering semi-retirement.

It wasn't until the 1946–47 season that the NBL reintegrated, with four different teams signing black players after a three-year hiatus.

The most high-profile of the four new signings was Dolly King. King had been the first black basketball player to achieve prominence at a top-level basketball program in college nearly a decade earlier when he captained Long Island University.

As LIU's star center and team leader, King alongside Ossie Schectman—the eventual scorer of the first BAA points—emerged as a dominant force in college basketball both locally in New York and nationally. Their first season together resulted in an undefeated 23–0 record, culminating in a victorious 1938–39 NIT championship, in the process beating more teams by over 30 points than they did by merely single-digits.[36]

Midway through his senior year, King left the LIU program to go professional. He signed with the New York Renaissance and simultaneously formed his own barnstorming team, the Dolly King Five, but the outbreak of World War II hindered their tours. King shut down his own team when he began to work in military aircraft production for the Grumman Aircraft Engineering Corporation, and soon after traded his spot on the Renaissance for one on the Washington Bears.

Managed by renowned radio personality Hal Jackson and bolstered by signings from the New York Renaissance, the Bears played exclusively on Sundays to accommodate players with essential jobs or military commitments. Their opponents ranged from top all-black teams to NBL, ABL, and service league teams.[37]

In their second season, the Bears were invited to the WPBT in Chicago, where they handily defeated the Minneapolis Sparklers and the Dayton Dive Bombers. In the championship game, they employed a quick passing attack to overcome the Oshkosh All-Stars 43–31 and clinch the title with a perfect 41–0 record, becoming the first professional team since 1909–10 to complete an undefeated season.

The Bears remained one of the top basketball teams on the East Coast for the next three years but were never invited back to the WPBT to defend their title. Abe Lichtman retired in 1946 and shut down the team after the 1945–46 season. Most of the Bears players returned to the New York Renaissance, but two didn't: Dolly King and Pop Gates.

After the Washington Bears disbanded, Les Harrison recruited King to join the Rochester Royals, noting his skills as a top-notch rebounder and reliable defender. However, King's role in Rochester was limited as a substitute center or occasionally as a starting power forward due to teammate injuries.

He faced racial taunting from opposing fans, notably during the playoffs against Fort Wayne.[38] Although Rochester avenged the taunts by defeating the Zollners in a 2–1 series, their season ended in disappointment with a Finals loss to the Chicago Gears.

Harrison and Leo Ferris together championed the cause of integrating professional basketball and decided that summer to each sign one of the two best Washington Bears players. While King signed with Rochester, Ferris signed Gates to the Buffalo Bisons, which soon relocated to become the Tri-Cities Blackhawks.[39]

Gates, a tremendous shooter capable of playing both forward positions, was often compared to Hank Luisetti, known as one of the greatest college players of that time. He was also very fast, an exceptionally smart player, and a skilled and disciplined defender, all of which helped him become the ideal supporting piece to Don Otten for the Bisons-turned-Blackhawks.

He had skipped college to play professionally for the New York Renaissance in 1938–39, where he earned a starting spot almost immediately and played a major part in winning the WPBT as a rookie, gaining swift recognition for his shooting prowess and his sharp cuts to the basket. Like King, he joined the Bears when offered a more lucrative deal by Abe Lichtman, and he finished second in scoring only to King when the Bears won the WPBT as well.

In the NBL, Gates found success as the starting small forward for the Buffalo/Tri-Cities franchise, finishing third in scoring and earning respect throughout the league for his contributions to the Blackhawks' playoff contention.

Handicapped by their midseason move halfway across the country, the Blackhawks found themselves in a tight three-way race for the bottom two playoff spots. In a crucial game against Syracuse, tensions escalated, leading to a physical and chaotic encounter where Pop Gates and opposing forward Chick Meehan may as well have both spent as much time plummeting to the court's floor as they did upright. Meehan, an overly aggressive defender on his best day, became more combative than usual as Gates couldn't miss on offense.

As the game neared its end with Syracuse ahead by 12 points, Gates and Meehan got tangled up while lunging after a loose ball and Meehan's face hit the floor hard. Meehan, fed up, got up and squared off against Gates, looking for a fight. As soon as Meehan raised his fists, Gates knocked him out cold with a punch later described as a "really beautiful wallop [that] would have shamed most boxers."

The scene erupted into a brawl with hundreds of fans storming the court and Gates had to be escorted off the floor by a combination of local police officers and National Guard troops. Meehan was hospitalized for over a month with serious injuries to his left eye and cheekbone.[40]

The incident marred Gates' reputation in the NBL and was a likely factor behind NBL teams failing to offer contract renewals to him, King, Bill Farrow of the Youngstown Bears, or Willie King of the Detroit Gems, causing the NBL to revert to a whites-only league yet again.

Speculation ensued that Gates' actions might threaten Jackie Robinson's chances of getting called up to the Brooklyn Dodgers, but Robinson made his debut with the Dodgers two months later. Packers center and Dodgers first baseman Howie Schultz arrived late to training camp due to his basketball commitments, and Schultz's tardiness gave Robinson just enough of a chance to stand out in order to take Schultz's starting spot and run with it. A month later, Schultz was traded to the Philadelphia Phillies.

Schultz's baseball career faltered after leaving the Dodgers and ended after a disappointing season with the Phillies, a short-lived return to Brooklyn, and a wrist injury soon after joining the Cincinnati Reds spelled the end of his baseball career.

When Doxie Moore and Ike Duffey cut a deal to add the Renaissance to the NBL as the Dayton Rens a year later, three of the four members of the second attempt at integration returned to the league. Dolly King only played one game in the NBL and Farrow suffered a career-ending knee injury in just his third game in Dayton, but Gates was once again a prominent member of the NBL, acting as player-coach and starting at shooting guard.

The Rens weren't world-beaters in the NBL but they held their ground in the NBL with Gates excelling in his dual role as player-coach, with an improved statistical output compared to his other NBL season, while Hank DeZonie, known for his faceup playing style, emerged as a valuable asset as the team's starting center.

Leading scorer DeZonie, along with Gates and future MLB All-Star George Crowe, formed a formidable trio, but a homesick DeZonie left the team in the middle of February, leaving the Renaissance short-handed on top of their already difficult situation.

Dayton ended the season with a 14–26 record, which was better than the teams from either Denver or Calumet could produce and should have qualified them for the bottom playoff spot in the Eastern Division. Since they were required to add the 2–17 record of the Detroit Kings, though, officially speaking they had a league-worst record of 16–43. Calumet, who went 21–41—1.1 percent worse than the Rens managed—made the playoffs instead.[41]

Following the season, Dayton was excluded from the merger between the BAA and NBL.

4

Black Basketball, the New York Renaissance, and Sidat-Singh Is Not a Hindu

Bob Douglas had founded the New York Renaissance decades earlier in the aftermath of World War I. A native of the Caribbean island of Saint Kitts, he immigrated to the United States at 20 years old and fell in love with basketball when he first watched a game in New York that same year.

In 1908, he cofounded the Spartan Field Club, a youth club dedicated to offering organized sports opportunities for black children. He formed two amateur basketball teams associated with the club, later deciding in 1923 to found one of the first professional basketball teams exclusively owned by, operated by, and featuring black men.

Organized professional leagues were off-limits to black players at the time, but the amateur game had recently experienced unprecedented growth and success within the black communities of East Coast cities.

Dr. Edwin B. Henderson, the first certified black physical education teacher in the U.S., introduced basketball to the black community in 1904 after learning the sport during a summer teaching course at Harvard University.

Initially met with skepticism, he cofounded the first black amateur athletic union, leading to the sponsorship of basketball teams by schools, "Colored YMCAs," and Howard University in Washington, D.C. Organizations in Baltimore and New York quickly followed suit.

Brooklyn's Smart Set Athletic Club, Harlem's Alpha Physical Culture Club, and Manhattan's St. Christopher Club represented the best black teams out of New York. They helped to create the all-black Olympian Athletic League (OAL). The OAL turned basketball into a major social event in the late 1900s as Harlem began to transform into a beacon of black American culture.

Smart Set, a dominant force in New York's black basketball scene, gained recognition by winning the title of Colored Basketball World Champions in 1907–08, in what would become a long-standing tradition for *The New York Age* to annually recognize the best black basketball team in the country.

Major Hart, owner of St. Christopher Club, attempted to professionalize black basketball by founding the New York All-Stars in 1910–11. The team faced vehement opposition due to the prevailing taboo surrounding playing basketball for money. The heavy criticism of the "evils of professionalism" took a toll on the All-Stars, far more than it did on white teams that benefited from the infrastructure of professional leagues, and they shut down operations after 1912–13.

At the same time that the first black professional team dismantled, though, amateur black basketball's first superstar arose.

Cumberland Posey, born into an affluent black family in Pennsylvania, became black basketball's first superstar after dropping out of Pennsylvania State University due to poor grades and both signing with the Homestead Grays in baseball's Negro Leagues, and forming his own basketball team, the Monticello Athletic Association. The Monticellos had no home arena and had to practice at night in a gymnasium where one of their players worked as a janitor, but despite their lack of facilities, the Monticellos quickly surpassed the quality of Pittsburgh's top white teams.

Posey invited Howard University's team, then the reigning Colored World Champions, to Pittsburgh to play against Monticello in 1911–12. Howard players didn't take his challenge seriously and only accepted the offer as a way of showing the upstart Pennsylvanian team "how basketball is played in polite circles." Monticello defeated Howard 24–19, with Posey leading the way with 15 points. This proved to black Americans that it was possible to put together a basketball team capable of large-scale success outside of the two main hubs of Washington, D.C., and New York and spurred a rapid escalation of the creation of black-owned amateur teams in midsize cities throughout the country.

The team was later sponsored by the Loendi Social & Literary Club, with Posey's father as president, and changed its name to the Loendi Big Five. While still playing for Loendi, he returned to college to finish his degree at Duquesne University, where he played basketball under the assumed name of Charles Cumbert for three years and led Duquesne in scoring. Riding the momentum of Loendi's victory over Howard, Cumberland Posey scheduled matchups against top black and white teams, but his collegiate commitments limited his playing time and Loendi's success declined until after World War I.

After returning from Duquesne, he became the Homestead Grays' manager and eventually gained majority control of the team. He developed a penchant for poaching players from other teams in the area, which he took to an extreme in basketball following World War I, when he recruited all of Pennsylvania's best black players to play for Loendi, leading to Loendi's overwhelming success as the Colored Basketball World Champions for four consecutive seasons from 1919–20 to 1922–23.

Posey utilized quick bursts of speed to gain an advantage getting around defenders, but his main strength lay in his shooting. While most players abided by a style of play which favored efficient shots from close range, Posey launched shots from as far as 25 feet away from the basket and fearlessly did so with a defender in close proximity, defying convention and keeping opponents on their toes.

Bob Douglas introduced professional basketball to the black version of the game, composing the majority of his initial professional team out of a combination of players from his amateur teams and castaways from the Commonwealth Big Five. (The departures of players from the Commonwealth team, including those who ended up filling out the original Renaissance roster, were primarily caused by a combination of (1) the existing debate within the black sports world regarding the morality of professionalism vs. amateurism and (2) the Commonwealth's financial instability.) The catalyst that made him decide to pay his players was when the amateur league that his Spartan Braves participated in ordered him to suspend two of his star players, Frank Forbes and Leon

Monde, for trying out for professional baseball teams and therefore breaching amateurism rules. He refused and was fined, which led him to realize that he could spend the money he was being fined directly on securing superior talent instead and left the league. Douglas' experiment seemed promising, given the thriving amateur game of the Black Fives era and Posey's stardom. The Renaissance's success was cemented when they added two Loendi players, Pappy Ricks and Fats Jenkins, to the team.

Ricks quickly became the Renaissance's top scoring threat, establishing himself as the most dominant offensive player in professional basketball during the late 1920s and early 1930s, consistently putting up high-teen point totals in an era where double-digit scoring was a rarity. Meanwhile, Jenkins joined the New York team late in the 1923–24 season, bringing not only his basketball skills but also his business acumen. As a member of the last eight Colored World Champions, Jenkins showcased his exceptional speed, craftiness, and ambidexterity on the court, and, despite standing at just 5'8", his impressive vertical leap even led to his occasional selection for jump balls.

Without a league to play in, organizing games posed a challenge for Douglas, with both white and amateur black teams hesitant to schedule a professional black team, and to top it off, the Renaissance had no home court.

The latter of those issues was solved when Douglas approached William Roach, a fellow British West Indies immigrant and real estate owner in New York, for permission to operate the team out of the Renaissance Ballroom & Casino. Roach had commissioned the building of the Renaissance Ballroom & Casino just a few years prior and it had quickly emerged as a prominent hub for black artistic and philosophical culture during the Harlem Renaissance, housing a premier jazz club that frequently showcased artists such as Duke Ellington and Louis Armstrong. In return for naming his team the Renaissance, Douglas gained the opportunity to use the historic venue.[1]

The Renaissance's unique court had a slippery surface, making dribbling difficult and prompting the team to adopt a pass-heavy offense that became their trademark. Led by Ricks, Jenkins, Forbes, and Monde, the Renaissance swiftly rose to prominence, winning the 1924–25 Colored World Basketball championship, the last year the title was awarded.

After assembling some of the best talent in the world, Douglas sought to join the newly established ABL the following year, only to face rejection from the league, unmistakably on the basis of race. In solidarity, the Original Celtics rescinded their own application. The Renaissance and Original Celtics had played against each other 10 times in the previous two years and had begun to develop a close rivalry forged by a foundation of mutual respect.

That rivalry would deepen during the late 1920s and early 1930s as the Renaissance gained talent and prominence. In 1929, Douglas signed Tarzan Cooper from the Philadelphia Panthers, another independent black team, and Cooper's athletic ability and uniquely formidable defensive presence propelled him to be widely recognized as the premier center of his era, and often as the greatest center ever seen. That same season, the Renaissance and the Original Celtics clashed in a three-game series billed as the World Basketball Championship Series, and although the Renaissance lost all three games, they left an indelible mark.

Earlier that season, the Renaissance ventured to the South for the first time, and in a game against a team from Louisville, Kentucky, were greeted by the presence of many of the Original Celtics in the stands rooting for them. Cooper and Original Celtics center

Joe Lapchick had grown to know each other well since Cooper's arrival to the Renaissance, and Lapchick rushed onto the court to embrace Cooper in a hug before the game. In the Jim Crow–era South, a white man and black man publicly embracing was considered scandalous and the Louisville crowd reacted with fury. A race riot nearly broke out, the game was canceled, and both teams were swiftly kicked out of their hotels. From then on, beginning with the World Basketball Championship Series that ended both teams' respective seasons that year, Lapchick and Cooper made a tradition out of not just embracing, but also exchanging kisses on the cheek before the start of every subsequent on-court encounter.

The Great Depression ended the financial viability of hosting games at the Renaissance Ballroom & Casino, compelling the New York Renaissance to embark on a three-year barnstorming tour across the nation. Noteworthy among their victories during this period was a resounding 37–20 triumph over the Cleveland Rosenblums, the reigning champions of the ABL, at the onset of the 1929–30 season.

In a world championship rematch with the Original Celtics in 1931–32, the Renaissance secured a narrow victory, earning the title of world champions for the first time. The following year, with Bob Douglas assuming the managerial role of the Renaissance Ballroom & Casino, the team reclaimed their former home court in Harlem, sparking a remarkable 88-game winning streak that persisted over 86 days both at home and on the road, doubling the existing professional record of 44 that the Original Celtics had set years earlier.[2]

In the subsequent years, the aging Original Celtics gradually faded from prominence, leaving the Renaissance without their long-standing rival by 1940–41. Over the span of 16 years, the two New York barnstorming powerhouses had faced off 156 times.

They laid claim to the world champion status for five consecutive years, from 1931–32 to 1935–36, and reinforced that claim in 1938–39 with the advent of the WPBT.

The Renaissance underwent a roster transformation in the late 1930s, with Willie Smith assuming the role of starting center, pushing Tarzan Cooper to power forward and backup center duties. The team signed college players, a practice they had not frequently done before, including Dolly King and Wilmeth Sidat-Singh, who became key parts of the team along with the veteran core and a young homegrown trio of Pop Gates, Puggy Bell, and John Isaacs.

In the first edition of the WPBT in 1939, the Renaissance reiterated their standing as the best team in the nation by surmounting the Harlem Globe Trotters and the Oshkosh All-Stars, with Smith, Cooper, and Gates leading the charge. Over the course of the next three years, they never returned to the WPBT championship game, losing in either the quarterfinals or semifinals to the Globe Trotters, All-Stars, and Detroit Eagles, before turning down their invitation to the tournament in 1943 once the Washington Bears had raided many of their key players.

Over the course of the next couple seasons, most of the players who had left for Washington returned to the New York Renaissance, the notable exception being Sidat-Singh.

Wilmeth Sidat-Singh, a multisport standout at Syracuse University, emerged as a basketball star in his senior year, leading the team in scoring, but his true acclaim came from his prowess as the star of Syracuse's football team, where he excelled as a tailback in a single-wing formation. He was known as one of the finest passers of 1930s college football, but his skin color stopped him from playing professionally in the segregated NFL.

Syracuse initially attempted to circumvent this barrier by presenting him as a "Hindu," leveraging his surname, which stemmed from his stepfather's Eastern Indian heritage. This ruse allowed Sidat-Singh to compete against teams that typically refused to face opponents with black players.

In Sidat-Singh's junior year, a column by *Baltimore Afro-American* sportswriter Sam Lacy exposed his true racial background, leading to his exclusion from a game against the University of Maryland. Syracuse lost 13–0 without him.

The next year, Duke University removed the clause that prohibited opposing teams from using black players at the urging of coach Wallace Wade, allowing Sidat-Singh to play against them and prompting other opponents, including Maryland, to follow suit, enabling him to compete in all football games during his senior year.

Because of the unofficial ban on black players in the NFL, Sidat-Singh found himself without opportunities in professional football, leading him to join a barnstorming team of ex–Syracuse players and also briefly play for the Rochester Seagrams in 1939–40. The next year he joined the New York Renaissance, excelling as a score-first, cutting shooting guard known for his quick bursts of acceleration.

After a season with the Renaissance, he was lured away to the Washington Bears along with several teammates. For the Bears he played a significant role, averaging 16.3 points per game and helping to plant the seeds for their undefeated season the following year.

In the wake of the devastating attack on Pearl Harbor, Sidat-Singh, driven by a desire to serve his country, initially joined the Metropolitan Police Department of Washington, D.C., which had lost many members of the police force who joined the military after the attack. The next August, Sidat-Singh enlisted as well.

Assigned to the renowned all-black Tuskegee Airmen's 332nd Fighter Group, he trained as a fighter pilot and flew aircraft manufactured at the same Grumman factory where his teammates worked. After completing successful training in Tuskegee, Alabama, he was transferred to Selfridge Field in Michigan in May 1943, marking the next chapter of his military service.

He took a short detour on his way north to Michigan to visit family and friends in Washington, D.C. On May 8, shortly after his arrival to his new military base, the *Baltimore Afro-American*—the same newspaper that had revealed his racial identity during his time at Syracuse—published a photograph capturing him proudly displaying his bomber jackets to his former Washington Bears boss, Hal Jackson.

On the very next day, May 9, 1943, Sidat-Singh's plane encountered an engine failure in the middle of a training flight and crashed into the middle of Lake Huron. After an exhaustive seven-week search, his body was recovered, still wearing his parachute tangled with the submerged plane's fuselage.

Sidat-Singh, only 25 years old, was mourned as the war's first loss of a prominent athlete, with his passing acknowledged by notable figures in black America, including boxer Joe Louis, who paid a visit to Sidat-Singh's grieving family.[3]

As the remaining players of the New York Renaissance reunited after their stint with the Washington Bears, it became evident that the NBL's top teams had surpassed the Bears as the nation's premier source of professional basketball. While they could still defeat many of the NBL's weaker and average teams, they struggled to keep pace with the Fort Wayne Zollners, led by Bobby McDermott, or the Chicago Gears, led by George Mikan.

In 1947, the Renaissance were upset in the first round of the WPBT for the first time ever when they lost 62–59 to the Toledo Jeeps, a largely unheralded group of players who had just finished their first NBL season with a 21–23 record.

The following year, the Renaissance made up for their previous season's shortcomings with a run to the WPBT championship, beating the Tri-Cities Blackhawks in the semifinals and only losing in the championship game to the Minneapolis Lakers by four points. Shortly after, the NBL extended an offer for the Renaissance to join the league, and having tried in vain for over two decades to get the New York Renaissance accepted into the largely segregated realm of organized professional basketball, Bob Douglas eagerly accepted the offer despite the challenging conditions that ensured a successful first season would be an uphill battle.

As discussions advanced for the BAA–NBL merger, Ike Duffey terminated the Rens' NBL contract, under pressure from the many BAA owners who owned their team's arena. The Harlem Globetrotters surpassed the Renaissance as the premier black team in the 1940s, drawing large crowds and ensuring lucrative profits for arena owners. To take advantage of that, Globetrotters owner Abe Saperstein orchestrated agreements with many BAA teams, facilitated by Warriors general manager and head coach Eddie Gottlieb, preventing the Renaissance's entry into the league. Saperstein aimed to maintain the Globetrotters' ability to recruit top black players for lesser salaries. Additionally, Saperstein strongly opposed the creation of the NBA, and the owners understood that defying his wishes on two major fronts in the same offseason would be detrimental to their financial interests. Frustrated and unable to compete with Saperstein's financial resources, Douglas leased the Renaissance to Saperstein, who absorbed many of the Renaissance's top players into the Globetrotters organization and rebranded the New York Renaissance as a Globetrotters development squad.[4]

The merger brought an end to the third significant attempt to integrate major league basketball. It also left Ike Duffey with only the Anderson Packers once again following the omission of Calumet from the merger.

Complicating the Packers' transition from the NBL to the NBA was the loss of Murray Mendenhall as coach, who Carl Bennett had hired to fill the Pistons' coaching position. Unable to attract high-profile coaches to Anderson, Indiana, Duffey appointed Howie Schultz, the team's center and most fundamentally sound player, as player-coach.

Under the weight of his dual roles, Howie Schultz's playing performances suffered, particularly on offense, but with an undersized and undermanned team, he was nevertheless forced to assume a majority of the team's center minutes and proved resilient against his most formidable opponents such as George Mikan and Adolph Schayes. Small forward John Hargis, the Packers' most multifaceted scorer, struggled with injuries at the start of the season, further complicating the start of Schultz's coaching career.

Frank Brian at shooting guard and Bill Closs at power forward stepped up as the main options for the Packers, compensating for the compromised contributions of two fellow starters. Closs, known as one of the better rebounders and defenders at his position, garnered praise for refining his finishing technique in an attempt to remedy his inclination to stray toward the perimeter, while Brian enjoyed newfound offensive freedom as the team's primary scoring option.

In a notable departure from their NBL championship-winning season, where a rigid adherence to teamwork prevailed, as exemplified by their unique scoring distribution, with seven players averaging between 7.8 and 9.9 points per game, and none surpassing that mark, the emergence of Brian and Closs as individual contributors was a striking deviation from the teams of the Mendenhall era. It worked, though, as Anderson claimed victory in their first three games and eight of their first 11, culminating with a convincing Schultz and Brian–led 111–91 win over Sheboygan to take the lead in the Western Division standings. Twenty-three points from Brian the next day in a win over the Hawks provided an added buffer.[5]

Just a day prior, the Waterloo Hawks team that Anderson beat had become the third team in the league to reach 10 losses, following the Nuggets and Celtics, but unlike the other two bottom-dwelling teams, their chances at making the playoffs seemed to have risen since the start of the season. Their 3–10 record was just a single game behind Tri-Cities, who had won six more games than them the previous year and were now tenuously holding the final Western Division playoff spot.

The Hawks boasted a competent frontcourt duo consisting of Dick Mehen and Harry Boykoff, whose professional careers became intertwined via their shared move from the Toledo Jeeps to Waterloo in 1948 and subsequent transition from the NBL to the NBA in 1949.

Mehen, a strong contender for the previous year's NBL MVP award, showcased his offensive prowess in the low post and face-up situations, leveraging his balance, strength, footwork, and anticipation to find easy scoring opportunities against even the best defenders.[6]

Boykoff, known for his shot-blocking and formidable hook shot, had faced the greatest challenge in adapting to the goaltending prohibition compared to other skilled goaltenders, but he remained a significant shot-blocking threat and lost no momentum offensively. As a senior at St. John's, he once scored 54 points against St. Francis College.[7] His role in the professional game wasn't to ever threaten to repeat that particular performance, but he settled into life as a very capable second option who had a knack for error-free play and couldn't be ignored as a threat to shoot from the midrange.

As the two most capable scorers on the team, Mehen and Boykoff traded world-class offensive performances in the early NBA games, but the Hawks often found themselves on the receiving end of lopsided defeats.

Outside of the post tandem and dynamic 5'11" second-year point guard Leo Kubiak, there were very few rostered players for Waterloo capable of keeping up with NBA stars or defending complex offensive threats. Boykoff, while an adept shot blocker, was heavy-footed. Kubiak could get steals but wasn't very effective at preventing scoring opportunities. Mehen was simply disinterested in defense. As a result, the Hawks often were the victim of a barrage of scoring from entire teams, rather than simply giving up a lot of points to one or two players.

In late November, the acquisition of Jack Smiley aimed to bolster the team's defense in an effort to keep pace with the Tri-Cities Blackhawks throughout the demanding season.[8] Smiley, a former member of the University of Illinois Whiz Kids, had served in the military during World War II and played a critical role in the Battle of the Bulge, firing a howitzer for 96 hours as an infantryman. After returning to basketball, he had a stint as a point forward with the post–McDermott Fort Wayne Zollners before being traded to Anderson, where he was unable to earn meaningful time on the court and struggled mightily on the offensive end in the few minutes he did play. After less than a month in Anderson, he was sold to Waterloo, who had many more minutes available for him and opted to make him their primary wing defender off the bench.

The defensive issues that spurred Waterloo to acquire Smiley also provided a reprieve for the Rochester Royals after their underwhelming start. In a two-game home-and-away series against the Hawks, they soared to easy wins with Bob Davies leading the way on both occasions, and Davies and the Royals carried the momentum into a narrow win over Washington, leading them past Fort Wayne in the divisional standings and closing in on the records of Chicago and Minneapolis.

Elsewhere in the Central Division, the St. Louis Bombers faced a challenge in integrating their summer acquisition, Mike Todorovich, into the rotation, with Ed Macauley and Red Rocha monopolizing playing time in the post.

A capable face-up scorer and respectable passer for a power forward, Todorovich had excelled in the NBL with the Sheboygan Redskins, beating out Jim Pollard for the 1947–48 NBL Rookie of the Year Award and making both an All-NBL First Team and Second Team before opting to return home after the merger.

Playing as a backup to an out-of-position Rocha and receiving around 25 minutes per game, Todorovich was unhappy with his reduced role and struggled to make his usual impact on either end of the court. To add insult to injury, St. Louis' 6–8 record was markedly worse than that of Sheboygan. Todorovich requested and was granted a trade to the Tri-Cities Blackhawks, where he was immediately inserted into the starting lineup and provided facilitation and defensive versatility to the team. In exchange, the Bombers received Mac Otten, a rookie post player who would bring the Bombers' bench some much-needed rebounding as they won four of their next five games in order to get their first winning record of the season at 10–9.[9]

Alex Groza quickly established himself as the NBA's breakout star as a rookie, exceeding even the impractically high expectations many had set for him as the highest-profile collegian since Mikan and Kurland. In his first few games, he scored 30-plus points twice and nearly kept pace with Mikan in their first head-to-head matchup. Just two days later against Rochester, he scored 43 points on 17-of-35 shooting while limiting Arnie Risen to 12.

With a quarter of the season completed and Minneapolis enjoying four wins out of their last five games, while Indianapolis continued to put up erratic performances, the much-anticipated rematch featured Groza and Mikan dueling in the paint, as Groza's 38 points more than matched Mikan's 33. Underwhelming outings from Jim Pollard and Vern Mikkelsen, who combined for a mere seven points, helped clinch an important win for Indianapolis by a score of 86–68.[10]

Meanwhile, the Warriors plummeted toward the bottom of the standings as Joe Fulks stumbled through a six-game stretch, unable to muster over 20 points in any contest, the longest such streak of his career thus far. The burly Ed Sadowski, formerly the BAA's premier interior force on offense, found it difficult to consistently score much more than 10 points with the growing number of tall centers, as well as the decline of his own athletic abilities, putting the 6'5" 240 lb. 34-year-old at a constant disadvantage.

One of the only significant sources of solace for Philadelphia was first-round pick Vern Gardner, the most rebound-savvy perimeter player in basketball as a rookie. Gardner, the fifth pick in the 1949 BAA draft, had been the star center for the University of Utah, with the high point of his collegiate career coming as a sophomore when he won NIT MVP after Utah pulled off a significant upset over the star-studded University of Kentucky in 1947.

The athleticism that allowed the 6'5" Gardner to thrive as a center in college translated to the professional game despite a drastic positional change to small forward and he staked his claim as the Warriors' most competent rebounder and finisher. In addition, his scoring savvy began to show, as he averaged 16.1 points in his first nine games. When he was sidelined by cellulitis in his foot and lower leg for two weeks,[11] the Warriors commenced a losing streak of seven games out of eight, with their sole victory narrowly achieved when their ultra-versatile lockdown defender of a point guard, George Senesky, blocked a potential game-winning layup by Kenny Sailors in the final seconds.

On the court, the Anderson Packers were as healthy as anyone in the league. Frank Brian was proving his scoring consistency, averaging 14.1 points through the opening 14 games of the season.

Roles were clearly defined. Brian was the primary scorer. Ralph Johnson was the primary ball handler and best long-range shooter. John Hargis excelled as a versatile scoring threat. Pivot plays ran through Milo Komenich, a power forward noted for his soft hands, willingness to face the basket from the perimeter, and smooth hook shot.

They retained their identity, though, running an offense at breakneck speed and pressuring the opposing offense to do the same. It was rare for the Packers to have a good shooting night as a unit, thanks to their tempo of play, but even rarer was it the case for them not to make their opponent shoot even worse. While Howie Schultz's play was suffering, his coaching was very impressive and he had created not just a winning team but one with a very unique on-court identity. Now holding the top spot in the Western Division by a considerable margin and with a record that only trailed the Nationals, Anderson was emerging as an early championship contender that teams were bound to fear matching up against come the postseason.

The financial situation of the Anderson Packers was less promising than the team's on-court performance. Their attendance hovered around 2,500 per game, under half that of similarly talented teams like Minneapolis, Syracuse, and New York. In little more than a month, Ike Duffey had lost $14,000, projecting a potential season loss of approximately $65,000.

It was also evident that Duffey was seeking a life change. On December 4, Duffey and his brother sold the Duffey's Inc. meatpacking company and its subsidiaries for $3,000,000.

During halftime of an 88–81 home win against Sheboygan the next day, in which Brian led the Packers in scoring with 17 points, Duffey addressed the crowd, assuring them that the Packers would remain in Anderson until the season's end but also urging fans to bring friends to future games. While allaying the worst fears of some, it implied that Duffey was prepared to sell the team and that the team's continued presence in the small industrial city seemed highly improbable unless attendance experienced a significant surge.[12]

The Celtics weren't selling tickets much better, but in their case the unexciting and inept basketball product was to blame. Boston hit a new low early in December when a loss to Indianapolis—their seventh straight—dropped them to a 4–14 record, below Waterloo, for the second-worst winning percentage in the league. This was not a team lacking in veteran leadership, between Sonny Hertzberg and center Bob Kinney, but a lack of consistent playing-time distribution on the part of head coach Doggie Julian continuously stymied the team's momentum.

Howie Shannon, the BAA's top rookie the year prior and technically the top pick in the summer draft, was less than inspiring and remained handcuffed to the bench behind a various rotation of five other wings, each of whom was capable of either scoring the most points on the team or struggling to get on the scoreboard at all, depending on the day.

Of those wings, forward George Kaftan was the best natural talent, having displayed his gift for scoring from near the basket in the latter half of the previous year, but he couldn't duplicate his previous season's work as a sophomore on more than the rare occasion. Nonetheless, a rare outburst such as his 34-point game against his hometown Knicks on November 26 provided something for Boston fans to root for.[13]

Tony Lavelli, the 1948–49 National Player of the Year for Yale, brought both excitement and uncertainty to the Celtics. Known for his incredible fadeaway hook shot and ability to draw fouls, Lavelli's performances on the court as a rookie fluctuated dramatically, as his outstanding games were often followed by those where he made minimal contributions, but his talent was undeniable.

Very much a known entity coming out of college, Lavelli had graduated as the fourth-highest scorer in NCAA history at the end of his four years at Yale University. In addition to refining the fadeaway hook shot to a near perfect level of technical proficiency with either hand, he was also elite at drawing fouls, an expert ball hawk and a capable rebounder of missed long-range shots. Despite his basketball success and the promise of a contract at near the price tag of many of the sport's best players, it wasn't a given, even after he was drafted, that he would ever become a Celtic at all.

Despite his basketball talents, music was Lavelli's true passion. He had studied musical composition and applied to numerous performing arts conservatories during his senior year at Yale. After selling three of his songs to Broadcast Music, Inc., Lavelli decided not to pursue a career in basketball and instead committed to attending the Juilliard School as a graduate student. Unbeknown to the Celtics, Lavelli had already committed to his musical aspirations when they drafted him 14th overall.

Months of contract negotiations between Lavelli and Celtics owner Walter Brown proved fruitless until Leo Ferris, acting on behalf of league president Maurice Podoloff, intervened. Ferris proposed a unique agreement that would incorporate Lavelli's music career into his contract. Lavelli would receive a $13,000 annual salary from the Celtics and an additional $3,125 from the league office for performing 25 halftime concerts on the accordion throughout the season. Although Lavelli joined the Celtics nine games into the season, his presence on the roster provided a sigh of relief for a team that had missed out on their first-round pick the year before.[14]

The other Eastern Division team adorned in green, the Washington Capitols, also proved to be unremarkable, at least in comparison to the team they had in the BAA Finals the previous year. With an aging roster and veterans playing key roles, their drop in performance was expected to some extent. However, the speed at which they went from one of the league's best to an 8–9 record following a promising 4–1 start was unexpected.

Offensively, Washington had fallen apart, surpassing their previous season's scoring average in only five of their first 17 games, and the main culprits for the dwindling firepower were the team's initial core duo of Bob Feerick and Bones McKinney. Between the addition of coaching duties to his responsibilities and recovery from the meniscus tear in his left knee that ended his season the previous spring, Feerick simply couldn't avoid showing signs of decline.

Before the BAA was founded, Feerick had a successful collegiate career at Santa

Clara and played for AAU teams on the West Coast. His connection with Red Auerbach, through military service, led him to the BAA after a season with Oshkosh. In the 1946–47 and 1947–48 seasons for the Capitols, he had been the only player in the league to finish both seasons in the top five in scoring, field goal percentage, and free throw percentage, and, while his numbers took a dip the following year, he became the first player in league history to shoot upward of 85 percent from the foul line in 1948–49, at 85.9 percent. In his prime one of the most prolific scorers basketball had produced, a composed floor general, and a deceptively versatile defender, his presence on the wing for Washington was invaluable to their success in their first three years.

Still hampered by his knee injury and visibly incapable of producing offense the same way he had, Feerick brought himself off the bench behind Chick Reiser to start the year, adapting to his reduced agility by playing closer to the basket. His difficult start was further highlighted by a condensed early December schedule where he only scored eight points in four games. By the end of that stretch, his average was 5.3 points in the first 11 games, on track for nearly an eight-point decrease from the previous year.

Contrasting with Feerick's serious approach to the game, McKinney established himself as an entertaining showman during his early years with the Capitols. He incorporated trick shots, including the occasional backwards free throw, and other gimmicks reminiscent of the Harlem Globetrotters, which endeared him to the fans but often resulted in inefficiency and vulnerability to opposing teams' defense.[15]

Under Feerick's slower offensive system, designed to suit the team's experienced roster, McKinney's offensive freedom was limited, leading to a decline in his overall impact. His role transformed into that of a spot-up shooter, a specialty he wasn't good enough at to justify, and his defensive shortcomings didn't help matters.

Washington turned to second-year center Jack Nichols as their beacon of hope. A late arrival as a rookie in 1948–49, Nichols broke through as a fantastic interior presence on offense, consistently scoring in double figures and leading the team in scoring during the playoffs.

Despite bringing a breath of fresh air to the team, a concerning pattern emerged as the team's performance suffered whenever Nichols played a prominent role. In the 21 games where he scored in double figures, the Capitols struggled with an 8–13 record, in contrast to their outstanding 30–9 record when he either scored less than 10 points or did not play.

Quick and slightly undersized for a center, Nichols' success often came against slower, taller centers like George Mikan and Bill Henry, also standing out in matchups against players like Kleggie Hermsen of the Chicago Stags, whom he scored 51 points against in two games. As it had done the year before, the team failed to capitalize on his performances and the Capitols lost in most of his best games, including splitting those two games against Chicago.

For Chicago's third matchup against Washington, Harold Olsen adapted to Nichols' success by starting 19-year-old Joe Graboski, the second-youngest player in the NBA, at center in order to take the plodding Hermsen out of the matchup equation. Graboski, only a year removed from high school, didn't allow Nichols the same advantages he had become accustomed to in the NBA and held the Capitols center to just four points in a 20-point Chicago win.[16] One game later, Washington lost to Minneapolis 93–76, with Mikan scoring 35 points on 23 shots, and fell to a losing record for the first time in almost two years.

The same day that Washington fell below .500, Sheboygan met the same fate after their sixth consecutive loss nullified their strong start to the season, this time against division rival Waterloo.[17] The underwhelming play of fleet-footed point guard Bobby Cook, who'd been a pleasant surprise through his scoring bursts on the fast break at the start of the season, was a factor, but the defensive shortcomings of Noble Jorgensen in the post had become apparent as the first four losses were all spearheaded by the opposing centers.

After the loss to Waterloo, Jorgensen fell ill with pneumonia and was hospitalized for two weeks, leading to Milt Schoon, a journeyman backup, stepping in to replace him.[18] Although Schoon lacked technical proficiency compared to Jorgensen, he possessed greater athleticism and physical strength. Schoon's biggest claim to fame was holding George Mikan to nine points in a game in college while playing for Valparaiso, but that was more a combination of sheer strength and a willingness to foul Mikan hard when necessary than out of defensive expertise. Regardless, this presented the possibility that Schoon could counter his own weaknesses by finding ways to limit the impact of star centers.

With the BAA's first two champions, the Philadelphia Warriors and Baltimore Bullets, much closer to the bottom of the division than to a winning record, change was desperately needed for both.

The Warriors' high-profile center Ed Sadowski was enduring his worst statistical season in years. Aging and hindered by his declining skills and the emergence of taller centers in the postwar era, Sadowski's defensive limitations became more apparent. His inability to protect the rim and guard against cuts made him a vulnerability. He remained a top-tier defensive rebounder, making up enough for the flaws in his game to warrant his continued presence as a starter, but the Warriors, a team with an inordinate number of rotational players who liked to shoot from distance, badly needed a capable offensive rebounder, which he was not as adept at.

Baltimore, without most of the talent that had helped the Bullets to a championship two years prior, desperately sought to revive their stagnant offense, which was on track to be the league's worst. Pinning his hopes on the possibility that Sadowski's rough start to the season was just a temporary rough patch, Bill Dyer traded Baltimore's starting center, rookie Ron Livingstone, to Philadelphia for Sadowski and cash.[19]

Selected as the sixth pick in the 1949 draft, Ron Livingstone was seen as Baltimore's defensive answer following the departure of all three of their centers that summer. His length helped him to be an ever-reliable source of rebounds, and the rest of his defensive game was quite good, but his offensive skills were lacking, between a nonexistent shooting touch and poor positioning instincts. He just so happened to be one of the top offensive rebounders among role players—exactly what the Warriors were looking for.

Sadowski's professional career was turbulent yet successful. Baltimore would be his 13th team in ten years since college. Despite suffering a fractured patella that cut short his time at Seton Hall University in the middle of an undefeated season, he went on to start for a WPBT-winning Detroit Eagles team, win two ABL championships with the Wilmington Blue Bombers, and become a key addition to Bobby McDermott's final championship team in Fort Wayne.

Always a top ten scorer throughout his career, the longer games, rules favoring up-tempo offenses, and a small pay rise had compelled Sadowski to leave the Zollners for the BAA in 1946–47 despite the NBL's monopoly on talent; it was no coincidence that his statistical prime coincided with the three years of BAA operation.

He initially hoped to play for the New York Knicks, but Joe Lapchick advised the team against signing him. His former coach at Seton Hall, Honey Russell, was coaching minor league baseball during the summer and didn't begin to assemble his Celtics roster until the end of baseball season, so Sadowski never received an offer from them either.

He ultimately accepted an offer from the Toronto Huskies that made him the highest-paid player in the BAA's inaugural season at $10,000 per year and gave him head-coaching duties as well as a key role as a player.

The Huskies' inaugural game presented a hopeful facade, drawing a sizable crowd despite basketball's limited appeal in Canada at the time. Sadowski's 18 points led the way. The game was indicative of many flaws, though, not least of which was Sadowski himself. His 18 points came in just over half of the game, as he fouled out with nine minutes remaining in the third quarter and the Huskies trailing by double digits.

It wasn't until after he was relegated to the bench that Toronto began to mount a comeback spearheaded by George Nostrand, Sadowski's backup, that gave them a slight lead in the waning minutes of the third quarter and kept them ahead until there were three minutes remaining. At that point, Sadowski, in order to appease the crowd, subbed in one of the Huskies' token Canadians, Hank Biasatti, who made a couple of key mistakes on defense. The Knicks ended the game on a 5–0 run and pulled out a close win.

Sadowski's preference as coach was to run a deliberate offense full of screens and off-ball movement in which each player on the floor touched the ball about three times per possession before opening up a scoring opportunity—often either an open long-distance shot for one of the guards or a pivot play revolving around Sadowski himself.

Much more of a players' coach than a strategist, his twice-daily practices consisted mainly of scrimmages and the occasional shooting drill. After the first few games were up, Toronto's games began to often devolve into Sadowski shooting drills as well, as he attempted a shot on well over a third of his team's possessions, inspiring a joke among his teammates when he suffered a minor shoulder injury that it was from shooting the ball so much.

After a respectable 2–3 start to the season, the team spiraled to a 3–10 record by the end of November. A blizzard further exacerbated their woes when they struggled to reach a game against the Providence Steamrollers. The team arrived late at the train station and were forced to travel the 545-mile journey by taxi. They lost 79–65.

After that game, Sadowski was nowhere to be found, rumored to be seeking a return to the Zollners in Fort Wayne. He didn't turn up for two days, with Huskies managing director Lew Hayman searching desperately for him. Eventually, under threat of league expulsion, Sadowski set up a meeting with Maurice Podoloff in New York and requested directly to be relieved of coaching duties and placed on a winning team.

Podoloff saw an opportunity to invigorate the Celtics, who were one of two large-market teams in the BAA without a winning record, and urged Hayman to get a deal done with Boston. Hayman refused and held out for better offers, suspending Sadowski as a player indefinitely and firing him as coach.[20]

Seventeen days after Sadowski's last game for Toronto, Hayman agreed to send Sadowski and backup point guard Ray Wertis to the Cleveland Rebels in exchange for starting forwards Leo Mogus and Dick Schulz, accompanied by a cash fee. Sadowski helped lead the Rebels to the playoffs, but they ended the season with considerable debt and folded. Toronto did as well.

Sadowski's long-awaited stint with the Celtics, where he ended up after Cleveland, proved to be a bittersweet affair. In his finest individual season yet, he finished in the top ten of every single statistical category tracked except for free throw percentage. Nonetheless, the Celtics hadn't improved much and featured the worst offense in the league. Disgruntled fans, seeking a scapegoat, turned their ire toward Sadowski.[21]

Ridding the Boston roster of Sadowski was Doggie Julian's first act as their new head coach, orchestrating a trade with Philadelphia centered around Chuck Halbert despite not having any long-term plans for Halbert, who would himself be traded the next January.

Despite significantly increased efficiency as a second option to Joe Fulks with the Warriors, Sadowski couldn't help push Philadelphia back into contention. Instead, the team endured its first losing season upon his arrival.

After a rough start to the 1949–50 season, a trade to Baltimore seemed to rejuvenate him, as he led the Bullets on a successful stretch of 5–4 in his first nine games on the team, averaging a team-high 16.7 points in that stretch, including his first 30-point game since departing Boston.

The addition of Ron Livingstone also infused renewed energy into Philadelphia. They also won five of their next nine games, including consecutive close games against the Bullets. Livingstone's strong performance, coupled with his ability to generate additional scoring opportunities through offensive rebounds, allowed Fulks to find easier scoring chances, resulting in an average of 19.7 points for Fulks during this period.

Rising back to a winning record and creating a gap between themselves and Sheboygan in the race for second in the Western Division, Indianapolis won a crucial away game against divisional leaders Anderson in a close defensive battle that took the Packers outside of their comfort zone. That snapped a seven-game away losing streak for the Olympians, who had proven to be a very good team but struggled a bit to adapt to the NBA's travel schedule. Alex Groza led the way with 30 points, his fifth 30-plus game of the season, something that had only previously been accomplished in the BAA by Joe Fulks (three times), George Mikan, and Ed Sadowski and in the NBL by Mikan.[22]

The Lakers, despite featuring the league's biggest star in George Mikan and one of the best all-around rosters in professional basketball, still weren't quite managing to differentiate themselves from the pack. On the same day the Syracuse Nationals reached a record of 16-1, the Lakers suffered a crushing 87–66 defeat to the Pistons. Mikan scored 27 points, but none of his teammates reached double figures and the opposing trio of Fred Schaus, John Oldham, and Charlie Black combined to outscore the entire Lakers team with 26 from Schaus, 23 from Black, and 19 from Oldham.[23]

Vern Mikkelsen showcased his value, yet his synergy with Mikan remained inconsistent. Jim Pollard, while a top four player in the league, was in the midst of one of the worst offensive stretches of his career; on this occasion he only scored a single free throw while yielding 26 points to Schaus. This marked the fifth game in a series of eight single-digit scoring outputs for him. Two games later, he shot 3-of-16 against New York.

The guard rotation's failures were just as significant to Minneapolis' struggles, which placed them at a merely respectable 12–6 record—just 1.5 games behind the Chicago Stags at the top of the Central Division but also only 2.5 games ahead of the St. Louis Bombers at the bottom—as the frontcourt's playing style adjustments remained a work in progress. Head coach John Kundla grappled with a surplus of guards without a true playmaking leader, dividing playing time between veteran Herman Schaefer and rookie Slater Martin at point guard alongside Don Carlson at shooting guard. The bench featured rookies Bob Harrison and Paul Walther, with Gene Stump contributing on the wing and small forward Arnie Ferrin also taking some backcourt minutes due to Mikkelsen's emergence. As a result, none of the guard rotation thrived and only Ferrin seemed on track to increase his impact.

Rookie point guard Slater Martin, who had excelled in the fast-paced game during his collegiate years at the University of Texas, had faced a decision similar to Mikkelsen's before the season. Initially inclined to join the Oilers and play alongside Bob Kurland while working for Phillips Petroleum, Martin changed his mind after being offered an office job instead of his desired hands-on machinery work.[24]

Taking his chances with the Lakers, Martin encountered a steep learning curve in Minneapolis. The team's offensive system relied heavily on slowing down the pace and feeding the ball to Mikan, meaning Martin's offensive duties were mostly relegated to passing the ball off to a more experienced teammate as soon as he crossed halfcourt and then running around off the ball. In order to carve out a consistent role backing up Herman Schaefer, Martin had to focus on becoming a tenacious defender while adjusting his offensive game.

Attempting to find a solution to the backcourt jam via addition rather than subtraction, Kundla bought the rights to Billy Hassett from the Tri-Cities Blackhawks.[25] Hassett was absorbed into the Lakers' guard rotation abyss, and after an excellent, if somewhat unpredictable, start to the season with the turbulent Blackhawks, he never scored more than eight points for Minneapolis.

On December 10, the Knicks and Stags played a close, physical game that ultimately went to overtime. Max Zaslofsky led Chicago in scoring with 22 points and Connie Simmons answered with 21 along with significant help from Carl Braun, Vince Boryla, and Dick McGuire. The game was ended by a buzzer-beating layup at the rim by Knicks point guard McGuire. With a 93–91 Knicks win, that was the first buzzer-beating game winner of the post-merger NBA.[26]

The Nationals' impressive 12-game winning streak came to an end via a slow-paced contest abundant with free throws, which they lost 69–63 to the Royals.[27] This allowed Rochester to surpass the Pistons in the standings. The Royals, boasting a solid and cohesive roster, featured the tenacious small forward Bill Calhoun, often described as a "defensive wizard," who seamlessly connected the swift guards with the rebounding tandem in the paint. Bob Davies and Bobby Wanzer constituted Rochester's backcourt and Calhoun started alongside power forward Arnie Johnson and center Arnie Risen.

Syracuse, as shown through the winning streak that gave them a dominant lead over the rest of the league, clearly had the best defense in the league and the roster most full of talented role players despite a lack of many household names.

Adolph Schayes had improved considerably from his rookie year in the NBL, with his 15.9 points per game so far making for a noticeable increase compared to the 12.8 he produced the prior year. His rebounding was also shaping up to be arguably the best in the league, only barely trailing the league-leading George Mikan despite significantly fewer minutes than the Lakers star.

Among the league's player-coaches, Al Cervi seemed to be the only one thriving at both roles. The next-best record from a team with a player-coach was the Indianapolis Olympians at 12–10, and Cliff Barker's playing time was infrequent as he was his own eighth option on the team, allowing for him to act as a bench coach for more than half of most Olympians' games.

Cervi also played fewer minutes than he would usually command for similar reasons, but, still one of the best perimeter defenders in the league, was a regular starter and played extended minutes against teams with high-scoring guards such as the Anderson Packers with Frank Brian and the Indianapolis Olympians with Ralph Beard.

He had the luxury of removing himself from the game to focus on strategic adjustments without compromising the team's performance more than he would've been able to on any other team in the league, with Ray Corley, Paul Seymour, Billy Gabor, and Fuzzy Levane all capable of running the offense, as well as Schayes' ability to find cutting teammates out of the high post.

Seymour in particular stood out as an heir apparent to Cervi despite mostly playing small forward, between his unwavering commitment to defense and his strong leadership at a young age. Only 21 years old at the start of the season, he was already in his fourth professional season, having left the University of Toledo for the NBL after just one college season in 1945–46.

In the NBL, he was the youngest player in the league as a rookie by nearly a year and a half but earned consistent playing time off the bench for the Toledo Jeeps, before leaving for New Orleans in the PBLA. For the New Orleans Hurricanes, he was the best player on both sides of the floor among teammates and opponents considerably more experienced than him. After the league shut down, instead of returning to the NBL, he signed with the Baltimore Bullets of the BAA, but he quickly returned to the NBL to join Syracuse after his role in Baltimore diminished to less than he'd gotten as a rookie in Toledo. Thanks to Leo Ferris' drastic overhaul of the roster the following offseason, he was already the longest-tenured National by the time of the merger.

Waterloo found themselves just half a game behind the Tri-Cities Blackhawks' playoff position in the Western Division, despite a lackluster start to the season. The frontcourt duo of Dick Mehen and Harry Boykoff carried the team, but recent struggles, including eight losses in their last ten games, cast a shadow of doubt.

Al Cervi (January 18, 1950) was the player-coach of the Syracuse Nationals, coaching the Nationals to the best regular season record in the league and leading them to the inaugural NBA Finals while also leading his team in assists. A key piece of an NBL championship four years earlier with Rochester, he was at this point most associated with his aggressive, dogged defense.

Denver guards Kenny Sailors and Jim Darden combined for 39 points against the Hawks on December 2 and 44 points two days later, exposing Leo Kubiak, the Hawks' starting point guard, as lacking the defensive prowess he had exhibited in the NBL. The Nuggets, who entered the back-to-back with a 1–16 record, won both times.

The Blackhawks, while not a strong team, enjoyed the advantage of being in the weaker Western Division. With four out of six teams from the division qualifying for the playoffs and one of those six teams being the Nuggets, they didn't need to even approach a winning record to contend for a place in the postseason, and their 6–13 record was on track to beat out Waterloo, which was all they needed to do to qualify.

Trading for Mike Todorovich proved to have a significant impact, especially once it became evident that he and Don Otten could coexist effectively. Initially experimenting with lineups, coach Red Auerbach tried Todorovich at center and benched Otten in favor of pairing Todorovich with second-year power forward Don Ray. After three consecutive losses, Auerbach reinstated Otten as the starter and shifted Todorovich to power forward.

Otten repaid him for the second chance with his best game of the year in a win against Boston, which led Auerbach to settle on three of his five starters going forward with Dike Eddleman at shooting guard, Todorovich at power forward, and Otten at center in the first semblance of continuity in his rebuilding process.

Eddleman, a rookie, entered the professional basketball scene with a remarkable track record as an all-around athlete. As a high school student, he was featured in the nationally circulated magazine *Life* for his exceptional abilities, going on to lead his basketball team to a state championship victory with a thrilling comeback and buzzer-beating shot. He also excelled in football and won three state high jump titles.

While serving in the military, Eddleman played for the Wright Kittyhawks, a renowned service league team coached by Chuck Taylor, of Converse shoe fame. Returning to Illinois in spring of the 1946–47 season upon discharge, Eddleman made his college

Dike Eddleman (1950) was a gifted all-around athlete whose athleticism had led him to be a track and field Olympian and college football record breaker. He provided a new dimension to the rebuilding Tri-Cities Blackhawks and helped propel them to a playoff spot while leading them in points as a rookie (Dee Lenzi personal collection).

football debut in the 1947 Rose Bowl, where he contributed to Illinois' 45–14 win over the previously undefeated UCLA. Playing the next two seasons as a wide receiver, punter, and punt returner, though the team didn't replicate that success in the following seasons, Eddleman established several records that remain unbroken, including career punt return average, longest punt return, and longest punt. He was drafted by both the NFL's Chicago Bears and the AAFC's Cleveland Browns.

Eddleman's college basketball career began during the ill-fated attempt to reunite the Whiz Kids after the war, limiting his playing time. His final two years with the Illini were significantly different, as he emerged as the team's leading scorer, became a second-team All-American and Big Ten Conference Player of the Year in 1948–49, and led Illinois to the Final Four, in which they were summarily dismantled by the Alex Groza–led University of Kentucky.

High jump remained his standout sport, though, as he secured five Big Ten individual titles and contributed to a national championship in 1947. He represented the United States in the 1948 Summer Olympics, placing fourth in the men's high jump event.[28]

Once in the NBA, he made an immediate impact, initially as Tri-Cities' starting small forward and soon moving to shooting guard, proving capable of scoring with his high-arching two-handed set shot from near-limitless distance, utilizing his change of pace while handling and distributing the ball during offensive lulls, and often assigned to guard the opponent's top scoring threats.

The contrasting skillsets of Eddleman, Todorovich, and Otten in the Blackhawks' lineup resulted in a complementary dynamic and a potential turnaround from their rough start seemed inevitable, a sentiment reinforced by two wins in their first three games starting together, the trio averaging a combined 43.3 points in that same stretch.

Meanwhile, Minneapolis overtook Chicago for the Central Division's top spot with a 90–81 Lakers win over Philadelphia, led by George Mikan's 28 points and supported by Arnie Ferrin's 17 points and Bob Harrison's 12 points and nine assists, effectively countering the scoring efforts of Vern Gardner and Joe Fulks for the Warriors.[29]

For Chicago, relying on Max Zaslofsky as the leading scorer and Andy Phillip as the playmaking force was a tried and tested path to success. Phil Brownstein coached a slightly slower offense than Harold Olsen had and the continued development of Phillip and Odie Spears, as well as the arrival of impact rookies Leo Barnhorst and Frank Kudelka, all contributed to a dip in Zaslofsky's individual offensive production, though, allowing him to conserve his energy for the latter stages of the season and playoffs.

Phillip had started to shine as one of the purest passers in the history of the sport the season prior. Compared to Bob Davies' penchant for no-look passes, between-the-legs dribbles, and other trick plays and emerging Knicks rookie Dick McGuire's constant, seemingly out of control feints and ball fakes, his style was more composed and calculated. With a keen eye on all his teammates, he paced himself, delivering precise two-handed passes to those cutting to the basket, often finding Odie Spears and Stan Miasek in favorable positions.

With both the system and the makeup of the team beginning to shift from existing primarily to complement Zaslofsky to a supporting structure for a backcourt tandem of the two, Phillip developed an early lead over the rest of the league in the assists column.

Kleggie Hermsen, a new arrival that summer from the Capitols who had started opposite George Mikan in the 1949 BAA Finals, brought championship experience from his time in Baltimore. Despite his limitations in mobility and his mediocre hands,

Hermsen effectively stopped most frontcourt players and disrupted passing lanes, ranking among the top centers in traditional defensive abilities. Offensively, he created space for cutters to operate, leading to a significant improvement in the efficiency of Spears and Stan Miasek from the year before.

The Capitols were the first to truly exploit him defensively via Jack Nichols, prompting Phil Brownstein to give playing time to Joe Graboski as a replacement for Hermsen. Graboski, a 19-year-old former Stags ballboy who had joined the team straight after finishing high school, held his own in some instances, but his lack of refinement was evident, highlighted by struggles against Connie Simmons in their 93–91 loss to the Knicks, as well as persistent mental lapses and unnecessary fouls.[30]

Those two factors caused Brownstein to make the twofold decision to keep Graboski in the rotation to aid his development while removing him from the starting lineup. Kleggie Hermsen regained his position as the starting center, and Ed Mikan, George Mikan's younger brother, faced the prospect of an imminent departure from the Stags.

As a rookie the prior year, Ed Mikan had shown glimpses of promise, albeit with occasional lapses, making him one of the few highlights in a relatively unremarkable draft class in terms of top-tier talent. Having quickly gone from a vaguely promising starter to not just relegation to the bench unit but also losing significant playing time to a teammate four years his junior, Mikan was sold to Rochester.[31]

The Royals had a pressing need for a "Mikan stopper" after three consecutive playoff losses to teams led by George Mikan. Ed emerged as a potential solution. In six games against Chicago in 1948–49, George had primarily faced off against his brother in three and against Miasek in three. Against Miasek, he averaged 34.3 points. Against his brother, he averaged just 22.7, fewer than he managed against all but one other defender, Charlie Black.

Ed Mikan's acquisition brought more benefits beyond this specific matchup, of course. With his athleticism and strength, his 6'8", 230 lb. frame provided a stark contrast to Arnie Risen and Jack Coleman, who were both built like beanpoles. He was a very capable rebounder, something that could become very valuable as a backup to Risen, considering the scarcity of strong rebounders on most teams' benches.

At first, Rochester attempted to split the center minutes between Risen and Mikan, but neither played well under those conditions, causing the team to heavily rely on Bob Davies and Bobby Wanzer's offense. Consequently, Mikan's minutes were significantly reduced except for in back-to-backs.

This adjustment coincided with a nine-game winning streak for the team, highlighted by an impressive 87–62 victory over Minneapolis.[32] During this stretch, Davies, Wanzer, and Risen were playing some of the most cohesive basketball they'd ever played together, with Davies' 16.4-point average during those nine games leading the way.

With both Rochester and Minneapolis returning to their usual winning ways, Fort Wayne was the team whose job was made much harder.

Rookie small forward Fred Schaus stood out as one of the top performers in his draft class, displaying impressive scoring ability and solid fundamentals. A lack of aggressiveness with the ball in his hands stopped him from scoring as often as he was capable of, but he still managed 15.4 points per game through the season's early days. During that period, though, he showed promise in that regard by increasing his free throw attempts from 3.7 to 6.1 per game, which would position him among the top players in the league if he could maintain this trend.

They faced a setback when point guard Curly Armstrong came down with an odontogenic infection after a strong start to the season.[33] The team struggled without him defensively, conceding 26.5 percent more points from opposing guards while he was out of the lineup than when he was available.

Leo Klier replaced Armstrong in the starting lineup, while John Oldham, Armstrong's backcourt partner, shifted to point guard. Although Klier was both a versatile scorer and a capable defender, he lacked the fundamental soundness to succeed as the Pistons' primary defender, which was the case during Armstrong's absence.

Another player affected by the defensive concerns was Bob Harris, the third pick in the 1949 draft, who saw a decrease in playing time. Despite being a good rebounder and showing promise as a versatile frontcourt player, his ability to match up against larger players and maintain a strong presence on the court raised concerns. Bob Carpenter, acquired from the defunct Oshkosh All-Stars, replaced him as starting power forward in mid-December. While Carpenter was full of grit and power, as well as utilizing his solid shooting stroke in spacing the floor offensively, his lack of height proved to be just as much of an issue as Harris' lack of strength, and Fort Wayne continued their slide from the top of the division to fourth.

While most teams' struggles came down to a few major problems that were, at least in theory, relatively straightforward fixes, Denver's numerous problems were simply overwhelming.

Kenny Sailors stood out as an effective scorer, but he was alone in that regard. The only other Nugget who had been a starter on any professional team before was Al Guokas, and that was on the previous year's Nuggets.

Dillard Crocker showcased incredible speed for a forward but undermined his value with poor shot selection. He took nearly 16 shots per game and made less than 30 percent of them, the worst efficiency of any player with his volume of attempts.

Jack Toomay was so full of hustle that it was as if his career depended on it. Which it did. He had played for four different teams in his two professional seasons and was utilized almost exclusively as a hatchet man. Toomay's prominence on the Nuggets was concerning in and of itself, considering he had been cut by the Bullets—also a losing team—in training camp.

Denver's offense was stagnant, their defense was below average at best, and it didn't take a rocket scientist to see how they'd started off the season 3–21. Furthermore, limited financial resources and a lack of desirable trade assets made it challenging to improve the team's situation.

Despite these obstacles, the Nuggets found a glimmer of hope in the acquisition of Floyd Volker, a versatile forward with experience playing alongside Kenny Sailors and Jim Darden during their national championship season at Wyoming. Although Volker had been riding the bench for the Olympians, he had previously strung together a pair of seasons as a utility role player for Oshkosh. While his career was built on versatility and interior scoring, the biggest addition he brought to the Nuggets was his ability to make the correct pass. Even Sailors, at point guard, was more comfortable scoring than distributing, making Volker's presence as an off-ball distributor a welcome change.

Still a far way off from competence, the Nuggets showed some improvement with Volker on the team. They kept games closer at the very least, and over the course of the next ten games they went 3–7 to double their number of wins. Volker had a considerable impact, averaging 11.9 points during that stretch.[34]

While not quite as poor as Denver, the Boston Celtics found themselves in a dire situation with a 7–14 record, heading toward their worst season yet, even after winning three straight games over Philadelphia, Sheboygan, and St. Louis on the backs of George Kaftan, Bob Kinney, and the relentless rebounding of power forward Brady Walker.

The Celtics lacked a star and an identity. Their roster was an eclectic mix of decent players, all too often Doggie Julian reacted to good individual performances by barely playing the player responsible in the next game, and the majority of the roster was either past their prime or nowhere near it.

Bob Kinney was primarily effective in the post against bigger opponents, but he was 29 years old and beginning to lose his agility. Sonny Hertzberg was the leader of the team, but in his three BAA seasons he had never been a double digit scorer. The team's few promising young players, namely George Kaftan and Ed Leede, faced their potential being hindered by the inconsistent rotations.

As a way to at least remedy that issue, owner Walter Brown applied the theory of addition by subtraction, waiving John Ezersky, a wing with a penchant for long-range shots whose presence cut into Leede's playing time, and selling lanky center George Nostrand, who was mostly useful for his height.[35] Boston's fortunes turned, as the three-game winning streak that brought them from 4–14 to 7–14 followed within a week. Kaftan scored double-digit points in each victory, having not previously done so all year in what had been a jarring regression from his performance the year prior.

Ezersky found refuge with Baltimore, a team he had previously played for, while Nostrand was acquired by Tri-Cities, largely due to Mike Fitzgerald anticipating a potential trade with another team desperately seeking additional bench size—a description fitting approximately 40 percent of the NBA's teams.

5

Trade Season, the BAA, and Three-and-a-Half-Million Dollars

On December 14 and 15, the Lakers suffered consecutive double-digit losses to the Knicks and Bullets, with George Mikan as their sole standout contributor. Mikan scored 38 points against New York and 34 against Baltimore. The rest of the team combined for measly totals of 46 and 34 points, respectively, in the two games.[1]

John Kundla's frontcourt experiment was yielding mixed results. While they achieved several blowout wins, the Lakers also lost plenty of games that they shouldn't have lost. Nonetheless, the undeniable talent of Vern Mikkelsen made it clear that reducing his playing time would be a disservice.

The logic behind Kundla's lineup was the natural extension of scientific basketball—the prevailing basketball ideology during the 1920s and early 1930s. Written by Original Celtics star Nat Holman in 1922, *Scientific Basketball* was the name of the first book espousing in-depth basketball strategy. Some of the points Holman emphasized included short passes, possession control, working the ball near the hoop or inside the free throw line, and employing shifting in man-to-man defense.[2]

The concept of Holman's that gained the most traction was focusing on close-range shots, which became synonymous with the scientific basketball philosophy as a whole and sparked a revolution in lateral offensive movement that persisted until the early to mid–1940s when Bobby McDermott's prominence shifted teams' focus to the impact perimeter shooting could have on cutters.

Kundla's utilization of a three-interior-player strategy aimed to maximize close-range scoring opportunities and create open perimeter shots when the defense collapsed to the inside. In practice, it meant Jim Pollard had significantly less room to operate in and denied him as much opportunity to utilize his finesse around the basket, while also leading the defense to suffer as the league's best shooters took advantage of Pollard's and Mikkelsen's adjustment to their new roles—the best in the league the year before, their defense was now merely average.

It seemed to be a tactical blunder, and some on the fringes raised doubts whether Kundla's impact on the Lakers' consecutive championships was instrumental or incidental. After all, he hadn't been the first choice for the job.

Joe Hutton, Hamline University's coach and athletic director since the early 1930s, had initially emerged as the favored candidate when Minneapolis first secured a team due to his transformation of Hamline's program into a powerhouse within the NAIB. When the Lakers contacted him about the job, he declined in order to keep coaching his son, who was entering his sophomore year at Hamline.

Kundla also had initially declined, unimpressed by the quality of play he had witnessed refereeing a PBLA preseason game and assuming the NBL was similar. Sid Hartman returned with a contract offer that would double his current salary, which he accepted.[3]

His coaching background was limited before the Lakers: at the College of St. Thomas, he had coached just one season and achieved a perfectly average 11–11 record. What had propelled him to second choice for the job was a distinguished playing career at the University of Minnesota that made him a popular figure in his adopted home state.

Once the Lakers job was his, what stood out the most about Kundla to a casual observer was a calm demeanor that set him apart from other coaches in the pros. The result was that he often fell under the radar compared to his star players and rarely attracted the warranted praise for their considerable success.

After the Lakers' two big losses to the Knicks and Bullets, they temporarily dropped back below Chicago and out of the top position in the Central Division, but Kundla stuck to his guns. Soon after, it would unmistakably pay off.

Sheboygan snapped their losing streak, after nine winless games since the foul-happy win over Tri-Cities, with another crucial victory over the Blackhawks. Noble Jorgensen's absence didn't make halting the negative momentum an easy task, but in his absence Bobby Cook and Max Morris stepped up and tried to right the ship.

Cook was a star small forward for the University of Wisconsin before joining the Redskins and transitioning to the backcourt. Though he was known as a sharpshooter, he exhibited a more disciplined approach to the role compared to others seeking to emulate Bobby McDermott. His greatest weapon was a push shot from near the free throw line resembling that of Hank Luisetti's. His greatest weakness was his defense, a deficiency shared by the team as a whole.

Morris, also a recently retired football star as a tight end and defensive end for Northwestern University and professionally for the Chicago Rockets and Brooklyn Dodgers, had simultaneously played in the NBL for the Chicago Gears and later for Sheboygan, missing about a third of most seasons because of his football commitments. Having retired from football in 1948, 1949–50 was Morris' first year where he had gotten to experience an offseason from professional sports, and he was having a bigger impact than ever before.

Morris' influence on Sheboygan's basketball team was significant, and with his football-honed toughness he manifested on the court as a whirling dervish of energy capable of imposing his will on the opposition as a highly impactful two-way star. His ability to draw fouls—only rivaled among NBA wings by Bobby Wanzer and Don Boven—and lead the team in attacking the defense translated into a shared aggressive mindset, with Jorgensen and Bob Brannum also in the top 20 free throw attempts in the league. As a team, they led the league.

They also led the league in points conceded. Through the first 19 games, no team was within three points per game of the number they allowed their opponents to score.

Seeking defensive help, the Redskins signed Jack Phelan, recently waived by Waterloo to make room for Jack Smiley.[4] Mostly known for being George Mikan's backup at DePaul as a freshman, Phelan's most common duty as a rookie was to act as an agitator in order to slow down bigger, more athletic, and more skilled post players.

His development in that role stemmed from battles with Mikan in practices at DePaul, when Mikan was already the most famous basketball player in the world and Phelan was a freshman who was five inches shorter, 50 lbs. lighter, and averaging more than 20 points fewer. He defended Mikan rigorously and learned the most effective positioning to force him into a tougher shot, often taking so much of a beating from Mikan's famously violent elbows in the process that he had to coat his arms with a heat rub to lessen the swelling.

In one practice, Phelan had Mikan frustrated enough that Mikan threw his elbow into the right side of Phelan's face and knocked out two of his molars. Phelan turned around and punched Mikan in the face, driving Mikan's glasses into the edges of his cheeks. Both players were sent to the hospital; Mikan needed stitches and had a permanent mark on his left elbow from Phelan's teeth. They boarded the train to New York later that day and DePaul finished as NIT runners-up the next week.[5]

The Knicks entered the latter part of December with an impressive 18-7 record, marking a significant improvement from their previous seasons of average results and frequent roster changes.

Carl Braun and Harry Gallatin returned as key players for the Knicks, with Braun continuing to be the team's most recognizable and important member, while Gallatin's role expanded following his strong playoff showing in 1948-49, despite splitting time between starting and coming off the bench. They were joined by New Yorkers Dick McGuire and Connie Simmons in the starting lineup, along with Vince Boryla, a do-it-all rookie forward best known for his participation in the 1948 Olympics. The fifth starter, when it wasn't Gallatin, was Ernie Vandeweghe.

The team's roster construction had many of the same features that were holding other teams back. Like Boston and Sheboygan, they lacked a clear number one option. Like Philadelphia, they had multiple important pieces, in Braun and Boryla, who favored outside shots. Like St. Louis, there was a considerable drop-off in talent from their starting five to the bench. Unlike all of those teams, they found success, winning 14 of their last 15 games after a 4-6 start and climbing to the second-best record in the league by late December, trailing only the Nationals.

As the youngest team in the NBA, with no starters older than 24, the Knicks were, in some ways, similar to the St. John's University teams Joe Lapchick had coached to a 334–130 record during the 11 years before he joined the Knicks. McGuire had even played two seasons for Lapchick at St. John's, easing his transition to the NBA and giving his coach one less thing to worry about as he paced the sidelines.

Before his coaching career, Lapchick was a standout player for the Original Celtics and Cleveland Rosenblums, generally recognized as the best center of the late 1920s and a pioneer as a playmaker from the pivot.

As a coach, his intense passion for the game was apparent above all else. In the 1944 NIT Final against DePaul, he drove himself into such a frenzy that he fainted in the second half. In the 1948–49 season coaching the Knicks, he fainted again and was hospitalized for over a week when Ned Irish traded away shut-down defender Tommy Byrnes against Lapchick's wishes. He routinely became so excited or anxious that he developed heart pains severe enough to render him incapable of delivering halftime team talks. The professional game and its heightened scheduling demands, travel, and job pressure only made those issues worse for him. On multiple occasions, he ripped off his suit jacket and stomped on it mid-game in a display of frustration. He once flung the empty chair next to him against a wall. In another incident, he launched a water tray into the air, drenching himself with water.

Despite these outbursts, he was one of the few coaches, like John Kundla, who rarely raised his voice in anger at his players. Lapchick initially lacked strong tactical skills and initially deferred to his players too often, later admitting that he felt out of place because he lacked a college education. He evolved as a coach by incorporating offensive strategies from his playing days and those of his former teammate Nat Holman, such as the give-and-go, and he maintained his focus on motivating his players and ran a disciplined team based on humanistic principles. Lapchick's approach fostered a culture where each player was expected to be a "coach on the floor."[6]

Under his guidance, St. John's became one of the nation's top basketball programs, producing talented players like McGuire, Max Zaslofsky, and Harry Boykoff. He won back-to-back NIT championships in 1942–43 and 1943–44.

By the late 1940s a very high-profile college coach based in New York with a prestigious playing career and regular appearances at Madison Square Garden, Lapchick provided a massive boost to the BAA's credibility when he left St. John's for the Knicks.

Fittingly, the Knicks as a franchise were also born out of the success of college basketball. Ned Irish, the charismatic team founder and president of the Knicks, wielded his position as the director of basketball at Madison Square Garden by leveraging the fame of New York's top college teams to entice the best teams nationwide, and with them, many thousands of fans.

Irish, known for his entrepreneurial spirit from a young age, had a knack for business ventures but followed his Wharton School enrollment by entering the newspaper industry. writing about sports for the *New York World-Telegram* and taking a side job as head of public relations for the NFL's New York Giants.[7]

The way he told the story, Irish's basketball origin story began when the *New York World-Telegram* assigned him to cover a game hosted by Manhattan College in 1932–33. When he arrived, the small gymnasium was so packed that he couldn't get in through the door and had to climb through a small window in a nearby office, tearing the pants of the best suit he owned.

According to Lou Black, the other journalist sent to cover the game, the story is entirely fabricated. Nevertheless, Irish told it constantly.

The following year, he approached John Kilpatrick, owner of the Madison Square Garden Corporation and the New York Rangers, with a proposal to rent out the arena for college basketball games at a cost of $4,000 per night. With financial backing from Tim Mara, owner of the New York Giants, Irish secured a deal that granted him exclusive rights to promote college basketball at Madison Square Garden as long as his profits exceeded the rental fee.

His inaugural promotion featuring New York University versus the University of Notre Dame and Westminster College of Pennsylvania versus St. John's University drew a crowd of 16,180 spectators and earned more than the necessary $4,000. He then continued to earn more than that time and again, cementing his position and enabling him to step in as acting president of the Madison Square Garden Corporation when Kilpatrick was called into military service during World War II. He was given a permanent vice presidency upon Kilpatrick's return.[8]

Irish's commanding "my way or the highway" negotiation tactics made him more than a few enemies in college basketball, but his opponents had little recourse but to either comply or forfeit the opportunity to play on the grandest stage basketball had to offer.

When the BAA was founded, assigning a franchise to New York was inevitable. As his popularity among basketball fans was rivaled only by his unpopularity among his colleagues, Irish was the obvious contender to receive the New York franchise but also the only one of the founding members for whom there was still an ownership dispute by the time the BAA's organizational meeting began.

Irish's rival bidder was Max Kase, the man most directly responsible for the original conceptualization of the BAA in the first place. The sports editor for the *New York Journal-American* since 1938, Kase rose to prominence outside of his natural realm of sportswriting in 1943 when he spearheaded efforts to use professional sports events to sell Series E bonds.[9]

The most impactful event arranged by Kase was the *New York Journal-American* War Bond Game in 1943 at the Polo Grounds, featuring an all-star team of players from the New York Yankees, New York Giants, and Brooklyn Dodgers against a military all-star team. Preceding the game was an exhibition featuring retired baseball stars, including seven Hall of Famers. Babe Ruth hit his final home run in that exhibition. This event raised approximately $800 million in war bond sales and pledges. The following year, Kase organized the Tri-Cornered Baseball Game, a three-way game between the Yankees, Giants, and Dodgers, raising an additional $56 million in war bond sales.

With a rising profile because of the war bond games, Kase's long-held vision of basketball succeeding nationally in major cities gained traction, and he already had Walter Brown onboard from over a decade prior. Once American Hockey League (AHL) president Maurice Podoloff signed on as BAA president on June 6, 1946, the league became official.

When Kase went to Irish proposing a BAA team based out of Madison Square Garden, Irish informed Kase that Irish's membership in the Arena Managers Association of America included a clause requiring any professional sports teams utilizing Madison Square Garden as their home arena to be owned by the Madison Square Garden Corporation. After that meeting, Irish pursued his own BAA team and Kase had to modify his proposed franchise for a smaller arena. The prospects of both men's franchises being admitted were slim to none.

Irish's cocksure pitch to the owners of the other BAA teams as to why he should get the franchise began, "I represent a corporation with more than three and a half million dollars in assets." He focused on the benefits that having a team owned by the Madison Square Garden Corporation offered, which, from a financial sense, were many and significant.

Throughout Kase's attempt to pitch his plan for a team at the 69th Regiment Armory, Irish repeatedly interjected with a refrain of "three and a half million dollars."[10]

For his bravado Irish was rewarded with a unanimous vote in favor of his ownership of the BAA's New York franchise. Given the existing commitments at Madison Square Garden and uncertainty surrounding the league's commercial viability, the team ended up playing 24 of their 30 home games at the very venue that Kase had settled on for his bid, the 69th Regiment Armory.

Irish conducted a vote among his Madison Square Garden employees to determine the franchise's name. Each employee submitted a name on a piece of paper and put it in a hat. The name written by more employees than any other was the Knickerbockers, a 19th century term synonymous with New Yorkers and popularized by writer

Washington Irving's first novel, which involved a literary character named Diedrich Knickerbocker.

Since the BAA didn't implement a draft until after its first year of existence, the original 11 teams relied on recruiting entire rosters under an initial salary cap of $55,000. That meant most teams, after signing their core players, filled out much of their remaining roster space with homegrown talent. Fifty-one out of the 141 players rostered by BAA teams on opening day of the league's inaugural season played for a team based in the same state as either their hometown or the college they attended.[11]

The Knicks, with nine New Yorkers on their roster, had the most homegrown players aside from the Pittsburgh Ironmen's 12 Pennsylvanians. In the late 1940s, New York had approximately 2 million Jews, good for slightly over 40 percent of the entire Jewish population of the United States and more than the entire population of Israel at the time. This was reflected heavily in the Knicks' roster, with three Jewish starters and a roster that was more than half Jewish.

A common refrain from crowds they visited as the away team, particularly in the three cities with segregationist policies, was "Pass the ball to Abe!" in a derogatory reference to Abraham, the father of Judaism. Crowds in Pittsburgh went a step further, creating their own anti–Semitic theme song for the Knicks by parodying the popular song "The Sidewalks of New York" with a version that replaced the final line of the verse with the lyrics, "here come the Jews from New York."

Following a 5–16 stretch that came on the heels of a 14–3 start, Irish and Neil Cohalan decided to split up the Jewish core of the team, reasoning that their presence invited too much abuse at road games and that they were so closely knit that it made the non–Jewish Knicks into outcasts of a sort.[12] By the time of the merger, basketball's best Jewish players, despite all being native New Yorkers, weren't Knicks. Adolph Schayes played for Syracuse, Max Zaslofsky played for Chicago, Harry Boykoff played for Waterloo, Sonny Hertzberg played for Boston, and Red Holzman played for Rochester.

That next year, they made a different social breakthrough when they briefly rostered Wat Misaka, a 5'7" nisei point guard whose defensive heroics for the University of Utah in the 1944 NCAA tournament en route to a national championship had made him a crowd favorite in Madison Square Garden at the same time nearly 120,000 American citizens of Japanese heritage in the western half of the country were being taken from their homes, systematically robbed of their possessions, and thrown into internment camps.

Misaka believed Ned Irish only drafted him in a bid to increase ticket sales because of his popularity with Madison Square Garden crowds from his collegiate career. That wasn't an unlikely supposition; Irish had a clear affinity for signing players with the express purpose of selling more tickets, whether it be from playing for New York colleges or from being crowd favorites as the star of an opposing team that visited Madison Square Garden.[13]

Nonetheless, when the Knicks added Misaka to the team, he became the first person of color signed to a BAA team. He only played three games for New York, but in doing so he also became the first person of color in to play in BAA history.

It was unknown to the public at the time, but Irish financially supported the league office in order to keep the league running beyond its first season. Almost every team and the league itself were dealing with unsustainable amounts of debt, but the Knicks were profitable from the start, and Irish didn't let anybody forget it.[14]

Their monetary success wasn't quite matched by the good but not great on-court product, and Irish didn't have much patience for a team that was merely good. The Knicks' roster turnover was constant despite their being one of just four teams (along with Chicago, Philadelphia, and St. Louis) to qualify for the playoffs in all three years of the BAA's existence.

By the halfway point of the 1947–48 season, none of the starters from the start of the first year remained. By the time of the merger, the 22-year-old Carl Braun was the longest-tenured player on the team.

Irish, recognizing Carl Braun as a valuable centerpiece from the beginning of his Knicks career, made every effort to construct a high-caliber team around him regardless of any restrictions or limitations on what was allowed.

It took him just half a year to first bend the BAA's rules to his advantage, recruiting and signing Lee Knorek while he was still playing college basketball for the University of Detroit Mercy despite a BAA regulation prohibiting the signing of college players until their graduation.

Though Detroit Mercy's athletic director, Lloyd Brazil, deemed Irish's actions "irregular and unethical," Maurice Podoloff sided with Irish on the grounds that Knorek

Carl Braun (shooting, October 25, 1952) was the leading scorer for the New York Knicks and top ten in the league, as well as the extension on the court of Hall of Fame coach Joe Lapchick's philosophy. He was widely regarded as the most skilled long-distance shooter in professional basketball following the retirement of Bobby McDermott. Also shown (from left): Dick Groat, Ray Felix, Harry Gallatin, and Mark Workman.

had already played over four years of college basketball, between three years at De Sales College, one year at Detroit Mercy after De Sales shut down, and one year at Denison University because of the V-12 Navy program.[15]

The next year, Irish went even further and selected Harry Gallatin with the 16th pick in the draft and signed him despite Gallatin having just completed his collegiate sophomore year, causing a stir as Gallatin had been drafted by the Baltimore Bullets in the previous year but couldn't sign then due to his underclassman status. Podoloff made an exception this time, citing that Gallatin had actually managed to graduate college in those two years, although the rule itself had not been modified to accommodate early graduates, making Gallatin a special case.[16]

Irish managed to bend the rules for several reasons: the favorable treatment he received stemmed from his previous financial contributions to the league office, the player war created a risk of Gallatin joining an NBL team that Podoloff wanted to avoid, Podoloff aimed to establish New York and Chicago as the BAA's most prominent teams, and Irish threatened to withdraw the Knicks from the league at the slightest inconvenience—a threat that wasn't unfounded, since he made more money at the time hosting college games than BAA ones.

Irish was dismissive toward small-market teams from the NBL, as they didn't help his gate receipts, an attitude that led to a feud with Ben Kerner resulting in New York and Tri-Cities refusing to recognize each other on their arena marquees before games. Irish's promoter mindset dictated his actions, and if he didn't see something as worthy of promotion, he considered it unworthy of his attention.

On December 14, 1949, even the defending BAA champion Lakers were snubbed by his marquee in the first post-merger matchup between the two teams in Madison Square Garden, the sign instead reading "Geo. Mikan v/s Knicks," as Irish figured Mikan was a bigger name than the Lakers as a team.[17]

The game itself mirrored the marquee, with Mikan scoring an impressive 38 points but lacking support from his teammates, while the Knicks, led by Carl Braun's 26 points and Dick McGuire's record-breaking 16 assists, secured a 94–84 win.[18]

Irish used his frustration over the inclusion of small-market teams as leverage to further bolster the Knicks' roster. He targeted Vince Boryla from the University of Denver and Ernie Vandeweghe from Colgate University, both highly sought-after prospects, and once again threatened to take the Knicks out of the NBA if he didn't get his way. With special arrangements made by Podoloff, Irish secured Boryla's rights before the draft and reserved Vandeweghe's rights to ensure they could select him later without risk, allowing Irish to draft Dick McGuire in the first round and still end up with both Boryla and Vandeweghe as well.[19]

Vandeweghe, hailing from Montreal, Quebec, became the NBA's first international player upon his debut. There had previously been seven in the BAA and nine in the NBL, but none remained in professional basketball by the time of the merger.

The selection of McGuire, rumored to be due to a slip of the tongue when attempting to instead draft Jack Kerris, proved fortuitous as he quickly established himself as one of the league's four elite point guards and an exceptional playmaker.

Boryla had a variety of ways to score and his ability to space the floor made him a crucial starter on a team largely lacking shooters, save for the greatest shooter in the league in Carl Braun. Vandeweghe, despite only being available for home games, as he was attending medical school at Columbia University, made significant contributions as a scorer when he took to the court, starting at shooting guard when available, with Carl Braun, Boryla, and Connie Simmons forming the frontcourt, and replaced in the starting five by Gallatin with Braun and Boryla each shifting down a position in his absence.[20]

The Indianapolis Olympians' biggest potential problems coming into the 1949–50 season had been on the wing, and that partially materialized early in the season when they struggled against teams with balanced attacks and strong wing threats. While Alex Groza and Ralph Beard were a resounding success as a rookie partnership and Wah Wah Jones fit the mold of a great third option, the rest of the roster was mostly a surplus of wings and forwards.

Bruce Hale stood out as the most skilled offensive player of the bunch, but, as the oldest player at 31 years old, that meant the somewhat inconsistent, formerly explosive wing playmaker was relied on far too heavily for his age and for being misaligned with the pace of a team featuring nine rookies.

Cliff Barker's impact on the court was limited by his coaching role taking precedence and a series of niggling injuries to start off the year. With his availability limited, he settled into a role backing up Hale at shooting guard while Joe Holland and Marshall Hawkins took on most of the small forward minutes.

Both workmanlike role players whose willingness to adopt an off-ball role which complemented their ball-dominant teammates, Holland and Hawkins were both full of hustle and played very physically for small forwards; Holland was a better rebounder and one of the best young forward defenders in the NBA, while Hawkins was a bit more natural of an athlete and much more comfortable with the ball in his hands.

In a surprising 88–79 loss to Baltimore, who were led by 23 points from Paul Hoffman and overcame 27 from Groza, Hawkins had a standout performance when he was given an increased role in Beard's absence, but he suffered a broken cheekbone late in the game.[21] Beard's absence, caused by a strained back, was brief and he was back for the next game, but Hawkins missed the next month. While Holland was the obvious choice to take on most of his minutes, this also meant additional pressure for both Hale and Barker.

As the regular season approached its halfway mark in late December and the playoff picture began to take shape, trade activity began to kick into high gear.

One notable trade had already occurred, separating former BAA stars Joe Fulks and Ed Sadowski, and it proved to have a positive impact on both players. Fulks, a highly skilled scorer with a versatile offensive repertoire, had started the season in a slump; his 18.3 points at the time of the Sadowski trade was still fourth highest in the league behind just George Mikan, Alex Groza, and Noble Jorgensen, but 7.7 points per game less than his average the previous campaign. In the two weeks following the trade, Fulks shot above his career average in all but one game and scored 20-plus points in five out of seven.

Similarly, Sadowski experienced a resurgence after a rough end to his time in Philadelphia, averaging 16.2 points in his first five games as a Bullet, and that was topped in the sixth game when he scored 30 in a 106–95 loss to Fort Wayne.

The Central Division had four of the league's strongest teams and it was a near guarantee, even at this early point in the season, that those four—Chicago, Fort Wayne, Minneapolis, and Rochester—would be the division's four playoff berths in some order.

There wasn't much pressure on the Pistons to make it out of the division, but the same couldn't be said for the other three teams. Chicago in particular was eager for real success, having experienced continually declining levels of playoff success and relevance through their previous three years despite initially being hailed as an exemplary BAA team.

Joe Graboski's brief breakout success dwindled, leading Phil Brownstein to move Stan Miasek from starting power forward to backup center to cover for him, coinciding with losses to Philadelphia, New York, Tri-Cities, Rochester, and Syracuse in just over a week. The decision to sell Ed Mikan to Rochester proved to be ill-considered, leaving them with a shortage of players capable of defending against tall or skilled centers. In the five subsequent games, opposing centers or otherwise post-centric players consistently led the opposition in scoring. That was in no way tenable when a run to the Finals almost certainly meant going through Minneapolis' George Mikan, Rochester's Arnie Risen, or both.

Recognizing the need for a solution, John Sbarbaro pursued a trade for George Nostrand, who, while considerably worse overall than the similarly available Don Otten, possessed similar post-defending abilities, was a better rebounder, came at a lower cost, and wouldn't cause the sort of positional overcrowding that had caused them to trade away Mikan in the first place.[22]

Tri-Cities got Gene Vance out of the deal, a versatile ex–Whiz Kid who had acted as a secondary ball handler and tertiary scorer for the Stags in previous seasons but had been holding out all season due to contract issues. His skills on both ends of the court, ability to run a fast break offense, and natural fit with the up-tempo Western Division made him a valuable addition to the Blackhawks, providing aspects of play Tri-Cities badly needed with both Warren Perkins at small forward and Whitey Von Nieda, who had taken over at point guard in wake of Billy Hassett's departure, in poor form.

The Olympians were also active on the trade market, with Babe Kimbrough having quickly scrounged up enough cash to buy a reinforcement in the wake of Marshall Hawkins' injury in the form of rookie guard Paul Walther.[23]

Walther had been the odd man out in Minneapolis. He had too much flair to his game and he needed more freedom of movement than a George Mikan–centric team allowed. With four shooting guards and two point guards ahead of him in the rotation, there was much less need for him on the Lakers than on the Olympians.

In Indianapolis, playing alongside Alex Groza, who was more adaptable than George Mikan, Walther had more leeway to showcase his skills. His high energy was encouraged, and he began to show flashes of dogged on-ball defense, but poor shooting limited his usefulness at shooting guard for a team that needed the floor spaced, and he was quickly shifted to be Ralph Beard's backup. While not a natural playmaker, he got involved on offense as an initiator and now made frequent cuts to the basket, which he had been discouraged from doing in Minneapolis.

In Walther's Olympian debut, a 104–92 win over Chicago, Groza scored 42 points.[24] This was already his third 40-point performance as a rookie, the three highest post-merger scoring performances with no other player having yet surpassed the 38 points that he and Mikan had both reached. Out of all the great scorers the NBA, BAA, and NBL had seen, Groza had surpassed each and every one of them with more than half the season remaining. Neither Mikan nor Max Zaslofsky ever scored 40 or more points as a rookie, and Joe Fulks only hit that milestone once during his rookie year.

In the depths of the Western Division, the Waterloo Hawks were providing Denver with some unexpected competition for the title of the NBA's worst team. Their meager 6–19 record, punctuated by plentiful blowout losses, did not inspire much hope, especially after a threesome of losses to Syracuse, Chicago, and Anderson marked their second winless back-to-back-to-back stretch of the season. Nearly halfway through the year, they were still without an away win aside from a two-point squeaker against the Bullets on the nominally neutral ground of Philadelphia.

The Hawks, a franchise with a brief and peculiar history, seemed an odd addition to the merger in the first place. The franchise began just the year before, in 1948–49, founded by Pinkie George, a 1920s bantamweight boxer turned manager and promoter.

George originally chose Des Moines, Iowa, as the city he would base his team out of, but a lack of enthusiasm from the city and a concerted effort from Waterloo, Iowa, community leaders led him to change his mind and relocate to Waterloo before the season began.

Waterloo had tasted the flavor of professional basketball once before during the fleeting presence of their Pro-Hawks in the PBLA. The Pro-Hawks were led by future NBA players Noble Jorgensen and Price Brookfield, but they nonetheless accumulated just a 1–5 record and attendance that failed to reach a thousand people more often than it surpassed 2,500.

Despite this, the city was sports mad, with enthusiasm sky-high after the Minor League Baseball Waterloo White Hawks won the Illinois-Indiana-Iowa League in 1947. Even after the PBLA went under, the City of Waterloo bought the portable court and hoops from the league in bankruptcy court, ostensibly for hosting state championships but ultimately to lure a new professional team like the one that would soon become a reality.

In homage to the Rath Packing Company, one of Waterloo's prominent employers alongside John Deere, the team adopted the name "Hawks" after a local naming contest. The choice was inspired by the Black Hawk meats produced by the company. That name, in turn, paid tribute to Black Hawk County, where Waterloo resides, named after the renowned Sauk war leader Ma-ka-tai-me-she-kia-kiak, commonly known as Black Hawk. Ma-ka-tai-me-she-kia-kiak was also the ultimate namesake of the nearby Tri-Cities Blackhawks.

George put his younger brother, Andy George, in charge of the Hawks while he was busy finalizing the creation of the National Wrestling Alliance. Andy, a war hero decorated with two Bronze Star medals for valor, had served in the Office of Strategic Services across various European theaters in World War II. Upon his return, he was the Pro-Hawks' manager of business affairs, giving him some brief experience in basketball prior to the Hawks.[25]

To establish credibility and distance the Hawks from the ill-fated Pro-Hawks, the George brothers appointed Charley Shipp as player-coach. As one of the most seasoned players in basketball, he was one of only two players to participate in every season of NBL history, along with Oshkosh's Leroy Edwards.

Shipp's career began immediately after high school, as he showcased his skills for the Hilgemeier Packers, later renamed the U.S. Tires due to a sponsorship change, starting in the 1933–34 season. The U.S. Tires became founding members of the MBC in 1935–36 and added Edwards, a standout player who had been the National Player of the Year as a sophomore at Kentucky the year before.

Edwards, renowned for his exceptional left-handed hook shot and extreme physicality, led the league in scoring and was, along with Johnny Wooden, one of the best players in the league.

While Edwards held the spotlight, Shipp's defensive and playmaking abilities, including his talent for delivering full-court outlet passes to Edwards, distinguished him far more than his reliable, but not outstanding, two-handed set shot from distance did.

Both players were extremely talented on both sides of the floor and both very tenacious defensive players when needed, exhibited strong passing skills, and effectively collaborated in pick-and-rolls, but the team as a whole wasn't great and finished with a 5–9 record, missing the playoffs.

They each left the team after 1935–36; Shipp went to Akron Goodyear and Edwards went to the Dayton London Bobbies.

In Akron, Shipp played a pivotal role for one of professional basketball's historically great teams. With Shipp playing alongside Ray Morstadt and Bob Cope, they employed a deliberate and controlled offense that limited opponents to low scores. Their regular season record was a remarkable 16–2, and they swept their way to a championship.

Edwards' London Bobbies excelled as well, winning the Western Division in the regular season, but he left for the independent Oshkosh All-Stars before the season ended. Although Dayton remained competitive, they forfeited the decisive third game of a playoff series against the Fort Wayne General Electrics and were eliminated.

With the reorganization of the MBC into the NBL, Oshkosh gained admission to the league for the 1937–38 season, and both Edwards and Shipp were once again both important players for two of the best teams in the league.

In January, Akron and Oshkosh were the league's two best teams, each with only one loss. Morstadt tore his Achilles tendon late that month, and his absence led to a collapse that allowed Akron Firestone to surpass them in the standings. Oshkosh ended the season with the best record at 12–2, led by Edwards, who became the league's leading scorer and won the NBL MVP award. Both Edwards and Shipp were named to the All-NBL First Team.

In the playoffs, Goodyear regrouped under coach Lefty Byers' strategy of utilizing their bench unit to play aggressively against the opposing starters, subsequently substituting in the regular starters to exploit the worn-out opponents. They swept Akron Firestone 2–0 and advanced to the inaugural NBL Finals against Oshkosh. After splitting the first two games, Akron secured the series victory in game three by successfully defending an early 10–1 run when Shipp, moved mid-game from guard to center, limited Edwards to only nine points.

Morstadt's injury had a lasting impact on Goodyear, leading to the defending champions' decline to a .500 record. Oshkosh, with Edwards as MVP once again, reached the championship game but fell short against Firestone.

In 1939–40, Shipp reunited with Edwards on the Oshkosh All-Stars. Led by a third straight MVP season from Edwards, 6'4", 225 lbs., and the strongest player in the NBL, and Shipp, with his improved shooting and court vision, Oshkosh again came up one point short in the deciding game against Firestone, their third consecutive loss in the Finals with all three coming down to winner-take-all games.

They finally earned a championship in spectacular fashion, sweeping both Akron Firestone and Sheboygan. The year after that, Edwards and Shipp had their best season together and finished with a 20–4 record and a second championship, this time over the Fort Wayne Zollners.

As the league contracted in the face of players leaving for military duty, Oshkosh's reign finally ended as the team missed out on a championship appearance for the first time since the league had become the NBL and even finished with losing records in subsequent seasons.

Shipp moved to Fort Wayne, winning his fifth championship but having a limited impact from the bench. Oshkosh experienced further decline with Shipp gone despite Edwards' highest-scoring season in nearly a decade.

With the additions of Bob Carpenter and Gene Englund, Edwards gracefully transitioned into a third option for the All-Stars while they regained their winning form, although playoff success remained limited. Edwards earned his final All-NBL selection in 1945–46, leaving him with eight (six times All-NBL First Team and twice All-NBL Second Team), the most of any NBL player. Shipp's seven tied Bobby McDermott for the second most selections.[26]

Shipp's time with the Zollners ended on a negative note due to his involvement in the brawl that also got McDermott sent out of Fort Wayne. He was sent to the Anderson Packers, where he played for a year and a half prior to being hired by Waterloo.

Among the most important signings for the first version of the Hawks in 1948–49 were three members of the recently disbanded Toledo Jeeps: Harry Boykoff, Dick Mehen, and veteran high-energy bench wing Dale Hamilton. He desperately attempted to add a fourth, sharpshooter Fran Curran, but Curran chose to sign with Rochester instead. The team, led by Boykoff and Mehen, had a mediocre season, finishing with a 30–32 record and missing the playoffs.

In the second half of their first season, Waterloo's issues were exacerbated as Shipp's effectiveness as a player was curtailed by a series of illnesses, an allergic reaction to wool, and a punctured foot from stepping on a fishing lure.

They did well at attracting a crowd, though, in large part due to their $0.85 tickets, and that gave Pinkie George enough confidence in his brother's running of the team that he gave away half of his interest to Andy and the other half to Shipp for free.

The Hawks were in the red by the end of the season. When the merger happened and travel costs multiplied, Andy George and Shipp couldn't afford to operate the team anymore and planned to follow Oshkosh in pulling out of the league between the merger and the season's start. Through a community fundraising effort, the team was kept alive, and new shareholders formed Waterloo Basketball Inc. to manage the team and elected Chris Marsau, a Rath Packing Company export salesman and minor league baseball executive, as chairman.

With financial backing intact, Waterloo not only retained their team but also acquired the rights to the bankrupt Calumet Buccaneers. The only Calumet player to actually make the switch to Waterloo was Stan Patrick, with aging stars McDermott and George Glamack both semiretiring. Six rookies Calumet drafted, though, signed for the Hawks, headlined by Don Boven and Wayne See.[27]

After briefly considering retirement to become a full-time coach, Shipp returned for a 17th and presumably final year as a player. With the team's guard depth having been depleted over the summer, Shipp played rotational minutes, primarily backing up Leo Kubiak at point guard. He had a limited role on the court but remained a solid defender and could be a professional nuisance capable of getting into the heads of less experienced players.

The Waterloo Hawks possessed an efficient lineup, with players like Mehen, Boykoff, and Patrick boasting high shooting percentages; however, their chances were often undermined by turnovers and fouls. The team's starting guards, Kubiak and See, played at a faster pace than the rest of the team, resulting in various unforced errors.

Don Boven, a versatile rookie who had excelled in multiple sports at Western Michigan, proved to be the team's most talented two-way player as a rookie starting at small forward. On the wing, Boven had to attempt to make up for the rest of the team's defensive shortcomings with physical defending of his own, but it rarely seemed to make enough of a difference for the team to win.

To address the shooting guard position, Shipp promoted rookie See, a relatively unknown player from Arizona State College at Flagstaff, to the starting lineup in Patrick's place. See had shown promise as a defender and penetrating threat off the bench, impressing Shipp with his tenacious defense and playmaking abilities, no doubt reminiscent of Shipp's own style of play.

The team's bench rotation included Ward Gibson, a versatile power forward who'd just completed a very good season with the Nuggets but wasn't finding many minutes backing up Mehen and Boykoff, and Bob Tough, an aging scorer with sporadic spot-up shooting ability and many defensive weaknesses.

Baltimore experienced a resurgence following the Ed Sadowski trade, winning five out of eight games, nearly surpassing Washington and putting a little extra space between themselves and the Warriors and Celtics in the bottom half of the Eastern Division.

Unlike most Sadowski-led teams, they were playing entertaining, up-tempo basketball. While they convincingly beat both the Lakers and Olympians during this period, perhaps the most encouraging game for them came in the form of the 95–106 loss to Fort Wayne in which Sadowski had scored 30 points. Not only was their new arrival playing better than he had in over a year, but Paul Hoffman also scored 25 and Carlisle Towery and Tommy Byrnes combined for another 31. It was a loss and involved pretty poor defense, but it was the highest-scoring regulation game that the Bullets had ever put together.[28]

Two players in particular deserve credit for this adjustment despite the addition of, Sadowski, a high-profile player who had become synonymous in recent years with rough and unappealing styles of basketball: Buddy Jeannette and Paul Hoffman.

Jeannette, who, though no longer in his prime, was still pretty fast and could lead a quick offense if needed, recognized the skills of rookie point guard Joe Dolhon, who was faster and had better shooting abilities. Accordingly, he began to increase Dolhon's time on the court and reduce his own.

Hoffman, showing improvement from his rookie season despite missing the previous year, averaged 15.9 points per game prior to Sadowski's arrival and only took a brief hit after he joined. His contortions while shooting near the basket confused the less defensively sound of his opponents and led to many three-point plays. More than anything, he had grown more accustomed to having the ball in his hands for a considerable amount of time, allowing Dolhon to adjust to starting in the NBA without having to fully run the offense as a rookie.

Unfortunately, both Hoffman and Jeannette were injured just two days apart as a five-game road trip approached, and Dolhon, as well as the entire team, would have a baptism of fire to look forward to. Hoffman's chest contusion courtesy of Wah Wah Jones' elbow wouldn't keep him out much longer than two weeks, but Jeannette tore a knee ligament in a collision with Bob Feerick, condemning him to crutches on the sideline and putting his career in doubt.[29]

The other Southerners, St. Louis, shouldn't have been as bad as they were. At 12–14, they would have still been on track to make the playoffs in either of the other divisions, but in the hypercompetitive Central Division, it would take a catastrophic string of losses from one of their divisional counterparts for the Bombers to have a real shot.

Despite the addition of Ed Macauley next to Red Rocha, who provided height in the post, the team struggled with rebounding against stronger opponents. What had made St. Louis stand out in the past was excellent ball movement and defense. While their defense was different from the Bombers' traditional aggressive style reliant on traps and forcing opposing centers to work hard to get the ball, it was still effective. The ball movement was less so.

Johnny Logan stood out as a star player for the St. Louis team during their BAA years, earning All-BAA Second Team selections in all three seasons. In the 1948–49 season, Logan had higher and more efficient scoring marks than ever before, enhanced by the third-most assists in the league, behind just Bob Davies and Andy Phillip. Without Logan's great season, they likely wouldn't have been a playoff team in 1948–49.

He came back down to earth in 1949–50 after a strong start to the season, though, with both his assisting and scoring numbers taking a noticeable hit. Belus Smawley, his longtime backcourt partner, underwent a similar drastic improvement in 1948–49, and was given a further increased role as Logan regressed. Nonetheless, this was also indicative of a two-pronged problem for St. Louis: Ken Loeffler's old motion offense had devolved into frequent isolation plays under his replacement as coach, Grady Lewis, coupled with unversatile players and insufficient shooters to turn a team that had originally been built on speed into the slowest team in the NBA.

Although Smawley's distinctive whirling two-handed jump shot was his trademark, both Logan and Smawley were above-average shooters at best. Macauley had a good shot for a center, but it was much preferred that he excel on the interior, attempting hook shots and fighting through traffic for layups. Rocha wasn't exactly a traditional post player, but his points often came from pick-and-rolls or fast breaks.

That left shooting up to starting small forward Ace Maughan. Due to the cramped spacing resulting from the inclusion of two natural centers in the lineup, Maughan was unable to fully leverage his superior athleticism in his optimal role of converting lobbed passes or offensive rebounds into scoring opportunities. As such, he was often relegated to being St. Louis' de facto sharpshooter to rescue them from challenging offensive situations. He'd been in this position before with the Detroit Falcons and failed miserably, having shot 24.1 percent on a team that went 20–40. Whether his impact on a given game would be positive or negative for the Bombers was anyone's guess.

Easy Parham, the primary bench player, had a finesse-based game and decent ball-handling skills but was a weaker shooter compared to the starters. Mac Otten, Bill Roberts, and Don Putman all also provided about a dozen minutes off the bench. Otten was a rebounding specialist and not tasked with much else, Roberts had been a backup in college and was only in the NBA because he was 6'9", and Putman had once been an effective change-of-pace scorer but was playing his way out of the NBA.

Christmas Day provided one of the most basketball-filled days of the regular season. On Christmas of 1946, the BAA had no games and the NBL had just one, but the schedule had gradually ramped up in the couple years since, and by 1949–50, only three teams got the day off.

On this particular Christmas Day, Alex Groza emerged as the top scorer with 28 points, although his team, the Olympians, faced foul trouble with six players fouling out and Malcolm McMullen even picking up a seventh foul. The Waterloo Hawks, down 84–72 with just 58 seconds remaining, found salvation in Charley Shipp's ingenious exploitation of the two-minute rule, a provision that rewarded non-shooting fouls in the game's final moments with a single free throw followed by a subsequent jump ball between the fouler and foulee.

With both Alex Groza and Wah Wah Jones already fouled out, Indianapolis lacked height and the Hawks strategically targeted backup power forward Malcolm McMullen and player-coach Cliff Barker with intentional fouls, aiming to exploit the jump ball rule in their favor. Neither player converted any of their last-minute free throws, allowing Waterloo to erase a 12-point deficit in less than a minute to force overtime. Ward Gibson scored on Waterloo's first two possessions in overtime, and the Hawks eventually slipped away with a desperately needed 97–93 win that put an end to a four-game losing streak and brought the Hawks within one game of Tri-Cities for the final playoff spot in the division. Don Boven's 17 points led a balanced scoring effort, with eight Hawks players contributing eight or more points each.[30]

Wins for Rochester (88–79 over Boston) and Minneapolis (72–58 over Fort Wayne) turned the leading spot of the Central Division into a three-way tie, with Rochester having the best season on paper, Minneapolis having the most talent, and Chicago having held a slight lead over both for most of the season. The next day, Chicago lost to Fort Wayne and both Minneapolis and Rochester won close games, jointly giving the Lakers and Royals the top spot in the division.

Philadelphia and the injury-riddled Baltimore Bullets had a hard-fought battle with playoff implications. A closely contested affair saw no individual player shine, but a late Ron Livingstone free throw sealed a nail-biting 64–63 victory for the Warriors, inching them closer to Baltimore in the standings.[31]

In a matchup between the league's two winningest teams, Syracuse hosted the Packers for their fourth meeting of the season. The game showcased the fast-paced, open style of play favored by both teams. Paul Seymour and Billy Gabor combined for 46 points to lead the Nationals to a win despite the best efforts of Anderson's Bill Closs, who countered with 20 points and stifling defense against Adolph Schayes.[32] Syracuse's win was their fifth straight, marking their third streak of five or more wins that season. The brilliance of their 23–3 record was only matched by the incompetence of Denver, who fell to a ghastly 3–25 after a loss to the flailing Sheboygan Redskins, who had themselves only won two of their last 12 games.

Washington won their Christmas Day game against St. Louis, but dropped two straight in two consecutive days following. With that, they had lost five of their last seven games to fall to a 12–14 record and just 3–8 away from home.

The Capitols still featured veterans Fred Scolari, Bob Feerick, John Norlander, and Bones McKinney, who were part of the successful starting five from three years prior, but the familiar roster did not mean familiar levels of success.

Auerbach's departure following the 1948–49 season had a more profound impact on the team than anyone had expected. He had run just about every aspect of the team when he was coach; Capitols owner Mike Uline was so aggressively hands-off that Auerbach later joked that he "didn't know the difference between a basketball and a hockey puck."[33]

Uline was the oldest owner by over 20 years to play a part in founding the BAA, already 71 years old by the beginning of the league's existence and 74 by the time of the merger. Born as Michiel Ulijn in Alem, The Netherlands, he immigrated to the United States when he was a teenager after flooding left his family financially ruined. For five years, he worked as a digger at a quarry in Cleveland, Ohio, until he had saved up enough money to purchase an ice plant at 21 years old.

Over the next 35 years, he grew the M. J. Uline Ice Company into an empire of over 30 ice plants and patented about 70 inventions, but his obsessive work ethic strained his family life and eventually destroyed his marriage. In 1931, he moved from Cleveland to Washington, D.C., without his wife or children.

Ten years after the move, Uline obtained a $600,000 loan to construct the Uline Arena next to his Washington, D.C., ice plant. The arena was originally intended as a skating rink, but the train tracks across the street negated that possibility because of the expectation that cinders from the steam locomotives would stick to the ice; instead, a roofed arena was built. The initial attraction was the Washington Lions of the AHL.

Uline Arena's seating was initially segregated, except for a one-time exception made for a Paul Robeson–headlined benefit concert organized by feminist activist Cornelia Pinchot for the Washington Committee for Aid to China. For boxing matches, Uline kept white and black patrons separated and for all other events he only sold tickets to white people. For years, Dr. Edwin B. Henderson led boycotts and pickets of Uline Arena, eventually gaining national attention. In January 1948, halfway through the Capitols' second season and after five years of organized protests, Uline relented and abandoned segregation as arena policy.[34]

In 1946, Uline, along with the league's many other arena moguls, had supported the establishment of the BAA and bankrolled a franchise based in the nation's capital. However, it's not D.C.'s status as the capital city of the United States, but in fact the United States Capitol—the building in which Congress meets—for which the franchise was named.

Red Auerbach's selection of signings for Washington's inaugural roster was distinctive in his inclination toward players from the service leagues. Of the 14 players who suited up for Washington in 1946–47, only Fred Scolari hadn't served in the military.

He had been drafted; he just couldn't medically qualify. Scolari had a perforated eardrum and was legally blind in his left eye—blind enough that he couldn't even see the top E on the Snellen chart when they tested his vision.[35]

Standing at just 5'10" and with a stocky appearance, he was given the nickname "Fat Freddie." On the first day Scolari showed up to training camp for the Capitols, Auerbach exclaimed that he "looked like some fat broad in slacks."[36]

His shooting form the result of a high school shoulder injury that made him unable to shoot a standard two-handed set shot, Scolari quickly launched the ball at the hoop, somewhat side-armed, from the right side of his hip, in a cockeyed adaptation of Hank Luisetti's push shot.[37]

Scolari went to Galileo High School in San Francisco, the same high school Luisetti had gone to a few years prior, but he missed out on making the varsity team due to his height. He then attended the University of San Francisco, and after the coach that recruited him quit, he played for the freshman team and then spent a year on the varsity team without playing a single minute. Without a role on the team and unable to afford tuition if he quit basketball, Scolari left the university and found work at Bank of America.

Turning to the AAU circuit, he played for the Salesian Boys' Club of San Francisco, making a notable impression at the AAU Tournament in Denver in 1942 with a 34-point performance. Over the next four years, Scolari continued to play for Bay Area AAU teams, earning recognition and common comparisons to Luisetti.[38]

With the Dardi Dandies, he was teammates with Bob Feerick for a couple weeks before Feerick left for Oshkosh without playing a single game for the Dandies. It was Feerick, Auerbach's eventual successor, who recommended Auerbach sign Scolari based on that brief experience.[39] Scolari also received an offer to join St. Louis from Ken Loeffler, who, as coach at the University of Denver for a year, had seen Scolari in person during an AAU tournament, but he opted to join the Capitols.

Feerick, Scolari, and McKinney formed the core of Auerbach's team for three years, consistently contending for championships but falling short. Scolari's transition from AAU forward to pro point guard was not seamless, with Feerick initially taking on ball-handling duties, but Scolari's shot was extremely effective in the BAA despite its unorthodoxy, and he was simultaneously an imaginative, dynamic scorer and an aggressive and tenacious defender in a similar mold to Al Cervi, particularly notable for having quick hands that made him one of the league's most reliable ball hawks.

In 1949–50, though, that trio was no longer capable of leading a team to success. Feerick was regressing heavily and couldn't be relied on to produce much more than 20 minutes per game. McKinney, while still starting, was having a very poor season owing to knee troubles of his own.

Scolari remained a key player, joined by the quick-footed jump hook extraordinaire Jack Nichols as the two most important players on the team. Feerick brought in McKinney's old Chicago Stags foe Chuck Gilmur and aging stars Chick Reiser and Chuck Halbert, but Halbert played spot minutes and Reiser, the second-oldest player in the league, while still an asset as a cutter and secondary ball handler, was increasingly inconsistent and below average on defense. Gilmur, known for his toughness, stood out as a strong defender and their most important bench player.

John Norlander, the Capitols' small forward ever since their founding, was benched in late November and replaced by Dick O'Keefe. O'Keefe, one of the Capitols' few positive surprises that season, had been a member of Washington's bench corps for two years already as a physical defender, and was beginning to find his shot, making him a better option to start than Norlander, a solid but streaky shooter who was a lesser defender and had been declining steadily throughout his career.

Against Syracuse on December 28, Nichols scored 27 points and Scolari and O'Keefe added 18 and 13, respectively, as the Nationals couldn't quite pull off a late comeback effort, making Washington just the fourth team to pull off a win against the red-hot Nationals.[40]

Meanwhile, Waterloo had an opportunity to cheaply add some extra scoring finesse for the rest of what seemed likely to be a long fight with their closest rival, Tri-Cities, for the bottom Western Division playoff spot after Johnny Payak was waived by Philadelphia.[41]

Payak had been college teammates at Bowling Green and high school rivals in Toledo, Ohio, with Waterloo guard Leo Kubiak. Having already succeeded at sharing the backcourt together, it had made sense for them to be reunited when Payak was let go by the Warriors. His stint in Philadelphia, where he was played out of position in the frontcourt, resulted in a meager scoring average of 2.2 points. Nonetheless, his addition offered potential wing support and familiarity within the Hawks' team structure.

Noble Jorgensen made his return to playing after three weeks out of commission following his bout with pneumonia . Restricted to only ten minutes per game, he contributed eight points, including a crucial tip-in that helped maintain a narrow lead in a 94–92 win over Waterloo.[42]

His teammates held their own in his absence, keeping Sheboygan just below a .500 record. Max Morris and Bobby Cook stood out during Jorgensen's time off, averaging 15.6 and 15.0 points, respectively, in that interval, and Brannum had a career game in Jorgensen's first game back, scoring 31 points—11 more than his previous career high.

Brannum's exceptional talent in high school was such that Adolph Rupp drove 700 miles to watch him play. At the end of the game, Rupp asked Brannum and his brother, Clarence, if they'd consider going to Kentucky.[43]

Clarence Brannum never got to play for the Wildcats; he was stricken down by typhus and partially paralyzed during the summer before his freshman year, so he stayed home in Kansas to recover. By the time he was fit to play, he opted to go to Kansas State instead.

Bob Brannum accepted the opportunity and became the focal point of Kentucky's team, becoming the first 18-year-old to be named an All-American since Columbia University's Ted Kiendl in 1908–09.

After a stint in the military during the war, Brannum returned to find a transformed Kentucky team and was relegated to be Alex Groza's backup. Rupp went so far as to remove Brannum from the traveling squad for the 1946–47 Southeastern Conference Tournament, so Brannum, frustrated by the snub, transferred to Michigan State University. At Michigan State, he played against his old team once, losing 47–45 but outplaying Groza and outscoring him 23–10.

Along with Brannum, Cook, Morris, and Jorgensen, Sheboygan also started Jack Burmaster, a tireless and reliable ball-moving, defensively intense shooting guard from the University of Illinois who'd spent his rookie year as a member of the last group of Oshkosh All-Stars. At 6'3", he was tall for a guard, which helped cause mismatches against teams that favored shorter backcourts.

The team's bench boasted several valuable players, including Milt Schoon, who filled in admirably at center during Jorgensen's absence, displaying relentless hustle and contributing in various ways, and the recently signed Jack Phelan. It also included experienced guards George Sobek and Walt Lautenbach.

Sobek, a smooth and savvy veteran known for his exceptional fundamentals and accurate shooting, had an impressive basketball background as an All-American at Notre Dame, a member of the renowned Great Lakes Bluejackets that were led by Bob Davies and George Glamack, and an important starter for the Toledo Jeeps.

Lautenbach, a versatile guard and former teammate of Burmaster in Oshkosh, stood out for his rugged defense, much needed on a team that was conceding 3.5 points per game more than the second-worst defensive team.

Both spent most of their time at point guard, with Bobby Cook's score-first approach having become a bit of a frustration for head coach Kenny Suesens, a pure point guard in his own playing days. Cook's offensive opportunism also complicated matters for the coach tactically, forcing him to rely on Brannum and Morris as primary distributors from the frontcourt. Cook had their highest scoring average outside of Jorgensen, but seemed to be trusted the least and was substituted the quickest.

6

The Celtics, the New Year, and You Just Can't Play Basketball with Glasses On

The Boston Celtics, a pitiful team through most of their short existence, experienced a positive turnaround as the year came to a close, marked by Gene Englund's return from retirement on December 6.

Englund, a lifelong Oshkosh All-Star, had retired after the All-Stars shut down but remained in high demand, eventually choosing to sign with the Celtics after meetings with the Olympians, Pistons, Blackhawks, and Hawks.[1]

Englund had made a name for himself in college, leading the University of Wisconsin to a national championship, and later became a key player for Oshkosh alongside Bob Carpenter, but an All-NBL First Team season by Englund en route to a championship series loss in 1948–49 wasn't enough to help keep the team afloat.

Englund, 32, became player-coach for a minor league phoenix club of the All-Stars, the Wisconsin State League's Oshkosh Stars, but after six games, he was headed to Boston.

In his first game back in the professional game, Englund scored 14 points, good for second on the team, in a loss to Indianapolis.[2] Boston won each of the next three, improving their record to 7–14 and closing the gap on the Warriors.

Before the final game of that short stretch, Boston strengthened their frontcourt with the addition of Bob Doll, a defensive specialist Ken Loeffler had based a significant part of his defensive schematics around in St. Louis.[3] When Loeffler stepped down following 1947–48, Doll had joined Denver but returned to the BAA when his rights were sold to Boston, retiring after that season. After he struggled to get a dry-cleaning business started up in Boulder Springs, Colorado, Walter Brown convinced him to rejoin the team, providing the Celtics with significant post depth alongside Englund.

The Celtics now had an 11-player rotation, enabling them to overcome poor individual performances and play cohesive team basketball. During the month since Englund's arrival, eight players averaged between eight and 11 points per game, with no one surpassing Kaftan's 10.7.

After the three-game winning streak, the Celtics split a pair of games against Minneapolis and dropped two close losses before racking up three more decisive wins to end December, with an 82–57 thrashing of the Bullets and 19-point wins over New York and Fort Wayne. For the first time all season, Boston passed both Philadelphia and Baltimore to find themselves on track for a playoff spot.

That spell of wins over decent-to-good teams was quite possibly the first time in the Celtics' history that they were in any way reminiscent of the Original Celtics for which they were named.

The Original Celtics, initially known as the New York Celtics, first emerged in the late 1910s as a semiprofessional basketball team composed mainly of teenagers from Manhattan's West Side. After a brief dissolution due to the founder's departure for World War I, the team was revived by Jim and Tom Furey, who added "Original" to the team's name for legal purposes. Run by Jim Furey, a 24-year-old Arnold Constable & Company cashier, the Celtics aimed to captivate audiences across the country, envisioning their team as basketball's equivalent of a circus.

With the addition of talented players like Nat Holman, Johnny Beckman, Joe Lapchick, and Dutch Dehnert, the Original Celtics established themselves as the predominant force in professional basketball. They employed a game focused on passing and cutting, with the give-and-go play between Holman and Beckman becoming their signature move. Defensively, they utilized a switching man-to-man defense. As their fame grew, they embarked on extensive tours, playing against a wide range of teams, including black teams, and breaking blue laws by playing games on Sundays.

Despite their success, financial troubles and legal issues plagued the team. Jim Furey's arrest for embezzlement resulted in his imprisonment, the team went through several ownership changes, and midway through 1927–28, they became property of the ABL.

The Original Celtics' superiority in the ABL had become a source of frustration for other teams, so league president John O'Brien sought to restore competitive balance by disbanding the team and scattering its players across the other teams in an ill-fated attempt to ensure parity.

Various attempts were made to revive the team, but it never regained its former glory. The franchise was ultimately sold to Abe Saperstein, owner of the Harlem Globetrotters, who used the Original Celtics as exhibition opponents before ceasing their operations.[4]

Walter Brown wanted a name for his BAA franchise that would appeal to Boston's Irish population and their rich heritage. The name "Celtics" not only had an Irish connection due to the Celtic Revival movement but also carried the prestige associated with the Original Celtics. Ironically, considering Jim Furey's first act as owner of the team was to change the name from the Celtics in order to avoid paying for naming rights, Brown paid Furey thousands of dollars for the rights to the name, and the Boston Celtics were born.[5]

The Denver Nuggets faced additional challenges when player-coach Jim Darden decided to step away from his playing duties and coach from the sidelines.[6] Darden had been contributing 9.6 points per game since coming out of retirement in late November, ranking third on the team behind Kenny Sailors and Bob Brown during that time frame.

With limited depth, especially in the backcourt, Darden's decision of who to replace himself with was a fairly straightforward one: either Al Guokas or Duane Klueh.

Guokas, Darden's backcourt partner the year prior, was known for his rebounding, defensive prowess, and team-oriented play. Three years prior, Al had been a passenger in the car accident that ended his older brother Matt's basketball career, but only suffered minor injuries himself.

Klueh showed a lot of promise as a scorer but fractured the talus bone of his foot in the third game of the season.[7] That caused him to miss 11 games and lose his early momentum. Klueh had potential as a scorer, specifically his soft touch on aggressive drives to the basket, but his decision-making needed polish.

Darden ultimately chose neither, instead opting to promote Dillard Crocker, a forward who was benched upon Floyd Volker's arrival. This put Crocker entirely out of position, but at 6'4" and 205 lbs., he had a significant physical advantage over guards that would hopefully translate into easy points and fewer losses.

The Tri-Cities Blackhawks, facing difficulties in distancing themselves from Waterloo and lacking a reliable starting point guard, saw Whitey Von Nieda as the logical replacement for the recently sold Billy Hassett. Von Nieda was expected to put more pressure on defenses with great body control near the hoop and a reputation as a great shooter, but his shooting had been off all season and further hindered by a recent corneal abrasion. After four games starting after the Hassett trade, he was benched in favor of Murray Wier.

Wier, although successful as a scorer off the bench, struggled to find his rhythm as a lead guard and failed to take charge of the offense, resulting in a five-game losing streak and the need for power forward Mike Todorovich to assume playmaking duties. Dee Gibson filled the point guard role upon his return from a broken hand that had kept him out for seven weeks so that Wier could return to his bench spark plug role, but that was only ever a temporary solution.

Days later, Mike Fitzgerald swung a trade to get them a point guard who could hopefully maintain a stranglehold on the starting spot, trading rookie wing Jim Owens, a ball hawk and streaky shooter fresh out of Baylor University, and cash to the Packers for Walt Kirk.[8]

Kirk wasn't a pass-first guard either and hadn't played in the backcourt until midway through the prior season, but his size advantage and scoring repertoire had made him a unique player to game-plan for since the switch to point guard. The Blackhawks' hope in acquiring him was that a starting lineup with no one shorter than 6'3" could provide an inherent advantage, and with Eddleman and Todorovich being joined by Gene Vance as players capable of promoting ball movement and Kirk not being as ball dominant as Gibson or Wier, that he would be able to use both his on-ball and off-ball skills routinely.

On December 31, the Waterloo Basketball Inc. board of directors made the decision to transition Charley Shipp from player-coach to a non-playing coach due to concerns about his ability to lead the team while playing. Publicly, Shipp agreed with the decision, stating that he would be able to do a much better job as coach without playing duties and that "it is hard to see everything that goes wrong when one is playing and coaching at the same time."[9]

In effect, this brought about an unceremonious end to the longest and winningest career in the NBA in the middle of Shipp's 17th season as a professional player and his 15th year in a major league. In his final game, two days prior, he had scored a single point from the foul line and recorded an assist in a 94–92 loss to Sheboygan. With Shipp no longer active, the Capitols' 35-year-old Chick Reiser became the new oldest player in the NBA, and the number of players remaining with more than ten years of professional experience was reduced to four: Reiser, Al Cervi, Dick Schulz, and the injured Buddy Jeannette.

A loss to Minneapolis in their next game, their seventh loss in the last eight, saw the Hawks' record careen to 7–22, with George Mikan scoring 35 points for the Lakers. That game closed out the decade, ending about an hour after the last of the other three NBA games that day: a Rochester blowout of the St. Louis Bombers, an upset for Washington over New York, and a close Pistons win over the Warriors after Philadelphia fumbled away a very winnable game with a 9-of-55 shooting stretch in the middle of the game.

The first half of the 20th century drawing to a close marked two months since the NBA's first game, with 241 others having happened since then and 315 yet to be played. Syracuse's 24–4 record was top of the Eastern Division and the league, while Rochester led the Central Division at 19–8 and Anderson led the Western Division at 17–9.

Minneapolis (20–10), Chicago (20–12) and Fort Wayne (17–11) remained within striking distance of Rochester, and Indianapolis (17–13) was now only two games behind Anderson after compiling five wins in their last seven games. New York (20–12), Washington (14–14), and Sheboygan (11–12) were likely playoff bound, while Boston (11–17), Baltimore (11–18), Philadelphia (10–19), Tri-Cities (8–19), and Waterloo (7–22) were all preparing to cast themselves deep into the throes of the race for a playoff spot. Only St. Louis (13–16) and Denver (3–26) were far from the playoff race, and the Bombers would have been in a far different situation had they been in either the Eastern or Western Division.

George Mikan held a commanding lead in the scoring title race, averaging 27.4 points per game, with Alex Groza as his closest competition at 24.4 points per game. The only other players within even 10 points of Mikan's averages were Joe Fulks, with an 18.1 point average, and Noble Jorgensen, with a 17.7 point average.

Mikan kicked off the new year with one of his best games of the season, scoring 38 points on 16-of-25 shooting in an 87–75 Minneapolis win over Anderson, while Jim Pollard added 20.[10]

For the Lakers, this was their fifth straight win and enough for them to tie Rochester atop the Central Division. A career-high 30 points from Frank Brian wasn't enough for the Packers; this was their fifth loss in seven games, and an Indianapolis win brought the Olympians within one game of Anderson.

Baltimore's January got off to a rocky start as they suffered convincing losses to Tri-Cities and Anderson, extending their losing streak to six games and dropping to fifth place in the Eastern Division. The trade for Ed Sadowski wasn't proving as successful as initially hoped, and Paul Hoffman and Buddy Jeannette's injuries had a significant impact on the team's performance.

Opposing teams knew to single out Sadowski, either as a target of overwhelming defense or of hard drives to try to get him into foul trouble. Unable to get to his normal spots or play as many minutes as normal, he dropped from 16.7 points per game before the Bullets' injury troubles to just 11.7 during them.

Walt Budko, more known as a hardworking hustler and rebounder than a scorer but more than capable of shooting from distance and handling the ball as well, and Carlisle Towery, the chief enforcer of the Bobby McDermott–era Fort Wayne Zollners, were the other frontcourt starters and the players who most needed to pick up the slack offensively. Budko managed to increase his scoring average to nearly equal Sadowski. Towery continued to play about the same level he had all year, averaging a little over nine points and playing tough defense, but he made waves across the league in a Bullets–Lakers game when he hit Jim Pollard from behind after a rebound. Pollard retaliated by throwing the ball at Towery's head, which Towery responded to by punching him behind his right ear, sending Pollard flying to the ground and starting a brawl that involved players, referees, and some spectators. Towery was thrown out of the game and later fined $50 by Maurice Podoloff, but he admitted no wrongdoing, later stating that his only regret was that he "should have hit him harder." Jeannette stood by Towery, suggesting he shouldn't have been thrown out and that he frankly should have hit Pollard earlier in the game.[11]

Tommy Byrnes, while rarely starting, was a crucial leader for the Bullets with a relentless motor, a winning mentality, and the ability to provide a shooting threat on offense and intensity defensively. Also in the frontcourt, Baltimore had Les Pugh, a lanky, perimeter-oriented center with a penchant for hitting clutch shots, and 6'5" Marv Schatzman, whose role was mostly rebounding and defense.

The frontcourt wasn't the problem, though; Bill Dyer had waived four underwhelming guards within the opening month of the season and a fifth two weeks later. That meant, with Jeannette and Hoffman injured, Joe Dolhon and minor league call-up George Feigenbaum were the only natural guards available during that losing streak.

To address this shortage, they brought in John Ezersky, a high-scoring sharpshooter recently released by Boston.[12] Banned from playing in college for allegedly accepting money from boosters, his winding path to the NBA involved a failed tryout with the MLB's Detroit Tigers, three years in the U.S. Army, and a year driving a taxicab before a season in the ABL earned him his way to the major leagues. Ezersky played for Tri-Cities, Providence, Baltimore, and Boston before returning to the hobbled Bullets following a short stint with the ABL's Hartford Hurricanes. Inconsistency and defensive ineptitude had kept him from ever sticking with a team for the full length of a season, but his natural skill for shot creation continually kept teams interested in him.

On January 4, 1950, Ike Duffey sold half of his shares in the Anderson Packers to the Packers Civic Committee, a group of about 50 local investors headed up by Bob Myers, a retired U.S. Air Force captain who now ran a building materials supplier, Myers Sand and Gravel, in Anderson.

In the background, Sid Goldberg, the general manager of the NBL's Toledo Jeeps years prior, had expressed interest in purchasing the franchise for $25,000 with intentions to relocate it to Toledo after the season. Duffey wanted to keep the Packers in Anderson if at all possible, so he made the offer to Myers that they could co-own the team for the remainder of the season, while Myers held an option to acquire the remaining shares at season's end or else Duffey would sell to Goldberg in the summer.[13]

Rochester was making a strong statement with their impressive performance, securing nine consecutive victories and making a very compelling case that they might be the best team in the league. Despite Bob Davies' slightly reduced role, the 30-year-old point guard continued to excel, exemplified by his stellar 32-point, seven-assist display in a close win over the New York Knicks.

Davies remained the linchpin of Rochester's success, while Bobby Wanzer, a valuable bench player in his first two years but now starting alongside Davies, showed consistent improvement and emerged as one of the league's best guards in his own right. Always primarily a streaky scoring threat, Wanzer's shot selection and his ballhandling were becoming major assets as well and he averaged 13.6 points during the winning streak, second only to Davies.

Although a minor knee injury that just wouldn't go away led to a significant increase in Arnie Risen's fouls and limited him to playing just over half of a game most of the time and the worst statistical output of his career, he largely retained his reputation as one of the best centers in professional basketball. Fortunately, rookie Jack Coleman, Ed Mikan, and former starting power forward Andy Duncan all provided relief minutes at near-starter quality, keeping his injury issues from holding the team back.

Bill Calhoun and rugged Arnie Johnson completed Rochester's starting unit, but the Royals also had a deep bench, with Coleman, Mikan, and Duncan joined in the bench rotation by Red Holzman and Fran Curran, a pairing dubbed "the Firemen" for their ability to put points on the board in a hurry.[14] Holzman's basketball acumen and ability to control various facets of the game made him one of the league's most intelligent players, while Curran's relentless hustle and sharp shooting from distance solidified his role as a valuable asset off the bench for the Royals.

The Denver Nuggets struggled immensely, only securing three wins in their first 30 games, putting them on track for a worse record than that of the worst BAA team (the 1947–48 Providence Steamrollers at 6–42) and all but two NBL teams (the 1946–47 Detroit Gems at 4–40 and the 1937–38 Columbus Athletic Supply at 1–12).

Kenny Sailors may not have been a natural point guard, but he embraced the role as a leader in Jim Darden's absence, achieving personal bests in points, field goal percentage, and assists, averaging 19.9 points over the last 20 games.

It remained the case, though, that Sailors wasn't of the quality needed from a first option—or even a second option—to build a winning team around. By this point, Bob Brown, Dillard Crocker, and Jack Toomay had all done a good job at proving themselves worthy of a roster spot; Brown and Crocker each averaged about 11 points and Toomay, previously notable mostly because he held the BAA's playoff record of eight fouls in a game, became one of the league's better offensive rebounders and cut down on his fouling significantly. None of the trio should've been relied on to that extent, though.

Floyd Volker, operating at power forward, demonstrated versatility by taking on passing duties when necessary, similar to Tri-Cities' Mike Todorovich. While Duane Klueh and Al Guokas substituted the guard positions, Jack Cotton, backing up Toomay at center, served as the primary frontcourt substitute. As one of the three returnees from the previous year, Cotton began the year as a starter but quickly lost his starting spot to Toomay. Cotton was an above-average rebounder and rim protector, but he was extremely unrefined technically and his mere presence within the Nuggets' rotation, as a player who had averaged just 2.5 points off the bench during his one college season at Wyoming, was indicative of the franchise's larger issues.

Off the court, the franchise faced financial challenges, and team president Dave Garland warned the players that the team was on track to only afford to pay half their guaranteed salaries. He promised the Nuggets would grant any trade requests players submitted due to the situation.[15]

Out to prove they weren't just the NBA's doormats, the Nuggets disrupted the league's balance with consecutive victories over the division-leading Anderson Packers, as Crocker's exceptional defense held Frank Brian to seven points in both.[16] The two losses for Anderson caused Indianapolis to tie them for the top spot in the Western Division.

That same day, Sheboygan upset the Minneapolis Lakers 85–82, not for a lack of effort from George Mikan, whose 42 points came just one short of Alex Groza's NBA record of 43 points in a game. Jim Pollard added 18 points, but the rest of Minneapolis shot 9-of-36 and poor defending allowed Max Morris to score 23 points on 16 shots and Bobby Cook to score 21 on 13 attempts.[17]

Mikan's journey to basketball stardom was far from predestined, hindered by his poor eyesight and a compound leg fracture, but a growth spurt propelled him from a modest height of 5'11" to 6'5" during his six months on crutches and an impressive 6'10" by the time he graduated high school.

Mikan first attended high school at the Joliet Catholic Academy in Joliet, Illinois. When he tried out for their varsity basketball team as a freshman, he was among the last two players cut from the team by the Rev. Fr. Gilbert Burns, Joliet coach, who is said to have told him, "You just can't play basketball with glasses on." Mikan didn't play again, aside from intramural leagues, for years.

He transferred from Joliet Catholic after one year to Archbishop Quigley Preparatory Seminary in Chicago, with the intent of studying to become a priest. He didn't play basketball for Archbishop Quigley until his senior year, and between having an hour-and-a-half commute and a part-time job as a roofer, even then he was only able to play on Wednesdays and Saturdays.

After scoring 24 points in a game against Leo Catholic High School, Mikan was offered a scholarship by DePaul University athletic director Paul Mattei, who was there initially to scout Stan Patrick on the opposing team.

During his freshman year at DePaul, Mikan's talent was largely overlooked by head coach Bill Wendt, leaving him searching for alternative opportunities. During Christmas break, Mikan traveled to South Bend, Indiana, to try out for coach George Keogan at the University of Notre Dame, hoping he could potentially transfer there. He scrimmaged against Notre Dame players and was completely out of his depth, clumsy and unable to keep up with smaller and quicker players. On top of that, his physical examination revealed he had a broken arch in his right foot. Keogan told Mikan not only that he had failed to make the team, but that he wasn't sure Mikan was cut out for basketball at all.

Wendt resigned from his coaching post at DePaul after the season following a 10–12 record, DePaul's first losing record since 1927–28. His replacement would be Keogan's top Notre Dame assistant coach Ray Meyer.

There were a lot of parallels between Meyer and Mikan that made them a natural fit together. They had both spent a portion of their high school education at Archbishop Quigley. They had both intended to become Catholic priests but were sidetracked by basketball dreams. Meyer had nearly taken the coaching job at Joliet Catholic a couple years prior to Mikan's short time there.

Meyer, unlike his old boss, saw potential in Mikan, even if developing him into a good player would take more time and hard work than with a typical player. He was intrigued by Mikan's height, though, and by the time that he began practices, he noticed that Mikan's work ethic stood out as well. There wasn't much to his game skill-wise at first aside from a decent right-handed hook shot, but there was enough there for Mikan to be worth Meyer putting extra time into.

Meyer employed unconventional training methods for Mikan, including boxing and dance lessons. He had Mikan guard 5'5" Billy Donato in practice to work on his speed and assigned him a goaltending drill to work on his timing. He had Mikan jump over a bench on hook shot attempts because he wasn't jumping high enough, and told him to shoot 300 left-handed shots every day to develop his off hand. Most famously, he invented what has since been termed the "Mikan Drill," in which Mikan made a layup with his right hand, rebounded with his left hand, made a layup with his left hand, rebounded with his right hand, and continued repeatedly. These efforts yielded remarkable results, transforming him into a near-unstoppable center and laying the foundation for his future success in the NBA.[18]

Minneapolis' loss to Sheboygan despite Mikan's best efforts was preceded by a winning streak of six games, leaving them with a 22–11 record, but 22–11 failed to distinguish them in the highly competitive Central Division. Even after escaping a possible upset against Boston 85–80 after overtime in the next outing, they trailed Rochester by a slim margin and held a mere one-and-a-half-game lead over Chicago and Fort Wayne. Rochester had a hard-fought battle of their own that day, only escaping defeat to St. Louis by two points after double overtime, thanks to a field goal by Fran Curran and a made free throw by Bob Davies to clinch the game.[19]

Fort Wayne's surprising ability to compete with renowned teams can be attributed to Murray Mendenhall's effective run-and-gun system, supported by Carl Bennett's decision to grant Mendenhall authority over rookie selections in the 1949 draft, and about half the team was composed of rookies. In the previous season under Bennett and Armstrong, Fort Wayne won just 22 games out of 60. With Mendenhall at the helm, their 22nd win of the 1949–50 season arrived with 33 games left to play.

On January 10, the Waterloo Hawks achieved their most significant victory of the season with an 86–84 overtime win against Syracuse, led by Harry Boykoff's 26 points and Don Boven's 22 points. Syracuse coach Al Cervi and owner Danny Biasone both had public freak-outs at perceived referee bias in the waning moments of the game, with Cervi breaking a chair and Biasone causing enough of a scene to be threatened with removal from the arena by Waterloo security. Syracuse attempted 45 free throws to Waterloo's 42, but they made only 24 of them and that was a deciding factor in the result.

In the immediate aftermath as the team celebrated their best result all year, Charley Shipp was called into Perk Purnhage's office and dismissed as Waterloo's head coach. They did have just an 8–27 record with more than half the season passed and had recently just lost eight games consecutively, but the timing of firing Shipp right after a win and just 11 days after requesting he end his playing career for the sake of full-time coaching was odd.

The decision shocked the players, who confronted the board of directors. The board revealed to them that the decision was motivated by the team's dismal financial situation rather than its performance.

Harry Boykoff was publicly shaken by how poor the team's outlook was—they were in such dire straits that they also had to release Stan Patrick and Bob Tough, both veteran role players, before their next road trip began—and the team all agreed to support Jack Smiley when he was named player-coach. Imminent improvement in on-court results wasn't coming, as they lost all three games on the road and fell to 8–30, but financially things were slightly more tenable.[20]

Though a petition for Shipp's reinstatement gained significant support and he later received coaching job interviews with other NBA teams, he never returned to the league. Shipp briefly led the Waterloo Rockets, a semiprofessional team, before joining Purdue University as an assistant coach. Shipp's health would deteriorate in the 1960s due to thromboangiitis obliterans, resulting in the amputation of both his legs. He later transitioned to a career in the collections department of a bank until his retirement.

The Sheboygan Redskins games were always among the highest-scoring games in the league, and despite being in a bit of a funk with four increasingly disastrous away losses in as many days, their first home game against the abysmal Nuggets was no exception. The final score was 115–92 and the win kept them from falling too close to the 11–21 Tri-Cities Blackhawks, but all the headlines from that game featured one particular player: Bobby Cook.

Cook scored 44 points, breaking Alex Groza's NBA scoring record by a single point despite ending the first quarter scoreless. His second quarter was nearly perfect, with 16 points on 6-of-7 shooting from the field and 4-of-4 from the free throw line. He added 12 more points in the third quarter as they began to pull ahead, and in the fourth they held a large enough lead that his teammates fed him the ball repeatedly in order to give him a chance to break the record. With half a

George Mikan (1948) had been the best and best-known player in college basketball during World War II and by 1950 was firmly entrenched as the best and best-known player in the professional game, en route to his fourth championship in as many years while leading the league in points and (estimated) rebounds. Midseason, he was voted the best player of the preceding 50 years, and he would be well on his way to breaking the sport's all-time scoring record within two or three years.

minute to go, he made an open one-handed push shot from long range assisted by Milt Schoon to surpass Groza's 43 points. He shot 18-of-33 for the game, with 10 of those misses coming in the fourth quarter when he was actively going for the record.[21]

That same day, for the first time in 30 games, the Lakers were led in scoring by someone other than George Mikan or Jim Pollard in their 89–73 win over St. Louis. Vern Mikkelsen's 31 points led the way in the best game of his early career, and the ease of Minneapolis' win combined with his 16-point impact on a win over Syracuse the prior day showed his rapid improvement and hinted at his potential to be a game-changer for the team.[22]

Indianapolis, without a loss in 19 days, was in equally encouraging shape as they retained their lead over the Packers atop the Western Division. Kentucky coach Adolph Rupp hadn't supported the idea of his old college stars teaming up in the NBA, but the Olympians were proving more than worthy of their existence and turning into a threat to contend.

Alex Groza stood out as a legitimate star, making a strong case for being the league's second-best player. Ralph Beard was among the very best of the guards too, and it seemed very likely the duo was destined to lead the greatest team in basketball once Mikan and Pollard exited their respective primes.

Wah Wah Jones, while not as flashy, was one of the best power forwards in the league too, although that comes with the context of the position being the weakest in the league with the exception of Adolph Schayes. Most impressive was how well-developed Jones' passing and shooting was for a rookie post player with a reputation for doing the team's dirty work.

Bruce Hale also proved his worth, albeit with occasional streakiness, while the absence of Marshall Hawkins did not significantly impact the team due to a solid wing rotation featuring Hale, Joe Holland, and Cliff Barker. Also receiving semi-consistent minutes off the bench were Malcolm McMullen, a tenacious power forward known for his gum-chewing habit during games, and Carl Shaeffer, a defensive ace on the wing who had been captured by Nazi German forces on the first day of the Battle of the Bulge and held for seven months in the Stalag Luft IV camp in Tychowo, Poland; by happenstance, the same prisoner-of-war camp Barker was being held at. Upon Barker's urging, Shaeffer was the first player Babe Kimbrough signed to the team outside of the five founding members.

As head coach, part owner, and player, Barker had what remains the most all-encompassing job in NBA history. Helpfully, he didn't have to do too much tactical coaching, since many of the players already knew every single play in his system from playing under Adolph Rupp, and a large part of his coaching role was simply man management. With 13 wins in the last 16 games, maintaining team chemistry came naturally.

George Mikan swiftly surpassed Bobby Cook's short-lived NBA single-game scoring record by becoming the first player to achieve 50 or more points in a game, scoring 51 against Rochester on January 14. The other eight Lakers on the floor scored just 26 points, and Minneapolis lost 83–77. The pattern had materialized that Mikan had to strike a balance between his own scoring prowess and involving his teammates, as they often failed to provide adequate support during his most remarkable scoring displays.[23]

The great individual performances, underscoring the significance of Mikan's presence in the Lakers organization, were still somewhat like wins for Minneapolis, though, as they owed much of their existence to him.

When Sid Hartman convinced Ben Berger and Morris Chalfen, prominent figures in the movie theater and entertainment industry, to invest in a professional basketball team, they purchased the struggling Detroit Gems franchise and established the Minneapolis Lakers, named for Minnesota's nickname as the "Land of 10,000 Lakes."

The Gems had been a historically awful franchise through their lone season in the NBL: they ended the season with 23 consecutive losses, only scored 60-plus points thrice, failed to even reach 40-plus points on seven occasions, and once managed to suffer an 83–41 drubbing by the Indianapolis Kautskys. They finished with a 4–40 record, 22 games outside of the playoffs despite a season only 44 games long. The average score of a Detroit Gems game was 48.6–63.0. When accounting for the drastic increase in tempo between 1946–47 and 1949–50, that would be equivalent to an average loss of more than twice as much as the hapless 1949–50 Nuggets.

Berger and Chalfen's decision to acquire the Gems, aiming to retain the team's records and secure priority in a potential PBLA dispersal draft, positioned the Lakers to sign Mikan without competition.

However, negotiations failed, and Mikan planned to start up an independent team instead of returning to the NBL. Hartman, assigned to transport Mikan to the airport, intentionally veered off course, causing Mikan to miss his flight. Mikan stayed in Minneapolis for an extra day and Berger and Chalfen increased their offer to meet Mikan's $15,000 per year salary demands, which he agreed to.[24]

In their rematch against the Royals, the Lakers bounced back with a convincing 85–72 victory. Mikan led scoring again with 25 but was helped by 16 points from Vern Mikkelsen and 15 from Jim Pollard, and Rochester had no one score more than the 13 points of Andy Duncan.[25] This win, coupled with a 26-point triumph over Boston two days later, put them atop the Central Division, overtaking Rochester and leading the division for the first time in nearly a month.

Washington won their fourth out of five games in a bid to turn around their poor run thanks to the duo of Fred Scolari and Jack Nichols, keeping a safe distance from the bottom three Eastern Division teams, but clutch play from the Knicks kept the Capitols from making up any significant ground compared to New York. New York beat the Capitols by one point in Washington's only loss of that stretch and followed it up by staging a 16-point comeback against the Celtics, with Carl Braun hitting a pair of clutch long-range shots, the second of which came in the form of an off-balance one-handed game-winner with one second left in the game.[26]

Sheboygan suffered a loss in their rematch against Denver, Jack Burmaster's 23-point effort made irrelevant by Max Morris, Bob Brannum, and Bobby Cook's combined 6-of-36 shooting. For Denver, Dillard Crocker led the way with 28 points on just 15 shots and Kenny Sailors added 24.[27] This result narrowed the gap between Sheboygan and Tri-Cities, as well as between Waterloo and Denver, making the Nuggets' prospects of avoiding the league's worst record more plausible.

Following the loss, the Redskins tried to shake off their malaise by signing Dick Schulz, a clutch veteran defender who had been a key part of Washington's championship-losing team the previous year and Baltimore's title-winning team two years prior.[28] Schulz, having recently been released by Tri-Cities, rejoined Sheboygan, where he'd spent three years playing for the Redskins during their three consecutive Finals losses from 1943–44 to 1945–46, and joined Milt Schoon as one of Sheboygan's two most important backups.

The Boston Celtics, just a couple weeks prior appearing poised to solidify themselves as a likely playoff team, followed up their 105–79 loss to Minneapolis with a 94–86 loss to the Philadelphia Warriors to complete a four-game backslide, allowing Philadelphia to tie them for fourth in the Eastern Division.

Dermie O'Connell, a speedy rookie point guard, had emerged as an unexpected hero during Boston's successful December stretch. However, a couple of subpar performances resulted in reduced playing time for O'Connell, as Sonny Hertzberg regained the starting point guard position.

Julian, after months of waffling between various backcourt pairings and not seeming to find one that worked aside from O'Connell and Ed Leede, coalesced around a guard pairing of Hertzberg and Howie Shannon.

Bob Kinney, the team's center, remained unaffected by Julian's rotation adjustments and played some of the best basketball of his career. George Kaftan, though not reaching his rookie potential, consistently contributed double-digit performances despite lineup changes and position shifts. In January, Kaftan secured a permanent starting spot at small forward after spending parts of the season variously starting at power forward or coming off the bench.

Alongside him would be some combination of Brady Walker and midseason acquisitions Gene Englund and Bob Doll. Englund retained most of the playing time, but Doll's defense could not be overlooked. For the time, they could make do by giving Englund backup center minutes as well as a decent amount as a forward, but there weren't enough minutes to go around in the frontcourt, and the result was that Julian tried to give more extended minutes per game to each of them by handing out occasional DNP–CDs. Despite establishing a more settled lineup, the team continued to grapple with the issue of lacking star power in their frontcourt, a problem reminiscent of their earlier struggles in the backcourt.

Before the establishment of the Celtics, Walter Brown's family had deep roots in sports, particularly ice hockey. His father, George Brown, had been instrumental in organizing the Boston Marathon and had a hand in various pursuits in amateur ice hockey as the director of athletics for the Boston Athletic Association for 16 years.

Following a disastrous fire at the Boston Arena in 1918, George advocated for its reconstruction, which eventually took place under the funding of Henry Lapham, the vice president of the Boston Athletic Association. When the arena reopened in 1921, George assumed the role of manager.

In 1924–25, the Boston Bruins joined the National Hockey League (NHL) and played their games at the Boston Arena. Seeking a better venue, Bruins owner Charles Adams supported the expansion of the Madison Square Garden Corporation into Boston, resulting in the creation of the Boston Garden.

When the Madison Square Garden Corporation sold the Boston Garden to the Boston Arena, creating the Boston Garden-Arena Corporation, Lapham made Brown manager of both.[29]

George Brown died of an intracerebral hemorrhage in 1937 and Walter took over managing both arenas, aged just 32. He had already made a name for himself as the founder and coach of the Boston Olympics amateur hockey team and had achieved success coaching the United States men's national ice hockey team. Additionally, Brown was involved in the establishment of the Ice Capades, a popular ice skating show that featured renowned figure skaters from around the world.

Brown's interest in professional basketball preceded even the founding of the NBL, stemming back to the beginning of his friendship with Max Kase in 1934. Kase, Brown, and Cleveland Arena owner Al Sutphin recruited other owners to join the BAA, and once Kase was denied his entry into the league in favor of Ned Irish's New York Knicks, Brown and Sutphin were, for all intents and purposes, the BAA's founders.

The Celtics' lack of BAA success was foreshadowed, though, by their very first home game against the Stags on November 5, 1946. When referee Pat Kennedy blew his whistle to end pre-game warmups, feisty backup center Kevin Connors—later renowned as Chuck Connors of *The Rifleman* fame—playfully launched a two-handed set shot from about 40 feet, unintentionally shattering the ill-installed glass backboard. The only other backboard the Celtics had access to was across town in the Boston Garden, which was hosting Gene Autry's World Championship Rodeo at the time, and no Celtics employees were willing to cross the bullpen in front of the storage closet. The Boston

Garden-Arena Corporation's director of public relations paid off a small group of drunk front-row fans to do the task. The game was delayed by over two hours and nearly half the fans had left by the time the Celtics actually started playing. Boston lost 57–55.

That wasn't the only thing that went wrong, by any means—Brown's first choice for head coach was Frank Keaney, the mastermind behind Rhode Island State College's famed up-tempo offense. When Keaney showed up for his interview, Brown was kept late by another meeting and Keaney left and refused to reschedule.

Brown ultimately hired seasoned ABL journeyman coach Honey Russell, then of Manhattan College. Russell spent the summer managing the minor league baseball Rutland Royals and insisted he couldn't begin his duties as coach until the baseball season was complete. Brown hired him anyway, but Russell's delayed arrival resulted in missed opportunities to secure valuable players, as other BAA teams had already signed them.[30]

After a public feud with Ed Sadowski in his second year, Russell was fired, prompting Brown to again reach out to Frank Keaney, who took the job this time around but had to step down just days later due to health concerns, leading to the hiring of Doggie Julian.[31] After a tough and tumultuous year in 1948–49, Julian's rebuild wasn't shaping out to be a quick success. A 13–24 record so far in 1949–50 left them in contention for the playoffs due to the underperformance of Philadelphia and Baltimore, but they were also on track to finish with a worse record than in any of their previous lackluster seasons.

Sheboygan and Fort Wayne played a thrilling game on the same day as Boston's loss to the Warriors, with the Pistons racking up a big 21–8 lead early in the game, the Redskins coming back in the second quarter to take the lead just before halftime, and the lead swinging back and forth throughout the second half. In the closing moments of the game, Charlie Black made a crucial free throw to tie the score, followed by a free throw from Dick Schulz that put Sheboygan back in the lead. Fort Wayne had possession, down one, and raced down the floor to get off a last-second shot. The ball came to Black and he made a one-handed push shot with five seconds left, securing the win for the Pistons.[32]

That would be Black's last shot as a Piston, as he and Richie Niemiera were traded to Anderson for Howie Schultz and Ralph Johnson later that night.[33]

Schultz, a better defender and larger player than Black, would bolster the Pistons' chances in the playoffs against opponents like Arnie Risen and George Mikan. Johnson, an upgrade over Niemiera, would assume the starting point guard role for Fort Wayne, allowing Curly Armstrong to come off the bench and conserve energy for the postseason. Both players were familiar with Murray Mendenhall's style of play from his time coaching the Packers, which would help to ease their transition.

The Packers' financial difficulties helped to spur the deal along, but Anderson business manager Doxie Moore wouldn't have agreed to the deal without the potential for the new arrivals to improve the team. Two years prior, Schultz and Black were paired together in the post and Anderson had showcased Schultz as the primary option, but Black had since developed into a stronger post scorer and passer. With Black's improvement and Niemiera's athleticism and willingness to drive to the rim, the trade aimed to enhance Anderson's already potent offense. The substitution of Niemiera in for Johnson also meant that Frank Brian would have more ballhandling responsibilities.

The trade left Anderson without a head coach, and instead of promoting a veteran player such as Frank Gates or Milo Komenich to player-coach in Schultz' place, Duffey assumed coaching duties himself—not unprecedented, but surprising and disconcerting given Duffey had never coached before.

Anderson played their first game with Duffey in charge the very next day. Black started at power forward while Komenich was shifted back to center. Brian was moved to point guard as Niemiera came off the bench and played limited minutes in his debut, and the 29 points Brian scored showed the possibilities that could arise from that positional change, but poor foul shooting by his teammates resulted in an 81–78 loss to Rochester.

The Chicago Stags faced setbacks in the standings due to a light January schedule featuring an eight-day break between games, falling behind divisional contenders Minneapolis and Rochester despite winning seven out of eight games since Christmas.

The team's success was primarily attributed to their star-studded backcourt pairing of Andy Phillip and Max Zaslofsky. Phillip was a top contender for the assist title, with only New York's Dick McGuire as his main competition, while Zaslofsky ranked among the league's top guards in scoring, trailing only Kenny Sailors.

The acquisition of George Nostrand affected Joe Graboski's playing time, solidifying Kleggie Hermsen's position as the starting center. However, Odie Spears emerged as a crucial frontcourt player for the Stags, excelling as a combo forward with his athleticism and defensive prowess complemented by a scoring touch on one-handers and hook shots near the basket.

Coach Phil Brownstein's adaptability, stemming from his unique background that included scouting for the Harlem Globetrotters while coaching Kelvyn Park High School, set him apart from other coaches in the NBA. This experience exposed him to a wide range of playing styles and allowed him to counter opposing teams more effectively.

Brownstein liked to switch between larger lineups featuring Spears and Stan Miasek in the forward slots and smaller ones, with Spears moving to power forward and rookie Leo Barnhorst often starting as a well-rounded small forward. Frank Kudelka, another rookie known for his electric scoring ability, frequently made an impact off the bench, particularly in clutch situations. Kenny Rollins showcased improved performance in a reduced role from his rookie year, occasionally playing alongside Phillip in the backcourt with Zaslofsky shifted to small forward for added versatility.

Zaslofsky scored 30 points in a victory against Tri-Cities—his first such game of the season—but the Stags failed to gain ground in the standings as both the Royals and Lakers also won.[34] They remained two and a half games behind Minneapolis, two games behind Rochester, and held a slim lead of just one and a half games over Fort Wayne.

Alex Groza scored 30 points of his own on that same day in a 104–87 win over Waterloo, strengthening Indianapolis' lead over the Anderson Packers by two games. Bruce Hale added 21 points, directly following up a 23-point performance against Denver in the previous game to string together his best two games as an Olympian so far.

Following that game, Marshall Hawkins was able to return to action after a 31-day absence due to his broken cheekbone. Incorporating him back into the team would prove to be a quandary for Cliff Barker, as Joe Holland and Carl Shaeffer had both benefited noticeably from Hawkins' absence, Barker himself and Hale also had a minor increase in scoring opportunities, and the team had gone from 15–12 at the time of the injury to 24–14 at the time of his return. Before the injury, Hawkins was earning minutes similar to those of Barker and Holland; during his absence, each of the other four wings had more playing time than Hawkins had gotten when he was healthy.

6. The Celtics, New Year, and You Just Can't Play with Glasses On

Meanwhile, any concerns about the Lakers' underwhelming start were completely forgotten after Minneapolis won 13 times in 15 games, with George Mikan averaging 28.8 points, Jim Pollard averaging 18.1, and Vern Mikkelsen averaging 12.5 during that stretch.

In the final game of a grueling stretch of away games on the East Coast, they followed up wins over Boston, Washington, and New York with a game against the Warriors, as Philadelphia fought to stay in the playoff race with a pair of recent wins over Sheboygan and Boston having halted a slide down the standings.

Trailing 89–84 with just six seconds left, Mikan sank a pair of free throws to narrow the gap to three, then outjumped Philadelphia's Jake Bornheimer in a two-minute rule-mandated jump ball and tapped the ball forward, directly to Jim Pollard, who was under the basket and swiftly made the score 89–88 with an open layup.

The Warriors inbounded with five seconds left and Slater Martin immediately fouled Chink Crossin while trying to strip the ball from him. Crossin made his free throw with four seconds to play and increased the Warriors' lead to two points.

This time during the jump ball, Mikan just grabbed the ball out of mid-air instead of tipping it to a teammate and started to bring it down the court himself, but Vern Gardner shoved him out of bounds to intentionally foul him. Mikan made a free throw to bring the game within one again and lined up with Gardner to face off for one final jump ball.

Mikan again tapped the ball to Pollard, but a Philadelphia defender knocked the ball out of bounds and secured the 90–89 Philadelphia Warriors victory. Mikan finished with 34 points, Pollard had 18, and Bob Harrison scored 16, but they couldn't quite overcome the 21 scored by Vern Gardner and 19 added by George Senesky for the Warriors.[35]

In the broader context, the Central Division teams were excelling in the NBA, amassing a combined record of 32–14 since the start of the calendar year. This meant trouble for Fort Wayne, who, despite winning seven of their last 10 games, found themselves falling further behind in the divisional title race. A 112–94 loss to the Indianapolis Olympians, led by Ralph Beard's 31 points and Wah Wah Jones' 29, separated even the third-place Chicago Stags from them by two games.[36]

Syracuse, still three games ahead of any team regardless of division and six games ahead of the Eastern Division's second-place Knicks, were 30–6 for the season and on track to finish with the best record in all of professional basketball since the 1938–39 Akron Firestones.

At home on January 22, they racked up a 43–34 lead over the Anderson Packers by halftime, but the Packers' recently acquired Richie Niemiera led a comeback that sent the game to overtime. Frank Brian took over the overtime period for Anderson, scoring seven of their nine points, leading them to eke out a 77–75 win on the back of his crucial free throws with six seconds left in the extra period.[37] This result brought an end to a 21-game home winning streak for Syracuse that extended back to the previous year's NBL playoffs. That loss had also been to Anderson.

The bottom half of the Eastern Division didn't fare any better than the top that day; the Boston Celtics suffered a humiliating defeat against St. Louis, scoring a mere 47 points and shooting an abysmal 19-of-97 from the field, marking a historic low for the team and the first sub-50-point NBA game since the merger.[38]

In the Central Division, the Chicago Stags failed to capitalize on their opportunity to climb up the standings against the Lakers, losing twice despite the absence of an ill Jim Pollard. George Mikan and Vern Mikkelsen led the way with 28 and 19 points in a

103–75 blowout in the first game. In the second game, Mikan scored 40 points, including 17 in the second quarter, surpassing Bobby Cook's single-quarter scoring record and securing his third 40-plus-point performance in less than three weeks.[39] The Lakers held on to a close lead over Rochester in the standings and Chicago was now closer to Fort Wayne's fourth place than Rochester's second place position.

The Olympians and Knicks dismantled their respective Western Division opponents; each had one of the most one-sided halves of the year that day. New York, hosting the Sheboygan Redskins, turned in a 57–30 second-half advantage en route to a 101–68 victory featuring 19 points by Connie Simmons, but the Knicks' outstanding play was upstaged by Indianapolis' 60–28 second-half run in their 107–69 win over the Waterloo Hawks.[40] New York remained steadily in second place of the Eastern Division, while the Olympians extended their lead over the Packers to three and a half games and Sheboygan's struggles were providing a window of opportunity for Tri-Cities to potentially overtake them.

After compiling a 1–2 record in eight days acting as the Packers' coach since trading away Howie Schultz, Ike Duffey relinquished his coaching role to Doxie Moore.[41] Most prominent for having been the NBL's final commissioner, Moore had been entrusted with basketball operations by Duffey as the Packers' business manager since the merger.

Moore's journey as a coach began with modest beginnings, coaching basketball and football at the high school level for about a decade after backing up Johnny Wooden on a national championship team at Purdue. After nine years as a high school coach, Moore joined the U.S. Navy during World War II.

With the Navy, after brief stints at Fort Schuyler and Fort H. G. Wright, Moore joined the University of Iowa's pre-flight school as a physical education coordinator, also serving on Jack Meagher's coaching staff for the Iowa Pre-Flight Seahawks football team that achieved a 10–1 record and a sixth-place national ranking.

Following the war, Moore was hired as the head coach for the Sheboygan Redskins, taking over from Dutch Dehnert. The team's president, Magnus Brinkman, believed that Dehnert's offseason residence in New York handicapped the team's roster-building abilities. Moore's commitment to living in Sheboygan year-round appealed to Brinkman, leading to Dehnert's departure and Moore's appointment.[42]

Moore's time coaching Sheboygan didn't exactly start smoothly: among the Redskins' five starters, Dick Schulz followed Dehnert to Cleveland, Steve Sharkey requested a sale to Syracuse where his family lived, and Mike Novak tried to jump leagues but ended up suspended from both, soon shipped out to Syracuse as well.

Despite the setbacks, Moore made significant signings, including Fred Lewis and Luther Harris, who became key scorers for the Redskins. Under Moore's guidance, the team achieved a respectable 26–18 record, but they were eliminated in a close-fought first-round playoff series against Oshkosh.

The addition of McDermott, the championship-winning player-coach of the previous NBL season, ruffled some feathers, and rumors that Moore was on his way out after a 6–5 start to the season were only quelled once Brinkman signed him to a two-year extension that promised to keep him in Sheboygan until the end of the 1949–50 season.[43]

Just five days later, a quarrel between Moore and several Redskins players resulted in Brinkman unofficially removing Moore from all his duties and sending him home early from a road trip for "important business reasons." McDermott was named interim head coach and Ed Dancker was named interim business manager.[44]

Also in the fallout from the incident, Harris was suspended indefinitely for insubordination and breaking of training rules, and Kenny Suesens, the joint-longest tenured player on the team, made an ultimatum that he would never play for the Redskins again as long as Moore was associated with the team. Suesens was released.[45]

After what amounted to an unofficial two-week suspension, Moore was officially removed as head coach and replaced by McDermott, instead taking on the position of general manager.

The most crucial reason for his return was that Sheboygan faced the risk of vacating a 59–48 win, as McDermott played Harris without informing the league of his reinstatement from suspension, which led Oshkosh owner Lon Darling to launch an appeal against the result. As it turned out, Moore had initially issued the suspension before being relieved of his responsibilities, but it was revoked when six Sheboygan players confronted Brinkman, declaring that if Harris was benched, they would refuse to play. Moore and Brinkman had to work together to handle damage control, which ended up being quite easy, since Brinkman had personally informed NBL commissioner Ward Lambert that the suspension had been lifted just before the game started.[46]

Less than a week later, Harris faced another suspension following his arrest for speeding and failure to observe a traffic sign. During his suspension, he was arrested once more for falsifying a $25 check.[47] He never played for the Redskins again and Moore sold him to Tri-Cities a month later. In the meantime, Moore also traded McDermott, purportedly for financial reasons but much more likely because he was losing control of the locker room, particularly Dancker and Lewis. Moore resumed coaching duties and Brinkman released a patently absurd statement that Moore had "always been coach."[48]

Sheboygan failed to bounce back from the turmoil. The Redskins finished with a 23–37 record, worst of their long NBL history, and it was largely a relief when Moore was appointed NBL commissioner, freeing them from their commitment to retain him as coach for two more years. Moore was no stranger to chaos. Even back in his high school coaching days, he once withdrew his team from the athletic conference after other schools unanimously rejected a rule change he proposed.[49]

Despite that, his reputation as a skilled coach, mentored by prominent basketball minds, remained intact. He had worked well with Ike Duffey so far in multiple domains and appointing him as coach didn't cost Duffey anything extra, so for the foreseeable future, Moore would be head coach of the Anderson Packers.

7

The Minor League Debate, the Future of the League, and Is President Podoloff Doing a Good Job?

During a period of 29 days encompassing 12 games, the Baltimore Bullets won only once, suffering an average loss of 14.3 points per game. The absence of Buddy Jeannette and Paul Hoffman's return before fully recovering contributed to their poor performance.

Hoffman's gradual return to full strength and the additions of Whitey Von Nieda and rookie Andy O'Donnell provided much-needed depth in the backcourt. Von Nieda, purchased from Tri-Cities, assumed a playmaking role when Joe Dolhon needed a rest. O'Donnell was a level-headed spot-up shooter from nearby Loyola University Maryland, jumping from college to the pros midseason. The Bullets won games against Philadelphia and Sheboygan and put up a respectable fight against the clearly superior Royals in Rochester. It also took two overtimes for New York to put them away, 79–77, with Carl Braun and Hoffman topping scoring for their respective teams with 19 points each, but that loss cost the Bullets their best defender, Tommy Byrnes, who limped off the floor with a sprained ankle.[1]

Despite the Knicks' win, their fourth in the last five days, they remained distant from the Nationals, who remained far ahead of the rest of the league at 31–7.

Surprisingly, key Syracuse players like Adolph Schayes, Al Cervi, and Paul Seymour were not performing at their best during recent games, with Schayes' scoring averaging only 12.0 points over the Nationals' last 10 games. Games were more competitive than they had been at the start of the season, but wins over very good teams like Anderson and Rochester still came with relative ease.

The fleet-footed Billy Gabor was the Nationals' leading scorer in recent weeks. Although he was Syracuse University's all-time leading scorer, Gabor's Nationals career had begun a bit slowly, so 20-plus points in five games within a month signaled that he was still as gifted a scorer as he had been.

A day after leading Syracuse with 20 points, most of them on the fast-break, in a 76–72 victory over Rochester, Gabor sought dental treatment for a toothache but discovered through X-rays that it was actually a broken jaw. In a game against Washington a month earlier, he was hit by the errant shoulder of Capitols' point guard Leo Katkaveck and had been unknowingly playing with a fractured jaw in the eight games since. He would have to wear a protective mask for the next couple games, but he had no reason to sit out, since he had already been playing through the injury.[2]

While the Packers were rapidly losing ground against Indianapolis after their four-player trade and coaching changes, Frank Brian was a notable benefactor of the trade on an individual level.

Liberated from the constraints of previous coaches' systems, Brian showcased drastic improvement from the previous two years, and his all-around excellence as a phenomenally fluid scorer with decisive playmaking and a knack for stealing the ball became widely recognized despite the occasional streakiness.

In the six games since Howie Schultz and Ralph Johnson were shipped out and Brian was moved to point guard, he scored 25 points or more five times, averaging an impressive 26.2 points per game, second only to George Mikan during that period. Notably, his increased scoring didn't impede the offensive contributions of teammates Bill Closs, John Hargis, and Milo Komenich, each of whom continued averaging over 10 shot attempts and maintaining their scoring averages. Defensively, the team suffered due to the loss of their best post defender and one of their best perimeter defenders in the same trade, but it was an expected consequence.

The Pistons fared even worse in the immediate aftermath of the trade with four consecutive double-digit losses, culminating in a 77–64 defeat against Baltimore that extended Fort Wayne's post-trade record to just 1–6, compared to 23–13 before the deal. This meant that the Pistons, at 24–19, were closer to the Central Division's last-place St. Louis Bombers, with an 18–24 record, than to the division's leaders, the 32–13 Lakers and 30–13 Royals, for the first time all season.

The issue may have had less to do with the trade than it did with the trade's aftermath coinciding with Fort Wayne's lengthiest road trip of the season. All six losses were road games and the win was at home, fitting for a team previously holding a 18–2 home record and a 5–11 record as visitors. Nonetheless, it was a worrying sign for the new-look Pistons, who were performing noticeably worse on both sides of the floor.

Charlie Black had been the Pistons' second-leading scorer at the time of the trade, so redistribution of playing time and shot attempts posed challenges. Improved performance from Bob Carpenter and the newly acquired Howie Schultz partially compensated, but that limited opportunities for Jack Kerris and Bob Harris and made the team less rotationally adaptable. The reduction in Curly Armstrong's playing time due to his illness and to accommodate Ralph Johnson, while not incidental, weakened their perimeter defense similar to his illness.

Baltimore's win over the sliding Pistons added intrigue to the Eastern Division's lower ranks; with Philadelphia's win over New York and Boston's loss to Rochester on that same day, the Bullets' victory led to a three-way tie for the fourth and final playoff place in the division. As Fort Wayne held a five-and-a-half-game lead over St. Louis and Tri-Cities surged ahead of Waterloo by six games in the midst of a winning streak, this was likely the only serious playoff race left, and it was closer than ever.

The situation was particularly disappointing for the Warriors, as Boston had yet to achieve significant success, while Baltimore had faced talent losses and injuries this season, offering them some justification. Philadelphia had been steadily declining since their BAA championship despite having retained Joe Fulks and Eddie Gottlieb.

The decision to stay or leave was simply business for the players, but Gottlieb's decision to remain with the Warriors was expected, given his deep-rooted connection to Philadelphia basketball that spanned decades.

Starting his basketball journey at the age of 10 in 1908, Gottlieb excelled as a guard in basketball, a quarterback in football, and a catcher in baseball. In a sign of things to come, at 15 he managed an amateur baseball team consisting mainly of players three or four years his senior.

In high school, he teamed up with Harry Passon and Hughie Black and they established themselves as Philadelphia's premier young basketball players, winning consecutive city championships from 1913–14 to 1915–16.

Beyond basketball, Gottlieb, Passon, and Black shared common backgrounds of poverty, Judaism, and as members of immigrant families who had fled the Russian empire to escape the anti–Semitic May Laws in the Pale of Settlement when they were young children. Gottlieb and Passon were both born in Kiev, Russia (now Kyiv, Ukraine) and Black was born in Mogilev na Dnestr, Russia (now Mohyliv-Podilskyi, Ukraine).

Though they went to separate universities, they kept in touch, and two years later, they reunited to form a basketball team again.

In the 1918–19 season, sponsored by Philadelphia's Young Men's Hebrew Association, their Philadelphia YMHA team joined the American League of Philadelphia (ALP), a local minor league, but finished with a 4–11 record, joint worst in the league.

The next season, the Young Men's Hebrew Association withdrew their sponsorship, believing the game to be excessively violent, and the trio turned to the South Philadelphia Hebrew Association instead and adopted the name Philadelphia Sphas. The South Philadelphia Hebrew Association also pulled their sponsorship soon after, prompting the trio to open a sporting goods store to fund the team.

The Sphas gradually improved, especially with the addition of Chick Passon, Harry's younger brother. By the 1921–22 season, the Sphas had a strong record and were poised to win their first championship, but the ALP disbanded before the season's completion.

In 1923–24, the Sphas broke through and won the Philadelphia League. With the addition of Davey Banks, the team improved their record and secured a spot in the championship series, defeating the Tri-Council Caseys to claim the title, after nonpayment and match fixing allegations led Tri-Council to forfeit the deciding game three. The league never recovered from the scandal, and the Sphas joined the Eastern Basketball League (EBL), a league that would go on to implode halfway through the season.

Around this time, there were efforts to nationalize the sport, akin to professional baseball and football. The newly formed ABL, spanning from Boston to Chicago, completed its first season with overall success, excluding the Boston franchise. Financially solvent thanks to Max Rosenblum, founder of Rosenblum's Department Store, and George Preston Marshall, operator of Palace Laundries laundromat chain, the ABL benefited from the guidance of Chicago Bears owner George Halas and NFL commissioner Joe Carr. With the exception of the Sphas, the Original Celtics, and the New York Renaissance, the ABL featured basketball's top talent.

Carr invited Eddie Gottlieb and Harry Passon to operate the ABL's new Philadelphia franchise and the Sphas joined the ABL. They incorporated non–Jewish players, and changed their name from the Sphas to the Philadelphia Phillies, then the Philadelphia Quakers, and finally settling on the Philadelphia Warriors, inspired by the Lenape indigenous people. While in the ABL, the Warriors experienced modest success, reaching the Eastern Division Semifinals in the 1927–28 season but being swept by the Original Celtics. After enduring financial losses of approximately $60,000 and selling off players, they left the league in 1928. They returned to barnstorming, reverted to their

Jewish roots, and reclaimed the Sphas name. Harry Passon retired as a coach, granting full organizational control to Gottlieb.

After operating as a barnstorming team for a year, the Philadelphia Sphas joined a new iteration of the EBL, requiring a roster rebuild. Led by rookies Cy Kaselman and Harry Litwack, along with forward Red Wolfe, the revamped Sphas outmatched the EBL and won three consecutive championships from 1929 to 1932. Only the Trenton Bengals, led by a host of former ABL players, managed to defeat the Sphas in a championship series the next year.

Following the 1932–33 season, a partial merger between the EBL and the New York–based Metropolitan Basketball League led to the creation of a new ABL with diminished salaries, smaller markets, and fewer teams. To maintain their competitive edge, coach Eddie Gottlieb reshaped the Sphas roster, adding players like Shikey Gotthoffer and Inky Lautman. With a young lineup averaging 22.6 years old, the Sphas embraced a philosophy centered on ball movement, inspired by the success of the Original Celtics and New York Renaissance. Gottlieb implemented a system based on short, cautious passes, constant movement, and finding open shots, with an emphasis on the shooting prowess of Kaselman and Gotthoffer. The remaining starters relied on scoring opportunities near the basket.

In the early 1940s, the Philadelphia Sphas experienced a period of transition and change in their playing staff. The team had managed to survive and thrive in the ABL, but with Cy Kaselman's generation of players aging and nearing retirement, it was clear that the roster needed rejuvenation. Long Island University became an important recruiting ground for the Sphas, with players like Irv Torgoff, Ossie Schectman, Butch Schwartz, and Art Hillhouse joining the team. This new group, along with Lautman's offensive leadership, led the Sphas to multiple championship appearances and two titles, culminating in the 1944–45 championship, their twelfth in the last 23 seasons.

When the name "Philadelphia Warriors" was chosen to represent Philadelphia's entry in the BAA, the connection between Philadelphia's newest team and the Sphas was evident in the name the Sphas had used in the ABL. Gottlieb wasn't the owner of the Warriors—that was Peter A. Tyrrell, a sports publicist and the general manager of the Philadelphia Arena known for his connection to the Ice Capades—but he might as well have been.

While stepping down as the Sphas' coach to lead the Warriors, Gottlieb retained ownership of the Sphas and appointed Litwack as the new head coach. Many key players were snapped up by BAA teams. Litwack's Sphas quickly declined, and before long, he left to become an assistant under Gottlieb.

The Sphas experienced their first losing season in 25 years in 1947–48, and in 1948–49 they finished 8–26, after which they shut down operations.[3]

In the NBA, the Warriors were becoming increasingly removed from their championship team and even further removed from the Philadelphia Sphas. Though they still had one remaining ex-Spha in the rotation in Jerry Fleishman, the 1949–50 Philadelphia Warriors lacked the ball movement that characterized Gottlieb's preferred style of basketball.

The Warriors' style had shifted toward long-distance shooting, which became less effective as center-centric offenses became more prevalent, but one that Gottlieb wasn't in a rush to halt, since it was a unique and entertaining way to play. Still, 1948–49 was the first losing season Gottlieb had been a part of in over a quarter century and

1949–50 was shaping up to be considerably worse. Worst of all was that the poor ball movement precipitated a slow pace of play, creating a cycle of limited opportunities for quality ball movement and diminishing entertainment value. Despite occasional victories in such circumstances, such as a January 28 win over New York 58–55, a losing team that produced seven games with less than 60 points scored was hardly an appealing product from a team in a first-year league. That win over the Knicks was the second time in just a week's time that Philadelphia had failed to reach 60 points.

There was no other rivalry as fierce as the one between the Tri-Cities Blackhawks and the Waterloo Hawks, and both teams profited significantly from bumper crowds whenever they hosted each other.

The animosity started in their first NBL encounter, when Iowans eagerly attended to support Murray Wier, the prodigal son of the University of Iowa, and Blackhawks coach Roger Potter deliberately delayed substituting Wier into the game until there were less than two minutes remaining in the game.[4] The arrival of Red Auerbach as Potter's replacement further fueled the hostility, as he frequently engaged in sideline outbursts and confrontations with referees.

During their third matchup of this season, Auerbach lost his temper when a pep band continued playing during a Blackhawk player's free throw attempt. He confronted the referee, Ed Bro, demanding a technical foul for the Hawks. Bro paused the game to request Waterloo coach Perk Purnhage tell the band to stop playing during free throws. When Purnhage's response was that he wouldn't until Auerbach went back to his bench and calmed down, Auerbach cursed up a storm, insulting everything from Purnhage's mother to his weight, until Bro had to physically separate the two out of fear that Purnhage would punch Auerbach. Later in the game, Auerbach also nearly came to blows with Waterloo's Dick Mehen and had to be escorted out of the arena by police when a Hawks fan took a swing at him after the game's conclusion.

Tri-Cities won amid all the drama, 85–79, with Mike Todorovich's 25 points leading the way.[5] The Blackhawks, having now won four out of their last five games, were beginning to look somewhat competent as long as you ignored Auerbach's antics, and they had improved in the standings to 16–24, just half a game behind the third-place Redskins in the Western Division standings.

Following their strong performance, the Blackhawks had hopes of being competitive in the postseason, prompting Mike Fitzgerald to continue making roster changes. The same day that Tri-Cities defeated Waterloo, Fitzgerald traded John Mahnken to the Boston Celtics for Gene Englund.[6]

Englund had expressed homesickness and a desire to return to the Midwest, especially after his playing time diminished significantly in Boston when Doggie Julian made Bob Doll the starting power forward and gave Brady Walker most of the reserve minutes for both post positions. With his family still residing in Oshkosh and his career winding down, Englund saw little reason to remain far away from his loved ones if he wasn't a valued player for the Celtics.

For the Blackhawks, this was a major upgrade. Mahnken had previously been an important player under Auerbach in Washington, but while he remained somewhat of a defensive anchor, his offensive skill had eroded and he had gone from being a contact-averse stretch big to an outright liability who struggled to keep up with Tri-Cities' fast-paced style of play and frequently faced foul trouble.

Julian, aside from seeking more than just cash for Englund, had admired Mahnken's game for nearly a decade. Statistics didn't show the whole picture of Mahnken's game; the foul trouble was a concern, but he had once been the top long-range-shooting center in the league. That sometimes resulted in frustrating offensive tendencies, but it had the potential to facilitate better coexistence among Bob Kinney and the Celtics' smorgasbord of cutting guards. His rebounding had been the best on the Blackhawks, and at 6'8" and 245 lbs., he stood as the Celtics' largest player, with no one previously surpassing Kinney's 6'6" and 215 lbs. The trade coincided with Boston's surprising release of Dermie O'Connell. The Bombers, needing all the bench help they could get, signed him on waivers.

Good news for Tri-Cities directly correlated with bad news for Sheboygan, and a 91–74 Sheboygan loss to the Packers the next day meant the Redskins were now merely tied with the Blackhawks for third in the Western Division.

This particular string of losses wasn't as eye-catching as the nine straight they'd racked up in early December, but the current situation was even bleaker. Unlike before, when they could attribute some of their losses to Noble Jorgensen's absence, this was a mostly healthy roster that was losing by embarrassing margins.

A 23-point loss to Anderson was one-upped by a 30-point loss to Indianapolis, which was in turn a less humiliating result than the double-digit home loss four days later to a 5–29 Denver Nuggets team that hadn't won an away game in 10 months.

Winning just three games out of the last 14 was bad, but precisely how poorly Sheboygan was performing was exposed by a 101–68 blowout loss courtesy of the New York Knicks. While allowing five Knicks players to shoot over 50 percent from the field was disappointing to say the least, the defensive shortcomings were no surprise at this point. Even on their best day, the Redskins typically allowed well over 80 points. The real problem was that they were no longer pairing their abysmal defense with a competent offense. In this particular loss, Noble Jorgensen had a minimal impact on the offense, shooting only twice and finishing the game with one point. Jack Burmaster shot 1-of-16. As a whole, the team went 22/79 and added a pretty poor 24-of-37 on free throws.[7]

Jorgensen, who had been a leading scorer before falling ill, failed to regain his previous form upon returning, averaging a mere 7.3 points in the month since he returned to action. The rest of the Redskins couldn't compensate for the substantial decline in their best player's performance, now more accurately their fifth- or sixth-best player if he couldn't return to fitness soon. Kenny Suesens attempted to restructure the offense with Max Morris and Bobby Cook as focal points. While Morris excelled in his role, Cook's inconsistency made it challenging to rely on him and launched Burmaster, a much more dependable defender than he was a scorer, into an inflated offensive role that he wasn't accustomed to.

Suesens had an opportunity for poetic justice as the coach of Sheboygan, hoping to stabilize the team and surpass Tri-Cities in order to face Doxie Moore's Anderson Packers in the playoffs, with Moore's coaching tenure in Sheboygan having led to Suesens' release.

Suesens came back to Sheboygan as a player-coach to conclude his playing career with the Redskins as soon as Moore left for the NBL commissioner job. He had been a part of the team since their inaugural NBL season in 1938–39, except for a brief stint with the Seattle Athletics of the Pacific Coast League after Moore waived him, the only thing that separated Suesens from having an uninterrupted 11-year career with Sheboygan. Only Eyre Saitch, who played for the New York Renaissance from 1927–28 to 1940–41, had a longer career as a one-team player.

The Sheboygan Redskins began as a local independent team in the 1920s and later turned professional in the late 1930s, making them the NBA's second-oldest team behind Rochester. Founded by Tony Posewitz, a shoe manufacturer and amateur baseball player-manager, the team was built around his younger brothers and their friend Carl Roth.[8]

Exhibiting remarkable talent and routinely winning games by as much as 20 or 30 points, they attracted renowned barnstorming teams like Bob Douglas' New York Renaissance, who had recently achieved the unofficial title of world champions and an 88-game winning streak. The Renaissance won 40–30.

The City of Sheboygan had a deeply troubling racial climate. Although it is unclear if there were official municipal laws enforcing residential segregation, numerous accounts suggest that Sheboygan operated as a sundown town, where black individuals faced expulsion or worse if found within city limits after nightfall.[9]

In contrast to the big picture of Sheboygan's racial relations, the Renaissance players were treated well enough that they returned three times the next year. The games between the Sheboygan Redskins and the Renaissance drew record crowds for the city. Other all-black teams like the Harlem Globe Trotters and Chicago Crusaders also made appearances in Sheboygan, although their reception varied, and instances of discrimination, such as being denied access to hotels and restaurants, occurred.

Nevertheless, the Globe Trotters held their first-ever preseason training camp in Sheboygan prior to the 1940–41 season. Among major league teams, only the Oshkosh All-Stars hosted the Globe Trotters more frequently, and only Oshkosh, Indianapolis, and Philadelphia played the Renaissance more often than the Redskins did.

After a game against the Chicago Crusaders in December 1936, Tony Posewitz signed the Crusaders' star center, Jack Mann, for the final three months of the 1936–37 season.[10] Mann didn't stay in Sheboygan past that season, but he was the best player on the team while he was there and integrated a team that was based in a city with a population of zero black people at the time of the 1930 census.

Local jewelry company owner Ed Imig formed a syndicate of Sheboygan businessmen to establish the Sheboygan Basketball Association and secure a spot in the NBL for the 1938–39 season. Ten of the co-owners and Sheboygan player Carl Roth were named to the board of directors, with the presidency changing hands each year. As the team lacked a permanent president, Roth assumed chief decision-making authority as the team's business manager.[11]

While the Posewitz brothers remained on the team, their careers were declining, and new talent like Ed Dancker, Rube Lautenschlager, and Paul Sokody joined the roster. After a losing season, Roth recruited Frank Zummach, an assistant coach from Marquette, as coach.

Under Frank Zummach's coaching, the Sheboygan Redskins experienced playoff success, reaching the NBL Finals in his second season but falling short to Oshkosh. After a disappointing 10–14 third-season record, Zummach resigned in protest when Roth signed rookie Ken Buehler to a higher salary than Dancker and Lautenschlager. Zummach's final season had coincided with Dancker's breakout performance, earning him a spot on the All-NBL Second Team.

Roth replaced Zummach with Moose Graf, who only lasted a little more than a month before being fired. Roth took over and guided the team to the second best record of the four teams still participating in the NBL during the World War II–affected 1942–43 season.

Every team lost players to the war effort, and for the Redskins that came in the form of Buehler joining the U.S. Navy with just one remaining game before the playoffs. Fortunately, the team had signed Buddy Jeannette through fan club fundraising, anticipating the possibility of Buehler's departure, just two weeks earlier.[12] Dancker, Jeannette, and Lautenschlager led the Redskins to sweep Oshkosh 2–0 and defeat Fort Wayne 2–1 en route to their first and only NBL championship.

Despite losing Jeannette, the team improved the following year by adding Mike Novak from the defunct Chicago Studebakers to pair with Dancker in the post, but the Fort Wayne Zollners had improved so much that it didn't matter. Sheboygan made the next three championships and lost them all.

Roth left the team to enlist in the U.S. Marine Corps in the summer of 1944 and the Sheboygan Basketball Association decided to prioritize stability by discontinuing their practice of rotating the presidency among board members. Magnus Brinkman, owner of the DeLand Cheese Distributing Company, was named president prior to the 1944–45 season and held the position throughout the Redskins' transition to the NBA.

The Redskins faced a tough challenge from the surging Tri-Cities Blackhawks, who had quickly closed the gap in the Western Division standings with a string of six wins in seven games. The Blackhawks' success was attributed to key trades in the backcourt, acquiring Gene Vance and Walt Kirk. In games with both new additions playing, the Blackhawks, who had been 7–16 before the first of the two trades, were 10–3.

Both Vance and Kirk were starters, pushing Dike Eddleman to small forward and causing tenacious defensive small forward Warren Perkins to now assume a bench role while still contributing significant minutes. Eddleman, Mike Todorovich, and Don Otten all played better with their new teammates than they had earlier in the year and the Blackhawks' defense had noticeably improved.

They weren't just beating teams like Waterloo or Denver either. Among the victims of their 6–1 stretch between January 22 and February 1 were Anderson, Indianapolis, New York, and Syracuse, all potential contenders vying for postseason home-court advantage. As Todorovich thrived with an average of 15.7 points over seven games, Eddleman, Otten, and Vance contributed 12.6, 12.1, and 10.1 points per game, respectively, and Murray Wier and Dee Gibson both proved to be threats to score double digits off the bench.

New York wasn't having the best time even without accounting for their loss to Tri-Cities. That was their third straight loss and 35 points from George Mikan the next day in a 96–81 Minneapolis win over the Knicks extended that streak to four.[13]

In early February 1950, Mikan was voted the greatest basketball player of the half century in a poll conducted by the Associated Press. Out of 380 sportswriters across the United States, Mikan received 139 votes, closely followed by Hank Luisetti with 123 votes. Nat Holman placed a distant third with 31, Chuck Hyatt of the University of Pittsburgh and numerous AAU teams received 16, and Alex Groza received 13. No other players received 10 or more and Joe Fulks was the only other active NBA player to receive more than a lone vote.[14]

Ned Irish's circumvention rules in assembling a talented Knicks roster had paid off, with players like Harry Gallatin, Vince Boryla, and Ernie Vandeweghe, all acquired through unconventional means, proving themselves to be very good NBA players and only going to improve over the next few years.

However, the rapid success of these individuals hindered the team's overall progress, as it left little time for Irish and coach Joe Lapchick to construct a supporting cast that could complement the strengths of their core players.

This affected Ray Lumpp, who had thrived as a scoring-oriented guard as a rookie but now had to adapt to a backup point guard role focused on distribution due to Dick McGuire's presence in the starting lineup. Rotation shooting guards Goebel Ritter and Bill van Breda Kolff saw reduced playing time to accommodate rookies Vandeweghe and Harry Donovan at their position.

Moreover, it was still uncertain which, exactly, of the Knicks' starters were their core players. With all five starters under age 25, no player could be ruled out due to a mismatch in their career timeline. Carl Braun, the team's top scorer, had seemingly plateaued in his third season. Vince Boryla possessed the potential to become a star, considering his scoring versatility, but often faded into the background due to his team-oriented style of play. Rookie Dick McGuire exceeded expectations and was in a two-player race with Andy Phillip to lead the league in assists, but the concept of building a team around a pass-oriented point guard with limited scoring abilities was unprecedented in major league basketball. Even Gallatin and Connie Simmons were potentially worth building around; while Gallatin was known for his work ethic, he was also already a dominant rebounder and proficient in face-up scoring, while Simmons had already proven himself capable of guiding Baltimore to a championship just two years prior.

A pressing concern was how to handle Ernie Vandeweghe's inability to travel for away games, leading to a different starting five when away from home. Vandeweghe's extended playing time on a road trip, made possible by his medical school's Christmas break, gave him a chance to show off his scoring touch, and 18 points against Chicago and 19 points against Denver helped build his case for more minutes.

Coach Joe Lapchick ultimately shifted Braun and Boryla to a full-time frontcourt partnership and benched Gallatin to accommodate Vandeweghe's full-time inclusion in the starting lineup. These changes, combined with the road trip, affected the team's momentum and the Knicks sank from their streak of 14 wins in 15 games to winning just 10 of the next 21. Despite securely holding second place in the Eastern Division, their path to the Finals depended on defeating Syracuse in the playoffs. To stand a chance against the formidable Nationals, they had to regain their best form. When school restarted in January, Vandeweghe resumed playing exclusively in home games and the rotations reverted to Lapchick's original plan.

On the opposite side of New York, Rochester continued to mount a strong challenge to Minneapolis in the Central Division. Although the Lakers had an impressive 13–3 January record that put them at 34–13, they couldn't shake off the 32–13 Royals even as Chicago and Fort Wayne began to find it difficult to keep up.

Bob Davies experienced a dip in form, failing to score in double digits during more games in January than in November and December combined. Arnie Risen's performance had continued to decline. He was the fourth-best scorer in the BAA in 1948–49, now he was the third-best scorer on his own team behind Davies and Bobby Wanzer.

In mid–January, Bill Calhoun was briefly sidelined with an illness, and Les Harrison inserted Jack Coleman as the starting power forward and moved Arnie Johnson over to small forward.[15] Johnson, at 6'5" and 236 lbs., was hardly small for a forward and the trio of Johnson, Coleman, and Risen made the Royals a very tough team to outplay in the interior.

7. Minor League Debate, Future of the League, President Podoloff

In a January 21 game against Anderson, Risen collided knees with Packers center Milo Komenich on the first play, forcing him to be substituted due to injury. He reentered the game a few minutes later but injured his other knee in the second half, preventing him from playing further.[16] Despite being unfit to play, Risen returned for several games on limited minutes before finally taking time off to recover after a 0-of-7 shooting performance with just one point scored in a loss to Baltimore.

Amid Risen's injury issues and Calhoun's absence, Bobby Wanzer and rookie Jack Coleman stepped up to take on leading roles for the Royals and kept the team afloat through a time that easily could have included more losses than wins if it weren't for the consistent 25- to 35-point combined outputs of that duo. Risen, who had taken a liking to Coleman and even helped negotiate his rookie contract, praised the fellow Kentuckian's performance, telling the media that Coleman had "been carrying the club for the past month." Coleman, a rugged rebounder and defender with excellent mobility for a center, had only been drafted 22nd overall in the previous draft, but filled in for Risen effortlessly and steadily improved throughout his first few months in the NBA, even outplaying Risen to some extent.

By that point, as January came to a close, it was widely known that several NBA teams were financially tenuous and Rochester owner Les Harrison floated the idea of dividing the NBA into a major league and a minor league, indicating his intention to propose it in the NBA's annual meeting that summer.

He suggested that minor league teams could operate with smaller rosters and be led by player-coaches to reduce costs, permitting even teams with attendance as low as 1,200 people to still break even.

Harrison's mistake was that he went out of his way to categorize teams into his proposed system: he named the

Red Holzman (left) and Arnie Risen (1948). Holzman was at this point relegated to being a key bench figure for the Rochester Royals, with his career beginning to wind down from the All-NBL talent he had been in the mid-1940s. Arnie Risen was extremely important for the Rochester Royals, taking the majority of the frontcourt offensive burden and tasked with matching up with George Mikan in their relatively frequent meetings. Although hampered by injury in 1949–50, he is still estimated to have led the Royals in rebounding, as well as placing third in scoring.

Bullets, Celtics, Stags, Lakers, Knicks, Warriors, Bombers, Nationals, and Capitols as major league teams; the Packers, Nuggets, Redskins, Blackhawks, and Hawks as minor league teams; and suggested the Pistons and Olympians could fit in either group.[17] This triggered a strong response from other team executives, many of whom were understandably upset and offended by the implication that their teams would in any way not be considered major league organizations.

The most indignant of all was Ben Kerner, whose Blackhawks were fifth in attendance and becoming so popular in the Tri-Cities, thanks to their recent success, that he was working on a concept for a flexible rubber wall that could expand the seating capacity of Wharton Fieldhouse as needed. He said that Rochester was more than welcome to leave the NBA if Harrison had issues with the NBA's organization and that if the league were to split, that Rochester should be included in the minors. In that same breath, though, he made sure to characterize Waterloo and Denver as "weaker teams" and favorably compare his Blackhawks to teams like the Royals and Nationals.[18]

Knicks coach Joe Lapchick, despite his team being among Harrison's selection of major league teams, branded the idea "ridiculous" and defended Tri-Cities and Fort Wayne, highlighting their competitive teams and financial success compared to Boston, Chicago, and St. Louis, three of Harrison's major league teams. He counter-proposed a complete geographical division of the league, with Western and Eastern teams playing separately until the NBA Finals.[19]

Eddie Gottlieb, single-handedly responsible for the league schedule, was more receptive to Harrison's idea than Lapchick's—Lapchick's proposal required reducing the schedule from 68 games to 54, and Gottlieb doubted the league's chances for survival with a schedule of fewer than 60 games—but did not fully endorse the idea of splitting the league, instead refraining from commenting any further other than an expression of surprise that there weren't two or three teams that had already dropped out. With more tact than Harrison had shown, he didn't specify which teams, but it was obvious that he was referring to Anderson, Waterloo, and Denver.[20]

Tri-Cities Blackhawks fans, misled by a local newspaper editor's claim that Eddie Gottlieb supported Les Harrison's idea, expressed their discontent toward Gottlieb during a game against the Warriors, booing and pelting him with wads of paper, with one man going as far as waving his hat in Gottlieb's face and cursing at him until Gottlieb hurdled the restraining ropes and chased the man down the aisle into the arms of a security guard. He clarified post-game that he was misquoted, acknowledging his belief in the league's unwieldiness, but that he lacked viable solutions, and that Syracuse and Tri-Cities were the two former NBL teams the BAA had specifically wanted in the merger.[21]

Even as a partisan former BAA leader, president of the NBA Maurice Podoloff wasn't at all happy with the notion that certain former NBL teams weren't up to snuff either. He received complaints from Kerner and Ike Duffey, with Kerner demanding Harrison be fined. While Harrison escaped a fine, Podoloff berated him for his inept handling of the situation and for going to the media before submitting a proposal to the league office.[22] The likelihood of Harrison's proposed league split materializing soon was effectively extinguished.

Podoloff, a Yale-educated lawyer, was born in Yelisavetgrad, Russia (now Kropyvnytskyi, Ukraine). Like Gottlieb, Kerner, and Ben Berger, he immigrated to the United States as a child with his family to escape anti–Semitic violence after the assassination of Emperor Aleksandr II. His family settled in Setauket, New York.

Moving to the outskirts of New Haven, Connecticut, Podoloff's father, Abraham, found work as an insurance agent and later established the successful A. Podoloff & Sons real estate company with strong ties to the local Republican Party.

Maurice and his brother Jacob joined the family business after college and played pivotal roles in its expansion, eventually representing Yale in acquiring the New Haven Hospital. In collaboration with lawyer Isadore Resnick, A. Podoloff & Sons acquired the property of the former Yale ice hockey team's arena, which had burned down, and formed the New Haven Arena Company to complete its construction. Nathan Podoloff, another brother, served as chief engineer and later became the arena manager.[23]

To provide the arena with a steady stream of events, Nathan and Maurice cofounded a minor league hockey team, the New Haven Eagles. The Eagles, minor league affiliates of the NHL's Boston Bruins, Montreal Canadiens, and New York Americans at various times, faced moderate success during their tenure in the Canadian-American Hockey League. In 1935–36, Maurice secured his first league office position as the secretary-treasurer of the Can-Am League.

By orchestrating a merger with the rival International Hockey League, which had undergone a drastic downsizing, Podoloff established the International-American Hockey League. As copresidents, Podoloff and John Chick helmed the league office, while both leagues retained the potential for independent operations. Following the final consolidation two years later, Podoloff assumed the role of the first president of the American Hockey League, skillfully steering the league through the tumultuous era of World War II and expanding its reach beyond the Northeastern United States, adding teams in Indianapolis, Washington, D.C., and St. Louis.[24]

The executive committee of the BAA initially pursued Asa Bushnell, executive director of the Eastern College Athletic Conference, for the role of president. When Bushnell's salary demands proved excessive, Chicago Stadium's Arthur Wirtz asked Cleveland Rebels owner Al Sutphin, who also owned the AHL's Cleveland Barons, about Podoloff's performance as AHL president. With Sutphin's answer, "He's doing a good job," the executive committee turned to Podoloff, who would take on the BAA position alongside his existing role as head of the AHL.[25] Within three years, he transformed the BAA from a market-driven, talent-deficient organization into the preeminent professional basketball league, compelling the long-established NBL to scramble to force a merger. When the merger went through, there was no question that it would be Podoloff running the NBA.

Podoloff had also discussed possibilities for the 1950–51 season, naturally having to plan ahead given the tumult the league faced surrounding the demise of the Oshkosh All-Stars. Publicly, he displayed a greater sense of optimism regarding small-market teams and the league's financial condition than the owners, even contemplating expansion to cities like Des Moines, Milwaukee, and Grand Rapids to increase the number of NBA teams to 20 and hinting at the idea of revisiting the original intended setup that included two divisions and two sections within each division.[26]

That also had to be put on the back burner for the foreseeable future, thanks to Harrison, as Podoloff had to quickly assemble a satisfactory plan for the upcoming season to assuage Kerner and Duffey's concerns. With limited time to flesh out his ideas, Podoloff simply assured them that each NBA team would play every other NBA team an equal number of times the next season—presumably two times at home and two times away, creating a 64-game schedule. Expansion and the introduction of conferences would have to wait.

8

Sales and Trades, the Playoff Picture Takes Shape, and Are Coaches People?

As debates raged among the league's decision-makers on the viability of big and small markets, some franchises in the former category were struggling just as much as those in the latter.

The St. Louis Bombers, amid a five-game losing streak, found themselves in a precarious position. Key players like Johnny Logan and Belus Smawley were underperforming, while top pick Ed Macauley contemplated retirement due to the physical toll of facing formidable centers night after night. Macauley was forthcoming in expressing his disillusionment, stating, "I used to love the game but I'm getting to hate it."[1]

As the Bombers faltered on the court, fan support dwindled, with a mere 1,487 attendees for a game hosting the Knicks barely surpassing 10 percent of the St. Louis Arena's capacity and a stark contrast to the enthusiasm during Macauley's debut just months earlier.[2]

Adding to the team's troubles, C. D. P. Hamilton, Jr., and Emory Jones publicly announced their intent to sell the franchise. Recognizing the Bombers' lack of profitability, the duo sought either a deep-pocketed investor capable of weathering the storm or a skilled promoter who could swiftly revamp the team's public image.[3]

Jones, formerly an internal auditor, assumed the role of arena manager for the St. Louis Arena in 1932 following its bankruptcy. Under his guidance, the venue expanded its repertoire, hosting diverse events such as ice hockey, figure skating, boxing, and notable occasions like the World Light Heavyweight Championship between John Henry Lewis and Bob Olin and a Wendell Willkie political rally that drew over 20,000 attendees.[4]

In 1941, Jones and Hamilton purchased the St. Louis Flyers hockey team and navigated them from the minor leagues to the AHL during World War II. Five years later, they established the Bombers in the BAA.

Jones hired Ken Loeffler, the sole original BAA coach with experience in professional, collegiate, and military leagues, to coach the Bombers in their debut season. After returning from World War II, Loeffler discovered that his coaching position at Yale University had been taken over by former MLB All-Star Red Rolfe. Refusing to accept an assistant role under a baseball player, Loeffler left and joined the University of Denver. His time there was short-lived too, as Denver reinstated the previous coach upon his return from military service, regardless of contractual obligations to Loeffler. The whole ordeal prompted Loeffler to publicly wonder, "Are coaches people?"[5]

Implementing a focus on conditioning and discipline once he got the Bombers job, Loeffler recruited mostly college rookies, believing continuous movement to be crucial for success in the professional game. His offensive strategy involved a continuous weave, while defensively the team started with a zone defense and shifted to man-to-man after substitutions. St. Louis started the season impressively at 21–8, but struggled after the BAA banned zone defense, and Loeffler eventually resigned over a bonus dispute following his second season with the team.[6] He went on to coach the Providence Steamrollers before returning to the college level.

Jones appointed Grady Lewis, a burly, skilled center who had a brief stint with the Bombers under Loeffler, as player-coach to replace him. Lewis expressed his intention to maintain the existing system, but the odds were always stacked against a rookie coach replicating the results of the iron-fisted 20-year veteran Loeffler.

As St. Louis continued to decline under Lewis' coaching in his second year, it became evident that he couldn't sustain Loeffler's basketball approach. Opposing defenses knew that St. Louis couldn't play up-tempo anymore because of a lack of depth and sagged off of shooters as they preferred the Bombers' perimeter players taking long-range shots over Ed Macauley getting post opportunities.

A St. Louis car salesman who had ties to the Harlem Globetrotters, Bob Soell, headed up a consortium of a dozen local businessmen aiming to purchase the team. Between his promoting skills and the money of his investors, Soell had a chance to be precisely what the Bombers needed, but he delayed making an offer until the summer, reluctant to assume the debts expected to accrue during the remainder of the season.[7]

Joe Fulks' rapid fall from BAA superstardom was an unwelcome sight for the nascent NBA, and for no one more than his coach, Eddie Gottlieb. After a lackluster return from a hip injury sustained during a drunken fall down his cellar stairs ahead of the 1949 playoffs, Fulks struggled to find consistent rhythm on the court.

He had 3-of-18, 4-of-22, 4-of-27, and 1-of-19 shooting nights within two weeks. Opposing fans took to taunting him by singing the pop song "Don't Cry, Joe (Let Her Go, Let Her Go, Let Her Go)" every time he missed a shot. Gottlieb, when asked about his team's inability to win, openly labeled Fulks the culprit, stating that he was now just an ordinary player.[8]

As quickly as his scoring had stopped, though, so did the slump. He averaged 19 points per game over a seven game stretch and then played one of his best games of the season against Tri-Cities, scoring 30 points to lead Philadelphia to an 83–72 win.[9]

Despite the improved performance, he dropped from third to fourth on the scoring leaderboard after a minor injury limited him to just two minutes in a game against the Knicks. Frank Brian, who had been consistently scoring over 20 points per game recently, surpassed him with a 33-point performance against Boston.

With Waterloo's loss to Boston the following day, the Hawks were eliminated from playoff contention, solidifying Indianapolis as the first team to qualify for the NBA playoffs. In many ways, this was mostly an example of how weak the bottom half of the Western Division was, considering five different teams throughout the league held better records than the Olympians at this point in time, but nonetheless, they were safe.

When Fulks' 30-point game spurred a Tri-Cities loss and Sheboygan pulled out a 68–65 win over Washington, it set the stage for a pivotal game between the Blackhawks and Redskins where the winner would gain a one-game advantage in the standings over the other. Tri-Cities took an early lead, and Sheboygan's inability to match them persisted after Bobby Cook injured his ankle in the first quarter. Tri-Cities won 86–71.

The Philadelphia Warriors heavily relied on Joe Fulks (right, March 19, 1949), as he had been the BAA's best scorer throughout the league's existence, as well as the architect of the Warriors' 1947 championship run. Both on-court complications and issues with alcoholism sapped him of much of his firepower that season, but he remained the Warriors' highest scorer. Coulby Gunther of the St. Louis Bombers at left.

Cook's X-rays revealed an avulsion fracture, leading to his extended absence.[10] Kenny Suesens promptly signed Stan Patrick, waived by Waterloo a month prior amid the Hawks' financial crisis, as a stopgap replacement. George Sobek, who joined the starting lineup while Patrick took over as the main bench guard, made an immediate impact by leading Sheboygan in scoring with 19 points in his first start, but couldn't prevent a loss to Syracuse, where Billy Gabor matched Sobek's output with 19 points of his own, while George Ratkovicz and Ed Peterson added 16 each.

Following the Denver Nuggets' announcement that players would receive only half their expected salary, two players, Al Guokas and Duane Klueh, requested a trade. Denver sold Guokas to Philadelphia and Klueh to Fort Wayne, allowing both players to return to their home state.[11] Fort Wayne, in need of wing depth, released Bill Henry to make room for Klueh. Henry immediately signed with Tri-Cities.

Bombers owner C. D. P. Hamilton, Jr., urged Ed Macauley to shoot more during a game against Indianapolis. The matchup drew a crowd of 8,487, the highest attendance for the Bombers that season, so this would naturally be an important game for Macauley to play well in.

Macauley responded to Hamilton's encouragement by scoring 29 points, leading St. Louis to a 76–64 upset victory. In the following game against Rochester, Macauley achieved a career-high 34 points on 20 shot attempts, but despite his efforts and Belus Smawley's 26 points, the Royals emerged victorious with a 90–84 win.[12]

Syracuse secured their playoff berth with six weeks left in the regular season, becoming the second team to do so, after the Boston Celtics lost to Chicago.

Adolph Schayes was the paragon of consistency for Syracuse, exemplifying unwavering consistency ranking in the top five for scoring, assists, and, unofficially, rebounding, with an overall impact comparable to the likes of George Mikan and Alex Groza. Despite being a year ahead in his professional career than Groza, Schayes was almost two years younger and the seventh-youngest player in the NBA. Schayes had ample room for growth and potential to become the NBA's leading figure once eventually.

The presence of players like Al Cervi, Billy Gabor, Alex Hannum, and George Ratkovicz provided a strong supporting cast that allowed Schayes to attack defenses with a diverse set of approaches offensively and focus most of his energy on rebounding while on defense.

Under Leo Ferris' leadership, the Syracuse Nationals made significant strides from their previous underwhelming NBL performance. Their owner, Danny Biasone, initially ran a basketball team as a side business to his bowling alley, but when he reached out to Leo Fischer to complain about the Royals' refusal to schedule a matchup, he was offered the opportunity to buy an NBL franchise.[13]

Facing competition from larger markets among other applicants, Biasone negotiated directly with Stanley Allmen to acquire the franchise slot from Allmen's disbanded Cleveland Transfers, securing entry into the league at double the $2,500 entry fee.[14] Minutes later, Ike Duffey bought Anderson's way into the league the same way by buying the defunct Pittsburgh Raiders. The Lakers were founded similarly the next season, acquiring the rights to the Detroit Gems for $15,000, making Biasone's $5,000 price seem like a great deal.

John Norlander of the Washington Capitols suffered a season-ending anterior cruciate ligament tear in a loss to the Hawks.[15] Guards Chick Reiser and Leo Katkaveck greatly benefited from Norlander's absence, with Reiser's penetration becoming even more crucial and Katkaveck securing 15 minutes of playing time each game after previously struggling to stay in the rotation.

The next day, Washington lost 71–59 to the Lakers, with player-coach Feerick turning back the clock to score a game-high 15 points but receiving little help. This loss was particularly disheartening as it marked their final game of the season against the Minneapolis team that had defeated them in the previous year's BAA Finals. They had lost all six matchups.

Sheboygan, without Bobby Cook, got revenge on Tri-Cities for beating them earlier in the week in the form of a 104–82 blowout win marred by a high number of fouls. Tri-Cities committed 48 fouls, while Sheboygan accounted for 41, nearing the 91 fouls the two teams had compiled early in the year. Eight players fouled out in total. Max Morris led the proceedings with 30 points, while Tri-Cities' Gene Englund scored 22 points. Sheboygan's win kept them just one game behind the Blackhawks in the standings.[16]

Meanwhile, the Indianapolis Olympians faced a slump, allowing Anderson to close the gap for the divisional lead. Anderson handed the Olympians their worst loss of the season with a score of 107–76. Frank Brian scored 20 points and Ed Stanczak, Milo Komenich, and John Hargis all scored 15 or more in order to pummel Indianapolis despite a solid 25-point outing from Alex Groza.[17]

This victory secured Anderson's playoff qualification and brought the Packers, at 27–21, within one and a half games of the Olympians, who lost their fifth game in the last six. Free from the fear of elimination, the Packers could focus fully on reclaiming the Western Division's top position from Indianapolis.

February 10 was the final day of the transaction season for the NBA's first year. After that, a moratorium would go into effect until the offseason, meaning the rosters in place as of the trade deadline would remain intact through the end of the playoffs aside from potential signings of free agents.

Eastern Division teams were actively exploring last-minute trade opportunities. Doggie Julian of the Boston Celtics initially pursued a deal with the St. Louis Bombers for Johnny Logan, but they refused to part with Logan, Red Rocha, or Ed Macauley. Julian pivoted to the possibility of acquiring Ace Maughan instead, but Lewis wanted a Celtics starter in return. Joe Lapchick of the Knicks wanted George Kaftan from the Celtics, but that deal didn't come close either.[18] Syracuse's Leo Ferris contacted nearly half the league inquiring about potential trades but preferred a straight cash deal without giving up any of Syracuse's own players, and teams weren't lining up to send their best players to the winningest team in the league without getting any talent in return.[19]

Prior to Chicago's game against Philadelphia that day, John Sbarbaro of the Stags engaged in negotiations with Eddie Gottlieb, proposing to trade Stan Miasek and Joe Graboski to the Warriors for Joe Fulks. Gottlieb's asking price was one of the mentioned players plus one of either Andy Phillip, Max Zaslofsky, or Odie Spears. Sbarbaro wasn't willing to part with any of those three and the deal broke down. Fulks missed the first 10 shots he took that night and the Warriors lost 83–76.[20]

By the end of the day, only one trade had actually been completed. The Washington Capitols traded Jack Nichols to Tri-Cities for Don Otten and $5,000 after a month of negotiations between Mike Fitzgerald and Washington general manager Bob Foster.[21]

Otten, who was no longer clearly the star of the Blackhawks less than a year after winning NBL MVP, was too slow and too big to fit with Auerbach's active playstyle, as Fitzgerald and Auerbach's aggressive rebuild made Tri-Cities almost unrecognizable from the previous year.

Nichols, a young and agile player, presented challenges for the Blackhawks when facing larger centers, but he and the recently acquired Bill Henry could be deployed similar to Auerbach's usage of Nichols and Kleggie Hermsen against George Mikan the year before. Astonishingly, this was the 15th transaction involving the Blackhawks since the season opener and Nichols became the 22nd player to join their team that season.

On paper, the long-term impact of Nichols would certainly outweigh that of Otten, but Otten's potential was already fully realized, and for an aging Capitols team, all that mattered was increasing the chance of pulling off consecutive playoff upsets against the Knicks and Nationals, neither of whom were built to stop the tallest player in the NBA. Given that all playoff-bound Eastern Division teams were in the league's bottom half in tempo, Otten was well-suited for the division.

Auerbach guided the Blackhawks to a surprising number of victories despite a complete and utter lack of continuity and low expectations, with a similar record to Bob Feerick, who had inherited a team Auerbach had just led to the BAA Finals.

It was apparent that Mike Uline's decision to offer Red Auerbach only a one-year contract was a colossal mistake. Feerick simply couldn't match his coaching prowess, and Auerbach, as the Capitols would need to in the coming years, had taken just months to fully regear his new team for the future.

The Central Division standings were finally relatively stable, with Minneapolis leading Rochester by a couple of games, followed by a three-and-a-half-game gap between Rochester and Chicago, and another three-and-a-half-game difference between Chicago and Fort Wayne.

Rochester and Fort Wayne faced off in a two-game series, marking Arnie Risen's return from injury. His rebounding was much needed for Rochester, but his minutes restriction prevented him and the other frontcourt players from gaining momentum. Bob Davies carried the Royals with 29 points in the first contest, but Fort Wayne emerged victorious with a balanced team effort.

The following night, the Pistons secured another win, 76–74. For the Royals, it was simply a case of too little, too late, as they once trailed 60–44 and couldn't quite come back from that deficit. Those two games knocked Rochester down to 35–16, equally close to Chicago as they were to catching up to the Lakers.[22]

Meanwhile, the Redskins' pursuit of reclaiming third place in the Western Division wasn't going as planned. In the first game of Tri-Cities' post–Don Otten era, Tri-Cities fell short 95–89 against Indianapolis despite Jack Nichols and Mike Todorovich leading the way with 18 points each.[23]

This gave Sheboygan a chance to surpass the Blackhawks, with two consecutive games against the league-worst Nuggets. They lost both.

Dillard Crocker and Kenny Sailors propelled Denver to a resounding 108–78 victory in the first, with Crocker scoring 32 points and Sailors contributing 29. Sailors followed that up with 27 points in the repeat win two days later.[24]

The struggling Baltimore Bullets were sold to a local conglomerate called Civic Sports of Baltimore, Inc., for $30,000, with Jake Embry retaining some shares but stepping down as president. Joe Rash, owner of a Food Fair grocery store franchise, became the new president, while Buddy Jeannette continued as coach and took over Bill Dyer's front office duties.[25]

With six losses in their last seven games following an 86–67 loss to Indianapolis, the Philadelphia Warriors, now two and a half games behind Baltimore, were coming dangerously close to falling out of the playoff race. For the team to finish the season with a winning record was now a mathematical impossibility, and the Warriors' poor performance felt peculiar, given the presence of Joe Fulks and Eddie Gottlieb.

There was also the matter that Philadelphia had the most prestigious professional basketball history of any city in the United States. The very first professional basketball league counted three Philadelphia teams and one right across the river in Camden, New Jersey, among its six founding members. Up until World War I, Pennsylvania continued to host the majority of the best professional teams and players in the world. In the same way that Massachusetts was the birthplace of basketball as a whole, Pennsylvania was the breeding ground of professional basketball, and the Warriors' languishing, alongside the Celtics, at the bottom of the Eastern Division as the end of the first NBA season neared was a poor tribute to this rich legacy.

Making things more difficult for Boston and Philadelphia was that the Bullets, one and a half games ahead of the Celtics and two and a half games ahead of the Warriors, were returning to full health for the first time since December, with Buddy Jeannette and Tommy Byrnes back from their respective injuries.

As Arnie Risen struggled to regain his fitness, Rochester posed no real threat to the Minneapolis Lakers, who won 92–70 with George Mikan scoring 34 points opposite his brother, and with Jack Coleman shifting to power forward to make way for Ed Mikan while Risen remained a substitute. Jim Pollard contributed an additional 21 points for Minneapolis. This was the tenth consecutive win for the Lakers, who were at the peak of their powers and had only lost three of their last 26 games.[26]

The following game against St. Louis, Mikan sealed the Lakers' victory with a clutch free throw after being fouled by Red Rocha with just two seconds remaining, ending the game with a 72–71 Lakers win with St. Louis unable to get a shot off.

Although he calmly sank the game-winning free throw, Mikan hadn't played great, as Macauley held him to 21 points on 6-of-22 shooting. This wasn't the first time Macauley limited Mikan's scoring, as he had previously held him below 20 on three previous occasions. The Lakers were kept in the game by Jim Pollard, who scored 25 points on 11-of-28 shooting.[27] The victory secured the Lakers' spot in the playoffs and extended their lead over the Royals to four games.

As they aimed to catch up with Minneapolis, Rochester would have to fight their next few battles without Arnie Risen, who had to return home to Kentucky as his father recuperated from a stroke. Risen was still clearly hobbled by his bad knee and had only averaged 4.6 points in restricted playing time in the five games since his return from injury, but his absence would be felt regardless.[28]

During this stretch, the Royals, led by Bob Davies, embraced a faster tempo that their Eastern Division opponents were not accustomed to, resulting in impressive victories. Against Boston, who had lost George Kaftan to a strained hamstring, Davies, Bobby Wanzer, Fran Curran, and Red Holzman all scored 15 points or more in a 94–73 blowout win.

In their game against the New York Knicks, who were missing Carl Braun with a thumb sprain, Davies took control and the team shot an impressive 38-of-63 from the field, securing a 105–92 victory. Although these wins didn't close the gap with Minneapolis, who refused to lose, they solidified the Royals' playoff qualification, and they were now five games ahead of the division's third-place team.

That third-place team was no longer Chicago, who had lost their last three games.

Fort Wayne had overtaken them by winning four of five games in five days following their consecutive wins over Rochester the previous week.

Led by Fred Schaus on offense, the Fort Wayne Pistons showcased a strong frontcourt with bruising big men who contributed both offensively and defensively. Bob Carpenter, alongside Howie Schultz, emerged as a key player and the team's second-leading scorer since the trade of Charlie Black. The Pistons also had rookies Jack Kerris and Bob Harris providing valuable depth options. Coach Murray Mendenhall often adjusted the lineup to give playing time for the rookies to develop, moving Schaus to the backcourt and Carpenter to small forward in order to slot either Kerris or Harris into the power forward position.

Ever since arriving in Fort Wayne, Ralph Johnson kept a stranglehold over the point guard position that had belonged to Curly Armstrong and John Oldham for the first half of the season. The shooting guard position saw fluctuating stability, with Armstrong alternating between starting and coming off the bench. Oldham's height allowed him to occasionally start alongside Johnson instead, while the arrival of Duane Klueh added another starting option. Leo Klier, who had started in Armstrong's place earlier in the year, found himself on the outskirts of the team's rotation due to Klueh's arrival, and now had only about a quarter each game to make his impact.

As the Pistons surpassed Chicago in the Central Division, the race between the other two Indiana teams, Indianapolis and Anderson, was tightening as the Olympians couldn't catch a break at the end of games.

First was against Waterloo, when they held a 74–73 lead with 11 seconds left after a clutch layup by Carl Shaeffer, who previously hadn't attempted a shot all game. Five seconds later, Bruce Hale fouled Waterloo's Harry Boykoff. Boykoff made the free throw, won the jump ball by tapping it to Dick Mehen, and scored the game-winning buzzer-beater when Mehen passed back to him. Waterloo won 76–74.[29]

In their next game, the Olympians squandered an 11-point lead to the Capitols when Don Otten outplayed Alex Groza in the second half and controlled the rebounding down the stretch. Chick Reiser hit a pair of free throws with 44 seconds left in the game to put Washington up 81–79 and the Olympians failed to equalize in their last two possessions.[30]

The following day, facing the Syracuse Nationals without Al Cervi, Indianapolis had an opportunity to take a late lead, but even four offensive rebounds on the same possession wasn't enough for the Olympians to come away with two points. George Ratkovicz finally wrangled the ball into Syracuse's control, prompting Wah Wah Jones to foul him. Ratkovicz made the free throw, won the tip, and Adolph Schayes sealed the result with a layup to finish off an 82–78 victory. With three losses that came down to the final minute, Indianapolis now only led the Packers by one game, and they would have been tied if it weren't for Kenny Sailors' 31 points and Floyd Volker's game-winning jump shot with 16 seconds left propelling Denver to a home win over Anderson.[31]

After that surprising 86–85 win, the Nuggets hosted Syracuse, who were now without an ill Billy Gabor in addition to Cervi, resulting in sloppy passing that Sailors and Dillard Crocker capitalized on. Sailors scored a season-high 33 points, leading Denver to an 89–78 win despite Schayes' 31 points for Syracuse.[32]

That was the Nuggets' fifth win in six games, a shocking development after a 6–39 start to the season. Most crucial to Denver's sudden change in fortune was Sailors' 27.3 points per game during the latest stretch, along with the improved contributions of Crocker and Bob Brown.

Denver needed a minimum of nine wins in their last 11 games to have a shot at playoff qualification, though, and the playoff window was closing rapidly as teams entered the final stage of the season. On the day Denver beat Syracuse, New York stamped their ticket to the playoffs when Baltimore blew a fourth quarter lead to the Pistons. Tri-Cities joined them with their own victory over the Bullets the following day. Seven of the 12 spots in the playoffs were now taken.

A total of 21,666 fans, an all-time world record for a professional basketball game, packed into the 17,000-capacity Chicago Stadium ahead of the Stags' game against Baltimore on February 21. Almost none of them were there to watch Chicago play.

Despite having never fielded a losing basketball team, the Stags were consistent recipients of dismal attendance, often attracting 5,000 or fewer spectators. In an effort to stem the bleeding, John Sbarbaro scheduled doubleheaders featuring other NBA matchups or the Harlem Globetrotters preceding the Stags' games.

This particular doubleheader featured the Harlem Globetrotters and the Minneapolis Lakers, considered the best black and white teams in professional basketball, respectively. The Globetrotters had previously won two out of three matchups against the Lakers largely due to the efforts of Marques Haynes, a lightning-fast point guard with an incredible top dribbling speed of almost six times per second; Goose Tatum, their "Clown Prince" with an iconic no-look hook shot and a unique blend of basketball and comedy; and the more straitlaced Ermer Robinson, who had hit an unforgettable buzzer-beating shot in their first win over the Lakers.

On this occasion, none of the Globetrotters players could contain George Mikan, and as a result, the game was a walkover. Mikan ended the game with 36 points as the Lakers won 76–60. Haynes was the sole double-digit scorer for the Globetrotters with 16 points, while Mikan received support from Mikkelsen's 13 points and Pollard's 12.[33]

The next day was the final game of the Lakers' month-long 14-game winning streak, and, at 43–13, they were closing in on the Syracuse Nationals' league-best 41–9 record. Against St. Louis, Minneapolis delivered the most lopsided victory of the year. Mikan scored 28 points, Pollard added 20, and the Lakers won 100–57.[34] Their 43-point margin of victory not only broke the NBA record, but also topped the BAA record margin of 39 and tied the NBL record set in 1945–46.

Minneapolis' early-season mediocrity had, at this point, pretty clearly been a temporary outcome of integrating rookies into the defending champion's roster, now having won 27 of the last 30 games.

Initially, John Kundla planned on continuing as he had the previous year, with Herman Schaefer at point guard, Don Carlson at shooting guard, Arnie Ferrin at small forward, Pollard at power forward, and Mikan at center; the same unit that had started in the 1949 BAA Finals. Only Mikan and Pollard remained as consistent starters by the time of their winning streak.

Schaefer was the Lakers' most experienced player and ensured their composed, Mikan-centric offense, prioritizing controlled plays over fast breaks and long-distance shots. Military service had caused him to miss both of the Zollners' championship seasons during his time as a Fort Wayne player, but he was a two-time champion anyway with Minneapolis, present for both their 1947–48 NBL title and their 1948–49 BAA title.

Carlson, who began his professional career with the Stags in Chicago, returned to his hometown Lakers as one of Kundla's initial signings after starting for Chicago in the inaugural BAA Finals. The other first signing was Tony Jaros, a streaky-shooting wing who'd started alongside Carlson both at Minnesota and for the Stags.

Ferrin, in his second year after an accomplished college career at the University of Utah, where he'd become the first four-time All-American in nearly two decades and starred for the 1944 national champions, had initially faced challenges breaking into the established rotation as a rookie but eventually became a permanent starter after getting a shot when Pollard was injured.

In December, shooting guard Carlson lost his starting position to Vern Mikkelsen, prompting Ferrin to shift to the backcourt and Pollard to small forward. Ferrin followed Carlson to the bench unit soon after. While Carlson experienced a slight decrease in playing time, Ferrin's minutes were cut in half.

His replacement was Bob Harrison, the Lakers' second-round pick in the 1949 draft. Harrison was a constant scoring threat, adept at driving to the basket and proficient in his long-range set shot. Nothing exemplified that more than the fact that he held the all-time men's record for points in a game, having once scored 139 points in a 139–8 win when he was in eighth grade.[35] Since then, he had rounded out his game to include playmaking skills and decent defense, and as a rookie he embraced the Lakers' system enough to produce about as many assists as field goals.

Being basketball's record-holder for scoring wasn't the only thing that made Harrison one of a kind in the NBA. Harrison, biracial with white and indigenous Native American ancestry, was also the unofficially segregated league's only self-avowed person of color. His father was a member of the Winnebago Tribe of Nebraska and received his education at the Hampton Normal and Agricultural Institute, an HBCU.[36]

In late January, rookies Mikkelsen and Harrison were joined by Slater Martin starting at point guard, replacing Herman Schaefer, who was beginning to lose a step defensively. Ever since Martin was added to the starting lineup, they hadn't lost once.

The frontcourt hierarchy was much more straightforward. Once Mikkelsen was a regular starter, only Ferrin remained as a frontcourt bench player, while Jaros, more naturally a shooting guard, could cover spot minutes at small forward. Both Mikkelsen and Pollard could shift to center if necessary, allowing Ferrin or Jaros to step in as small forward while Mikan, Mikkelsen, or Pollard needed rest. It still wasn't optimal to have no other post player, so to remedy that, Max Winter signed Bud Grant, a power forward who had just been ruled ineligible, midseason, from the University of Minnesota.

Bob Feerick's coaching decisions and the absence of John Norlander due to injury proved costly for the Capitols as they lost a winnable game against the Knicks. The seven-inch mismatch between 5'10" Fred Scolari and 6'5" Carl Braun allowed Braun to repeatedly drive into the paint and use his size to score with ease over Scolari and score 38 points on 10-of-18 shooting while attempting an NBA record 26 free throws. To make matters worse for Washington, Bones McKinney exited the game with a broken hand that Feerick predicted would keep him tethered to the bench for the next three weeks.[37]

In the Capitols' subsequent game against Boston, the Celtics oddball trio of Tony Lavelli, Howie Shannon, and Bob Doll combined for 49 points in a comfortable win that put one and a half games between themselves and the Warriors. Ed Leede and Shannon scored 22 and 18 points, respectively, in the next game as Boston defeated Baltimore and drew even with the Bullets for fourth place in the Eastern Division.[38]

Syracuse erased a 49–30 halftime deficit to the Olympians by holding Indianapolis to just 18 points in the second half as Adolph Schayes and George Ratkovicz doubled down on bringing the game directly to Alex Groza.[39] This doomed the Olympians to their fifth consecutive loss and the Anderson Packers once again were at the top of the division.

Arnie Risen returned from family leave and Rochester managed to end the Lakers' winning streak, despite trailing 25–10 by the early second quarter. Risen's week off allowed his knee to heal enough that he was finally capable of playing more than half a game of basketball, but George Mikan had his way with his rival big man, outscoring Risen 39 to seven.

Mikan and Vern Mikkelsen accounted for all but two of the Lakers' first-quarter points, and that set the tone for how Minneapolis would play the entire game. Every single member of the Lakers backcourt went scoreless, and as Red Holzman took charge of the game in the second quarter and launched a comeback effort that Bill Calhoun and Bob Davies would soon join in on, Mikan had very little help to ward off the Royals. Aside from Mikan, Mikkelsen contributed 14 points and Pollard scored 10, while the impact of the other seven Lakers consisted solely of one made free throw from Tony Jaros. The Lakers were finally beaten, 66–64, and Rochester, in doing so, extended their own streak to five consecutive wins.[40]

The next day, Rochester was tasked with staving off a St. Louis Bombers team that had both Ed Macauley and Belus Smawley putting together top-notch offensive games. Macauley scored 31 points on 19 shots and Smawley added 19 points on 13 shots.[41]

The Royals continued their winning ways against the Bombers, however, narrowly prevailing when reserve power forward Andy Duncan, who was only in the game because of his teammates' foul trouble, tipped in a missed shot attempt just before the buzzer sounded. Rochester won 81–79, with Bob Davies leading them in scoring with 18 points. St. Louis' loss guaranteed the Fort Wayne Pistons a playoff spot.

With their season a lost cause, Denver shifted its focus from competitiveness to financial survival. With the worst team in the NBA, the Nuggets rarely received much fan support, and even reducing player salaries by half couldn't prevent the franchise from operating at a deficit. General manager Hal Davis devised an unconventional solution by selling the rights to their remaining home games to visiting teams for $1,500 each. Denver would now end the season with ten consecutive away games.[42]

Against the Hawks, Denver had an opportunity to narrow the gap with Waterloo to one game and potentially climb out of the NBA's gutter. However, Harry Boykoff and his Hawks teammates dominated the rebounding battle, resulting in Waterloo having 29 more shot attempts than Denver. Despite Dillard Crocker's 26 points, the game was never close after the first quarter, and Waterloo secured a comfortable 100–76 win.[43]

Star power defined the inter–Western Division game between Indianapolis and Sheboygan that day. The forward pairing of Max Morris and Bob Brannum led the Redskins, with Morris scoring 26 points and Brannum adding 20 points and 8 assists. Indianapolis relied on the usual suspects of Alex Groza and Ralph Beard. Those two combined with Bruce Hale to combine for 85 points, just one less than Sheboygan's total. Despite the one-sided score of 107–86 in the Olympians' favor, Sheboygan found solace in Bobby Cook's return to action after a three-week absence in which the Redskins had gone just 2–7.[44]

Beard and Groza made history as the first teammates to score 30 or more points each in a single NBA game. This feat had only occurred once before in professional basketball, when Max Zaslofsky and Gene Vance, playing for the Stags a year earlier to the day, scored 35 and 30 respectively. Beard recorded 13 assists alongside his 34 points, becoming the first player ever to produce a game with 30-plus points and 10-plus assists.

Syracuse continued to assert their status as the best team in the league, boasting a 44–9 record after defeating the fatigued and foul-prone Stags, who were playing their ninth game in as many days. The Nationals' success was evidence that team basketball was just as viable as Minneapolis' and Indianapolis' style of play and an indicator of Al Cervi's man management skills, especially considering none of their role players began the season with a particularly impressive pedigree.

Adolph Schayes had shown signs of becoming an important player as a professional ever since very early in his college career, and Al Cervi was well-known for being one of the greatest players in basketball before he even arrived in Syracuse. Out of the other starters, though, Billy Gabor had averaged just 6.1 points as a 26-year-old rookie the year before. Paul Seymour, at small forward, had been a starter for less than half a season's worth of games in his previous three seasons combined, and two of their three options at center had been career bench players up to that point.

Alex Hannum, who started in the post next to Schayes in most games, had backed up Gene Englund in Oshkosh the year before, and George Ratkovicz, who was proving to be quite offensively capable at both power forward and center, had been stuck on the bench behind George Mikan, Arnie Risen, and Don Otten in the three previous successive years. Ed Peterson had started the year before for Syracuse, but that was mostly due to limited options, and this year, even with the presence of the other two higher in the Nationals' rotation cutting into his playing time, his performance improved significantly.

From the bench unit, wings Johnny Macknowski and Fuzzy Levane, as well as rookie point guard Ray Corley, added hustle and spurts of energy to distract from the abundance of big men. Macknowski, like Cervi and Seymour, was a defensive asset, with great anticipation on that side of the ball and a reliable long-range set shot on offense. Corley was a steady ball handler, considering his lack of experience, and his presence allowed Cervi to ramp down his own workload for the sake of his coaching role. Levane, known for his shooting ability and veteran experience, found himself relegated to the last spot in Cervi's rotation, mostly useful as an unofficial bench coach whenever Cervi was in the game.

Bob Feerick upended the tail end of the Capitols' season a bit when it became public news on February 27 that he would be stepping down at the end of the season to take the open Santa Clara University coaching job.[45]

This decision likely meant the end of his playing career as well; juggling a collegiate coaching job and a professional playing career wasn't unheard of, but doing so with teams nearly 2,500 miles away from each other would be a logistical impossibility.

Feerick had been replaceable as a player ever since his knee injury, his coaching tenure wasn't outstanding, and it wasn't much of a surprise that he would return to his alma mater eventually, but with 10 games left in the season, plus, in all likelihood, the playoffs, his imminent departure had the potential to seriously impact team dynamics, especially with Mike Uline's reluctance to offer long-term contracts meaning Feerick's replacement would likely be a player-coach chosen from the existing roster.

9

Baltimore vs. Boston vs. Philadelphia, a Crowd of Just 700, and King Fulks

The arrival of March brought the harsh reality of playoff eliminations to several teams.

Denver suffered without Kenny Sailors as they faced Tri-Cities, falling to the Blackhawks despite a 27-point effort from Dillard Crocker. The Blackhawks won 97–80 with Mike Todorovich and Murray Wier tying for a team-high 17 points and Dike Eddleman adding 16. Now 11–44, Denver's playoff hopes were officially dashed.[1]

In the Central Division, Fort Wayne's collective effort led to a 75–70 Pistons win despite Ed Macauley's 23-point effort, and when Chicago defeated Washington by one point, the Bombers' death knell rang—Chicago was now qualified for the division's final playoff spot and St. Louis, on the same day as Denver, was eliminated. The Capitols and Stags met again the next day and clutch play from Fred Scolari, who scored 28 points, secured a 91–88 win for Washington.

With the playoff race still tight, Boston faced crucial away games against Baltimore and Philadelphia. Baltimore led with a 22–36 record, while Boston was just half a game behind at 21–36 and Philadelphia just one game below the Celtics at 21–38. After a Baltimore loss to New York, the Celtics' matchup against the Warriors could potentially propel them ahead of the Bullets into fourth place or allow the Warriors to tie for fifth.

Boston took an early 7–0 lead and maintained control through the rest of the half with a selfless offensive approach, but in the second half, Vern Gardner and Ron Livingstone made it difficult for Boston to grab rebounds. Quality passing all-around ensured numerous scoring opportunities for Leo Mogus and Gardner, who scored 27 and 20 points, respectively. Joe Fulks played only seven minutes, shooting 0-of-4 from the field and 0-of-1 from the free throw line. For the first time in his career—in the NBA, BAA, service leagues, college, or high school—Fulks completed a game of basketball scoreless.[2]

Gardner, Livingstone, and George Senesky had become crucial for the Warriors as Eddie Gottlieb reworked the system midseason to be less reliant on Fulks. Gardner's versatility on defense and boundless motor were what attracted the Warriors to him, who initially sought to mitigate Fulks' defensive shortcomings, but his finishing ability led him to often be a more potent scorer than Fulks as well.

Gardner wasn't particularly comfortable with the ball in his hands for a small forward, having primarily played in the post during his college career. As such, his scoring opportunities primarily came from cutting rather than driving. Gottlieb adopted a pivot strategy utilizing Livingstone as a high-post playmaker to find Gardner or other Warriors players on cuts.

Senesky, the starting point guard for the Warriors, transitioned from an offensive star in college to a defensive standout by his rookie season. After serving in the U.S. Army and gaining coaching experience there, Senesky recognized the importance of defensive play and focused on it despite having led the NCAA in scoring and earned National Player of the Year honors in 1942–43. In this defensive role, he played a key part in a BAA championship.

Now in his fourth season, Senesky expanded his skills to include passing and playmaking, taking on the role of the team's primary playmaker after Howie Dallmar's retirement. He thrived in this role, finishing fifth in the league in assists. This season, he was on track to repeat that.

Alongside him in the backcourt, Chink Crossin had retired from the Warriors to pursue a career in television but changed his mind and rejoined the team 12 days before the start of the NBA season.[3] His late return resulted in a rusty start, but he gradually regained his form and reclaimed his starting position in January.

Leo Mogus, humorously referred to as "Marco Polo" around the league due to his journeyman career, began the season as a backup but received more playing time as it became evident that Fulks was declining.[4] By February and March, he was starting just as often as Fulks was, earning more minutes in most games, and becoming a consistent source of interior scoring, as he averaged 17.0 points over a period of 15 games.

Aside from whoever of Fulks or Mogus didn't start on a given day, Jake Bornheimer was the first guy off the bench. Livingstone's backup at center, Bornheimer impressed with his scrappiness and mobility. Guards Nelson Bobb and Jerry Fleishman, who both specialized in long-range shooting, made up the rest of the rotation.

By beating the Celtics, Philadelphia caught up to Boston in the standings, trailing Baltimore by only half a game. The next day, Baltimore was blown out by Minneapolis, 28 points from Tony Lavelli wasn't enough for Boston to overcome the Knicks, and the Warriors were now tied with the Bullets for fourth in the division.

The Packers faced a grueling stretch of five games in five days as they duked it out with Indianapolis for the Western Division title. The Olympians, conversely, had no more back-to-backs, and three of their final four games were going to be at home against either Waterloo or Denver, neither of whom had ever beaten the Olympians in Indianapolis.

Anderson and Indianapolis had two games left against each other, though, one in Indianapolis and one in Anderson, and those would, in all likelihood, decide the divisional title. Before then, Anderson had a relatively easy win over Denver, though, while Indianapolis lost to Tri-Cities. Jack Nichols played his best game since being traded to the Blackhawks, scoring 22 points and holding Alex Groza to seven points on 2-of-11 shooting, and set the tone for a 96–83 win.[5]

The Warriors then toppled Minneapolis 66–61, with four players in double figures but none scoring more than George Senesky's 14.[6] Philadelphia's victory catapulted them past Baltimore, giving them sole possession of fourth place in the Eastern Division for the first time since November 8, when they were 1–3 and Baltimore and Boston were both winless.

That only lasted for one day, when Carlisle Towery of the Bullets single-handedly launched a Baltimore comeback against Chicago with four straight baskets to tie the Warriors once again, a game and a half above the Celtics.[7]

The Syracuse Nationals and Minneapolis Lakers faced off in their final regular-season matchup, with the two teams expected to finish the season with the NBA's two best records. Syracuse, despite having lost three of their previous four games, led the league at 45–12 and the Lakers weren't far off at 47–15.

Despite an early lead by Minneapolis, a scoring run led by Adolph Schayes gave Syracuse the lead until the second quarter. The game remained competitive, with Syracuse countering each Lakers' surge. Mikkelsen fouled out early in the fourth quarter and a series of fouls hindered Minneapolis in the final few minutes. Syracuse won 84–75, with Schayes scoring 28 points to Mikan's 29.

The Nationals' trio of centers—Alex Hannum, Ed Peterson, and George Ratkovicz—held Mikan to 9-of-29 shooting from the field, but Mikan's first points of the game, in the form of a hook shot, led him to reach 1,700 total points for the season, two more than the all-time record for a professional basketball season, which he had set at 1,698 the season prior.[8]

The Tri-Cities Blackhawks had found stability, now targeting a .500 record or higher with a 29–32 record and five games remaining, with an 8–5 record in that period slightly surpassing the season-long winning percentages of playoff-bound Anderson and Indianapolis. With the trade deadline passed, the team had achieved a month of roster continuity. Before the deadline, the longest Tri-Cities had gone without making a roster move was 16 days.

The evolution of the Blackhawks' starting lineup throughout the season amid the flurry of transactions was complicated, to say the least, and Dike Eddleman was the only player to remain a starter for the Blackhawks all season long. Under Roger Potter's leadership, the starting lineup consisted of Billy Hassett, Whitey Von Nieda, Eddleman, Warren Perkins, and Don Otten, but it took just six games, and two games into Red Auerbach's tenure as coach, for that to change, with Von Nieda benched and eventually sold, Eddleman moved to shooting guard, Perkins moving to small forward, and Don Ray taking the power forward position. Ray's time as a starter was short-lived as Mike Todorovich joined the team; around that same time, Murray Wier took over as point guard upon Hassett's departure to Minneapolis. Less than a week after being benched, Ray returned to the starting five in Perkins' place, a decision that was reversed less than a month later, around the time Dee Gibson took Wier's starting spot.

That was the final change in the lineup before the trade of Otten for Nichols, but since then, Auerbach had continued to make adjustments, introducing Walt Kirk and Gene Vance as the new starting backcourt. Eddleman returned to the frontcourt alongside Todorovich and Nichols, while Gibson and Perkins were relegated to the bench.

The frontcourt trio of Eddleman, Mike Todorovich, and Jack Nichols formed the team's core, with Todorovich leading in points and assists. Kirk was the weakest link out of the starting five, and as a result, Auerbach, in addition to keeping both Gibson and Wier in the rotation, often paired Vance with Eddleman in the backcourt, with Perkins inserted as the other wing. Ray was largely made redundant by the additions of Gene Englund and Bill Henry in the frontcourt and, not long removed from his time as a starter, was now the last player off the bench.

Rochester, with Arnie Risen closer to normal than he had been since January, was inconspicuously beginning to catch up to Minneapolis. With back-to-back wins over Fort Wayne coinciding with the Lakers' loss to Syracuse, the Royals' winning streak was extended to nine and they were now just a game and a half behind Minneapolis with six games left to make up the remaining margin. Standing in the way of that was the sprained ankle of the Royals' star point guard, Bob Davies, which he suffered in the third quarter of the second game against the Pistons. With just over two weeks until the start of the playoffs, he wouldn't have much time to rest his ankle and recover. For the immediate future, Red Holzman would take the reins of the backcourt and Risen and Bobby Wanzer would have to share most of the scoring load.

The Anderson Packers continued their winning streak by defeating Tri-Cities with a strong second-half performance, outscoring their opponents 44–25 in the final 16 minutes en route to an 88–77 win. Brian led the way with 26 points and Anderson's lead over Indianapolis increased to a game and a half.[9]

With 15 games scoring 20 points or more out of the last 22, Brian was crucial to the Packers, but the elimination from playoff contention of Denver, despite Kenny Sailors, and St. Louis, despite Ed Macauley, indicated that a one-man show alone was not sufficient for success.

The Packers' unique counter-attacking system and fast-break style posed a distinct challenge for opponents. John Hargis, who shifted from small forward to shooting guard after the Pistons trade, excelled at stretching the defense with a catapulting, low-arcing shot, but his speed, fluidity with the ball in his hands, and efficient scoring made him a seamless fit next to Brian in the backcourt.

Charlie Black, a center while at Fort Wayne, moved back to power forward with Anderson. While this move allowed him to play his natural position, he had to adapt to a more outside-focused role.

Komenich, once Black's backup, took over as the center. Often operating out of the high post on the left side, Komenich's left-handedness, shooting range, and agility despite standing 6'7" and 220 lbs. made him a unique challenge for tall opposing centers.

In previous seasons, Closs primarily contributed as a defensive bloodhound who came off the bench to pester high-scoring power forwards and centers. His timing had always been his biggest plus and led him to grab plenty of rebounds and deflect the ball out of opposing players' hands, but his offensive game steadily improved, and now as a starter he was the Packers' second-highest scorer and best rebounder.

As with the Lakers, the lack of frontcourt backups meant Anderson attempted to keep two of the frontcourt starters on the court at all times to fill the two post positions. Hargis or Ed Stanczak often filled in at small forward when one of the trio rested. The other three members of the bench were all guards or wings, the recently acquired Jim Owens and Richie Niemiera as well as 30-year-old veteran Frank Gates.

In their upcoming game against the Olympians, Anderson had the opportunity to extend their divisional lead or allow Indianapolis to narrow the gap. The game began with a series of back-and-forth runs, until Alex Groza stole the ball on three consecutive possessions in the third quarter, leading to a Groza jump shot, a Paul Walther bank shot, and a Ralph Beard three-point play, giving the Olympians a four-point lead. Black and Closs soon fouled out and Indianapolis took advantage, ultimately winning 107–93. Beard scored 16 points in the fourth quarter alone for Indianapolis and finished with 30 points on 11-of-24 shooting.[10]

Three months after first being stricken with pneumonia, Noble Jorgensen's quality of play had begun to bounce back as he scored 18 and 21 points in consecutive games. With Jorgensen returning to form and Bobby Cook back from his broken ankle,

Sheboygan was as much of a threat to pull off an upset in the playoffs as anyone, despite their poor record.

Against Minneapolis, Jorgensen continued his scoring streak with 23 points, simultaneously holding George Mikan to a career-low eight points, his lowest scoring total since his freshman year at DePaul. With Mikan only playing about 20 minutes, Vern Mikkelsen and Tony Jaros stepped up, with 19 and 17 points, respectively, leading Minneapolis to a comfortable win by a score of 90–73.[11]

Eddie Gottlieb figured he could force Mikan to replicate his poor game the following night by instructing his players to foul him as soon as he touched the ball in order to limit him to one point per possession instead of two, since non-shooting fouls only led to a single free throw.

At first, the method worked even though Mikan was making his free throws at an inordinate rate, simply because the league had not anticipated a coach employing an intentional fouling tactic throughout the entire game, rather than as a last-minute act of desperation. Gottlieb, as a member of the NBA Rules and Competition Committee, was aware of, and partially responsible for, that oversight. The Warriors controlled the course of a slow-paced, ugly game until they held a 60–48 lead with eight minutes remaining, courtesy of both his tactic and Jim Pollard's persistence despite a 2-of-19 performance out of fear that a pass to Mikan would again result in one free throw attempt instead of a chance for two points.

As the number of Mikan foul shots rose into the high teens, Ron Livingstone and Mike Novak both fouled out, forcing Joe Fulks—five inches shorter, 55 pounds lighter, and notoriously poor at defense—to guard Mikan. Bob Harrison cut Philadelphia's lead to 10 with a long-range bomb, and after that, Mikan and Vern Mikkelsen were responsible for every Minneapolis Lakers point until the end of the game. A Mikan hook shot gave the Lakers the lead with one minute and 18 seconds left, and Minneapolis won 68–65, led by Mikan's 34 points. Eighteen of them, on 21 attempts, were free throws.[12]

Had Gottlieb succeeded, it would have put Philadelphia on track for the playoffs. Without the win, they remained half a game behind Baltimore and tied with Boston.

Baltimore had lost that same day, to Washington, with just three wins in the last 11 games failing to be enough to separate them from Philadelphia and Boston. The return of Buddy Jeannette and Tommy Byrnes proved underwhelming, with Joe Dolhon and Carlisle Towery retaining their respective starting spots.

While the Capitols celebrated their victory against Baltimore, it was secondary in importance to the return of Bones McKinney, whose broken hand had only kept him out for 16 days instead of three weeks, as originally expected.[13]

The Knicks, Washington's likely first round playoff opponent, faced the absence of Connie Simmons. With Simmons dealing with lower back pain caused by a sprained anterior sacroiliac ligament, Joe Lapchick opted to rest Simmons in preparation for the playoffs.[14]

With Simmons sidelined, Harry Gallatin became the full-time starting center and Ray Lumpp joined the away version of Lapchick's lineup.

Against St. Louis, the Knicks fought back from a 10-point deficit and forced overtime. With the score tied and two seconds left in overtime, Ernie Vandeweghe took the throw-in and chucked the ball across the half-court line to Carl Braun, who gathered his bearings and launched a set shot from nearly 35 feet out. As the shot was in the air, the buzzer sounded, and the ball went in. New York won 80–78.[15]

The Hawks and Nuggets met for one final battle of the season between the league's two worst teams, and a Denver loss would solidify their status as the NBA's worst team while a Waterloo loss would formally eliminate the Hawks from the playoffs.

The game was never close. Waterloo was up by 16 at halftime and their lead only kept extending from there, as they won 97–68. Denver center Jack Toomay's 18 points could not make up for Waterloo's all-around attack of six double-digit scorers. Denver was officially the worst team in the NBA and would finish the season so, irrespective of future results.[16]

Waterloo's fate now depended on the very Denver team they'd just doomed to the bottom of the NBA standings to pull off a victory against the Redskins in Sheboygan. They didn't. In a 115–92 Sheboygan win, Jack Burmaster scored 26 points, supported by Milt Schoon and George Sobek with 18 and 17 points off the bench. As a team, they had 48 assists, six more than the previous record, led by Bobby Cook's 11. Sheboygan secured their playoff spot, leaving fourth place in the Eastern Division as the final playoff spot up for grabs. Waterloo's postseason hopes were officially extinguished.

That same day, Indianapolis overcame the Anderson Packers for the second time in three days. Their records were now tied at 35–25.

The race for the final playoff spot continued, with a week and a half left in the season. While a team effort from Baltimore proved capable of taking down the Simmons-less Knicks, and a combined 42 points from the Warrior duo of Leo Mogus and Chink Crossin was enough to subdue the Bombers, Boston lost 78–59 to the unyielding Rochester Royals, whose winning streak extended to ten. The next day against Washington was more of the same. Additionally, leading scorer Bob Kinney's season was ended by a leg injury, and he joined George Kaftan on the sidelines.

Washington further made headlines by appointing Bones McKinney as their new coach to succeed Bob Feerick come season's end.[17] With Feerick departing and John Norlander nursing his injured knee, it seemed likely that McKinney and Fred Scolari would be the sole remnants of the original Capitols players come fall. Although McKinney's antics had diminished this season compared to previous years, questions nonetheless arose regarding his ability to embody the requisite professionalism for coaching. Two seasons prior, McKinney's response to a disagreeable foul call was once a grandiose, sarcastic bow during Joe Fulks' free throws, proclaiming that "in the pros, you have to salaam to King Fulks." That comment earned him his second technical and subsequent ejection.[18]

Chicago hosted another doubleheader, with a game between the Anderson Packers and New York Knicks preceding the Stags' clash with Fort Wayne. Max Zaslofsky's 24 points outdid Fred Schaus by one in the latter game, a 90–88 Chicago win that narrowed the standings gap between the two teams to just one game in Fort Wayne's favor.[19]

The Packers and Knicks engaged in a relentless back-and-forth contest, with Carl Braun's impressive 36-point display unable to shake off the resilient Packers. A free throw from Brian tied it up, and when Anderson ended up with the ball one final time, he sank a shot with three seconds left that gave the Packers the win, 91–89.[20] This outcome restored Anderson's half game lead over the Western Division.

In the final game between any of the three teams still in the playoff race, Baltimore hosted the hobbled Celtics. Despite a valiant effort by Tony Lavelli, who scored 23 points, the Celtics fell short as the Bullets prevailed with a 79–75 victory.[21] This outcome gave Baltimore a 25–39 record, followed by 24–41 from Philadelphia and 22–42 from Boston.

Connie Simmons' absence was felt by New York, who, after opening with a 5–3 lead over the Lakers, only scored three more points for the rest of the quarter, falling behind by 20–8 and never leading again for the rest of the game. Harry Gallatin's early foul trouble forced Gene James, who was just 6'4", to defend Mikan during most of the third quarter. Mikan scored 18 points in that quarter, breaking his own record from earlier in the season, and Minneapolis ultimately won by 21.[22] This was Minneapolis' 50th win of the season, as they became the first major league basketball team since the 1907–08 East Liverpool Potters to win a half century's worth of games or more in a league season.

The Olympians eked out a 90–89 win, catching back up to Anderson in the standings until Anderson beat Sheboygan the next day. The day after that, Indianapolis narrowly defeated the Syracuse Nationals after Alex Groza stole the ball from a stalling Al Cervi and Cliff Barker made a one-handed push shot on a 3-on-2 fast break to give the Olympians a late lead, once again tying the Packers.[23]

Grady Lewis displayed Ed Macauley's versatility against Boston, matching him up with Bob Doll at center on offense but taking advantage of Red Rocha's presence on the team to allow Macauley to defend small forward Tony Lavelli. Macauley contained Lavelli to a mere four points while delivering an impressive 31-point performance on 11-of-18 shooting. A 13–0 surge for St. Louis in the fourth quarter was crucial in helping the Bombers pull away for an 86–76 win, eliminating the Celtics from playoff contention.[24] The fourth seed in the Eastern Division had come down to Baltimore and Philadelphia, with the Bullets still holding on to a one and a half game lead. With just two games remaining for Philadelphia, even a single Warriors loss or Bullets win would result in a tie at worst, while any additional success for Baltimore would guarantee a place in the postseason.

The Philadelphia Warriors next faced Anderson in a game characterized by sloppy play. with interceptions and bad passes littered throughout the game. George Senesky held Frank Brian to 3-of-15 shooting but Bill Closs held Joe Fulks to 3-of-16 shooting, and Philadelphia prevailed after overtime.[25]

Away to Minneapolis, the Bullets got off to a competitive start with a 34–34 tie halfway through the second quarter, but things took a turn for the worse and the Lakers outscored Baltimore 62–28 in the final 30 minutes. George Mikan scored 34 points, Vern Mikkelsen added 16, and no Bullet scored more than John Ezersky's 11.[26] Baltimore's lead over the Warriors shrank to half a game.

The Boston Celtics, with nothing but pride on the line, fought hard against the Knicks, and Tony Lavelli willed them back into the game with two minutes left, scoring thrice consecutively to bring the score level. A Carl Braun tip-in with three seconds remaining threatened to undo Lavelli's hard work, but Lavelli unleashed a hook shot from half-court as the buzzer sounded that miraculously found its mark. However, a clutch layup from Harry Gallatin in overtime sealed an 88–84 Knicks win. Lavelli and Doll's 28 and 21 points, respectively, were matched by 26 from Gallatin and 23 from Ernie Vandeweghe for the winners, while Dick McGuire tied the single-game assist record at 16.[27]

Al Cervi nearly reached that same mark for Syracuse the very next day in a game against the Sheboygan Redskins, assisting on 14 of his teammates' field goals as well as scoring 12 points of his own as the Nationals topped the Redskins.[28] This win confirmed Syracuse would finish with the league's best record even if they lost their final two.

Indianapolis comfortably defeated Denver, with Alex Groza's 36-point display helping extend their lead over the Packers to one game. With just one game left on both teams' schedules, the best Anderson could hope to do was tie Indianapolis.[29]

Despite playing against a Bombers team who was at a similar talent level, had been out of playoff contention for weeks, and didn't even have their head coach present with Grady Lewis away scouting for the upcoming draft, the Bullets didn't have enough firepower to overcome St. Louis.[30] Just days before, Baltimore had seemed destined for a playoff spot. Now, they were even with the Warriors at 25–42. The Warriors' game against Washington the next day and Baltimore's against Rochester on the final day of the regular season would determine the outcome of both teams' season.

In Boston's final game, against the New York Knicks, Lavelli struggled to replicate his previous heroics, scoring only 3 points on 1-of-12 shooting. However, Bob Doll, Ed Leede, and Brady Walker combined for 64 points, keeping the Celtics in the game. Free throws turned out to be Boston's kryptonite, as they went 12-of-25 from the foul line. Worst of all, Jim Seminoff and Sonny Hertzberg both missed go-ahead free throws at the end of regulation that would have clinched the game for Boston, but instead regulation ended at 88–88. They lost 98–96 after two overtimes.

This was Boston's seventh consecutive defeat and their fifth straight loss at home, transpiring in front of a crowd of approximately 700 fans. That remains the NBA's lowest-ever attendance with the exception of the crowdless 2020 NBA Bubble.[31]

Five days later, Doggie Julian resigned as Boston's coach, commenting, "I don't think I am tough enough for professional basketball." He returned to the NCAA to coach Dartmouth. Julian's inconsistent rotations and rumors of poor man management were called to task as possible reasons for his departure with one year left on his contract, but Walter Brown, despite accepting Julian's resignation, expressed that he was caught off guard by the coach's decision to leave and didn't have an immediate choice for his successor. The immediately available possibilities seemed to be backup guard Jim Seminoff and assistant coach Art Spector.[32]

Julian had compiled a 47–81 record with the Celtics split across the BAA and NBA, and his return to college basketball would begin very poorly, as Dartmouth won only three of 26 games in his first year, but he turned things around once he added his own recruits and eventually led Dartmouth to back-to-back Ivy League championships and three appearances in the NCAA Tournament, remaining their head coach until his death.

The Celtics' record-low attendance was outnumbered tenfold by the crowd at the game between the other two most under-supported former BAA teams, Chicago and St. Louis. Ed Macauley's 35 points led the Bombers to a comfortable victory, and he broke George Mikan's record of 28 points in a half, scoring 30 by halftime before resting most of the second.[33]

In Philadelphia's crucial final game, they faced off against the Washington Capitols, who had been a bogey team for the Warriors over the years, winning 18 of the previous 25 matchups between the two.

The Warriors couldn't afford to come into the game scared, though, and Joe Fulks, despite having gone the previous eight games without scoring in double figures, quickly asserted himself by making an early layup and extending the lead with a jump shot, setting the tone for the game. Soon, Philadelphia led 9–1, and before long, 24–7.

Fred Scolari struggled under George Senesky's defensive pressure, resulting in one of his worst performances of the season with just six points on 1-of-12 shooting and a single assist. Fulks had saved his best game in over a month for the most important of Philadelphia's season, delivering a standout performance with a game-high 24 points, and the Warriors' forceful 85–59 win put them half a game ahead of Baltimore. This meant the Bullets would have to win their last game or else they would be eliminated from playoff contention by a Warriors team that had trailed them all season.[34]

Rochester's Bob Davies returned from injury and played a pivotal role in their 77–74 win, a result that extended their winning streak to 14, brought them their fiftieth win, and shortened the Lakers' lead over them to just one game. Syracuse also achieved their fiftieth win, defeating the Tri-Cities Blackhawks 89–88 after overtime.

The Olympians, in their final game of the year—a second consecutive home game against Denver—had a chance to end their season by rendering Anderson's result irrelevant. A loss would give the Packers one final chance to tie them for the divisional title. Coincidentally, the game took place in Owensboro, Kentucky, less than 150 miles away from Lexington, where the former University of Kentucky players had spent their college days.

Indianapolis got off to a hot start and the game was never in doubt after they established a commanding 32–14 lead by the end of the first quarter. The title of Western Division champions was going to be theirs. The Olympians' ball movement and ability to create easy scoring opportunities was such that their hosts' nets began to wear out, and Cliff Barker—who had made a 63-foot shot to set Kentucky's all-time record for field goal distance with his final shot in Lexington the year before—replicated his famous feat with a three-quarter-court shot that drew a standing ovation from the crowd. The Indianapolis Olympians finished their regular season with a 110–73 win, with Ralph Beard and Alex Groza scoring 23 and 21 points, respectively, to clinch the divisional title.[35]

Denver finished their season with 10 consecutive losses. This was their fourth such streak of the season, something they'd also done three times the year prior in the NBL and no other franchise in NBA, BAA, or NBL history had done more than twice in a season.

While their start to professional basketball didn't indicate it much, the Nuggets boasted as proud a legacy as the NBA's best teams.

William Haraway, a Denver-based Piggly Wiggly district manager, founded the Denver Pigs as a local amateur team in 1928. Much of his inspiration to create a basketball team came in the form of his sports-loving son, Frank, who was confined to a wheelchair as a result of Pott disease. Frank recovered enough to use crutches instead for most of his life and spent 44 years as a sportswriter for *The Denver Post*.

After a few years confined to competing for Denver's city championship, Haraway entered the Pigs in the 1932 AAU championship. They lost in the first round, 26–21, to a team representing the Brown Paper Mill of West Monroe, Louisiana.

While at the AAU Tournament though, Haraway noticed the talents of the Northwest Missouri State Teachers College team coached by Hank Iba that had gone 81–8 over the previous three seasons. Haraway recruited three of their starters for the 1932–33 season and hired Glenn Jacobs from New Mexico Normal University as the team's coach, with Jack McCracken, who skipped his senior year to take Haraway up on his offer, standing out as Denver's star. To comply with amateurism rules, they also worked for Piggly Wiggly.

They pulled off an upset of the three-time champion Wichita Henrys that season, but fell short, losing in the third round of the 1933 AAU tournament.

The following year, they added Ernest Schmidt, the first player in NCAA history to score 1,000-plus points in their college career, to their roster. Schmidt's presence on the Pigs allowed McCracken to play more on the outside and focus on playmaking. They advanced further in the AAU Tournament, losing 31–30 in the quarterfinals to San Francisco Olympic Club after McCracken fouled out.

Haraway discovered another talented player, Lifschultz Fast Freighters' Ace Gruenig, during the 1934 tournament, and Gruenig's skills as a mobile center with a terrific sweeping hook shot, paired with the subsequent move of Schmidt from center to forward, turned Denver into AAU favorites after a 34–1 regular season record. A defensive meltdown late in the second half of the quarterfinals cost them a 10-point lead over the eventual champion Southern Kansas Stage Lines.

The Denver Pigs were rebranded as the Denver Safeway Stores after Safeway bought Piggly Wiggly's parent company. Glenn Jacobs reworked Denver's play style to be more fast-break-oriented, but they crashed out in the quarterfinals for the third year in a row, despite having a team built to win the tournament, this time after guard Bob Dowell committed a foul with the score tied and no time remaining on the clock. The day after the loss, Jacobs resigned as Denver's coach. Schmidt retired to take a job at GMAC.

Ace Gruenig (1939) was the most-awarded AAU player ever. A center known for his sweeping hook shot, he paired with Jack McCracken to win three AAU titles for the Denver Nuggets.

Everett Shelton was appointed as the team's new coach, and under his guidance, the Safeway Stores clinched the AAU Championship 43–38 over the Phillips Oilers. Gruenig, McCracken, and Tex Colvin were all named AAU All-Americans, the first three of any Denver players to earn that honor.

With Ralph Bishop, the only collegian on the gold medal–winning 1936 U.S. national team, added to Denver in the effort to defend their championship, Denver Safeway Stores went on a 29-game winning streak. The Rev. Dr. James Naismith hailed them as the "greatest team" he had ever witnessed, with particular praise reserved for McCracken. However, their bid to defend the championship was thwarted by the Healey Motors on the last possession of the game.

Following the game, Denver went from disappointment to a team in peril when Safeway withdrew their sponsorship due to a $68,000 tax bill resulting from a recently passed law.

Unable to quickly find a sponsor and with Shelton and all of the players out of a job, Haraway had to scramble to find solutions. In less than a month, Shelton and every player except for Gruenig and McCracken were gone.

Haraway switched his attention from securing a sponsorship to securing his two stars, and teamed up with Denver's branch of the United States Junior Chamber of Commerce to help Gruenig and McCracken both get new jobs, as well as Bishop, who had already left for New York but was willing to come back. This allowed Haraway to enter the 1938–39 season without the need for a sponsor and led to the team being rebranded, upon the suggestion of *The Denver Post* sportswriter Ray McGovern, as the Denver Nuggets, referencing the Pike's Peak Gold Rush.

McCracken was promoted to player-coach, and despite the changes, the Nuggets had a successful season with a 29–3 record and an AAU tournament run that culminated in a 25–22 win over the Phillips Oilers.

That fall, Haraway died of complications from an emergency appendectomy, leaving the team without its strongest advocate. Without him, the lack of a sponsor became a problem, with the number of players on the team decreasing to as few as eight. That lack of depth resulted in a title loss to the Oilers in 1939–40 and a failure to reach the championship game in the next season.

They had a resurgence in the 1942 AAU Tournament, clinching their third championship in six years, but the onset of U.S. involvement in World War II led Denver not to schedule a regular season entirely the next year and the Nuggets never recovered. Denver lost four more championship games in the next six years, all to Phillips.[36]

Wyomingite newspaperman Hal Davis joined as business manager to rebuild the team prior to their last AAU season. A year later, Davis successfully lobbied for the Nuggets to turn professional and join the NBL, but his rebuilding process proved to be tough when three starters left the team in consecutive years. Adding Kenny Sailors for the Nuggets' inaugural NBA season was a relative coup, but it couldn't prevent a league-worst 11–51 record.

Now their only consolation was the impending top choice in the 1950 NBA draft. The presence of territorial picks meant that one of the draft's prize prospects, Villanova's Paul Arizin, would likely already be a Philadelphia Warrior by the start of the draft, and it wasn't out of the realm of possibilities that Holy Cross' Bob Cousy and City College's Irwin Dambrot would be similarly taken by the Celtics and Knicks, respectively, but Chuck Share, a 6'11", 235 lb. defensive wunderkind from Bowling Green, would definitely be available for them to choose.

On March 19, 1950, the final day of the 1949–50 NBA regular season, three of the inaugural season's conclusive games had implications on playoff seeding.

One of the games that didn't featured Waterloo and Tri-Cities, who were tied 77–77 with four seconds left in the game after Jack Smiley exploited the two-minute rule by instructing his players to repeatedly foul the 5'9" Murray Wier. Johnny Payak began to drive around Gene Vance for a chance at the game winner. He fumbled the ball, and Vance almost tied him up, but Payak swept the ball loose and made a twisting shot from eight feet out just before the buzzer to conclude a disheartening season for Waterloo with a memorable moment and a thrilling 79–77 win over their rival.[37]

In the Nationals' closing game against Anderson, Adolph Schayes stood out with 20 points, leading Syracuse to a 72–67 victory. This solidified their record at 51–13, the best record in professional basketball since that of the 1946–47 Washington Capitols.

St. Louis, once again led by Johnny Logan as a makeshift player-coach, was stagnant and overly reliant on Ed Macauley. Macauley did his job well, scoring 24 points and causing both Kleggie Hermsen and George Nostrand to foul out, but with Logan preoccupied, Belus Smawley out with a twisted knee, and a slumping Red Rocha and Ace Maughan responsible for only one made basket each, the Stags won 80–64.[38]

Fort Wayne needed a victory against the Lakers to maintain tied for third place in the Central Division, and they weathered a Mikan-led 11–1 run to find themselves with a tied score and a chance at the last shot of the game. Ralph Johnson drove toward the basket and attempted a shot in traffic, and when Bud Grant fouled him on the shot attempt with five seconds left, Johnson made both free throws and the Lakers couldn't respond before time expired. A 67–65 win ensured that Fort Wayne finished the season tied with Chicago for third place in the Central Division.[39]

Minneapolis' loss meant that a win for Rochester would be enough to tie for the divisional lead as well,

Jack McCracken (1939) was a longtime player-coach for the Denver Nuggets who paired with Ace Gruenig to win three AAU titles for the Denver Nuggets and won a fourth with the Phillips Oilers. James Naismith held particularly high regard for the way he played.

a possibility that would throw the entirety of the Central Division's playoff picture into chaos.

The stakes were higher for the Royals' opponent, Baltimore, though, who were fighting to avoid the end of their season. Rochester quickly took control, building a 14–4 lead within four minutes. Bill Calhoun and Bobby Wanzer led the charge with strong performances, while three other Royals players also reached double figures. Despite Bob Davies shooting 1-of-10, Rochester cruised to a 97–66 victory. This win secured Rochester's tie with Minneapolis for the regular season divisional title and extended their winning streak to 15 games, surpassing the previous record set by the Lakers.[40]

Baltimore ended their season having squandered a game-and-a-half lead over the Warriors in five days, losing 14 of their last 20 games, including the final four. They were the fifth and final team to officially miss the 1950 NBA playoffs. Buddy Jeannette had already been promised the coach and general manager jobs going into the 1950–51 season by the new ownership, but the Bullets had never missed the playoffs before, either in the BAA or the ABL, so regular season elimination in their first NBA season was a significant disappointment.

Paul Hoffman, having just finished the season as the Bullets' top scorer, capped off the year by announcing his retirement from basketball and proclaiming it "the worst professional sport as far as the player is concerned," citing the demanding schedule, overwhelming contractual obligations, corner-cutting by owners, and the constant fear of being traded or released.[41]

Ultimately, he changed his mind and came back to the Bullets just a couple months after accepting a teaching and coaching position in Atlanta, Georgia. By the time he came back, Jeannette had retired from the playing side of things—concluding a 12-year professional career that resulted in four championships—and Ed Sadowski had also quit, playing one final minor league season while transitioning into a career in public relations. Sadowski retired as the 11th-highest scoring player in the then–52-year-history of professional basketball in a league format.

The 1949–50 NBA season came to a close, 561 captivating games after the merger brought the league to life. The Syracuse Nationals finished with the league's best record of 51–13, compiling a 79.7 percent winning percentage, followed closely by the Rochester Royals and Minneapolis Lakers at 51–17. Next best after that were the Indianapolis Olympians, who went 39–25. The Nationals and Olympians, winners of the Eastern and Western divisions, respectively, received $2,500 each, while the second-place teams earned $1,500. The battle for the extra $1,000 prize between the Lakers and Royals remained undecided.

Other teams with winning records consisted of the Chicago Stags, Fort Wayne Pistons, and New York Knicks, all of whom ended the season with 40–28 records, and the Anderson Packers, who compiled a 37–27 record.

That left nine losing teams: the 32–36 Washington Capitols, 29–35 Tri-Cities Blackhawks, 26–42 St. Louis Bombers, 26–42 Philadelphia Warriors, 25–43 Baltimore Bullets, 22–40 Sheboygan Redskins, 22–46 Boston Celtics, 19–43 Waterloo Hawks, and 11–51 Denver Nuggets. Since there were eight teams with more wins than losses and 12 playoff spots, four of these teams—Washington, Tri-Cities, Philadelphia, and Sheboygan—would still have a chance to redeem themselves in the playoffs. For the other five, the 1949–50 NBA season was officially over.

Boston and Baltimore had their worst seasons thus far. Washington, St. Louis, Philadelphia, Sheboygan, Waterloo, and Denver also had worse records than they'd ever previously managed, countered by the Syracuse Nationals, Minneapolis Lakers, and New York Knicks each pulling together the best seasons of their existence.

George Mikan set a new professional basketball scoring record with 1,865 points (27.4 points per game), surpassing his own record from the previous BAA season of 1,698 and becoming the NBA's first scoring champion in the process. Alex Groza finished second with 1,496 points (23.4 points per game), breaking the record for points by a rookie that Joe Fulks had set back in the BAA in 1946–47. Five other players—Frank Brian (1,138 points, 17.8 points per game), Max Zaslofsky (1,115 points, 16.4 points per game), Ed Macauley (1,081 points, 16.1 points per game), Adolph Schayes (1,072 points, 16.8 points per game), and Carl Braun (1,031 points, 15.4 points per game)—finished with more than 1,000 points in the season.

Dick McGuire, as a rookie, led the NBA in assists with 386 (5.7 assists per game), while Andy Phillip wasn't far off with 377 (5.8 assists per game). Alex Groza broke the old BAA field goal percentage record by 5.5 percent by making 47.8 percent of his field goal attempts. Forty-five players played in every game their team played all season. Ed Sadowski, due to the timing of his midseason trade from Philadelphia to Baltimore, played 69 games despite no team playing more than 68.

The NBA tasked 69 sportswriters with voting on two five-man All-NBA teams as the BAA and NBL had both done before it. George Mikan received 68 out of 69 first-team All-NBA votes. Mikan was joined in the All-NBA First Team by Jim Pollard, Bob Davies, Alex Groza, and Max Zaslofsky. The most controversial omission from the first team was that of Adolph Schayes, whose exclusion meant that the Nationals had no first-team All-NBA players despite finishing with the league's best record.

Schayes was voted into the All-NBA Second Team, along with Al Cervi, Ralph Beard, Frank Brian, and Fred Schaus. Honorable mentions included Kenny Sailors, Carl Braun, Dick McGuire, Dick Mehen, and Andy Phillip. Both Mehen and Phillip had been among the top five vote getters in a similar poll that featured NBA coaches instead of sportswriters two months prior; in that poll, Zaslofsky and Beard were both absent.

Both Cervi and Pollard earned their fifth all-league recognition, with Cervi having received All-NBL First Team honors three seasons in a row from 1946–47 to 1948–49 and All-NBL Second Team in 1945–46, and Pollard having been named an AAU All-American in 1945–46 and 1946–47, All-NBL First Team in 1947–48, and All-BAA First Team in 1948–49. With Charley Shipp's career having ended midseason, they became the second most awarded active NBA players, just one all-league selection away from Buddy Jeannette's retiring record of six.

The league lacked official individual awards, but George Mikan was unanimously awarded the Sam Davis Memorial Award, which served as an unofficial equivalent to an MVP, while Alex Groza received the *Sporting News* Rookie of the Year honor.

10

The Playoffs

There was only one day off between the end of the regular season and the beginning of the playoffs. That wasn't ideal, since the entirety of the Central Division's playoff seeding remained uncertain, Minneapolis and Rochester having tied for the top seed in the division while Chicago and Fort Wayne tied for third.

Tiebreakers were necessary for both pairs of teams in order to determine playoff seedings. The Lakers would face the Royals, with the winner becoming the top seed and playing the loser of the Stags–Pistons game. The loser of the Lakers–Royals game would then face the winner of the Stags–Pistons game. The Royals hosted the Lakers, while the Pistons hosted the Stags, and each tiebreaker game was a winner-takes-all situation. For Minneapolis and Rochester, the tiebreaker was for more than just seeding; the winning team would get a $1,000 payout from the league office as divisional winners on top of the $1,500 both franchises had already received.

Results were more conclusive in the other divisions. In the Eastern Division, the one seed Syracuse Nationals would host the four seed Philadelphia Warriors, and the two seed New York Knicks would host the three seed Washington Capitols. In the Western Division, the one seed Indianapolis Olympians would host the four seed Sheboygan Redskins and the two seed Anderson Packers would host the three seed Tri-Cities Blackhawks.

The playoff format consisted of best-of-three series, where the higher seed played the first and third games at home, while the lower seed hosted the second game. The winners of each series progressed to the divisional finals, adhering to the same rules.

To resolve the unique challenge of narrowing down three divisions to two championship contenders, the league introduced a format where the team with the best regular season record among the three divisional finals winners would earn a bye to the NBA Finals. The other two teams would then compete in the NBA Semifinals for the remaining spot. Unlike the previous rounds, the NBA Finals would be a best-of-seven series, with the team with the superior regular season record hosting games one, two, five, and seven, while the other team would host games three, four, and six.

In the first of the tiebreakers, Fort Wayne big men Howie Schultz and Bob Harris played exceptional defense, limiting the Stags' center rotation to a combined 4-of-24 shooting from the field. Chicago's point guard, Andy Phillip, also struggled, shooting just 3-of-19 with Ralph Johnson defending him. Fort Wayne's Fred Schaus led the offensive charge with 18 points and six assists. The Pistons defeated Chicago 86–69, securing the third seed in the Central Division and setting up a matchup against the loser of the tiebreaker between Minneapolis and Rochester.[1]

Before the matchup for the top seed in the division began, a fan presented Red Holzman with a miniature set of boxing trunks and gloves, referencing a recent altercation with Harry Donovan of the Knicks. The game began as a near-deadlock until Herman Schaefer made three successive running hook shots to open up a 13–8 Minneapolis lead. Rochester fought back, tying the game at 19–19 and eventually taking a 23–20 lead with free throws from Bobby Wanzer and a set shot by Bob Davies before the end of the quarter.

Red Holzman's insertion into the game as a substitute in the second quarter and his subsequent scoring on three consecutive plays helped Rochester to establish a 43–33 lead over Minneapolis shortly before halftime. Despite Minneapolis' strong shooting, Bob Davies helped the Royals maintain their lead with nine third-quarter points, and Rochester held a 70–62 advantage with eight minutes left in the game. The Lakers made a small comeback with contributions from George Mikan, Vern Mikkelsen, and Jim Pollard, but Rochester's solid play and sloppy Lakers fouls allowed Rochester to maintain the lead.

The Lakers rallied and took a one-point lead with two minutes remaining. Arnie Risen quickly responded for Rochester, but Fran Curran fouled Mikan on the floor, allowing him to tie the game with a free throw. With possession and a tied score, the Lakers held the ball, passing it around without attempting a shot. Rochester, hesitant to commit a foul, played along. When the clock had ticked down far enough for the Lakers to begin looking for a shot, Risen's defense prevented Mikan from receiving the ball. With only three seconds left, Tony Jaros launched a set shot from 40 feet and the basket miraculously went in. Fran Curran of Rochester had one final attempt from half-court, but it missed the mark. The Lakers won 78–76 and were Central Division champions.

Mikan led with 35 points while Schaefer contributed 12 points and seven assists. Pollard posted an underwhelming nine points, while Davies' 26 points and six assists proved crucial but were ultimately in vain. While Risen did a great job keeping the ball out of Mikan's hands in the final possession, the Royals would need more than the eight points he scored in this game going forward. This game set the Central Division playoffs: as the one seed, the Minneapolis Lakers would host the four seed Chicago Stags, and as the two seed, the Rochester Royals would host the three seed Fort Wayne Pistons.[2]

The postseason began with three playoff games on the same day as the second tie-breaker. The New York Knicks and Washington Capitols faced off in game one, which had to be moved to Uline Arena in Washington, D.C., due to a scheduling conflict at Madison Square Garden with the NHL's New York Rangers. The Capitols had the opportunity to take a 1-0 lead if they could secure a win on their home court before games two and three shifted to New York.

The Knicks entered Game 1 with wavering momentum, having lost five of their last seven games. However, they received a boost with the return of Connie Simmons, who had been sidelined due to a sacral injury. Simmons' presence was crucial as the Knicks faced a size disadvantage in the frontcourt against the taller Capitols' centers Don Otten and Chuck Halbert. While Ernie Vandeweghe was unavailable for Game 1 due to medical school exams, he would be present for the remainder of the playoffs.

The Capitols finished the season with a relatively better record than New York, winning six of their last 10 games. However, they struggled defensively against average teams and were further hindered by the absence of enforcer Chuck Gilmur, who sprained his ankle in the final game. Additionally, their performance against the Knicks was poor; they lost five out of six games, as Carl Braun and Dick McGuire were unfazed by Fred Scolari's defensive efforts.

Even with Simmons' return, the Knicks had difficulty containing Otten and

Halbert's rebounding. Strong defense from Scolari and Bob Feerick allowed the Capitols to gain a lead in the second quarter, but a scoring spurt by Carl Braun inspired the Knicks to finish the half with a 7–0 run and narrow the deficit to three.

As Braun continued to be the source of most of New York's offense throughout the second half, Washington attempted to repeatedly pummel the post with Otten and Halbert, but Simmons and Harry Gallatin stood their ground. Still, Scolari pushed the Capitols to an 80–71 lead with five and a half minutes remaining.

From there, a Dick McGuire steal launched a Knicks comeback that included five straight points from Braun. With two minutes and 15 seconds remaining, the Knicks took the lead 84–82 when McGuire drove, unimpeded, from New York's side of the court all the way to the basket for a layup. Washington kept the game close, and a tip-in by Otten brought the game within one point at 88–87 with 10 seconds left, but Braun looked past the Capitols' inbound press to lob the ball the length of the court to an open Gallatin for the layup that sealed a 90–87 Knicks victory. With a 1–0 series lead, the Knicks only needed to win one of their remaining two home games to advance.

The Capitols had stubbornly relied heavily on forcing the ball inside to Otten, who struggled to make shots, missing an astonishing 25 out of 29 attempts, although he drew plenty of fouls and finished the game with 20 points, second on his team to Scolari, who scored 23 points on 8-of-14 shooting. Braun contributed 26 points and 6 assists, compensating for McGuire's minimal impact, while Boryla added 20 points.[3]

The Packers, defending champions, entered their series against Tri-Cities as a streaky team, displaying unpredictability in their results compared to their championship-winning form.

The Blackhawks had lost seven times out of nine against the Packers and, having finished the season losing four of their final five games, couldn't stand by and hope to pull off an upset without making significant changes.

Tri-Cities had struggled at the point guard position throughout the season, with multiple players taking turns but none among the team's top three in assists per game. Facing the high-scoring guard Frank Brian of the Packers, Red Auerbach chose to pair Dike Eddleman and Gene Vance as the two guards, aiming to utilize Vance's defensive skills against Brian and exploit a height advantage in the backcourt.

In the regular season, whenever Eddleman was in the backcourt, the Blackhawks had started Warren Perkins at small forward in his stead, but Perkins was nursing a twisted ankle and would have to play limited minutes. With the only bench players really capable of stepping into a playoff starting position being centers Gene Englund and Bill Henry, that necessitated Mike Todorovich and Jack Nichols to also move over a position and serve as the two forwards. Gene Englund was recovering from a foot infection and was not available for Game 1, leading to Henry, who had seen limited playing time since February, starting at center.

The game began with Todorovich, proving Tri-Cities didn't need a natural point guard in their starting five, assisting Nichols right off the opening tip. The teams remained evenly matched, tying the score 16 times in the first three quarters. Eddleman's four fouls in the first half disrupted the Blackhawks' strategy, but Nichols' scoring kept Tri-Cities in the game, leading to a 49–44 advantage in the third quarter.

With seven minutes and 20 seconds left in the game and the score tied at 63–63, Brian scored to put Anderson ahead, and not long after, assisted John Hargis to double the lead. Jim Owens stole the ball in the backcourt seconds later and dumped the ball off to Brian for a layup, and the score was 69–63. Four Tri-Cities starters fouled out, leaving them at a disadvantage as the Packers clinched the game with a 26–14 run that resulted in an 89–77 final score. Nichols scored 27 points for Tri-Cities, but Brian and Hargis each had 17 points for the Packers and Owens, off the bench, scored a team-high 19. Anderson now held a 1–0 series lead.[4]

The Olympians won the last seven games of the season. The Redskins lost the last five. It didn't take a rocket scientist to differentiate between Indianapolis' 39–25 record and Sheboygan's 22–40 record. Injuries had impacted the Redskins' performance throughout the year, but their record with all of their starters playing was still below that of most NBA teams, standing at 16–24.

Beyond that, there was a chance that they still weren't at full strength. Bobby Cook had only been averaging 7.3 points since returning from his broken ankle, and that number fell to just 4.0 in the final stretch as he also banged up his knee.

Indianapolis had less reason to be concerned about Cook's status than Sheboygan did—he had struggled against them in the face of Ralph Beard's intensity all year and that played a part in the Redskins having lost five times out of seven against them.

As the game got under way, it quickly became apparent that Cook's injuries were still affecting his performance. In response, Kenny Suesens opted for a backcourt duo of George Sobek and Jack Burmaster, reducing Cook's minutes.

Sheboygan kept pace with the Olympians to start the game, which quickly descended into a battle of free throws between Noble Jorgensen and Wah Wah Jones, with Alex Groza on the bench with early foul trouble. When Sheboygan's Bob Brannum joined him on the sideline for the same reason, Indianapolis capitalized and closed the first half with a strong 17–7 run.

The Redskins stormed back, but after a hook shot by Ralph Beard gave the Olympians a 67–65 advantage, Sheboygan spent the rest of the game trying to play catch-up. Despite narrowing the gap to 86–85 with five seconds left, Sheboygan was unable to touch the ball again or intentionally foul, allowing Indianapolis to run out the clock. Beard led the Olympians with 17 points, supported by Joe Holland and Cliff Barker, while the Redskins trio of Burmaster, Jorgensen, and Brannum scored 19, 18, and 16 points, respectively, with Cook adding just one point. Indianapolis took a 1–0 lead in the series.[5]

The day after that, Syracuse began their series against Philadelphia, the teams having only played twice in the regular season, with both games resulting in Syracuse victories. Both Joe Fulks and Vern Gardner had played a bit above their average in those games, and Fulks' pivotal 24-point contribution in the Warriors' final regular season game was worthy of consideration.

Al Cervi's key decision coming into the series was who to start at center, having rotated between Alex Hannum, George Ratkovicz, and Ed Peterson. Cervi went with Ratkovicz to maximize offensive firepower.

Fears of Fulks' resurgence materialized as he and Gardner each began the game shooting well and the Warriors took an early five-point lead that they held onto through the first quarter, which ended 24–20. On the contrary, Adolph Schayes couldn't make a shot.

The Nationals gained momentum with a series of free throws, and after a pair of field goals from Ratkovicz, had gained a 32–29 Syracuse lead as Fulks started to miss and continued to shoot, but it wasn't until Cervi substituted himself for Ray Corley midway through the second quarter that the Nationals seized full control. Corley's impressive performance, sinking five out of seven long-range baskets in six minutes, propelled Syracuse to a double-digit lead at halftime, and that lead only increased as Schayes shifted his focus to facilitating plays for Ratkovicz and Cervi in the second half.

Schayes only managed five points on 1-of-10 shooting but contributed with six assists. Ratkovicz led the Nationals with 25 points, while Cervi, Corley, and Hannum added 13 each and Syracuse won 93–76. Fulks, after a promising first quarter, became the Warriors' biggest problem; shooting 4-of-20, he was ejected from the game for a flagrant foul out of frustration after Billy Gabor stole the ball from him. Chink Crossin, with 20 points, and Vern Gardner, with 19, played generally good games, but an inquest of the Warriors' entire playing staff was imminent if they didn't put up a better fight in Game 2. The regular season had been rough enough. Syracuse led the series 1–0.[6]

In more semifinals action, the Knicks faced the Capitols again, aiming for a swift series victory after winning in Washington and now playing at home. With Ernie Vandeweghe back, the Knicks went with their traditional home lineup, including Dick McGuire and Vandeweghe in the backcourt, and Carl Braun, Vince Boryla, and Connie Simmons in the frontcourt, with extensive minutes for Harry Gallatin at both post positions off the bench.

This shift meant Braun would be defended primarily by Dick O'Keefe, who succeeded at keeping Braun mostly out of the flow of the game. The aging Capitols struggled to keep up with the young Knicks, resulting in tactics like shirt-pulling and wrestling to disrupt their offense. These tactics helped Washington stay in the game, but the absence of Chuck Gilmur, their most notoriously dirty player, meant these fouls had to be propagated by Reiser, Feerick, and Bones McKinney, all veterans Washington couldn't easily do without in a postseason game.

With Don Otten adjusting well, not allowing Simmons to force him out of position as much, Joe Lapchick gave extended playing time to Gallatin so that the Knicks could better compete for rebounds and loose balls. Gallatin outfought the Washington centers on both sides of the floor and often found himself as the recipient of pinpoint passes from McGuire as the duo maintained an offensive flow while Braun struggled, but Scolari's 14 first-half points kept Washington in the game until the Knicks finished the half strong with a 10–1 run led by Gallatin and McGuire.

During the third quarter, Scolari tripped over a folding chair while running along the sideline to get back on defense. He landed on his left foot wrong and initial concerns were that he may have fractured his left ankle, although X-rays later confirmed that it was just a sprain. For Scolari, that was the end of the game.

Washington struggled without Scolari, as Reiser and Leo Katkaveck couldn't replace his impact. The Knicks took advantage of this and easily defeated the demoralized Capitols, ultimately winning 103–83. Otten scored 21 points for Washington, while Reiser had 15. The Knicks had three backups scoring in double figures, with Gallatin leading with 20 points. McGuire had 14 points and six assists to lead the starting lineup, while Braun was limited to just 10 points. The Knicks swept the series 2–0 to become the first team to advance to the Eastern Division Finals. Washington's season came to an end.[7]

This marked the end of Bob Feerick's career with the Capitols. The next season, he would, as expected, take the head coaching position at Santa Clara leading the team to remarkable success, including an appearance in the Final Four in 1951–52 and subsequent runs to the Elite Eight. He would return to the NBA 12 years later.

Both the Minneapolis Lakers and the Chicago Stags were in poor condition for their playoff matchup. The Stags were exhausted from playing their 17th game in 26 days, and the Lakers were entering the playoffs with George Mikan's knee heavily bandaged, Vern Mikkelsen and Herman Schaefer playing through minor back injuries, and Tony Jaros' impact weakened by a knee strain.

Mikan's success against Chicago in the regular season led to Phil Brownstein instructing the Stags to foul him often. The more the Lakers had to rely on Jim Pollard instead of Mikan, the better the Stags' chances were, although fouling Mikan too often could compromise their own X factor, Spears, who performed exceptionally well against Minneapolis.

Unfortunately for Chicago, Mikan wasn't missing many of his free throws and Mikkelsen made all of his six attempts. While Mikan wasn't efficient from the field, he scored 30 points and Minneapolis won. The Lakers pulled ahead in the second quarter, and Chicago's poor shooting and rebounding, along with Brownstein's questionable strategy of refusing to substitute out any of his starters until they fouled out hindered their efforts to catch up. Minneapolis won the game 85–75, with Mikan, Pollard, and Mikkelsen leading the scoring. Minneapolis took a 1–0 lead in the series.[8]

Rochester and Fort Wayne were the last of the six first-round series to tip off. Just two hours before the game, the Royals faced a setback when Bill Calhoun injured his back while trying to clear his snow-covered driveway. This forced Les Harrison to make lineup changes, moving Arnie Johnson to small forward and inserting Jack Coleman as a temporary starter until Calhoun recovered.

While limiting Rochester's rotational options, this gave the Royals' starting lineup a distinct height advantage. Murray Mendenhall countered by starting the Pistons' three tallest players, pairing Howie Schultz and Bob Harris in the post while putting little-used reserve center Clint Wager at small forward against Johnson. Fred Schaus moved to shooting guard while John Oldham and Bob Carpenter were benched.

The first quarter had the makings of a close game until Fort Wayne took the lead with a 7–0 run. They continued their momentum into the second quarter, while the Royals hit a cold stretch. The Pistons' lead grew to 48–26 before Ed Mikan spearheaded a 9–0 run from the Royals' bench unit to make the halftime score less embarrassing.

The Royals narrowed the gap to 90–84 by the end of the game, but it was the closest they ever got. Mikan, Wanzer, and Pep Saul each scored 15 points for the Royals, but Bob Davies' nine points were underwhelming and Risen was ineffective on both ends of the court. Wager, for Fort Wayne, matched Schultz's game-high 18 points, the most he had scored since 1944–45. Fort Wayne became the first team to steal home advantage, particularly impressive considering Rochester had only lost once at home during the regular season. Fort Wayne led the series 1–0.[9]

Al Cervi defied expectations and continued to rotate the center position in the postseason, swapping out George Ratkovicz for Alex Hannum despite Ratkovicz having led the Nationals in scoring in their Game 1 win. Hannum immediately rewarded Cervi by making three consecutive shots and helping Syracuse burst out to a 9–1 lead. Eddie Gottlieb also made a change for Philadelphia that was hard to miss, benching the profligate Joe Fulks in favor of Leo Mogus.

Philadelphia overcame an early disadvantage with an 18–7 run before halftime. They held the Nationals scoreless in the last four minutes of the half, giving them a slight lead. Both teams struggled to maintain a significant lead throughout the game, with sporadic scoring and a slow pace, but Philadelphia held control heading into the fourth quarter with a 44–39 lead.

In the closing minutes, Leroy Chollet's shot and free throw gave Syracuse a 47–46 lead. Cervi added a basket, but the Warriors fought back with George Senesky and Vern Gardner scoring. The Warriors went up 53–51, but failed to score again. As Syracuse breezed toward the final buzzer with an 8–0 run, the only remaining combat came between Paul Seymour and Joe Fulks, who threw a few punches at each other in the final minute after Seymour shoved Fulks away from a loose ball. The Nationals won 59–53, led by Schayes' 16 points. Gardner scored 17 for Philadelphia. Syracuse swept the series 2–0 and advanced to face the New York Knicks in the division finals.[10]

Indianapolis faced a pivotal moment: a win could seal the series with a sweep, but they needed to step up after a narrow victory against the playoffs' worst team. They played into Sheboygan's patented up-tempo style, with both teams' offenses firing on all cylinders. By halftime, Indianapolis led 53–49, not far off from the final score of the Syracuse–Philadelphia game.

Sheboygan started the second half with a 7–1 run, sparking a back-and-forth battle. Bob Brannum beat the buzzer to give the Redskins a 69–68 lead going into the final quarter. Wah Wah Jones tied the game, but Sheboygan regained the lead with a Max Morris jump shot, and they held on to the lead, ultimately winning 95–85. Alex Groza scored 26 points for Indianapolis, but Brannum led things for Sheboygan with 17 points and seven assists and Morris had a spectacular all-around game. The series was now tied 1–1, and the deciding Game 3 would be played in Indianapolis.[11]

In the other Western Division playoff game, Red Auerbach countered the Packers differently than Barker did with the Redskins. He used a slow half-court offense to take Anderson out of their comfort zone. The strategy paid off, as Tri-Cities seized a 31–21 lead by halftime.

Tri-Cities got a bit lax in the third quarter and Anderson prevented the Blackhawks from extending their lead despite nine third-quarter points from Jack Nichols. The Packers closed the gap to 66–60 with six minutes left but Tri-Cities increased it back to 71–62 with three minutes left.

The Blackhawks stopped shooting for the rest of the game, forcing the Packers to foul. Seven straight Anderson points as Tri-Cities missed most of their late free throw attempts closed the gap to two anyway, and Anderson soon trailed just 72–71 with a minute and 12 seconds left after Mike Todorovich's free throw was offset by a Bill Closs set shot.

The Blackhawks still stalled and refused to shoot, leading to Anderson fouling and Todorovich scoring another free throw. Todorovich won the ensuing jump ball and Bill Henry was fouled, making another free throw for a 74–71 lead, but Frank Brian brought the margin back down to one by racing down the court for a layup with 39 seconds to go. Don Ray's free throw made it 75–73, but Anderson tied the game as Stanczak tipped in his own missed shot for a 75–75 score.

The Blackhawks held on to the ball for the final shot, which Bill Henry missed with three seconds left, but Bill Closs fouled Nichols while battling for the rebound and Nichols sank the free throw to make the score 76–75. The buzzer sounded before Ed Stanczak could get a shot off for Anderson. Brian scored the most points with 26, while Nichols had 23 for the winners. The series was tied 1–1, and the deciding Game 3 would be played in Anderson the next day.[12]

In Game 3, the Blackhawks fell behind 10–3 and failed to score a field goal within the opening seven minutes. Eddleman single-handedly dragged Tri-Cities back into the game with four consecutive baskets, including two from near half-court, narrowing the score to a 15–13 Anderson advantage, and two more long-range shots put the Blackhawks within a point.

The game remained close through the first half of the second period, with Tri-Cities leading 33–32 with five and a half minutes left in the half, but John Hargis scored six straight points to give the Packers a five-point lead, and the rebounding of Anderson's frontcourt, especially from Closs, was vital to Anderson expanding their lead. As Hargis continued to score at will, the Blackhawks' chances to win slipped away. Hargis scored 21 points on 13 shots, with all of his points coming in the second and third quarters. Eddleman finished with 23 points, but zero other Blackhawks made more than two field goals. Anderson won the game 94–71, and, with it, the series 2–1. The Packers would advance to the Western Division Finals, awaiting the outcome of the decisive Game 3 between Indianapolis and Sheboygan.[13]

Fort Wayne, with a chance to send home the higher-seeded Royals, took an early lead but the Royals came back strong. Rochester followed that up by making one field goal in the entire second quarter, allowing the Pistons bench unit, led by Bob Carpenter, to take the lead. At halftime, the Pistons led 40–32.

Les Harrison, realizing that, without a change, his team was 24 minutes away from playoff elimination, inserted Ed Mikan as power forward, moved Jack Coleman to small forward, and placed Arnie Johnson in the backcourt opposite Fred Schaus. The Royals, led by Risen and Johnson, started winning the rebounding battle and gradually recovered from their deficit. With just over two minutes remaining, Mikan made two free throws, tying the score at 68–68.

Carpenter and Wanzer exchanged baskets, keeping the score close. With three seconds remaining, Wanzer found Johnson for an open shot from 25 feet out. Johnson missed, Fran Curran went for a put back and missed too, and the game went into overtime tied 70–70.

Jack Kerris scored with a hook shot for Fort Wayne in overtime, followed by four points from Carpenter, giving the Pistons a five-point lead. Risen and Johnson fouled out, but Coleman's free throw and field goal narrowed the gap to 76–74. Mikan tied the game a few seconds later.

Carpenter hit a hook shot from the left side of the hoop, and a sloppy Rochester inbounds play resulted in a foul that sent Kerris to the line for a free throw that gave Fort Wayne a 79–76 lead with six seconds remaining.

With Rochester's last chance being to make a timely shot, foul immediately, and win a jump ball in order to get the last shot, Bob Davies' full-court pass to Mikan was inaccurate, and Mikan fumbled the ball to Coleman, who made one final shot but without enough time for it to matter. Losing 79–78 after overtime, Rochester's season ended in the first round, despite their having won their last 15 regular season games..

Risen scored 17 points and Johnson had 15. Davies' six points, as well as his 4-of-17 shooting over the course of the series as a whole, was an atrocious showing from one of the best players in the league. Carpenter led Fort Wayne with 27 points off the bench, while Kerris and John Oldham also made significant bench contributions. Fort Wayne swept the series 2–0 and advanced to the Central Division Finals. Rochester was eliminated in the first round for the first time in their history.[14]

Only two first-round series were undecided: one with George Mikan and the

Minneapolis Lakers, and the other with Alex Groza and the Indianapolis Olympians. The Lakers held a 1–0 series lead, while the Olympians were in more danger as they were facing the threat of elimination. Late in the second quarter, Indianapolis scored 14 points, taking a six-point lead at halftime. Redskins guard Jack Burmaster injured his back in a fall amid that run. He attempted to return but could only last 11 seconds before being substituted out for good.

George Sobek fouled out early in the third quarter and joined Burmaster on the sideline, but the absence of both of Sheboygan's starting guards didn't hinder the team much, with Stan Patrick and a hobbled Bobby Cook taking up the helm of the backcourt while Noble Jorgensen battled Groza. When Groza accidentally deflected the ball into the hoop attempting a rebound, the Redskins took a 50–49 lead. Inspired by Patrick, who made his first four shots after entering the game to replace Sobek, Sheboygan pressed ahead and extended their lead to 64–55.

Joe Holland and Wah Wah Jones effectively limited Sheboygan's ball movement to Bob Brannum. With Burmaster unavailable and Cook playing hurt, that meant Max Morris had to exert so much energy on both sides of the game that he routinely hung his head and arms limp whenever the ball went out-of-bounds or a foul was committed.

Groza and Beard led the Olympians to a 22–6 run, giving them a convincing seven-point lead with six minutes left. Indianapolis' two stars and Paul Walther brushed off Sheboygan's final challenge for the lead to secure a 91–84 Olympian victory. Groza's 30 points and Beard's 24 proved too much for the Redskins to handle without a healthy Bobby Cook. For Indianapolis, the series had been far too close for comfort, but nonetheless they won the series 2–1 and advanced to face the Anderson Packers in the Western Division Finals.[15]

George Mikan scored seemingly every time he touched the ball against Chicago in Game 2 of the Lakers–Stags first-round series, despite Kleggie Hermsen playing well enough defensively on him that Phil Brownstein kept him in the game until he fouled out in the final seconds.

Max Zaslofsky was just as much of a scoring threat for the Stags as Mikan was for Minneapolis, and as the game became a one-on-one battle between them, neither team gained an advantage. Andy Phillip and Jim Pollard were disappointing, and Arnie Ferrin and Odie Spears stepped up as the top supporting performers for the Lakers and Stags, respectively.

The Lakers held a slight lead until Spears tied the game with four minutes left. Mikan responded in kind with three baskets in a row and Chicago couldn't catch back up. Mikan scored 34 points while Zaslofsky scored 31. Minneapolis won 75–67, sweeping the series 2–0, and the Lakers advanced to the Central Division Finals against the Fort Wayne Pistons.[16]

The Eastern Division Finals between the Nationals and the Knicks kicked off the second round of action, with both teams having swept their first-round opponents and not having had to deal with tiebreakers like the Pistons and Lakers did. New York and Syracuse had only played twice in the regular season due to scheduling, with Syracuse winning both games, in large part because they held both Carl Braun and Connie Simmons to far lower than their normal scoring averages. So despite Vince Boryla defensively matching up extremely well against Adolph Schayes, the Knicks entered the series having never beaten Syracuse in the NBA.

Syracuse struggled initially, while Braun, Simmons, and Dick McGuire gave New

York an early 11–4 lead. The Nationals caught up, but a trio of first-quarter fouls by Alex Hannum proved detrimental and necessitated his substitution. His replacement, George Ratkovicz, missed a load of shots, as did almost everyone on the Nationals roster not named Adolph Schayes, and the Knicks took a 28–20 lead.

In the third quarter, Syracuse benefited from the Knicks' foul trouble. Schayes and Ratkovicz capitalized on some free throws, narrowing the gap somewhat throughout the period's first six minutes. Schayes' fadeaway jumper brought the Nationals back within two and they trailed just 64–60 by the quarter break.

That four-point Knicks lead reappeared consistently through the fourth quarter, as stalling tactics begat fouling. The game turned into a free throw contest, with the score reaching 72–68 with five minutes left. Al Cervi narrowed the margin to two points with a pair of foul shots, but Braun's push shot extended the lead back to four points. Cervi fouled out, and Braun's subsequent free throw expanded the Knicks' lead to 75–70 with three minutes and 15 seconds remaining.

Schayes made two free throws for Syracuse, cutting the deficit to three points. The Knicks' stalling then went into high-gear, and in an effort to get the ball back, both Schayes and Hannum fouled out in the final minute. The Knicks missed their free throw on both occasions. Harry Gallatin fouled out for the Knicks moments later.

Two more free throws by Billy Gabor narrowed the lead to one, and Johnny Macknowski's contested layup gave Syracuse the lead at 77–76 with just 17 seconds left. Macknowski had a chance for a three-point play but missed the free throw.

Braun took a long-range shot with seven seconds left, hoping his teammates would rebound in case of a miss. Gabor fouled him, giving Braun another chance to put New York ahead with a pair of free throws. He missed the first, made the second, and the score was tied. Overtime followed after Fuzzy Levane missed a potential Syracuse buzzer-beater.

Macknowski started overtime with a free throw, but Braun's three-point play put the Knicks ahead 80–78. Peterson made consecutive hook shots, giving Syracuse an 82–80 lead. Chollet extended their lead with a layup, and the Knicks' chances slowly slipped away. Braun scored 22 points and McGuire added 15, but Syracuse won 91–83, and while Ed Peterson and Leroy Chollet were the overtime heroes, Schayes' 26 points were imperative. Joe Lapchick lambasted the refereeing as biased, declaring, "I was so mad after the game I could have hit somebody." Nationals general manager Art Deutsch sent Lapchick a basket of grapes, implying it was just "sour grapes." Syracuse led the series 1–0.[17]

Minneapolis and Fort Wayne had faced each other six times in the regular season, with the Lakers winning four times and the Pistons winning twice. In the three match-ups since Howie Schultz became a Piston, Schultz and Bob Harris held George Mikan under 20 points twice, something that could only be said of that pairing and Ed Macauley. That ability to limit Mikan and force the result to depend on Jim Pollard and Vern Mikkelsen would come in handy if they could harness it in the Central Division Finals.

Familiarity bred animosity as heated arguments barely avoided breaking out into brawls between Schultz and Pollard, Mikan and Curly Armstrong, and Mikan and Fred Schaus. A second-quarter run by Minneapolis that heavily featured Mikan and Herman Schaefer gave the Lakers a 21-point lead by halftime and Fort Wayne couldn't come back. Mikan scored 24 points, Mikkelsen added 18, and Carlson contributed 14 points to secure the win. Pollard had a rough game, allowing Schaus to produce 20 points while only shooting 2-of-14 in his own right, but it didn't matter and the Lakers won 93–79, giving them a 1–0 series lead.[18]

Despite beating Anderson five times in their seven regular season encounters, Indianapolis needed to step up from the way they played in their first-round series to avoid elimination by their in-state rivals. They barely avoided being swept by Sheboygan and lost by a larger margin in Game 2 than their two wins combined, and that was against a losing team with a key player barely able to contribute. Anderson, despite struggling against the Packers in the regular season, had experienced players with championship experience, the perfect recipe to punish an underperforming young team.

Doxie Moore changed his team's strategy against Indianapolis, sacrificing fast breaks and focusing on rebounding, utilizing Anderson's relative height advantage. Milo Komenich engaged Alex Groza on offense to tire him out. The Packers maintained a small lead and a strong start in the fourth quarter put them ahead 67–57 with just under seven minutes to go.

Paul Walther scored two consecutive baskets and Groza made a free throw, reducing the Packers' lead by half before Anderson responded with a Komenich tip-in. Groza then scored a hook shot, a free throw, and a lean-in jump shot, bringing the Olympians within two points at 72–70.

Wah Wah Jones was fouled by Ed Stanczak and sank a free throw to cut the lead to one. Jones fouled Stanczak back the next play, and on the other end, Stanczak's elbow collided with Jones' orbital cavity, causing him to bleed from two gashes near his right eye. The game was paused for Jones to receive medical attention, and Jones was out for the rest of the game with his eye heavily bandaged.

Malcolm McMullen made a crucial defensive play for the Olympians by tying up Richie Niemiera and forcing a jump ball. Despite being four inches shorter, Niemiera outjumped McMullen, but he tapped the ball directly into the path of Groza, who drove to the basket unimpeded and tied the game at 74–74.

Groza stole the ball from John Hargis, scored, and increased Indianapolis' lead to 77–74 the next time down the court courtesy of a free throw, and that was the last scoring of the game. He ended with 31 points while Jones had contributed 17 before getting injured. Beard, playing through influenza, scored just two points, both from the foul line. Anderson had four double-digit scorers but couldn't match Groza. Indianapolis led the series 1–0.[19]

With Fort Wayne facing a potential loss that could end their run, Minneapolis quickly took a 4–0 lead, thanks to early baskets from Slater Martin. The Pistons' aggressive defense led to frequent fouls on George Mikan. Howie Schultz had four fouls in the first quarter and Mikan punished Fort Wayne by making each of his first 12 free throw attempts. If it weren't for Fred Schaus' standout performance, the Pistons would've been far outplayed within a few minutes. As it was, it took until the third quarter for Minneapolis to extend their lead to 74–59.

Schaus boosted the Pistons in the fourth quarter, closing the gap to 79–75 with four minutes remaining. Jim Pollard yet again struggled to score, but in the second half he took on a distributary role as the Lakers briefly extended their lead to seven but lost it, ending up ahead 85–82 with 48 seconds left. After that, Pollard successfully picked out Vern Mikkelsen streaking to the hoop for a layup to bring the lead back to five and did the same with Herman Schaefer to put the game out of reach, securing an 89–82 victory for Minneapolis. Mikan's 37 points were nearly matched by Schaus' 33, but the Pistons lacked support from other players, with Schultz's 2-of-17 shooting and inability to

Jim Pollard (1948) was George Mikan's right-hand man in Minneapolis. A versatile and extremely athletic forward, he had the ability to lead a team but was willing to take a step back and focus on aspects of the game other than scoring for the greater good of the team en route to a multitude of championships. He was top ten in the league in both scoring and assists and made the All-NBA First Team.

contain Mikan contributing to their loss. Pollard only scored 6 points but racked up 12 assists, a season-high for non–point guards, while Martin and Arnie Ferrin added 11 points each. The Lakers won the series 2–0 and advanced to the next round.[20]

Which round, exactly, was uncertain. If Syracuse lost their series to New York,

Minneapolis would head straight to the NBA Finals, but if the Nationals won against the Knicks, Syracuse's better regular season record than the Lakers would give them the bye, and the Lakers would have to face the winner of the Western Division Finals in the NBA Semifinals for the chance to claim the second Finals spot. After a day without any NBA action, Game 2 of both series would commence.

The more the Knicks and Nationals saw of each other, the less they liked each other. Game 2 saw fewer fouls and less provocation between players than Game 1, but the tension between the in-state opponents was visceral. One of the Nationals' traveling fans, Dan Kelly, was arrested mid-game for pelting the court with spitballs. A Knicks fan stormed the court and shook the basket stanchion while a Syracuse player was taking a free throw. Referee Arnold Heft, criticized by Knicks coach Joe Lapchick after Game 1, faced jeers from the Syracuse bench and ended up giving a technical foul to Al Cervi for failing to control his players.

Adolph Schayes was taken out when he racked up his third foul early in the second quarter, allowing Vince Boryla to exploit a mismatch with Alex Hannum, and back-to-back fast breaks resulting in easy layups for Harry Gallatin and Boryla put the Knicks up 30–22.

New York stayed ahead as the Nationals made a flurry of substitutes. Excellent free throw shooting from Boryla, Carl Braun, and Goebel Ritter increased the Knicks' lead to double digits.

At halftime, New York led 42–33. Syracuse quickly narrowed the gap to four points with a free throw from George Ratkovicz and two long-range set shots by Johnny Macknowski. New York responded with a push shot by Dick McGuire, a Braun jump shot, and a pair of Connie Simmons free throws. Syracuse only managed a single free throw in return, which brought New York's lead right back to nine.

With nine minutes remaining, Ratkovicz's layup kickstarted a Syracuse run. Schayes contributed with four free throws and a hook shot, while McGuire made a set shot for the Knicks. After Schayes sank a set shot of his own, Syracuse had cut New York's lead to 71–70.

McGuire drew a foul and Simmons tapped the missed free throw attempt in to get the Knicks back on track. Fuzzy Levane narrowed the gap again with a set shot, but Ritter's free throws sealed the result. Schayes wasn't remarkable, shooting 3-of-12 for 14 points, but Syracuse's backcourt really struggled, with Cervi and Billy Gabor combining for just five points on 1-of-13 shooting. Boryla's 21 led the way for the Knicks, who pulled out a critical home win despite taking 16 fewer shots. With an 80–76 win, New York tied the series 1-1. The deciding game 3 would be in Syracuse.[21]

Indianapolis played Game 2 against Anderson shorthanded. Wah Wah Jones couldn't play as a precaution after getting six stitches around his eye and sporting a bruised cheekbone. Ralph Beard didn't make the trip, bedridden with influenza. In their stead, Carl Shaeffer joined Joe Holland and Alex Groza in the frontcourt while an out-of-position Cliff Barker replaced Beard at point guard.

Regardless of missing playing personnel, Indianapolis got out to an early lead, but Anderson closed the gap and eventually took the lead at 31–30 after a 20–9 run. They went back and forth until Frank Brian beat the buzzer on a 30-foot shot and the Packers went into the half with a two-point lead.

In the second half, Charlie Black played heavy help defense to assist Milo Komenich in keeping Groza in check, and with neither Beard nor Jones there to take the pressure off him, the Olympians quickly fell behind, with John Hargis' shooting playing a major part. Anderson scored 48 points in the second half to beat the Olympians 84–67. Both teams had balanced scoring, but Groza was limited to just 11 points. The series was tied 1–1, with the deciding Game 3 scheduled for Indianapolis.[22]

The Western Division's deciding game was a day earlier than the Eastern Division's. Beard and Jones both returned; it was simply too important to miss.

Indianapolis fell behind early and spent most of the game playing catch-up. They managed to take the lead at halftime, but the Packers, led by Hargis and Black, regained control and were ahead 47–39 after 10 more minutes of action.

Jones ignited an 8–0 run to tie the game, but the Packers quickly regained the lead with a 6–0 run of their own. The Olympians fought back to even the score again at 54–54. Jones and Holland scored to give Indianapolis a brief lead, but Anderson reclaimed it with two free throws, and with Indianapolis intentionally fouling as the Packers stalled Anderson, extended the margin to 64–61 with less than two minutes remaining.

Jim Owens scored a layup and Frank Gates made a free throw, extending Anderson's lead to 67–61 with 32 seconds left. When Bill Closs made a mistake on defense, it allowed Holland to cut to the basket uncovered for an open layup, and an Olympian steal resulted in Groza barging through Black and Komenich to get to the rim for a layup of his own. The Olympians were back within two points.

Indianapolis had to foul to regain possession with just 20 seconds left. The Packers missed the resulting free throw, but Anderson kept control of the ball after an offensive rebound and stalled long enough for the buzzer to sound before Indianapolis could do anything. Groza scored 26 points in the loss, with Jones adding 13. Brian led the way for the winners with 14 and four other players scored in double figures. Anderson, winning the series 2–1, became the first team since the merger to win their division in the playoffs without winning it in the regular season. The Packers, with a worse regular season record than Minneapolis, Syracuse, and New York, would have to play in the NBA Semifinals to qualify for the NBA Finals, regardless of the Eastern Division Finals' outcome.[23]

If Syracuse won, the Nationals would automatically receive a bye to the Finals and Minneapolis and Anderson would have to fight for the second Finals spot. If New York won, Minneapolis would get the bye and New York and Anderson would battle in the Semifinals. In both cases, the Packers' opponents would hold home advantage in the Semifinals and the team with a bye would hold home advantage in the Finals.

Vince Boryla and Ernie Vandeweghe scored early for the Knicks, but Syracuse quickly gained an advantage, exposing Vandeweghe's defensive lapses, and Syracuse took leads of 16–11, 21–14, and 26–18 by the end of the quarter.

McGuire and Vandeweghe helped put the Knicks ahead by a score of 38–37, but Adolph Schayes and Gabor regained control for the Nationals and Syracuse had their lead back by halftime. Johnny Macknowski extended Syracuse's lead early in the fourth quarter and they held on for the win. Schayes scored 24 points, Ratkovicz had 18, Gabor scored 17, and Cervi contributed with 14 points and 10 assists. Paul Seymour held Carl Braun scoreless throughout the first half, while Boryla was benched for poor defense. The 91–80 decision secured the Nationals a spot in the 1950 NBA Finals against the winner of the Minneapolis–Anderson matchup.[24]

After Anderson took a 4–2 lead to kickstart Game 1 between Minneapolis and Anderson, Doxie Moore instructed the Packers to stall, even with the first quarter barely under way. Minneapolis fans didn't take too kindly to that, booing Anderson players relentlessly throughout the game, and neither did Lakers coach John Kundla. The first quarter ended with a score of 7–7.

Kundla originally planned to split defensive duties against Frank Brian between Slater Martin and Herman Schaefer, but with Brian and Charlie Black the only Anderson players attempting to score and Martin and Vern Mikkelsen doing a tremendous job together at stopping them from doing so, Kundla pivoted toward the quick, defensively inclined rookie Martin.

The Lakers' frontcourt of Jim Pollard, Mikkelsen, and George Mikan took over in the second quarter, and Minneapolis soon had a double-digit lead. Anderson's slow game faltered, and the Lakers weren't letting up.

By the time Kundla finally had mercy on the Packers and brought in the reserves, Minneapolis led 68–39. Afterward, Kundla publicly criticized Moore's decision-making, explaining that the stalling gave the Lakers time to adjust to their poor early shooting without falling behind. Brian struggled with 2-of-12 shooting due to Martin's defense, Black scored only one point, and Hargis managed four. Milo Komenich, in addition to allowing 26 points from Mikan, shot 2-of-15. The Lakers finished with a 75–50 blowout victory, leading the series 1–0.

After a humiliating defeat, Moore acknowledged his shortcomings but expressed hope for redemption. He remarked that he had believed the Packers' best chance at victory against the Lakers to be conserving energy in the first half to match their pace in the second. While they were comparatively older, it was surprising to suggest they would be outrun by the Lakers, considering Anderson's aggressive fast breaks during the regular season. Regardless, the Packers couldn't keep up with the Lakers in the second half, even with the early stalling.[25]

Following Mel Taube's resignation as head coach of Purdue University's basketball program after a disappointing 9–13 season, a diverse pool of coaching candidates emerged, including UCLA's John Wooden, Butler's Tony Hinkle, and Tennessee's Emmett Lowery. Wooden withdrew his application after UCLA offered him a ten-year, $12,000 per year contract extension which included a clause paying off his mortgage loan.

On the morning before Game 2 of the NBA Semifinals, it became public knowledge that Doxie Moore had also applied.[26] Moore wasn't the only NBA head coach looking for a new job, although he was the only one imprudent enough to do it while in the middle of a playoff series. Ever since Tri-Cities' elimination from the playoffs, Red Auerbach had been actively searching for a new job despite being the highest-paid coach in the league and having been with the Blackhawks less than a full season. The John Mahnken–Gene Englund trade with Boston was completed against Auerbach's explicit wishes and the relationship between Auerbach and Kerner had deteriorated since then. Auerbach reportedly applied for the jobs at Purdue, Michigan State, and Northwestern, and he was one of the first two candidates reported on as meriting serious consideration for the University of Maryland coaching role, replacing the underperforming Flucie Stewart.[27]

Minneapolis and Anderson's second game started off a lot closer to how professional basketball was supposed to be played than their previous meeting. The Packers changed their strategy and played their normal intense game of fast breaks, and tied the score at 43–43 after falling behind by six points in the first quarter despite facing difficulties in containing George Mikan.

Moore's theory about the Packers' losing energy in the second half against the Lakers proved correct. In the third quarter, Anderson struggled with rebounding, allowing Mikan and Vern Mikkelsen to lead an 8–0 start to the half, mostly scoring off of tip-ins. By the end of the game, Mikan and Mikkelsen had combined for 18 points on tip-ins alone.

Mikan simply overwhelmed Milo Komenich. At times, Komenich had help from Charlie Black, Bill Closs, John Hargis, or Ed Stanczak, and all that did was allow Mikkelsen to shine. Slater Martin neutralized Frank Brian once again, and like the game before, it wasn't close by the end. Brian only scored four points, and his inability as the league's third-leading scorer to produce more than 10 points over two games made Anderson's position unsustainable.

Mikan scored 32 points, Mikkelsen scored 23, and a 90–71 Lakers win meant that Minneapolis had swept the series 2–0 with ease and was heading to the NBA Finals against the Syracuse Nationals.[28]

Doxie Moore wasn't offered the Purdue job.

With the impending inaugural NBA Finals to be contested between the Nationals and Lakers, one remarkable coincidence was that the Finals contenders were the only two teams in the NBA with a non-white player.

Bob Harrison was widely recognized for his Native American heritage. He was not the only person of color in the NBA, rather the only one known publicly at that time. Leroy Chollet, the rookie small forward for Syracuse who sank a crucial layup in overtime of the Nationals' Game 1 win over New York, was multiracial but passed for white during his career.

Chollet had excelled at Loyola New Orleans, leading them to an NAIB Championship title as a freshman in 1944–45 with an impressive 12.5 points per game. The 49–36 championship game win over George Pepperdine College, in which Chollet scored a game-high 18 points, would be the last game he ever played for Loyola.

Chollet's younger brother, Hillary, was the highest-regarded football prospect in Louisiana that year and was projected as a star halfback and kick returner. He initially committed to Louisiana State University but switched to Tulane, LSU's biggest rivals.

An upset LSU fan suspected the Chollets were black due to Hillary's olive complexion and dark, curly hair. He conducted genealogical research and discovered that their father's maternal grandmother, Rosa Olinde, was a black woman born into slavery. This made the brothers one-eighth black, legally classified as "negro" under Louisiana state law at the time.

Tulane quietly disenrolled Hillary Chollet after receiving a letter revealing his ethnic lineage. He instead went to Cornell University, leaving the segregated South. After facing academic misconduct charges at Loyola, Leroy Chollet transferred to Southwestern Louisiana Institute, where he would play with another brother, Al. Six games into the season, Leroy and Al were both mysteriously ruled ineligible at the same time—just over a week before a scheduled game against Tulane.

The Chollet family followed Hillary to upstate New York to escape the racially motivated harassment. Leroy continued his college career at Canisius, where he would attract the attention of the Nationals over the next three years. Al Chollet claimed for the rest of his life that the Chollets were run out of town.[29]

11

The Finals

April 8, 1950, was the first day of the 1950 NBA Finals.

Two nights earlier, three armed robbers broke into the Eastwood Sports Center that Nationals owner Danny Biasone ran, bound and gagged janitor Alex Bukowsky at gunpoint, and stole a 500-pound safe containing $7,240 in cash and an additional $8,000 in checks. Two thousand dollars of the money belonged to the Syracuse Nationals organization. A few hours later, papers from the safe were found floating in the Erie Canal, leading police investigators to believe that the robbers had succeeded in opening the safe, stolen the money, and disposed of the safe by dumping it in the canal.[1]

This was just one of 21 reported burglaries believed to be connected in a five-month period in Syracuse. Five weeks later, the same trio broke into a residence less than a mile away, but their plans were thwarted when alerted police closed in on them.

A confrontation ensued, resulting in gunfire exchange between the burglars and the officers. Joseph DePasquale sustained critical injuries, while Paul Grmusha was fatally shot. The remaining burglar, Sam Amato, managed to escape but was subsequently apprehended. Amato and DePasquale were sentenced to 40 to 60 years in state prison for first degree burglary. The stolen safe was eventually recovered in Onondaga Lake, devoid of its cash but still containing the $8,000 in checks.[2]

The Nationals' players couldn't afford to worry about that; they had to focus on finding a way to beat the Lakers at home twice in a row. Minneapolis and Syracuse had split their two regular season matchups, with the contrasting performances of Jim Pollard for Minneapolis and Adolph Schayes for Syracuse the biggest difference between a win and a loss for each team. While Syracuse would undoubtedly need Schayes to be at his best, Al Cervi's tactical approach coming into the series wasn't as concentrated on Schayes as it was on himself and Billy Gabor pushing the tempo and the team as whole taking high-quality shots to mitigate the likely advantage Minneapolis would have with rebounds.

At the same time, Cervi was strangely reserved about Syracuse's chances to win the series given their superior record and home advantage, commenting that "with that Laker lineup, it's the same as playing five men against six." He wasn't alone with that opinion; Pistons general manager Carl Bennett tabbed Minneapolis as favorites to win the championship ten days prior and Doxie Moore was bold enough after the Packers' elimination to suggest the Lakers would sweep Syracuse 4–0. Of course, both had self-serving reasons to make such a prediction, having each been knocked out by the Lakers, but the same couldn't be said about Knicks coach Joe Lapchick, who concurred.

Cervi started with a lineup of himself at point guard, Gabor at shooting guard, Paul Seymour at small forward, Adolph Schayes at power forward, and George Ratkovicz at center. John Kundla started Slater Martin at point guard, Arnie Ferrin at shooting guard, Jim Pollard at small forward, Vern Mikkelsen at power forward, and George Mikan at center.

The Lakers started the game like they were out to prove Bennett and Moore right. Mikan made two hook shots, Pollard followed them up with a tip-in, and Mikan then made a free throw to rush out to a 7–0 Minneapolis lead. Gabor put the Nationals on the scoreboard, but Syracuse remained behind for the rest of the half. Nothing was working to stop Mikan from continuing to score at ease, as Cervi swapped out Ratkovicz for Ed Peterson and then Peterson for Alex Hannum. The Nationals weren't out of the game, though, losing just 34–30 by halftime.

Two points each from Hannum, Seymour, and Schayes helped close the gap, but only by two as the Nationals allowed buckets from both Pollard and Mikan in that time frame. When Mikan converted a three-point play, the Lakers went back up by five. Schayes and Cervi each responded with a basket, and when Mikan fouled Schayes, Schayes made the game-tying free throw. Seymour was fouled the next time down the court and gave Syracuse a 42–41 lead, their first of the game.

Mikan countered with a hook shot from the pivot and Mikkelsen made the front-end of two free throws, the second of which Pollard tipped in, putting the Lakers back in front, but a pair of baskets from Peterson tied the score again at 46–46. Mikan broke loose for another hook shot to put Minneapolis ahead and Schayes returned the favor with a long-range set shot from along the baseline. When Hannum made a push shot despite a foul and sank the free throw as well, Syracuse established a three-point lead that they eventually expanded to seven, including a foul shot by Schayes that resulted from Mikkelsen's sixth foul. Mikkelsen was replaced in the lineup by Bud Grant. Mikan then scored six points in a row and Pollard made a free throw to tie the game at 61–61 with five minutes and 40 seconds to go.

Schayes drove to the basket and finished a layup through contact, and when Grant was whistled for a foul on the shot, Schayes sank the free throw to complete the three-point play and give the Nationals a three-point lead. Mikan and Seymour traded foul shots as Syracuse stalled in an attempt to stop the Lakers from coming back, but Bob Harrison stole a loose ball and raced down the court in a fast break to make an open layup that cut the Nationals' lead to just one at 65–64 with two minutes and ten seconds remaining. The Lakers had to foul, and Harrison fouled Seymour, who made a free throw to extend the Nationals' lead to two. With one minute and 15 seconds remaining, Pollard handed the ball off to Grant, who tied the game with a one-handed set shot from just behind the free throw circle.

The Nationals made a conscious effort to hold onto the ball for the final minute of the game, but instead of waiting until the last second, Cervi found an opening with seven seconds left, snuck past Martin, and put up an underhand layup. Mikan blocked the shot and grabbed hold of the rebound. He found Harrison on the left flank with an outlet pass, and Harrison let a shot fly from one dribble inside of halfcourt with one second left. He swished it. All Syracuse had time for was a wildly inaccurate full-court shot by Seymour before it was official that Minneapolis had won the series opener, with Bob Harrison having made a game-winning shot from around 40 feet out in the first ever NBA Finals game. Harrison dedicated his game-winner to his wife, Ruth, who was celebrating her birthday that day.

Harrison scored eight points and the shot that had put the Lakers in the position for a game-winner was Grant's only two points of the game. Foul trouble limited Mikkelsen to six points while allowing Schayes and Ratkovicz, the two players he spent significant time defending, to score 19 and 13, the most and second most on the Nationals. Syracuse's backcourt duo of Cervi and Gabor combined for just five points. Mikan scored 37 points, although only on 13-of-35 shooting from the field. Pollard added 14 points. With their 68–66 win to lead the series 1–0, the Lakers took away home advantage from Syracuse.[3]

After the game, Cervi cursed up a storm about "those lucky Lakers." Syracuse may have lost the battle, but Nationals players were adamant they'd win the war, and the dramatic ending that caused heartbreak for Syracuse players and fans alike lit a fire under them and led Billy Gabor to proclaim, "We can take the Lakers four straight from here."[4]

Cervi continued to adjust his lineup, returning to Hannum as starting center instead of Ratkovicz, and it was a Hannum push shot that kickstarted the back-and-forth first few minutes of Game 2. Trailing 17–16 at the end of the first quarter, Syracuse substitutions had a profound impact on the game when Johnny Macknowski and Ratkovicz sparked the Nationals to a 32–27 lead.

A 5–0 run consisting of a free throw by Ed Peterson, a set shot by Fuzzy Levane, and a driving layup by Ratkovicz extended the Nationals' lead to ten with three minutes left in the second quarter. Midway through the third quarter, that lead had doubled, with Gabor and Schayes guiding Syracuse to a 62–42 lead. Mikan took over the game from then on as the Lakers battled their way back, but the deficit was too large for Minneapolis to overcome and the Nationals won 91–85. Mikan scored 32 points, Pollard added 16, and Grant scored 12 off the bench, but Mikkelsen once again underperformed and only ended up with six points. The Nationals had significant contributions from almost every player, most significantly Ratkovicz, who led them in scoring with 17 points, most of them coming as Syracuse accumulated their lead.[5]

With the series tied 1–1 after back-to-back games in Syracuse, the Nationals and Lakers had four days off to rest before Minneapolis' first home game of the series, which would actually be in nearby St. Paul, Minnesota, because of scheduling conflicts with the Lakers' usual Minneapolis Auditorium. That didn't mean that the NBA was on pause, though. The very next day would be the NBA's annual meeting in New York and, right after it, the 1950 NBA draft.

The league meeting wouldn't be a simple one.

The implementation of the territorial pick had been one of the most contentious issues throughout the existence of the BAA, and with it having been in effect for one draft now with two territorial selections (St. Louis' of Ed Macauley and Minneapolis' of Vern Mikkelsen) having been made, the specifics were bound to be reviewed once again.

Fort Wayne in particular wanted the rules to be changed to increase the range of territorial pick eligibility from within 50 miles of a team's arena to within 100 miles. They had an unmistakably insincere reason for advocating for this; the most sought-after center in the draft and likely first pick overall, Chuck Share, had attended Bowling Green State University just over 80 miles away from Fort Wayne and the Pistons were desperate to add a young star center. At the same time, they had a legitimate argument that the territorial pick, as it stood, was bad for the league, particularly from a parity standpoint.

Every college within 50 miles of Fort Wayne combined to produce just one NBA player, Ralph Johnson. If the league increased that to 100 miles, players from Bowling Green, the University of Notre Dame, Western Michigan University, and the University of Toledo, all of whom had produced NBA players, would be eligible for the Pistons to select.

Other small-market teams were in the same boat; Waterloo didn't have a single college that had ever produced an NBA, BAA, or NBL player within 50 miles. Sheboygan was limited to selecting players from Marquette University with the current system and the new proposal would allow them to select players from the University of Wisconsin, including Don Rehfeldt, an All-American who was expected to be among the top picks in the upcoming draft. On the other hand, the Philadelphia Warriors and New York Knicks had the luxury of multiple top-tier college programs to choose territorial picks from. The Pistons hoped that the addition of the Midwestern former NBL teams since the last annual meeting would give them enough of a collection of sympathetic owners to force through an amendment to the rule in time for Fort Wayne to select Share with a territorial pick.

The Pistons weren't alone in bringing their own individual agenda to the meeting. The Boston Celtics had intended on playing a series of four exhibition games against local opponents to end their season, but Podoloff forced them to cancel the games because they were scheduled to take place while the playoffs were still ongoing. Walter Brown bristled at Podoloff's embargo on postseason exhibitions and, already frustrated by the Celtics' failing to make a profit and preoccupied by an arena dispute with the College of the Holy Cross, Brown openly threatened that the Celtics were "going to demand a lot of concessions at the draft meeting ... and if we don't get what we want, that will be the end of pro basketball in Boston."[6]

The Anderson Packers, as Ike Duffey prepared to sell the rest of his stake in the team to the Packers Civic Committee as part of the deal they'd come to in January, were also bound to have some demands of the league—chiefly, putting down in writing the promise Podoloff had previously made to Duffey that each team would play every other team an equal number of times in 1950–51.

The biggest threat to the league's hierarchy, though, was Ned Irish. For once, he hadn't preemptively spelled out what he planned to advocate for, but that brought little comfort to the other owners who realized quite plainly that the New York Knicks always got everything they wanted and Irish had only gotten more bold with his demands as time went on.

Another question that would inevitably come up is what would happen with the St. Louis Bombers.

After the end of their last game of the season, Emory Jones addressed the fans with a statement about the future of the team, "There are three things we can do: sell the players and franchise for somebody else to operate, sell the players' contracts if we intend to liquidate, or proceed with the intention of operating next year."

Bob Soell's consortium made a preliminary bid of $30,000 for the team, a figure that was flatly rejected. Two other groups of St. Louis businessmen also began negotiations with Jones behind closed doors.[7]

One possibility that gained a bit of traction was for the team to copy the Olympians' player-owner experiment and sell the team to Ed Macauley, Belus Smawley, and Johnny Logan. The issue with that was that the prospective Indianapolis player-owners had been given a loan to make the purchase, and for that reason the NBA was far less likely to go out of its way to initiate a sale to the Bombers trio.

Ben Kerner of the Tri-Cities Blackhawks got involved in the bidding war with the idea of buying the team in order to dissolve it and transfer the rights of all of the Bombers' players to the Blackhawks. Most probably would never get a chance to make the team, but the addition of Ed Macauley, Johnny Logan, Belus Smawley, and Red Rocha to a team that already had enough talent to make the playoffs would surely turn Tri-Cities into one of the league's best teams. His offer wasn't one that Jones was willing to accept, though. Although Kerner told Jones he was willing to improve his bid if one of the three St. Louis groups outbid him, Jones rebuffed him, letting him know that if any of the St. Louis groups met his asking price, he would accept without further negotiation in order to keep the team in St. Louis.[8]

Three days before the annual meeting, that changed. Two of the local ownership groups dropped out and only Soell remained. Jones conceded that he would have to seriously consider offers that would include relocation if Soell couldn't make an offer in the territory of $35,000. The chances that the Bombers would remain in St. Louis were rapidly diminishing, and while Jones refused to take the possibility of the team remaining under current ownership off the table, he was operating as if a sale had to be imminent if the franchise were to survive.[9]

It certainly was not the case that every team had been a source of steady profit. That was apparent in some cases even to the casual observer. When it came down to it, only nine of the 17 teams were moneymakers—Fort Wayne, Indianapolis, Minneapolis, New York, Rochester, Sheboygan, Syracuse, Tri-Cities, and Waterloo. Anderson and Philadelphia broke even. Baltimore, Boston, Chicago, Denver, St. Louis, and Washington all lost money.

Podoloff described the monetary loss as a function of "growing pains." He also had grave concerns about the setup of the league that he hadn't previously made known to the public.

He breached the topics of travel difficulties, scheduling imbalances, and the awkwardness of how having three divisions led to Syracuse's bye round. A possible solution he brought up: shrinking the league to 10 or 12 teams.[10]

In an effort to ensure that teams in the red could survive their financial issues, and implicitly as a way to reduce the number of teams in the league if at all possible, Podoloff then announced that the NBA league office would require each team to pay a $50,000 "performance bond" of $15,000 in cash and $35,000 in bonds to the league office within a week.[11]

Not every owner was happy about that. $50,000 was as much money as some of the stingier teams spent on their entire playing rosters, and while the expectation was that Podoloff would use the money to the benefit of all teams, the league office's favoritism toward certain teams was no secret and worries that Podoloff would use it to prop up certain large-market teams that were losing money—namely Chicago—were prevalent.

Most concerned was Ike Duffey. He gave the league office an ultimatum that the league had to formally adopt a rule to either give each team equal schedules or guarantee revenue sharing of gate receipts between every team. Neither Podoloff nor a majority of NBA owners agreed to either proposal.

In response, Duffey said that he couldn't in good faith pay the performance bond to the league. That was all Podoloff needed to hear in order to have reason to expel the Anderson Packers from the NBA. The league office bought the team from Duffey for $25,000, dissolved the franchise, and ended the meeting early. The remaining 16 teams would hold another meeting two weeks later, after performance bonds had been submitted, at the Stevens Hotel in Chicago.

After April 10, the Anderson Packers ceased to exist as an NBA team, just five days after being eliminated from the playoffs. The Packers probably wouldn't be alone; Podoloff remarked in the meeting that "10 teams, or 12 at the most" would be ideal. Sportswriters immediately began guessing who the unlucky teams would be. Denver, St. Louis, Waterloo, Sheboygan, Boston, Tri-Cities, Chicago, and Baltimore were all mentioned as possible casualties over the next few days.[12]

It was no secret what Podoloff himself preferred: a few weeks prior, he made that clear when he said that "basketball never prospered in the old days because it was operated by small independent owners who couldn't stand a few losing seasons. A few years ago, the owners of the buildings took an interest. Some of them have had to go along with losing teams for three or four years, but they're willing to stick."[13] Whether that was true was questionable; six of the ten founding teams of the BAA persisted, only a slightly better ratio than the six of 12 teams from that same season's NBL arrangement, but the former NBL teams, especially with Duffey no longer around as an advocate, were certainly the ones that were in the biggest position to worry.

The next day, Red Auerbach resigned as head coach of the Tri-Cities Blackhawks, citing poor health. Auerbach had lost about 25 pounds over the course of the season and was taking weeks to recover from a cold. In addition, his four-year-old daughter, Nancy, was battling asthma and couldn't spend extended time in Moline without aggravating her symptoms. In all likelihood, he would be announced as the University of Maryland's new coach within the week, a job that would significantly reduce his salary but would have fewer games, less travel, and allow him to be with his family year-round.[14]

Although Ben Kerner didn't expect to lose Auerbach and the Blackhawks' having to search for their fifth coach in as many years wasn't an encouraging situation, Tri-Cities was lucky enough to have a highly regarded unemployed head coach declare interest in the position right away.

Pops Harrison had coached the University of Iowa to a 98–42 record since being hired in 1942–43 and was off to a 9–2 start to the 1949–50 season before he was sidelined by a kidney operation and eventually fired amid a falling-out with Iowa's athletic director. He'd coached Murray Wier in college, so he already had a connection to the Tri-Cities team, and there was no way he was going to stay in college basketball if he could help it, as he publicly feuded with his old employer over how the NCAA itself operated. Harrison wanted the job and he was quite likely going to be the most qualified candidate, but his exit from Iowa stemming from a clash of personalities was somewhat troubling, considering Kerner was hands-on enough to rarely avoid conflict with his coaches. Other possible candidates included Doxie Moore and Charley Shipp, each of whom had coached in the NBA this season.

The Lakers and Nationals met again. For Syracuse, the focus would be on winning one of the next two games in Minneapolis so they could take back home advantage before Game 5. John Kundla was worried that exact situation might play out, remarking after a practice the day before the game, "If we play the way they practiced today, we are in for trouble tomorrow night."[15]

What Kundla didn't yet know was that Syracuse was weakened by the absence of Billy Gabor, who had tonsillitis, and the possible limitation of Adolph Schayes, who had a cold. Johnny Macknowski would start in Gabor's place.

Alex Hannum kept George Mikan in check to start off the game, but that didn't stop Vern Mikkelsen from connecting on consecutive tip-ins of Mikan's missed shot attempts to open the game as Minneapolis grabbed an early 4–0 lead.

Seven minutes and 45 seconds passed before Mikan scored his first points of the game, but Minneapolis had a 12–11 lead at that point anyways, and he scored seven points in the next few minutes to give the Lakers a 21–15 lead by the end of the quarter. The Lakers boosted their lead to nine before the Nationals came right back into the game with an 8–0 run. Hannum was the driving factor of the comeback, but Syracuse would've needed to dig themselves out of a much deeper hole if it weren't for Macknowski, who tallied 12 points in the first half, at the end of which the Lakers led 42–39.

Minneapolis' lead increased to seven when Mikan scored from right beneath the basket and Jim Pollard added a pair of free throws. Schayes responded with a couple of foul shots for the Nationals, Hannum added a push shot, and Schayes sank another free throw and a jump shot with Minneapolis' only answer being two points from Arnie Ferrin. Macknowski sank a jump shot from long range and, all of a sudden, Syracuse had tied the game at 48–48 with seven minutes and 50 seconds left in the third quarter.

Mikan grabbed the lead back for the Lakers, soon followed up by another basket from Mikkelsen, and Mikan responded to a Macknowski free throw with a shot that put Minneapolis up by five. On the next play, Paul Seymour twisted his ankle and had to sit out the rest of the game. While Seymour wasn't playing particularly well, shooting just 2-of-11, his presence as a defender and as a secondary playmaker in Gabor's absence was tactically important and the absence of him and Gabor combined was too much for the Nationals to overcome. They quickly fell behind by double digits and ultimately lost 91–77. Mikan and Mikkelsen played one of their best games together, scoring 28 and 27 points, respectively. Mikan also added eight assists, more than any center ever had in a playoff game before. The Lakers post duo's proficiency was only rivaled by Macknowski, who scored 25 points on just 14 shots. Every one of Macknowski's eight field goals was from long range. Schayes was largely uninvolved, only attempting eight shots all game in addition to conceding more points to Mikkelsen than he had allowed from a matchup in any other game all season. Al Cervi was even worse, shooting 0-of-6 and scoring two points. Even if Syracuse had been fully healthy, having their two All-NBA players combine for 14 points—just one more than the Lakers' third-highest scorer, Pollard—would have given them quite the uphill battle to fight. Minneapolis led the series 2–1.[16]

A conversation with a fan at the game about the future of the league following the Anderson Packers' demise prompted Maurice Podoloff to give an impromptu speech to the media present in the Minneapolis crowd.

First, he announced that Noble Jorgensen had been sold from the Sheboygan Redskins to the Tri-Cities Blackhawks. This meant a few things; the Blackhawks' planned to move Jack Nichols to power forward so he didn't have to get entangled in post battles as often, Ben Kerner had almost certainly given up on the possibility of buying the St. Louis Bombers and pairing Nichols with Ed Macauley, Pops Harrison's chances of getting the Tri-Cities job were astronomically high since they now had both of the NBA's only two University of Iowa alumni in Jorgensen and Murray Wier, and the Sheboygan Redskins' position in the NBA was likely more tenuous than expected.

He admitted as much, calling the Redskins "weakened" by the trade and also referring to Denver as "in a difficult position," implying that both teams, as well as Waterloo, had likely played their last NBA game. He also revealed the league office had submitted a bid to buy the St. Louis Bombers in order to dispose of the team like they had done a few days prior with the Packers. Podoloff was well on his way to cutting down the number of

NBA teams significantly from what he was now willing to openly refer to as "an impossible situation" of a first-year, 17-team league.[17]

After that, he had to take a flight to Chicago for a meeting. That meeting would consist of himself, Leo Ferris, and Ben Kerner representing the league, Sheboygan Redskins president Magnus Brinkman, Waterloo Hawks president Chris Marsau, and representatives from possible ownership groups from Anderson, Indiana; Des Moines, Iowa; Grand Rapids, Michigan; Racine, Wisconsin; and Sandusky, Ohio. There, Podoloff would propose an "affiliated league" to the NBA as a compromise in order to avoid fully ousting the teams from league-organized professional basketball. This way, Sheboygan and Waterloo would be able to hold on to the rights of as many players as they could afford to, unlike the expelled Anderson and as would likewise be St. Louis' fate should they fail to accept the league's offer. There would necessarily be a lower budget, smaller rosters, and a shorter schedule, though. The league would consist of eight teams; presumably the seven cities represented at the meeting and one of three other interested parties: Green Bay, Wisconsin; Hammond, Indiana; or Bob Soell's ownership group from St. Louis, Missouri. Altogether, this proposal was conspicuously similar to the sort of minor league Podoloff had been quick to suppress when Les Harrison publicly suggested it two and a half months prior.[18]

Both Billy Gabor and Paul Seymour would be ready to go for Game 4, which was now decidedly the most important game of Syracuse's season. Slater Martin had fully compromised Al Cervi's impact on the series' first three games, so Cervi took this as a chance to mix things up by bringing himself off the bench, moving Gabor to point guard in order to slot Johnny Macknowski into the starting shooting guard position in the wake of his 25-point game while still bringing Seymour back into the starting five.

George Mikan opened the game's scoring by finishing a fast break layup despite contact from Alex Hannum, resulting in a three-point play. Hannum retaliated with a fast break three-point play of his own, drawing a foul from Mikan, and after that, the Nationals began to use a full-court press in a bid to keep the game fast-paced and put extra pressure on Minneapolis' guard pairing of Martin and Arnie Ferrin. Hannum scored each of the game's next three field goals as the Nationals established a 9–6 lead over the Lakers, with all nine of Syracuse's points coming from Hannum.

While Hannum and Adolph Schayes were keeping Mikan and Mikkelsen from getting any scoring momentum early on, Jim Pollard kept the Nationals from getting too far ahead by capitalizing on his own teammates' mistakes, tapping in a long-range miss one play and grabbing a ball that Mikan fumbled and driving in for a layup the next. After Gabor earned himself a technical foul for throwing the ball too hard in the direction of referee John Nucatola, the Lakers tied the game with a free throw that made the score 14–14, and when Martin made a pair of baskets without retort, Minneapolis held a four-point lead. They conserved that lead for the rest of the quarter and led 27–22 coming into the second quarter.

Syracuse raced back with an 11–3 run that included scoring from all five of the players on the floor (four starters plus Cervi in Seymour's place) to put the Nationals back in the lead before long. The game stayed tight for quite a while until, three minutes into the third period, Mikan took over the game and led the Lakers on a 11–2 run to give Minneapolis their first double-digit lead of the game.

Schayes led a comeback with a jump shot and a three-point play and it wasn't long before Syracuse was back within three points. Mikkelsen drove past Cervi for a layup, but before the Nationals could answer, Gabor and Pollard had a brief tussle at mid-court. They were issued a double-foul with each player earning a free throw. Pollard made his and Gabor missed his. Hannum and Fuzzy Levane each hit a shot to bring the Nationals behind by only a score of 59–57, but Mikan drew a shooting foul, made his first free throw, missed his second, and tipped in his own miss to increase the Lakers' lead to five before the end of the quarter.

For the next eight minutes, the Nationals trailed by between five and 10 points until Cervi made three consecutive foul shots to close the gap to a 70–67 Minneapolis lead. Herman Schaefer made a turnaround jumper from the free throw line and Mikan tipped in a missed Mikkelsen free throw, putting the Lakers up by seven with four minutes left. Syracuse had to resort to fouling after that, and even after Martin and Mikkelsen fouled out for the Lakers, it was too much of an uphill battle for Syracuse. Mikan, despite his slow start, ended up with 28 points, although it was on 8-of-26 shooting. Pollard and Mikkelsen added 17 and 14, respectively. Schayes and Hannum led the way for the Nationals with 18 points apiece, but there wasn't much aside from that duo keeping Syracuse in the game. Gabor and Seymour each failed to score more than a single free throw, Ratkovicz scored merely four points in his first single-digit game of the playoffs, and Macknowski and Cervi each scored in double digits but combined to shoot just 4-of-17 from the field. Minneapolis won 77–69 to extend their series lead to 3–1.[19]

Magnus Brinkman was defiant in his response to the suggestion that the Sheboygan Redskins belonged in what would certainly amount to a minor league. He attended Podoloff and Ferris' meeting in Chicago out of courtesy, but there was no convincing the president of a team that had nearly just upset a one seed in the playoffs, turned a profit when nearly half the league didn't, had won a championship unlike 10 of the remaining 16 teams, and had successfully operated for more than 20 years that his franchise was one of the NBA's weak links.

The day after the meeting, he made it clear that he wanted no part of an affiliated league. The Redskins had enough surplus money to pay the NBA's required performance bond, and Brinkman planned on paying it and securing his team's spot in the NBA, but first he wanted a guarantee that he wouldn't be giving the league $50,000 just to get shafted anyway. Remaining in the NBA was still the ultimate intention, but there was no mincing of words: if Sheboygan was ultimately booted out of the NBA, Brinkman wouldn't go down without a fight and the Redskins would "be the nucleus of a new league which will not be associated with the NBA."[20]

Chris Marsau of Waterloo, who had a harder time coming up with the funds to stay in the league but was also able to after a fundraising effort, had ostensibly similar views to Brinkman but a much more diplomatic approach, refraining from commenting aside from that Waterloo would remain in major league professional basketball regardless of what anybody else ultimately decided.

Meanwhile, the fragile state of the St. Louis Bombers was leading owners other than Kerner to declare their interest in buying the team in order to add St. Louis' top players to their existing teams. Joe Rash of the Baltimore Bullets announced his intention to submit a bid for the team and give Buddy Jeannette a chance to form the next season's Bullets out of a combination of Baltimore and St. Louis players.[21] St. Louis officials made the suggestion that Ned Irish was also interested in buying the team for the sole purpose of bringing Macauley to the Knicks, but the Knicks issued a public denial of their interest.[22]

11. The Finals

Game 5 and every game onward was do-or-die for the Syracuse Nationals, with three consecutive wins needed in order to recover from their 3–1 series deficit. That was poised to be a significant uphill battle considering the Lakers had only lost three straight games once before in their history, in the form of a four-game losing streak near the beginning of the 1947–48 season just after Mikan joined from the Chicago Gears.

Cervi reverted the Nationals' starting lineup to the one including himself instead of Macknowski that was commonplace for Syracuse, but doubled down on the full-court press he introduced in the previous game, which had been a relative success despite the loss, suggesting "that is the only way to beat them, and we have to win tonight." Cervi also asserted that his team would be more competitive going forward because of Schayes and Gabor no longer fighting the illnesses they dealt with in Minnesota, clarifying that Schayes hadn't been quite able to play "his regular brand of ball" so far in the series.[23]

The Lakers, on the other hand, didn't have many adjustments to make. Coming off of two fairly convincing wins and with only one more needed in order to claim the championship, playing Game 5 away from home was less daunting than it would have been if the series was tied 2–2. There was also the unique factor of having shot worse than Syracuse in all four games but still coming away with three wins, something that highlighted how thoroughly Minneapolis' frontcourt was able to outrebound Syracuse despite generally above-average performances from Schayes, Alex Hannum, and George Ratkovicz on the part of the Nationals. John Kundla was characteristically reserved with his comments, stating just that his team was healthy and that Syracuse was a good team that was tough to beat at home but that he hoped Minneapolis would win.

The game started off slowly, and after Mikkelsen converted on a putback of a miss by Mikan, both teams came up short each of their next four possessions before Paul Seymour responded with the Nationals' first points of the game in the form of a layup assisted by Gabor.

Mikan and Jim Pollard each scored a field goal to give the Lakers an early 6–2 lead, but Johnny Macknowski sparked a brief run for the Nationals and converted a three-point play to give Syracuse their first lead of the game at 8–7 with five minutes left in the first quarter. Before the quarter's end, the lead changed hands three more times and was tied twice, with five quick points from Mikan giving the Lakers a 16–14 lead a quarter of the way into the game.

Macknowski tied the score with a shot from long range, and after Pollard and Adolph Schayes traded free throws, Schayes made a jumper to put Syracuse back in front. Mikan tightened the Nationals' lead to one with a foul shot, but George Ratkovicz answered with one of his own and Schayes sank a shot from long range to make the lead four. Mikan made another free throw and Mikkelsen tossed in a shot from right under the basket for Minneapolis' first field goal of the quarter to bring the game back within one in the form of a 22–21 Syracuse lead.

No other Laker made another field goal for the rest of the second quarter. Cervi sank a foul shot and followed it up with a driving layup on the next possession. Macknowski made a shot from long range to increase Syracuse's lead to six, and after a Macknowski free throw, Cervi and Ratkovicz each also sank long-range shots, Ratkovicz's from 30 feet out. Mikkelsen made a free throw to halt the Nationals' run at 10–0, but Paul Seymour and Schayes combined for five straight points soon after and Syracuse was ahead 37–22.

The Lakers reached a boiling point and Mikkelsen and Ratkovicz squared up for a fight, although it was broken up before it ever began. Right as the quarter came to a close, Mikan and Schayes also nearly came to blows after they got too physical with each other fighting for a loose ball, but they were swiftly ushered off to their respective locker rooms.

All in all, Syracuse outscored Minneapolis 24–8 in the second quarter to lead 38–24 at halftime, and the Nationals continued to race ahead with a team effort. With five minutes left in the game and a 73–52 Syracuse lead, John Kundla effectively conceded defeat by pulling Mikan out of the game. Bud Grant and Don Carlson led a late Lakers rally, but it was far too late to matter and Minneapolis didn't get back within single figures until the final seconds. The Nationals extended the series to a sixth game with an 83–76 win. Mikan led all scoring with 28 points and Mikkelsen added 17, but Jim Pollard was barely involved in the game and the eight-point contributions from both Grant and Carlson came after Minneapolis was already out of the game. Nineteen points from Schayes topped the Nationals' scoring, but particularly important was the drastic improvement of Syracuse's backcourt, with Macknowski, Seymour, and Gabor each scoring 12 points and Cervi scoring 10. Minneapolis led the series 3–2 and the two teams were heading to Minneapolis for Game 6.[24]

The University of Maryland hired Bud Millikan, head coach of Newton High School in Newton, Iowa, and a former star guard for Oklahoma A&M University, as their next coach after some confusion when a verbal agreement to coach Southwest Missouri State University, which he later rescinded in order to take the Maryland job, was leaked to the media. This meant Red Auerbach was still looking for a job following his resignation from the Blackhawks, although he'd actually pulled out of the running for the job shortly prior, stating, "I wouldn't take the [Maryland] job if they offered it to me."[25]

With the likelihood of St. Louis continuing to host the Bombers the next season diminishing, a number of Bombers players made it clear that they had no plans to stay with the team in the event of relocation, a revelation that ended any last chance of prospective ownership groups from other cities retaining an interest in buying the team.

That left just Bob Soell as a potential buyer aside from the league office. On the evening of April 22, Soell also rescinded his offer after it became clear that his valuation of the team and that of C. D. P. Hamilton, Jr., and Emory Jones were far removed from each other. Hamilton held a press conference hours later announcing his plans to accept the league office's offer and dissolve the franchise during the meeting in two days.[26]

Actually on their home court for the first time all series with their first two home games having been in neighboring St. Paul, the Lakers were looking to make serious improvements in order to win in front of their home crowd instead of allowing Syracuse to force a Game 7 back in Syracuse. Reflecting on the Game 5 loss, Kundla remarked, "I can't remember when we had a worse night shooting," and hinted that he thought they should be favorites to win Game 6 if they could turn their shooting performance around. Mikan concurred that it was "just one of those nights" but was fully confident in winning at home.[27]

Syracuse was still in the series, thanks to their inspired performance in the previous game, but they were far from safe. It remained the case that the Lakers had only lost in the Minneapolis Auditorium once in the last 14 months, and a Minneapolis win this time would mean a Minneapolis championship.

Pat Kennedy, the NBA's chief referee and one of the two assigned to Game 6, was ill and had to miss the game. His emergency replacement was Jim Beiersdorfer, a

Cincinnatian who Cervi had openly criticized for a supposed Midwestern bias throughout the season. The game progressed just seven seconds before Cervi began shouting complaints at Beiersdorfer.

Mikan opened the scoring with a tip-in, and that was just the start of a fantastic individual first quarter for him in which he scored 14 points. That was interrupted, however, by a fight between Pollard and Seymour underneath the Lakers' basket a minute and a half into the game. Players from both benches ran onto the court to get involved, as did quite a few fans—most notably golf administrator Harry Robinson, Jr., a Lakers fan, who sprinted 60 feet down from the upper level of seats to get down to the court. Ultimately, Minneapolis Police Department officers had to break up the brawl and send everyone back to their seats. The game continued without any of the players being punished.

Fights became the theme of the first half; as a plethora of missed free throws (mostly by Ratkovicz and Hannum) caused the Nationals to slip behind, Macknowski threw a punch at Pollard after Pollard fired the ball at Macknowski's face in anger at Macknowski having elbowed him too hard too many times without getting called for a foul, and Gabor briefly scuffled with both Don Carlson and Slater Martin in separate incidents.

Mikan and Pollard led the scoring to help Minneapolis grab a 10-point lead early in the second quarter, while Schayes had to sit on the bench after having been called for four fouls in the first quarter. Macknowski's shooting was the only thing keeping Minneapolis' lead from getting even more out of hand, but Don Carlson stepped up and got past Gabor for a couple of easy layups and the Lakers were ahead 51–39 at halftime with 28 points coming from Mikan alone, a record for postseason points in a half. Schayes, on the other hand, was still without a field goal.

The Nationals relied on fast breaks to try to catch up, but sloppiness on those fast breaks coincided with good shooting by Martin and Bud Grant for Minneapolis as the Nationals began to over-defend Mikan and the Lakers' lead continued to grow to an irreparable figure for Syracuse to come back from. With six minutes left in the third quarter, Mikan knocked Cervi to the ground as Cervi was trying to beat Carlson to a loose ball and Carlson landed on Cervi's arm while diving for the ball. Cervi was incensed when neither referee called a foul on either Mikan or Carlson and charged at referee John Nucatola, shouting that this was the worst officiating he had ever seen, with a string of expletives mixed in. Nucatola called Cervi for an unsportsmanlike conduct technical foul and banished him from the game. From there, the Nationals fell apart, ending the quarter behind 81–56. Even a 39-point fourth-quarter outburst for Syracuse led by Schayes, matching the Nationals' entire first-half scoring effort, wasn't enough to close the gap much and the Lakers won 110–95.

Mikan scored 40 points on 13-of-20 shooting, becoming the first player to score 40 points in a postseason game since the merger, coming just two points from breaking the all-time postseason single-game scoring record he'd set the previous year in a 1949 BAA Finals game against the Capitols, and becoming the first player in the history of professional basketball to score 40 or more points on 20 or fewer shots. Pollard scored 16 points and dished out ten assists to become the first player in basketball history to have multiple games with double-digit assists in the same playoff series. Herman Schaefer scored 12 points on six shots, Carlson scored 10 points on five shots and also had six assists, and Martin made all four of his field goal attempts en route to a nine-point game. Vern Mikkelsen only shot 1-of-11 and ended up with more fouls (six) than points (five), but it didn't affect the result. For the losers, Schayes led the way with 23 points on 13 shots and Macknowski added 17 points off the bench, but Gabor, Ratkovicz, and Seymour combined for 9-of-38 shooting and Cervi only compiled three points and two assists before his ejection.[28]

After winning the series 4–2, the Minneapolis Lakers were the inaugural champions of the NBA. As champions of the NBL in 1947–48, BAA in 1948–49, and now the NBA in 1949–50, the Lakers became the first team in 37 years to win more than two consecutive major league professional basketball championships, the only previous team to have achieved this feat being the Troy Trojans from 1909–10 to 1912–13. To make this accomplishment all the more impressive, the Lakers had only existed for three years and therefore were yet to have ever failed to win a championship.

For rookies Vern Mikkelsen, Slater Martin, Bob Harrison, and Bud Grant, as well as mid-season acquisition Billy Hassett, this was their first championship. It was Arnie Ferrin's second championship in a two-year career thus far, Jim Pollard's third championship in three years, and George Mikan's fourth championship in four years. Don Carlson and Tony Jaros, although Jaros made a minimal impact in the playoffs because of his injury, won their third championship in a row with the Lakers after having lost in the BAA Finals together as rookies with the Stags. Herman Schaefer also won his third, having lost two championship series earlier in his career with the Fort Wayne Zollners.

John Kundla, as head coach of all three of the Lakers' title teams, was now a member of the exclusive club of professional basketball's three-time championship head coaches, joining Eddie Gottlieb, Bobby McDermott, Paul Sheeks, John Donlon, and Johnny Whitty.

Kundla called his team the best of the three champions he'd coached, even going as far as to say the previous season's Lakers "would've been a dead duck" during this season with how much tougher the post-merger NBA was than the BAA or NBL. Cervi went a step further and said the Lakers were "the greatest team that ever won a pro title" and predicted Minneapolis wouldn't lose another home game for the next two years.

The complementary nature of both coaches in regard to their teams and each other didn't stop Cervi's vitriol toward the referees. The Syracuse player-coach complained, "This entire playoff series has been officiated so poorly it is a disgrace. They've ruined the games for the players. I'm not mad at anybody but the officials.... Either the officials better improve or all of us better quit trying to play basketball."[29]

12

Expulsion and Integration

While Al Cervi was just venting his frustrations and had no intentions of quitting basketball, it was possible that the same thing couldn't be said about Walter Brown. On the day of the decisive Finals game, Brown announced his bid to purchase the Bombers' rights for $25,000, outbidding Joe Rash and Ned Irish. The one thing stopping the deal from being finalized was that the NBA league office objected, a move that led Brown to take an aggressive stance that the Celtics should be granted the rights of all St. Louis Bombers players and first choice among Anderson Packers players or else he'd pull out of the league.[1]

Once the remainder of the postponed annual meeting took shape on April 24, it became clear that Brown not only lacked leverage, he also didn't have nearly as complete of a deal with C. D. P. Hamilton, Jr., and Emory Jones as he'd thought. Representatives for the Madison Square Garden Corporation, in place of a vacationing Ned Irish, submitted a bid of $30,000 for the Bombers and Brown wasn't able to match it.

Brown backed down and united with the majority of other owners against the sale. By a majority vote, the NBA vetoed the sale of the St. Louis Bombers to the Madison Square Garden Corporation. The league office instead paid the proposed $30,000 price and suspended the St. Louis Bombers franchise, reducing the number of NBA franchises to 15.[2]

With both the former Packers players and the former Bombers players needing to be assigned to their new teams, a dispersal draft would be held in conjunction with the afternoon's 1950 NBA draft, in reverse order of the league standings just like for incoming rookies.

Babe Kimbrough, president of the Indianapolis Olympians, reintroduced the possibility of enacting a schedule that would guarantee every team the same number of games both at home and away, echoing Ike Duffey's previous demand. The Olympians, feeling disadvantaged by hosting popular teams only once throughout the season, believed they were being deprived of fair gate receipts. Realistically, travel constraints wouldn't allow this to be particularly feasible even if there wasn't a significant divide between the goals of large-market teams and small-market teams. Only Western Division owners (not including Ben Kerner of the Tri-Cities Blackhawks, who aligned himself with the former BAA establishment) had any concern for unequal scheduling, and most of them were already fighting for their very existence. The proposal was overwhelmingly rejected.[3]

Similarly, Fred Zollner's proposal to expand territorial rights from 50 to 100 miles received a negative response. The move would undeniably help small-market teams more than large-market teams, logistics would pose a challenge with a few colleges within 100 miles of multiple different teams, and there was no hiding the fact that this was a blatant attempt to change the rules for the sole purpose of getting Chuck Share onto the Pistons.

Kerner had the most unique proposal, suggesting that the NBA should switch from four 12-minute quarters back to four ten-minute quarters like the NBL had done and like the NCAA still was. None of the other owners agreed with him on that, including those who had come from the NBL.

Magnus Brinkman arrived with a proposal that was just as aggressive as Brown's, although in his case it was more of a desperate gamble to avoid the inevitable than a misguided attempt at a power play. He presented a set of three conditions necessary for him to post the performance bond on behalf of the Redskins. Firstly, the league would need to reverse its decision on the recently denied equalization of schedules measure. Secondly, the NBA had to guarantee that Sheboygan would be part of the NBA itself, not an affiliated league as previously suggested. Finally, Brinkman insisted on the adoption of "better business methods" by the league.[4]

At the onset of the meeting, Podoloff addressed each owner personally, inquiring about their willingness to pay the $50,000 fee. Sheboygan, Waterloo, and Denver all answered in the affirmative, coming as somewhat of a surprise and undermining the presumed intent of the fee.

The Chicago Stags, on the other hand, were the one team planning to remain in the league that hadn't come up with enough money.

Even with the team's poor attendance and subsequently insufficient finances, the city remained an integral part of Maurice Podoloff's NBA vision. To ensure the Stags' survival until the end of the season, the league office had already provided them with $40,000, and in that same spirit, Podoloff extended the Stags' performance bond payment deadline until June 1. While the Stags were safe from immediate dissolution, it was heavily insinuated that the rest of the league expected the Stags to be under new, more savvy ownership soon.[5]

In the afternoon session, Podoloff put forth a motion to exclude Denver, Waterloo, and Sheboygan from the 1950–51 NBA schedule. Every Eastern Division team, every Central Division team, and the Tri-Cities Blackhawks voted in favor. Denver, Waterloo, and Sheboygan, naturally, voted against it. Babe Kimbrough of the Indianapolis Olympians attempted to abstain, but Podoloff threatened Kimbrough that he was willing to include Indianapolis in the ouster, so Kimbrough reluctantly went along with the majority to make the vote unanimous among the remaining teams.[6]

The Sheboygan Redskins, Waterloo Hawks, and Denver Nuggets were officially no longer members of the NBA, and the NBA now had 12 teams which could be organized into two divisions instead of three. On a provisional basis, the 1950–51 NBA season's Western Division would consist of the Chicago Stags, Fort Wayne Pistons, Indianapolis Olympians, Minneapolis Lakers, Rochester Royals, and Tri-Cities Blackhawks. The Eastern Division would remain unchanged, with the Baltimore Bullets, Boston Celtics, New York Knicks, Philadelphia Warriors, Syracuse Nationals, and Washington Capitols all still in the league.

Less than ten minutes after being dismissed from the NBA, Brinkman, Chris Marsau, and Jerry L'Estrange held a meeting of their own in the same hotel.

L'Estrange was already on the Nuggets' board of directors before stepping into Denver's general manager position to replace Hal Davis, who resigned at the end of the season after four years with the team. A former Marquette University football player and World War I veteran, L'Estrange had a background in insurance and had previously served on the board of directors for the Oshkosh Giants minor league baseball team. In 1948–49, he had relocated to Denver and began his involvement with the Nuggets.

The trio had realized the expulsion of their teams from the NBA was a likely outcome ever since the Anderson Packers had folded, so they already had a plan in place to establish a new professional league in the image of the NBL to rival the NBA.

Recognizing the inevitable direction of the three departing teams, the NBA took proactive measures to foster a more amicable relationship between the leagues. Shortly after the meeting adjourned, select members of the NBA's executive board left and engaged in preliminary negotiations to establish a peace treaty between the NBA and the envisioned new league.

The NBA proposed four interleague regulations aimed at maintaining a harmonious dynamic: conducting an audit of NBA finances to distribute the rightful shares to the departing teams, honoring existing player contracts with no unauthorized transfers between leagues without compensation, scheduling exhibition games between NBA teams against Sheboygan and Waterloo (but not Denver), and implementing a joint draft system.

Brinkman, Marsau, and L'Estrange accepted the first point easily, as the money coming from the league office, ultimately $1,995 each, would help them begin to fund their own league before other teams even joined. They were also fine with respecting existing contracts, since that meant they could get extra money out of NBA teams for players like Dick Mehen, Kenny Sailors, and Bob Brannum if those players wanted to move back to NBA teams, but they were hesitant to formalize that legally. The prospect of hosting exhibitions against NBA teams also held little appeal for them, since the NBA teams wanted half the money from gate receipts to cover travel expenses.

The draft was a tougher topic. Both leagues wanted a joint draft, but each side had a wildly different idea of what that would be in practice.

The NBA wanted to give Waterloo the rights to Dick Schnittker of Ohio State University and Sheboygan the rights to Don Rehfeldt of the University of Wisconsin, conduct two or three rounds of selections for NBA teams exclusively, and all remaining college graduates would be deemed undrafted free agents who could sign with anyone that reached out to them regardless of league. Schnittker and Rehfeldt were both consensus NCAA All-Americans at the power forward position, both probable top five picks in the upcoming draft, and Schnittker was largely considered one of the top two forwards, alongside Paul Arizin, in all of college basketball. There were, though, concerns that Schnittker, also a defensive end for Ohio State's football team, was considering signing with the NFL's Cleveland Browns instead of playing basketball professionally, so whether the Hawks would even get anything out of that possible draft setup was questionable, and giving up the possibility to sign either 24 or 36 players in exchange for the rights to just two was a lousy tradeoff, especially for a startup league.

The new league wanted to structure the first round of the draft with teams' selection positions based in reverse order of their record the previous season, the team with the fewest wins selecting first, with a draft order of 1. Denver, 2. Waterloo, 3. Boston, 4. Sheboygan, 5. Baltimore, 6. Philadelphia, 7. Tri-Cities, 8. Washington, 9. Chicago, 10. New York, 11. Fort Wayne, 12. Indianapolis, 13. Rochester, 14. Minneapolis, and 15. Syracuse, and all subsequent rounds would alternate between the leagues every pick. That would mean the NBA would cede three of the top four picks, likely losing out on

Rehfeldt, Schnittker, and Chuck Share, as well as half of all prospects outside of the first round, to a league that didn't even exist yet.

Ultimately, the two sides were way too far apart and the idea for a joint draft was scrapped. The NBA would go ahead with its draft and its dispersal draft after the rest of the issues brought up in the meeting were resolved, with an order of 1. Boston, 2. Baltimore, 3. Philadelphia, 4. Tri-Cities, 5. Washington, 6. Chicago, 7. New York, 8. Fort Wayne, 9. Indianapolis, 10. Rochester, 11. Minneapolis, and 12. Syracuse for both. The new league likely wouldn't conduct a draft at all and would just sign players on a first-come, first-serve basis once all of its teams were decided. What was certain was that, just as there had been between the BAA and NBL, there was a player war brewing, at least when it came to incoming rookies.

The trio heading up the new league hired as commissioner recent Anderson Packers coach Doxie Moore, who had been the final NBL commissioner. They admitted each of their own three teams as franchises and reserved a fourth spot for Lon Darling, longtime owner of the Oshkosh All-Stars back in the NBL, to operate a team in either Oshkosh or Milwaukee.[7]

From there, the biggest questions were what the league's rules were going to be and who else would be in it. Magnus Brinkman proposed that the NBA rules largely be kept, including the expansion to six fouls from the five that the NBL had used, but wanted to revert to 40-minute games so that teams could have the option of using fewer reserve players in the event of a financial crisis and still be able to compete. Chris Marsau reasoned that the 40-minute games would lead to lower scoring like there had been in the NBL and that the lower scores would make it easier for people to characterize it as a minor league. As such, they came to a consensus that the new league would play 48-minute games like the NBA.

The optimal number of teams, it was decided, was ten, so that would require six new teams in addition to Denver, Oshkosh/Milwaukee, Sheboygan, and Waterloo. By the end of the day, they had received applications from groups representing 13 other cities: Anderson, Indiana; Colorado Springs, Colorado; Des Moines, Iowa; Evansville, Indiana; Grand Rapids, Michigan; Kansas City, Missouri; Omaha, Nebraska; Rockford, Illinois; Sioux City, Iowa; St. Louis, Missouri; St. Paul, Minnesota; Terre Haute, Indiana; and Toledo, Ohio. The city Brinkman would give highest priority to in the immediate future was Omaha, because a team based there would solve a lot of problems with the logistics of teams traveling so far west to Denver.[8]

Podoloff tried to publicly characterize the three teams' departure as voluntary resignations from the NBA, pointing out that none of them paid the $50,000 performance bond while ignoring that they had all been willing to pay it had they been guaranteed a spot in the league the next season. Brinkman refuted him, saying, "Any way you look at it, we were kicked out. We did not resign. They simply wouldn't have us in and told us so in the morning meetings." Podoloff was also dismissive of the new league's potential impact on the NBA, suggesting the NBA had an inherent advantage at attracting talent because they had the bigger arenas and operated in larger markets, while Brinkman retorted that big arenas weren't much of an asset when they were filled with empty seats.[9]

The NBA's final major issue to tackle in the meeting was how to appease Ned Irish now that they had denied him the rights to the St. Louis Bombers players. They had gone forward with getting rid of most of the small-market teams, which Irish and

Minneapolis Lakers co-owner Ben Berger had long advocated for, but that did very little to help the Knicks in any way other than a supposed effect on the prestige of New York's opponents.

In practice, Irish had very little interest in 10 of St. Louis' 11 players that buying the team would've given him access to, all he really wanted was Ed Macauley, because he believed a young star center like Macauley was all the Knicks needed to become the best team in the NBA.

Now that Macauley was off the board in terms of possible additions, the Knicks' options were limited. Macauley certainly wasn't going to be available with six teams having a chance to draft him before New York, Red Rocha and Milo Komenich didn't have enough star power to be upgrades over Connie Simmons at all, and Chuck Share, who the Knicks weren't as eager to pick as most teams anyway, had no chance of being available by the seventh pick in the draft. That was the extent of prominent NBA-eligible centers that the Knicks could use.

Irish's solution to this problem, like it often had been, was in the form of a threat to pull the Knicks out of the NBA altogether. He informed his proxies present at the meeting to give the other NBA owners an ultimatum: the majority of the NBA's other 11 owners would vote to integrate, or else the New York Knicks would no longer be an NBA team.

The first sign that the Knicks would push for integration, aside from Irish having voted for it against the wishes of most of the other BAA owners the year prior, had been right before the start of the playoffs when Joe Lapchick was asked about the players he thought would be the best prospects in the 1950 draft class. Among them, he listed Chuck Cooper of Duquesne University and Bucky Hatchett of Rutgers University, both black players, after quipping that "there may even be a couple of negro players in the league next year."[10]

Neither of those players were the answer to Irish's problem or the source of his show of force. Cooper was one of the best all-around centers in college basketball and a second-team All-American, but at 6'5" he wouldn't be tall enough to play center in the NBA, and expectations were that he would pass up the NBA to play for the Harlem Globetrotters anyways. Hatchett was a high-scoring athletic forward for Rutgers and a multisport athlete drawing interest from the NFL's Baltimore Colts, but that also didn't fit Irish's needs.

The player Irish wanted to add so badly that he was willing to take his team out of the NBA, a move that would possibly doom both the Knicks and the NBA itself, if the league didn't vote to fundamentally change the standards of eligibility, was Don Barksdale, star of the Oakland Blue 'n' Gold in the AAU.[11]

Barksdale was already a man of many firsts when it came to racial integration. In 1946–47 while playing for the University of California, Los Angeles, he became the second black basketball player (after George Gregory of Columbia University in 1930–31) to be named a consensus NCAA All-American when he was selected to the All-American Second Team. That same year, Barksdale and his UCLA teammate Dave Minor became the first two black players named as All–Pacific Coast Conference players as UCLA won the conference.

While playing for UCLA, Barksdale ran one of the two black-owned record stores in Los Angeles, which gave him the opportunity to come in constant contact with entertainers such as singer, musician, and actor Nat King Cole, who would later become the first black man to host a nationally aired American television show.

Connections he made with people like Cole let him break into the entertainment industry after he graduated, and after he moved to Oakland, California, to play for the Oakland Bittners, Barksdale became the first black radio disc jockey in the San Francisco Bay Area while working for the radio station KLX and the first black television host in the San Francisco Bay Area while hosting *Sepia Review* on KRON-TV; he also founded Blue & Gold Beer, the first black-owned beer distributor in the San Francisco Bay Area.

After Barksdale led the Bittners, the same team Jim Pollard and Bill Calhoun had played for the year before, to the semifinals of the AAU Tournament as a rookie, Oakland was selected as one of the eight teams to participate in the Olympic Trials in advance of the 1948 Olympic Games in order to select the roster of the United States national team that went on to easily win the gold medal.

While the starting lineups of the Olympic Trials' two finalists, the Phillips Oilers and the University of Kentucky, would compose the majority of the team heading to the Olympics, there were four other roster spots reserved for the best performers on the losing teams, so after Barksdale led the Bittners in scoring with 14 points in a 57–55 loss to the Denver Nuggets, he still ended up making the team alongside five players from Phillips, five players from Kentucky, Vince Boryla from the Nuggets, Ray Lumpp from New York University, and Jackie Robinson from Baylor University. When he was named to the team, a controversial move that provoked significant racist backlash and only was possible thanks to the continuous lobbying of Olympic Basketball Committee member and Oakland city council candidate Fred Maggiora, Barksdale became the first black basketball player to represent the United States national team.

Before the Olympics started, a brief series of exhibitions was played between the Oilers (plus Barksdale and Robinson) and Kentucky (plus Boryla and Lumpp). The third of the three games was in Lexington, Kentucky, where Barksdale couldn't stay at the same hotel as his teammates because of the strictly enforced policies of racial segregation the state of Kentucky had. Instead, Adolph Rupp, Kentucky head coach and United States national team assistant coach, arranged for Barksdale to stay in the house of a local black physician, Dr. J. R. Dalton. While staying with the Dalton family, Barksdale received a death threat warning him against playing for the Oilers in Lexington, but he played anyways, scoring 12 second-half points to lead a comeback victory for the Oilers, and in doing so, became the first black player to play against Kentucky in Kentucky's home arena. As they won the Olympic gold medal the next month, Barksdale scored the third-most points on the team while coming off the bench, behind just Bob Kurland and Alex Groza.

In 1949, Barksdale led the Oakland Bittners to an AAU championship and became the first black AAU All-American, helping the Bittners win their first title ever and toppling an Oilers team that had won each of the previous six years' championships. Back when he was in high school, Barksdale had been cut from his school's basketball team every year because the coach had a policy of only allowing one black player on the team at the time, and in college, Barksdale had to play two years for Marin Junior College before he was given an opportunity to play for a well-known basketball program, but he overcame those obstacles to become an Olympic gold medalist and the star player on an AAU champion.[12]

The Baltimore Bullets, Boston Celtics, Rochester Royals, Syracuse Nationals, and Washington Capitols voted for integration. The Chicago Stags, Indianapolis Olympians,

Don Barksdale (1948) was a pioneer in both basketball and entertainment. The second black NCAA All-American ever and the first black Olympic basketball player for the United States, he led the Oakland Bittners to break the Phillips Oilers' streak of six consecutive AAU championships, catching NBA attention. It was with the intention of signing Barksdale that Knicks owner Ned Irish pushed for the league's integration.

Minneapolis Lakers, Philadelphia Warriors, and Tri-Cities Blackhawks voted against it. The Knicks, as a formality, abstained from the vote in order to show their seriousness about leaving the NBA if it didn't pass. The deciding vote came down to Carl Bennett, general manager of the Fort Wayne Pistons. He voted "yea," completing the voting tally at 6–5 in favor of integrating the NBA.

As the team representatives exited the room for a second break in the meeting, with nothing left to do except conduct the draft, Eddie Gottlieb confronted Bennett in the hallway, lamenting, "Carl, you son of a bitch, you just ruined the league! In five years, 75% of the league is going to be black. We won't draw crowds. People won't come out to see them."[13]

Before the NBA draft came the dispersal draft for teams to select former members of the Anderson Packers and St. Louis Bombers.

With the first selection, the Boston Celtics selected Ed Macauley from the St. Louis Bombers.

With the second selection, the Baltimore Bullets selected Red Rocha from the St. Louis Bombers.

With the third selection, the Philadelphia Warriors selected Bill Closs from the Anderson Packers.

With the fourth selection, the Tri-Cities Blackhawks selected Johnny Logan from the St. Louis Bombers.

With the fifth selection, the Washington Capitols selected Ace Maughan from the St. Louis Bombers.

With the sixth selection, the Chicago Stags selected Frank Brian from the Anderson Packers.

New York and Indianapolis both forfeited their picks, which would have been the seventh and eighth selections.

With the seventh selection, the Fort Wayne Pistons selected John Hargis from the Anderson Packers.

With the eighth selection, the Rochester Royals selected Charlie Black from the Anderson Packers.

With the ninth selection, the Minneapolis Lakers selected Mac Otten from the St. Louis Bombers.

With the tenth selection, the Syracuse Nationals selected Belus Smawley from the St. Louis Bombers.

In the second round, Boston selected Ed Stanczak from Anderson, Baltimore selected Bill Roberts from St. Louis, Philadelphia selected Milo Komenich from Anderson, Tri-Cities selected Richie Niemiera from Anderson, and Washington selected Don Putman from St. Louis. In the third round, Baltimore selected Jim Owens from Anderson and Philadelphia selected Frank Gates from Anderson. In the fourth round, Philadelphia selected Easy Parham from St. Louis. Dermie O'Connell of the Bombers, Jake Carter of the Packers, D. C. Wilcutt formerly of the Bombers, and Rollie Seltz formerly of the Packers both went undrafted and were free to sign with any team.

Philadelphia was the only one of the 12 NBA teams to utilize the territorial pick rule that day, forfeiting the third overall pick in the draft to preemptively select Paul Arizin from Villanova University, college basketball's 1949–50 National Player of the Year and breaker of the NCAA record for the most points in a season with 735 (as well as second all-time in points per game with 25.3, behind Ernie Calverley's 26.7 in 1943–44).

This meant that the first round would proceed with the same order minus the Warriors, and the previously designated fourth pick the Tri-Cities Blackhawks held would now hold the third pick, with every selection after that also moving up one spot.

Paul Arizin (1949) was a smooth-scoring forward for Villanova University and the winner of the 1950 College Basketball Player of the Year. In the 1950 NBA Draft, the Philadelphia Warriors used special dispensation by way of his territorial rights in order to select him before the draft began. He was the third player selected as a territorial pick.

12. Expulsion and Integration

With the first pick overall, the Boston Celtics selected Chuck Share from Bowling Green State University.

With the second pick overall, the Baltimore Bullets selected Don Rehfeldt from the University of Wisconsin.

With the third pick overall, the Tri-Cities Blackhawks selected Bob Cousy from the College of the Holy Cross.

With the fourth pick overall, the Washington Capitols selected Dick Schnittker from Ohio State University.

With the fifth pick overall, the Chicago Stags selected Larry Foust from La Salle University.

With the sixth pick overall, the New York Knicks selected Irwin Dambrot from the City College of New York.

With the seventh pick overall, the Fort Wayne Pistons selected George Yardley from Stanford University.

With the eighth pick overall, the Indianapolis Olympians selected Bob Lavoy from Western Kentucky University.

With the ninth pick overall, the Rochester Royals selected Joe McNamee from the University of San Francisco.

With the tenth pick overall, the Minneapolis Lakers selected Kevin O'Shea from the University of Notre Dame.

With the eleventh pick overall, the Syracuse Nationals selected Don Lofgran from the University of San Francisco.

Walter Brown kicked off the second round of the draft by selecting Chuck Cooper from Duquesne University, making Cooper the first black player to be chosen in any NBA draft (with none having also been selected by any team in any of the three BAA drafts).

The room was initially silent, as everyone in the room, for or against the NBA's integration, realized the gravity of Brown's selection of Cooper. Finally, one of the owners who had voted against integration said, "Walter, don't you know he's a colored boy?"

Brown responded, "I don't give a damn if he's striped or polka dot or plaid, Boston takes Charles Cooper of Duquesne."[14] Whether Brown could actually add Cooper to the Celtics remained a question, since Cooper had joined the Harlem Globetrotters five weeks earlier and had already played 18 times for the Globetrotters, earning limited minutes as the backup center to Nathaniel Clifton.

Cooper eventually wasn't alone as the only black player selected in the 1950 NBA draft, as the Washington Capitols, a team whose home arena had been segregated until just 27 months prior, drafted Earl Lloyd of West Virginia State College in the ninth round with the 100th pick overall, making Lloyd the first NBA draft pick to come from an HBCU and the second black player to be drafted.

The first offer to buy the Chicago Stags came almost immediately, from Waterloo Hawks founder Pinkie George at a cost of $40,000 with the intention of keeping the Stags in Chicago but a backup plan of eventual relocation to Des Moines if Chicago's lack of support for the team continued for more than a couple years. John Sbarbaro signaled that he would wait for other offers and would make his decision on the sale of the Stags on June 1, the day of Chicago's deadline to pay the performance bond to the league office.[15]

On April 26, the Washington Capitols became the first team to sign any black player to an NBA contract, signing both Harold Hunter and Earl Lloyd.[16]

Hunter, a speedy 5'10" point guard from North Carolina College at Durham, had gone undrafted the day before but had led North Carolina College to a Colored Intercollegiate Athletic Association championship in 1949–50 and proved to be the best offensive player in the conference in the meantime.

Lloyd had also played in the CIAA and had led West Virginia State to two consecutive conference championships in 1947–48 and 1948–49, with a 30–0 record in 1947–48 serving as the highlight of his collegiate career. As a 6'6" center, his remarkable lateral quickness for his size and knowledge of defensive positioning made him an optimal defensive specialist prospect for the NBA despite how far he'd fallen in the draft, but the presence of Don Otten and Chuck Halbert already occupying the center position in addition to his height disadvantage meant he would almost certainly have to switch to power forward for Washington.

Although the two signed with the Capitols on the same day, Hunter was the official first black player to sign because his college coach, John McLendon, had accompanied the two to Washington to advocate for them and suggested Hunter sign first, using the excuse that Hunter should go first because he was shorter than Lloyd but in actuality simply wanting the player he had coached to be the first black NBA player.

They were soon joined in Washington by a third black player, Harry Taylor, a collegiate teammate of Hunter who, like Lloyd, was a 6'6" center.[17] Taylor had a reputation of being a capable scorer and was particularly well regarded for his hook shot.

Walter Brown hired Red Auerbach as the replacement to Doggie Julian and the third head coach in Boston Celtics history, signing Auerbach to a two-year contract at $8,000 per year . With Ed Macauley and Chuck Share leading the list of names added to the Celtics since the last time Boston had played a game, Auerbach already had more talent on his roster than either Honey Russell or Julian had ever had in Boston, and he made an explicit point that he would make any additional trades that he had to in order to improve the team, as he had at Tri-Cities, declaring, "I don't give a darn for sentiment or names," decrying the idea that having "local yokels" on the roster for attendance's sake was in any way a good idea, and endorsing Brown's draft selections of Macauley as "the second-best center in the league to Mikan" and Share as the would-be first pick selection of "11, at least, of the dozen league teams."[18]

Auerbach's successor at Tri-Cities was named four days later. Ben Kerner surprised many by selecting retired University of Minnesota head coach Dave MacMillan instead of Pops Harrison.[19]

MacMillan held the distinction of having the earliest association with professional basketball among NBA personnel, having first played as a utility player off the bench for the South Side Germans in 1910–11.

It was that early association with the professional version of the sport as a player, his mentorship of John Kundla at Minnesota, and having produced NBA players Don Carlson, Kleggie Hermsen, Tony Jaros, and Bud Grant that led Kerner to overlook MacMillan's merely respectable college record of 297–192 and the fact that he'd only won a single conference championship since the 1922–23 season. Kerner secured his services with a three-year contract, recognizing the potential of his offensive-minded play style that always seemed to get the most out of quick players for a team that had just added Johnny Logan and Bob Cousy to the backcourt.

Chuck Cooper announced his intention to join the Celtics and become one of the NBA's first black players with a simple statement: "I am very much interested in joining

Boston and will be waiting to talk terms with them." Abe Saperstein, believing he held indefinite rights to Cooper, threatened Walter Brown that if the Celtics pursued negotiations with Cooper, the Harlem Globetrotters would never play in the Boston Arena or Boston Garden again. Brown, while realizing the financial ramifications of no longer being able to host the Globetrotters, accepted the consequences, although not without pointing out that he didn't think it should be such a big deal, since Cooper wasn't an established member of the Globetrotters.[20]

The Waterloo Hawks signed Pops Harrison as general manager less than a week after he lost out on the Tri-Cities coaching job.[21] Harrison's first move in charge of the Hawks was to sign Chuck Share, the NBA's first draft pick, to a two-year contract.[22] Even more than the obvious boost in talent this would provide Waterloo, this served as a coup for the new league and a sign that the exiled former small-market NBA teams had enough pulling power to compete with, at a bare minimum, the less successful NBA franchises for top-level young talent.

Share would get to team up with two of his former college teammates from Bowling Green State University in Leo Kubiak and Johnny Payak. Waterloo coach Jack Smiley was thrilled with the addition of basketball's 6'11", 230 lb. prize rookie and characterized his upside as "potentially another George Mikan, with plenty of height and speed," and Boston was left without the possibility of adding one of the most promising young players in the sport to an aging frontcourt on a team lacking particularly dynamic players. With Ed Macauley also having not signed yet and the new league possibly including a team from St. Louis, chances were that the Celtics, desperate for new talent, might end up with neither of their most exciting offseason additions.

On May 13, the new league that had promised to rival the NBA was officially founded at the Morrison Hotel in Chicago. The league would operate as the National Professional Basketball League (NPBL), an obvious homage to the NBL, and the representatives of prospective teams in addition to the cofounders in Denver, Sheboygan, and Waterloo included the former owners of the NBL's Indianapolis Kautskys, Oshkosh All-Stars, and Toledo White Chevrolets, plus a community group with some overlap with the group Ike Duffey had planned to turn the Anderson Packers over to before the team shut down. Magnus Brinkman was introduced as president of the NPBL, operating alongside commissioner Doxie Moore to provide a two-pronged executive of the league based on the NBL model, instead of allowing a single executive unchecked reign over the league as Maurice Podoloff had in the first year of the NBA and in the BAA before it.

Brinkman announced that temporary league offices had been set up in Lafayette, Indiana, and that prospective teams' applications to the NPBL would be considered and decided upon within 30 days. Each team would have to post a $3,000 fee to join, and the three founding members had already done so.[23] Three other teams also were granted charter membership to the NPBL, as Denver, Milwaukee/Oshkosh, Sheboygan, and Waterloo were joined by Anderson and St. Louis to form six out of what Brinkman promised to be "at least eight and probably 10 teams."[24]

The first correspondence the NPBL received from the NBA was an ultimatum that they not approach any more players the NBA had rights to. Since Waterloo's signing of Chuck Share, Milwaukee had begun recruiting second pick Don Rehfeldt, St. Louis had made it clear that their plan was to snatch Ed Macauley and Johnny Logan away from Boston and Tri-Cities, respectively, and Doxie Moore had identified Warriors territorial pick Paul Arizin as a rookie worth trying to bring to the NPBL regardless of team.

Maurice Podoloff told Brinkman and Moore that he had $100,000 of league office money with which he was willing to help NBA teams launch a player war against the NPBL and that he was willing to bring lawsuits against the NPBL and fight them all the way up to the Supreme Court of the United States if he had to.

Moore responded by leaking the telegram Podoloff sent to him in its entirety to the press. Moore also branded Podoloff "insane" to believe Denver, Sheboygan, and Waterloo "were going to go home … and fold up," emphasized that "professional basketball will be played in Sheboygan long after Podoloff is dead," and stated that, while he didn't want a player war, that's exactly what would happen if Podoloff continued to treat the NPBL with the "minor league" disdain he'd previously treated the NBL to.[25]

A week later, Moore announced the NPBL had granted its seventh franchise to St. Paul, Minnesota, and that the team had already hired Fort Wayne Pistons starting center Howie Schultz as its player-coach, a role he'd previously fulfilled in Anderson. Schultz, the first NBA veteran to jump ship to the new league, held no reservations about recruiting other players already under contract by NBA teams and went out of his way to imply in his introductory press conference that he would offer Vern Mikkelsen a sizable contract to leave Minneapolis for St. Paul.[26]

Following Schultz, the former Anderson Packers post duo of Charlie Black and Milo Komenich rebuffed Rochester and Philadelphia, respectively, to become the second and third players with NBA experience to leave for the upstart league, instead opting to stay put and join the NPBL's new Anderson team. It wasn't long, either, before Schultz succeeded in getting another NBA starter to join him in St. Paul, with Kleggie Hermsen leaving the Chicago Stags to join the St. Paul NPBL team.[27]

Don Barksdale turned down a $10,000 contract offer from Ned Irish that would have had him join the New York Knicks.[28] His basketball career was thriving in the AAU, where for three consecutive years he had been named as an AAU All-American and would for the second consecutive year lead Oakland to the championship game, although this time they would lose to the Phillips Oilers. So was his business career thriving: Blue & Gold Beer was doing well enough that he could now afford to sponsor the team himself, he had changed the Bittners' name to the Oakland Blue 'n' Gold prior to the 1950 AAU Tournament, and he was planning the grand opening of three ice cream parlors in Oakland later that month. Furthermore, the Olympic Basketball Committee had just offered the Blue 'n' Gold a chance to represent the United States as the United States national team in the inaugural 1951 Pan American Games, and Barksdale wasn't inclined to turn down a chance to represent his country for the second time.

With Barksdale declining to join the Knicks, Irish had to pivot to his second-choice center, Nathaniel Clifton. Clifton, known for his large hands that helped him to be a particularly excellent ballhandler for a center but also a very capable multifaceted scorer, was who Irish had wanted to sign the year prior when he first started lobbying for integration, and Clifton had been openly willing to join the Knicks for a year prior to that.

Clifton first started playing basketball at DuSable High School in Chicago, where he quickly improved from a clumsy player mostly on the team because of his height to one of the top players in Illinois. After high school, he played for Xavier University of Louisiana for one year, where he immediately earned the starting center spot and stood out offensively on a slow-paced team, with his best game coming in the form of a 42-point scoring outing against Benedict College.

His time at Xavier was cut short by military service after just one season, as he served in the U.S. Army during World War II in the French protectorate of Morocco, Vichy France, Belgium, and Nazi Germany. After returning from military duty, Clifton turned professional instead of returning to college, but the start of his professional basketball career was a complicated and somewhat controversial season.[29]

At first, he played for the New York Renaissance, but after two months, he left midseason to join the Dayton Metropolitans. Just a week later, Clifton left Dayton to sign with the Detroit Gems of the NBL, but his time in Detroit consisted of just one exhibition game before he returned to the Metropolitans two days after first leaving Dayton. He stayed in Dayton the rest of the season, but rejoined the Renaissance for the WPBT without alerting anyone on the Metropolitans, breaking a contract clause and leading Dayton Metropolitans president Dick Harper to threaten to sue the Renaissance if they played him, a threat that ultimately came to nothing.[30]

Nathaniel Clifton (left) and Joe Lapchick (1950). Clifton was the best black player of the late 1940s, spending time with both the New York Renaissance and Harlem Globetrotters. When the New York Knicks signed him, he became the first black player with prior professional experience to join the NBA. Lapchick, who had been the premier center of the late 1920s, was a highly respected coach in his third year with the Knicks. Having honed a close friendship with many members of the New York Renaissance during his playing career, he was the principal force behind the integration of the NBA.

Clifton's second season was much less eventful, as he spent the season with Dayton before returning to the Renaissance for the WPBT. It also brought him great success and recognition from some of the best teams in the world, as Clifton led Dayton to win the championship of the minor league All-American Basketball League and then averaged 23.7 points for the Renaissance in a run to a WPBT championship loss that included a strong showing matched up against Don Otten in a win against Tri-Cities and 24 points against George Mikan (although Mikan scored 40 on Clifton) in the championship loss to Minneapolis.

Abe Saperstein signed Clifton to the Harlem Globetrotters in the summer of 1948 to a $10,000 contract, matching Fats Jenkins' pre–Great Depression annual sum for the joint-highest salary a black player had ever received to play basketball.[31] He proved Saperstein right to pay him so much, as he became the centerpiece of the more pragmatic stylings of the team while surrounded by flashier teammates such as Goose Tatum and Marques Haynes.

Three more times over the course of the next two years Clifton had a chance to play against Minneapolis and Mikan again, with a four-point win and two double-digit losses, and while he never got much better at slowing Mikan down, he was the most consistent producer on the Globetrotters during those games, averaging 14.8 points.

By the end of the 1949–50 season, Clifton was tired of the Globetrotters' arduous barnstorming schedules and the relationship between Clifton and Saperstein was rocky. Clifton was surprised to learn about the higher salaries of top NBA players compared to the Globetrotters and came to the conclusion that Saperstein was exploiting his monopsony over black basketball to artificially reduce his players' salaries. Saperstein was frustrated by Clifton's baseball career, where he played with minor league affiliates of the Cleveland Indians, which took away from his time with the Globetrotters.[32]

There was just one year left on Clifton's contract with the Globetrotters, and now that the NBA had integrated, the likelihood was that Clifton would leave at the end of that season. Angry at Walter Brown over the drafting of Chuck Cooper, Saperstein figured that helping out one of the Celtics' divisional opponents add a better player than Cooper would be the best form of revenge and reached out to Maurice Podoloff to arrange the $15,000 sale of Clifton's contract to the New York Knicks, making Clifton the first black player with prior professional experience to join the NBA.[33] Minor league baseball meant Clifton would arrive late to training camp, so he was the second black Knick by a couple weeks. John Rucker, fresh out of Erasmus Hall High School in Brooklyn, beat him to it but was already waived by the time Clifton got there.[34]

With the NPBL showing no signs of backing off of NBA players, Podoloff retaliated by signing Dick Mehen, Harry Boykoff, and Kenny Sailors to contracts with the NBA, with the express purpose of weakening the NPBL by taking Waterloo's two highest scorers and Denver's leading scorer off their teams. Which team they would each play for now that they were back in the NBA would be decided at a later date, but for now they were expressly contracted to the NBA league office.[35]

After securing that trio of new players, Podoloff embarked on a trip to Europe to observe Saperstein's marketing tactics on the Harlem Globetrotters' first tour of Europe, a series of 73 games spanning across Portugal, France, Switzerland, Belgium, Italy, West Germany, and the United Kingdom. Podoloff's trip to Europe meant that the Chicago Stags' timeline to make a decision on ownership of the team and payment of the $50,000 performance bond would be extended from June 1 to June 20, upon his return.[36]

The Baltimore Bullets doubled the number of black players in the NBA in one day when they signed four, although there was no real chance they would all make the team. Bucky Hatchett, the forward Joe Lapchick had endorsed as a potential draft pick, was one, and signed along with him were Dave Minor of the Oakland Blue 'n' Gold, a streaky backcourt scorer and jump shot pioneer who had costarred with Don Barksdale at UCLA and then followed him to Oakland, where he became the second black player to make an AAU All-American team behind just Barksdale; Ben Bluitt of Loyola University Chicago, a power forward equally capable of stretching the floor with long-range shots and fighting for rebounds; and Lenny Rhodes of the University of Toledo, who had started at center despite standing just 6'4" and would have to switch positions in the pros but had proven his worth as a defensive expert having once limited Chuck Share to six points in a game despite a seven-inch height difference.[37]

Doxie Moore canceled the membership of the new St. Louis NPBL team after they failed to secure an arena to play in, ending their existence after just 22 days. That brought the NPBL back down to six franchises, but on the same day that St. Louis folded, Moore announced two new teams had been selected, pending payment from the prospective owners, to bring the league up to eight teams, the minimum number Magnus Brinkman had suggested at the league's foundational meeting.[38]

One of those teams would be in Dayton, Ohio, and Indianapolis Olympians starting shooting guard Bruce Hale, who had been stationed in Dayton during part of World War II, was believed to be a minority owner and the impending player-coach, again taking away another important player from the NBA. The other team would be in Toledo, Ohio. Moore announced that he was still considering adding two more teams in order to start the league with ten franchises, specifically mentioning Duluth, Minnesota; Muncie, Indiana; Omaha, Nebraska; and Sioux City, Iowa, as contenders for NPBL teams.[39]

A week before the Stags' deadline to pay the performance bond and guarantee their spot in the 1950–51 NBA season, reports began to circulate that Maurice Podoloff and Abe Saperstein, both still in Europe, were discussing the possibility of Saperstein buying the Stags.[40] Chicago had always been a winning team; the Stags' four consecutive winning seasons since their foundation in advance of the 1946–47 season were only matched by the Rochester Royals and New York Knicks and their all-time winning percentage in major league professional basketball was only behind Rochester, Minneapolis, and Washington out of the 12 NBA teams. They simply hadn't attracted enough attendance to be profitable, something that could surely be fixed with basketball's greatest promoter at the helm if Saperstein bought the team.

Two days before the deadline, Saperstein bought the Chicago Stags for $50,000. Upon his acquisition of the team, he made a bold announcement about his plans to overhaul most aspects of basketball operations, although he made it clear that this would be a wholly separate venture from the Harlem Globetrotters and that the Globetrotters would continue to operate as a barnstorming team without any affiliation to the NBA.[41]

He had good reason for keeping the Globetrotters and Stags as separate as possible. There was nothing to be gained and plenty to be lost by merging the teams and putting the Harlem Globetrotters, for all intents and purposes, in the NBA; the Globetrotters held greater public recognition and financial stability, boasting larger crowds, lower salaries, and a higher number of games per year compared to any NBA team. The NBA's decision to integrate had the potential to change that in the long term, but it remained the fact that their February loss to the Lakers had been better attended than any game between two NBA teams all year. Joining the NBA would likely diminish the Globetrotters' prestige, reduce their schedule, compromise their unbeatable image, and potentially require abandoning their trademark comedic style.

Throughout their existence, the Harlem Globetrotters transcended the traditional boundaries of a basketball team, incorporating showmanship and entertainment into their games, but Saperstein claimed that it took until 1939 for the flair of the individual talents on the team to become a crucial factor in the Globetrotters' identity.

As the story goes, fans attending a game in Woodfibre, British Columbia, directed racial slurs toward the Globe Trotters during warm-ups and guard Runt Pullins urged his teammates to retaliate on the court. They proceeded to establish an absurd 112–5 lead, provoking the crowd's anger. To defuse the tension, the players resorted to showcasing basketball tricks for the last few minutes, a solution that Saperstein encouraged them to incorporate on a regular basis whenever they got large leads.

In all likelihood, that story was a fabrication designed to distract from the most probable actual origin of the Globe Trotters' "clowning." They are known to have shown off extraordinary feats of ball handling and absurd tricks that prioritized entertainment value over the rules of basketball for years before 1939.[42]

Actor Thomas D. Rice popularized the character of Jim Crow in the 1820s, portraying an enslaved black man through blackface performance, exaggerated language, and stereotypical traits. Rice's act gained immense popularity, leading to the emergence of minstrel shows featuring white actors in blackface and perpetuating racist stereotypes. Over time, all-black minstrel shows also gained popularity in the Northeast, as audiences were curious about a supposedly more authentic look into how black people lived, something that was propagated by promoters of the shows advertising with a focus on white audiences getting a chance to see black people act "naturally." Black minstrel performers did add some elements of authenticity by including tongue-in-cheek humor about white society and some serious discourse on issues that affected black communities such as slavery and religion, but even these continued to reinforce harmful stereotypes and solidify racist beliefs.

Not long after the rise of black minstrelsy came the emergence of black baseball, with the first recorded game between all-black amateur teams taking place in 1859. Bud Fowler became the first black professional baseball player in 1878, and William Edward White, born into slavery but passing as white, made his debut in the major leagues a year later. Moses Fleetwood Walker and Weldy Walker became the first openly black major league players in 1884. Full segregation began to go into effect in baseball over the course of the next couple decades, and it would be 63 years before Jackie Robinson broke baseball's color line again.

The Cuban Giants, formed in 1885 through the merger of three amateur teams, became the first openly professional all-black baseball team. Despite having no Cuban players, the team strategically adopted the name to foster positive business relationships with Caribbean nations and understanding that taking on the name of an island with strong American support for its independence from Spain would potentially stave off some level of racial animosity.

Managed by Cos Govern, a Danish West Indies native with a background in hospitality and acting, the Cuban Giants incorporated elements of minstrel show–inspired comedy into their games, establishing the first instance of clowning in professional sports. This style of performance was emulated by other early black baseball teams and enjoyed popularity among diverse audiences. However, as black baseball sought greater respectability in line with white baseball, the practice gradually faded away, with only smaller barnstorming teams continuing the tradition as a novelty act by the late 1910s.

Abe Saperstein was aware of the baseball roots of clowning and the controversy that accompanied it at the time he brought the Harlem Globe Trotters into existence, as his first job in professional sports had been working as a promoter for Walter Ball's black barnstorming baseball team. While Saperstein may not have initially been aware of the direct connections between clowning and minstrel shows when he introduced it with the Harlem Globe Trotters, it became a contentious issue within Negro league baseball during the 1930s due to the Ethiopian Clowns and the Zulu Cannibal Giants. Not only was Saperstein still involved in baseball at this time, he became owner of the Zulu Cannibal Giants in 1937 and was responsible for some of the most objectionable forms of the Cannibal Giants' clowning, including painting players' faces and bodies with faux–African tribal patterns and having them play shirtless while wearing only grass skirts and jungle-themed headdresses.[43] He had every reason to go out of his way to fabricate a story that distanced the clowning of the Harlem Globe Trotters from that seen in baseball, just as with the supposed origin story of the Globe Trotters' clowning from that 1939 game in Woodfibre.

Saperstein, born to a Jewish family from Russia and raised in Chicago, harbored dreams of playing professional sports, and participated in basketball, baseball, football, boxing, and track in high school. His height of just 5'5" made a career as a basketball player an unlikely endeavor, though, and he failed to make the team at the University of Illinois.

After a year at Illinois, Saperstein dropped out of the university to work as a park supervisor and start up a semiprofessional basketball team called the Chicago Reds. It was through his work managing the Reds that he met Ball and got his introduction to managing professional teams.

In late 1926, Dick Hudson, a prominent fullback in the NFL, sought a white promoter for his Chicago basketball team, the Giles Post American Legion, to expand their reach beyond Illinois. He consulted Ball, who recommended Saperstein for the job.

Giles Post, purportedly an extension of the Eighth Regiment Five of Chicago, coholders of the 1923–24 Colored Basketball World Champions title, consisted of Hudson, future NFL player Joe Lillard, and the starting lineup of the previous year's Wendell Phillips High School team. Saperstein began his association with the team by booking an 18-game tour of small Wisconsin cities from December 1926 to January 1927.

When a financial dispute caused much of the team to part ways, Saperstein joined Tommy Brookins and Hudson in founding a new team called the Thomas Brookins Globe Trotters, while Giles Post became the Savoy Big Five and later the Chicago Crusaders.

As booking agent for the Globe Trotters, Saperstein established the team's presence by scheduling as many games as possible, a plan that briefly worked well until he overbooked them and had to secretly recruit the Savoy Big Five to tour as the Globe Trotters in Wisconsin while the Globe Trotters were in Michigan. Brookins confronted him about it, but instead of firing Saperstein, Brookins moved on from sports to tour the world as one half of the vaudeville act Brookins and Van, giving Saperstein the opportunity to take over the team.

Saperstein reorganized the team to feature just five players, with Saperstein owning two sevenths and each player owning one seventh of the Harlem Globe Trotters, a name change aimed to create a false impression of traveling from New York while also highlighting their composition of black players. With a limited roster, any absence due to injury or illness required Saperstein to step in.[44]

They played a lot of games and won the vast majority of them, embracing a willingness to make flashy passes and shoot from anywhere on the floor for the sake of flamboyance alone. Inman Jackson, joining in 1930–31, pioneered the role of the team's "Clown Prince," orchestrating their entertaining antics.

Throughout the 1930s, as their winning percentage, while playing against mostly amateur and semiprofessional teams, solidified at about 91 percent, Saperstein made it his goal to schedule a Colored World Championship against the New York Renaissance. He faced repeated rejection from Bob Douglas, who viewed the Globe Trotters' style as a disservice to both the sport and the public perception of black athletes.

With the addition of Ted Strong, the Harlem Globe Trotters embarked on their first international tour and began to compete against major league teams in 1935–36. The

Globe Trotters' first game against a major league team resulted in a loss to the Duffy Florals of Chicago, the eventual MBC champions that year, but the following season finished with a victory against the Whiting Ciesars. In 1937–38 and 1938–39, they played the Oshkosh All-Stars five times, and after four losses, finally triumphed 37–31 in their fifth encounter.

The 1938–39 season culminated in their participation in the inaugural WPBT, with reinforcements from Babe Pressley and Bernie Price. After beating an International Harvester company team and a group of former DePaul University players, the Globe Trotters got the chance Saperstein had hoped for when their semifinal opponent was the New York Renaissance.

Their height and weight disadvantage against the Renaissance proved to be significant, as the Globe Trotters fell behind quickly. The Renaissance controlled the pace and led 15–10 at halftime, but the Globe Trotters made a comeback in the second half. Late shots by Babe Pressley and Larry Bleach brought the Globe Trotters within two points, but a breakaway layup by Tarzan Cooper clinched a 27–23 victory for the Renaissance and a spot in the WPBT championship.[45] The Globe Trotters settled for a consolation game, which they won against the Sheboygan Redskins.

The following year, the Globe Trotters had a chance for revenge and defeated the Renaissance 37–36, with 20-year-old newcomer Sonny Boswell leading the way with 19 points. After beating the minor league Syracuse Reds in the semifinals, the Globe Trotters met Chicago in the WPBT championship and overcame a 29–21 deficit with a 10–0 run to end the game, capped off with a game-winner by Price.[46]

They couldn't defend their title the next season, losing in the quarterfinals to a Detroit Eagles team led by Buddy Jeannette and Ed Sadowski 37–36, and similar stories followed, with eliminations to the Oshkosh All-Stars, Dayton Dive Bombers, Brooklyn Eagles, and Chicago Gears between 1942 and 1945. In fact, they lost 17 of the next 22 times they faced off against NBL teams. After that, they never returned to the WPBT again.

Saperstein signed Negro league baseball player Goose Tatum to join the team in 1940–41. Two years later, Tatum was drafted to the military, and he returned to the team (whose name had gradually changed from the Harlem Globe Trotters to the Harlem Globetrotters during the first couple years of World War II) in 1945 to find Inman Jackson retired and Ted Strong enlisted. Embracing the role of the "Clown Prince," Tatum began to incorporate antics such as bouncing the ball off his head in the direction of the basket for free throws and organizing comedic football and baseball routines for all five on-court players to participate in. He was by no means just there for clowning purposes, though; with his ball handling, defense, and hook shot acumen, he was one of the five best players in the world at his peak.[47]

At the end of the 1945–46 season, instead of participating in the WPBT, the Globetrotters played an exhibition against the recently crowned NBL champion Rochester Royals. They took an early lead and never relinquished it, beating the Royals 57–55, although Rochester was without Bob Davies for that game. At the start of the next season, they held a rematch and Rochester won handily, 60–49.

Late in the 1947–48 season, the Harlem Globetrotters faced off against the Minneapolis Lakers, who were in their first year and featured George Mikan and Jim Pollard. This version of the Globetrotters was better than ever, with Langston University's ballhandling wizard Marques Haynes and military league star Ermer Robinson joining Goose Tatum and Babe Pressley to lead the team. With 17,823 people in attendance at Chicago Stadium, the game looked like it would get out of hand early, with Minneapolis jumping out to a 9–2 lead, but the Globetrotters kept the Lakers from extending that lead despite Mikan's 18 points by halftime, and they managed to contain Mikan's scoring in the second half with Tatum and Pressley double-teaming him often. Both Tatum and Pressley fouled out, but the Globetrotters clawed their way back into the game, eventually tying the game at 59–59 with a minute and a half left. Mikan then missed three consecutive free throws that could've given the Lakers the lead back.

With time running out, Haynes flipped the ball to Robinson, who was nearly 30 feet away from the basket. Robinson launched a one-handed jump shot, which he'd been 0-of-3 on from long-range so far in the game, and time expired while the ball was still in the air. It went in, confirming the Harlem Globetrotters win over the Minneapolis Lakers, 61–59, with Robinson's 17 points and Haynes' 15 leading the way.[48]

The Globetrotters' victory served as a high-profile example that the best black players could triumph over their white counterparts, elevating the Globetrotters' popularity and permanently altering the state of race relations in professional basketball. That was made even more apparent when the Lakers went on to win the NBL championship

Harlem Globetrotters, 1947–48 season. Standing, from left: Abe Saperstein, Babe Pressley, John Netherly, Ted Strong, and Winfield Welch; kneeling, from left: Ducky Moore, Ermer Robinson, Sam Wheeler, Boid Buie. One of the two nationally known black teams prior to integration, the Globetrotters made national headlines when they beat the Minneapolis Lakers twice in a row in the late 1940s.

without any real semblance of difficulty. The next year, the Globetrotters beat the Lakers again, 49–45, and even following that up with three consecutive losses of 15-plus points to Minneapolis before the end of the 1949–50 season couldn't take away the fact that they'd beaten the 1945–46 NBL champion Royals, the 1947–48 NBL champion Lakers, and the 1948–49 BAA champion Lakers. In the eyes of many, they were the best team in the world, and Abe Saperstein certainly wasn't going to disagree with that.

Following the 1949–50 season, the Globetrotters gained further acclaim by introducing the world of professional basketball to many of the top prospects in the 1950 NBA draft, including territorial pick Paul Arizin, second pick Don Rehfeldt, and third pick Bob Cousy, in the form of the College All-Stars. The Globetrotters had played against various College All-Stars teams for a decade at this point, but this would be an 18-game series, traveling across the country in a nationwide tour with an average attendance of 10,075 people, revenue of over $350,000, and 11 Globetrotters wins compared to just seven losses.[49]

After that, Saperstein brought the Globetrotters, sans Nathaniel Clifton, busy playing minor league baseball, across the Atlantic Ocean for the first time. Between May and July of 1950, they would play against the Stars of America—a team mostly composed of players from their designated touring opponents but led by two NBA players in Leo Barnhorst and Tony Lavelli—70 times in the nine European countries of Portugal, France, Switzerland, the United Kingdom, Belgium, Italy, West Germany, Denmark, and Norway. They would then take a brief detour to Northern Africa to play five games in Algeria and two in Morocco before heading home.[50] It was during this trip that Saperstein and Maurice Podoloff negotiated Saperstein's acquisition of the Chicago Stags.

Saperstein's first step toward fixing the finances of the Stags was moving them out of the Chicago Stadium to the Chicago Coliseum, an arena change that would drop the Stags' seating capacity from 17,000 to 6,000 but cost the team considerably less in rent and would give the Stags more independence as a franchise without requiring the same level of reliance on arena moguls as in the past.[51]

As it turned out, Toledo didn't even have any representatives at the meeting in which Doxie Moore granted them a franchise alongside Dayton, and while they weren't out of the running for an NPBL team, the funding wasn't there yet and the NPBL only had seven teams, with just Dayton officially joining the previously existing six.[52]

The eighth team to join, rather, was from Grand Rapids, Michigan, and featured NBL veteran George Glamack among its minority owners and acting in dual roles as a player-general manager.[53]

Glamack, nicknamed "The Blind Bomber" because he was so nearsighted that he couldn't clearly see the basket and instead used the lines on the court to triangulate where to shoot at, first burst onto the basketball scene at the University of North Carolina, where he became the second player ever to win multiple National Player of the Year awards (after Hank Luisetti) with consecutive such honors in 1939–40 and 1940–41, capped off by a 31-point performance in the last game of his collegiate career to break a single-game NCAA Tournament record for scoring (previously held by Jimmy Hull of Ohio State, with 28 points) that stood until 1950.

After graduation, he joined Akron Goodyear, where he led Goodyear in scoring as a rookie and helped them to their first playoff appearance since their 1937–38 NBL championship. After a stint in the U.S. Navy during World War II, Glamack joined the Rochester Royals for their first NBL season in 1945–46, and his proficiency at hook shots even from a decent range out and his hustle while rebounding complemented a Royals team led by Al Cervi and Bob Davies that won the championship that year.

After another run to the NBL championship game the following year, this time resulting in a loss, Glamack was sold to the Indianapolis Kautskys. where he would pair with Arnie Risen in the post, but Risen was sold to Rochester later that season and Glamack was also on his way out of Indianapolis soon after without any success on the Kautskys. In 1948–49, he was the leading scorer for the hapless Calumet Buccaneers, but when Calumet's players were bought by Waterloo, he had no interest in playing for the Hawks. He signed with the Wilkes-Barre Barons of the ABL for the 1949–50 season, but in the middle of preseason, he reversed course and retired. The Grand Rapids NPBL team would be his return to professional basketball after a year of retirement.[54]

Along with Glamack would come the NBL's biggest star, Bobby McDermott, signed as Grand Rapids' player-coach for the upcoming season.[55] Ever since the breakup of the Chicago Gears, McDermott's career had been on the decline. A brief renaissance as player-coach of Tri-Cities that followed up his 16-game tenure at Sheboygan also ended in disappointment when he was fired midseason amid organizational disappointment at failing to contend for a championship in 1948–49 and philosophical differences with key players, and in order to avoid a power struggle between McDermott and his replacement, Roger Potter, Leo Ferris shipped him off to Calumet to finish out the season before he played another game.

At Calumet, McDermott became teammates with Glamack, and after a brief flirtation with retirement, he signed up to be player-coach for the Wilkes-Barre Barons. There, he focused mostly on his coaching and made little impact as a player, averaging just 6.8 points per game on a team that made a first-round playoff exit.

The fact that Glamack and McDermott were going to form the core of the new Grand Rapids NPBL team together was great as a legitimization of the idea of the NPBL continuing the NBL's legacy, but any possibility of a 36-year-old McDermott and a recently retired Glamack having a significant impact as players on an NPBL team only served to strengthen the NBA's argument that the NPBL was little more than a minor league.

Next to be added to the NPBL was Omaha, Nebraska, the city Magnus Brinkman had always wanted to add because it would make road trips west to Denver less brutal.[56] Despite the addition, the league remained at eight teams, because the Dayton NPBL team dropped out of the league. When they first joined the NPBL, Bruce Hale had been assured by the University of Dayton vice president, Father Charles Collins, that the University of Dayton Fieldhouse would be available for the Dayton NPBL team, but the board of the university's athletic department voted against it and the Dayton NPBL team was without an arena. Without an arena, they couldn't play, so Doxie Moore provisionally revoked their membership, but with hopes of finding a new arena in a smaller city near Dayton, like Troy, Ohio, instead of turning down the franchise altogether.[57] Until that was figured out, though, Hale was back on the Olympians.

A report came out from the Associated Press that same day quoting Moore as saying that the NPBL might have to fold before it could even start in the wake of Dayton having to pull out, a significant change in tone from a month prior when Magnus Brinkman was adamant that the league would happen even if no other teams joined Denver, Sheboygan, and Waterloo, citing the successful operation of a four-team NBL in the 1942–43 and 1943–44 seasons.[58]

The story seemed somewhat suspect for that very reason, with the compounded factor of the report's general inaccuracy, with the explanation given for the league potentially not going ahead being based on the factually incorrect assessment of the league only having seven teams, with Grand Rapids left out of a listing of NPBL teams in the report entirely.

Sure enough, Moore immediately denied having ever said anything of the sort, saying, "We are definitely going ahead," confirming that Dayton's bid wasn't necessarily off the table yet, mentioning other possibilities but clarifying that he wouldn't select another team for the sole sake of having eight teams, and suggesting that the story was likely planted by an NBA executive in an effort to convince players who wanted to leave the NBA for the NPBL that the NPBL was a considerably more unstable league.[59]

After returning from the Harlem Globetrotters' European tour, Chuck Cooper signed a contract with the Boston Celtics to become the 11th black player under contract with an NBA team, one of two on the Celtics along with Rabbit Walthour, who had spent the previous season with the ABL's Harlem Yankees.[60] Cooper was the last black player to join the league during the 1950 offseason, with the Baltimore Bullets, Boston Celtics, New York Knicks, and Washington Capitols integrating their teams and the other eight teams all opting against immediate integration. Only Cooper, Nathaniel Clifton, and Earl Lloyd would remain on NBA rosters by the next season's tip-off.

Even now that they were in different leagues, the rivalry between the Tri-Cities Blackhawks and Waterloo Hawks continued. After weeks of NPBL teams recruiting and signing players already on NBA rosters, the Blackhawks became the first NBA team to bring legal action against an NPBL team by filing a restraining order against the Waterloo Hawks and the NPBL as a whole.

The injunction was centered around the claim that the Hawks had approached several Tri-Cities players—namely Dike Eddleman, Noble Jorgensen, Walt Kirk, and Murray Wier—with contract offers, to such an extent that players had complained to Ben Kerner about being harassed by NPBL representatives. Waterloo did sign Wier, but initial reports suggested the Blackhawks had waived Wier upon his request in order to allow him to sign with the Hawks without controversy.

Noble Jorgensen was the player that Tri-Cities' case most relied on, and he testified that Pops Harrison, representing Waterloo, offered him a $8,000 contract and then increased his offer to $10,000. Harrison countered that the calls were strictly personal calls, and since the Blackhawks had no physical evidence of a contract offer, there was no way of proving any wrongdoing by Waterloo in a court of law. Eddleman testified that Harrison never offered him a contract and neither Kirk nor Wier was called to testify. Furthermore, Blackhawks general manager Mike Fitzgerald revealed under questioning that he had contacted four NPBL players—Dick Mehen, at the time a member of the Hawks, and Bob Brannum, Max Morris, and Jack Burmaster, all on the Sheboygan Redskins—about the possibility of switching to the NBA despite being under contract with NPBL teams. Judge Henry Graven ruled that there was not sufficient evidence to issue a restraining order against the Hawks.[61]

In Boston, it was announced that Walter Brown would go from president of the Celtics to the team's majority owner as he teamed up with Lou Pieri to buy the team from the Boston Garden-Arena Corporation. The Boston Garden-Arena Corporation had lost approximately $460,000 running the Celtics for four years and were glad not to have to worry about operating a professional basketball team at a loss anymore, and Brown would now have control of the team he built without having to worry about approval from the same board of directors he dealt with as president of the arena corporation.[62]

Pieri, the operator of the Rhode Island Auditorium, owner of the Providence Reds ice hockey team in the AHL, and cofounder of the Ice Capades, had basketball experience as the one-time head coach of Brown University's basketball team and owner of the Providence Steamrollers of the BAA. While the Steamrollers didn't survive the merger, they operated for all three years of the BAA's existence, and Pieri was enthusiastic to return to professional basketball with his investment in the Celtics in large part because of the hiring of Red Auerbach as head coach.

An NPBL press release stated that the league had decided to set the number of franchises in the NPBL for its inaugural season as eight, contrary to suggestions Magnus Brinkman had previously made that the league was considering increasing to ten teams. With eight teams accepted into the league, that was no surprise, but the bigger deal was that the press release listed by name only seven teams as members.[63]

The Milwaukee NPBL franchise was no longer listed as a member of the league, and there was no mention of them at all. Like the previous offseason, when Milwaukee had to drop out of the NBA before the season even began, the issue was an inability to secure an arena. Lon Darling's next step would have to be attempting to raise money from the general public in Oshkosh in order to operate the franchise in Oshkosh like he had done with the All-Stars in the NBL. After an underwhelming fundraising drive, Darling pulled out of contention for an NPBL team, ending a chance at his and Oshkosh's return to professional basketball and folding the last remaining major league professional basketball franchise of the 13 original NBL teams from the 1937–38 season. Darling never returned to professional basketball and died less than a year later of a heart attack at just 48 years old.

Also announced by the NPBL at the time were a decision on the permanent location of the NPBL league office, which was to be moved to Waterloo; a rule stipulating that, in the event of a team dropping out of the league midseason, games against them would be stricken from the standings; the creation of a soft trade deadline that would be enforced at the halfway point of each team's schedule instead of on a specific date and allow for the possibility of exceptions with the approval of the commissioner; and discussion on the introduction of a potential rule to allow players who foul out to reenter the game during the final five minutes of regulation.[64]

A week later, the NPBL completed their eight-team setup by admitting a franchise based in Louisville, Kentucky. The Louisville NPBL team was explicitly designed in the model of the Indianapolis Olympians, with player-owners running the team, and in doing so, brought the biggest exodus of NBA players to the NPBL. Don Otten of the Washington Capitols, Odie Spears and Kenny Rollins of the Chicago Stags, and Don Ray and Dee Gibson of the Tri-Cities Blackhawks banded together to become the Louisville NPBL team's five co-owners, as well as its likely starting lineup.[65]

The NPBL now had the eight teams it needed to start up its inaugural season: Anderson, the Denver Nuggets, Grand Rapids, Louisville, Omaha, the Sheboygan Redskins, St. Paul, and the Waterloo Hawks.

Abe Saperstein continued his shakeup of the Chicago Stags by rebranding the team and ridding it of the Stags name altogether. From now on, the franchise would be called the Chicago Bruins, named after the Chicago Bruins teams that George Halas had run in the ABL from 1926–27 to 1930–31 and in the NBL from 1939–40 to 1941–42.[66]

While Saperstein had moved quickly to make business moves to promise success, his lack of roster moves was discouraging. In nearly three months in charge of the team, he had failed to sign a new head coach or re-sign any of the team's veterans, having already lost two frontcourt starters to the NPBL in Odie Spears and Kleggie Hermsen and risking the departure of more players including Max Zaslofsky and Andy Phillip. Just why he hadn't signed a single one of these players yet with the regular season soon approaching was unknown.

Just as had happened with St. Louis, Toledo, Dayton, and Milwaukee, the NPBL's plans had to be changed again when a team unexpectedly dropped out of the league, this time Omaha, who also couldn't find an available arena. Given the Omaha NPBL team was a logistical near necessity for the league, their nonexistence had the potential to spell disaster, but almost immediately, the NPBL lined up a replacement franchise in Kansas City, Missouri.[67]

Denver, Kansas City, St. Paul, and Waterloo would make up the NPBL's Western Division. Anderson, Grand Rapids, Louisville, and Sheboygan would make up the Eastern Division.

With just under a month before the start of NBA preseason, the Chicago Bruins finally made their first signings of the new season, re-signing Max Zaslofsky and signing first-round pick Larry Foust. Four days after signing the pair, Abe Saperstein pulled the Chicago Bruins out of the NBA and disbanded the team, citing "total failure of the NBA to deliver the franchise and the players in accordance with promises made."

Saperstein claimed he received "exactly nothing" from the NBA in exchange for his money, having not been given any sort of proof of ownership of Chicago's NBA franchise that he needed in order to sign players or protect him from lawsuits challenging the validity of his ownership of the Bruins.

During that time, nearly half of the 11 players who'd spent the previous year with Chicago had signed with NPBL teams and three of Chicago's first four draft picks had either signed with NPBL teams or begun their coaching careers, in large part because there was no option to negotiate with Chicago until Saperstein legally owned the franchise, leaving the Bruins exceptionally short-handed.

When Saperstein told Maurice Podoloff he needed compensation for the players he lost, Podoloff offered him $15,000. Saperstein countered that he didn't want the extra money, he wanted quality basketball players, and instead submitted a list of nine players around the league that he would accept any four of as full compensation. Podoloff agreed to assign him players, but failed to do so even three days after the agreed-upon deadline, so Saperstein backed out of the deal, leaving the NBA with just 11 teams.[68]

With the NBA heading into its second year and the NPBL heading into its first, both leagues had to face an extra unexpected hurdle over which neither had control. On June 25, 1950, the Korean People's Army of North Korea invaded South Korea with the express support of Chairman Mao Zedong of the People's Republic of China and chairman of the Soviet Union Joseph Stalin. The plan was to conquer South Korea in an effort to reunify Korea as a communist state run by North Korea premier Kim Il-sung.

Two days later, the United Nations Security Council adopted Resolution 83, which determined North Korea's invasion to be a "breach of the peace" and recommended "that the Members of the United Nations furnish such assistance to the Republic of Korea as may be necessary to repel the armed attack and to restore international peace and security in the area." Cuba, Ecuador, France, the United Kingdom, the United States, and Taiwan voted for the resolution, Yugoslavia voted against the resolution, and Egypt and India did not vote, leading the resolution to pass 7–1.[69]

12. Expulsion and Integration

That same day, on June 27, President of the United States Harry Truman announced that he was deploying aerial and naval troops to South Korea in order to prevent the communist military takeover of democratic South Korea. Soon after, the U.S. Congress passed, and President Truman signed, a bill extending the authority of the Selective Service System military conscription agency to draft men between 19 and 26 years old into the U.S. military.

On September 27, New York Knicks star Carl Braun was inducted into the U.S. Army and ordered to report to Fort Devens in Ayer and Shirley, Massachusetts, for basic training.[70] As a draftee, he would spend the next 21 months serving in the military and therefore miss the next two NBA seasons in their entirety.

Braun was the first NBA player lost to military conscription during the Korean War. He wouldn't be the last.

Chapter Notes

Chapter 1

1. Mozley, Dana. "BAA, NBL Join in 18-Club Loop." *Daily News* (New York, NY). August 4, 1949.
2. O'Donnell, John. "Denver Nugget Team Stopped Before 3,450." *The Democrat and Leader* (Davenport, IA). August 30, 1949.
3. "Cage Loop Meets." United Press. August 11, 1949.
4. "Pro Court Loop Splits Up Into Two Divisions." Associated Press. August 11, 1949.
5. "Eddleman Tallies 48 Points as Blackhawks Stop Ft. Wayne." *The Daily Times* (Davenport, IA). December 18, 1950.
6. Reddy, Bill. "Keeping Posted." *The Post-Standard* (Syracuse, NY). February 13, 1952.
7. Rosen, Charley. *Sugar: Micheal Ray Richardson, Eighties Excess, and the NBA*, p. 159. University of Nebraska Press, 2018.
8. Rosen, Charley. *The Chosen Game: A Jewish Basketball History*, pp. 81–83. University of Nebraska Press, 2017.
9. "Pro Court Loop Splits Up Into Two Divisions." Associated Press. August 11, 1949.
10. Johnson, Claude. *The Black Fives: The Epic Story of Basketball's Forgotten Era*, pp. 386–389. Abrams Press, 2022.
11. "Oshkosh All Stars Reach End of Line, Franchise Forfeited." *Oshkosh Daily Northwestern*. September 9, 1949.
12. Smith, Russ L. "NBA Realigns Into Three Divisions; Opens Oct. 29." *Waterloo Daily Courier*. October 10, 1949.
13. Schumacher, Michael. *Mr. Basketball: George Mikan, the Minneapolis Lakers, and the Birth of the NBA*, pp. 77–79. Bloomsbury USA, 2007.
14. Triptow, Richard F. *The Dynasty That Never Was: Chicago's First Professional Basketball Champions*. Richard F. Triptow, 1997.
15. Nelson, Murry R. *The National Basketball League: A History, 1935–1949*, p. 180. McFarland, 2009.
16. Shevlin, Maurice. "National League Withdraws from Basketball Group." *Rochester Democrat and Chronicle*. April 9, 1947.
17. Nelson, Murry R. *The National Basketball League: A History, 1935–1949*, p. 201. McFarland, 2009.
18. Gould, Todd. *Pioneers of the Hardwood: Indiana and the Birth of Professional Basketball*, pp. 151–153. Indiana University Press, 1998.
19. "Olympians Clip Denver, Knicks Edge Past Stags." Associated Press. November 2, 1949.
20. Hahn, Alan. *New York Knicks: The Complete Illustrated History*, p. 49. MVP Books, 2012.
21. Gould, Todd. *Pioneers of the Hardwood: Indiana and the Birth of Professional Basketball*, pp. 54–57. Indiana University Press, 1998.
22. McClellan, Michael D. "The Arnie Risen Interview." Celtic Nation, December 9, 2018. https://www.celtic-nation.com/blog/2018/12/09/the-arnie-risen-interview/.
23. Montieth, Mark. "Arnie Risen Introduced Indianapolis to New Era in Pro Basketball." NBA.com, September 14, 2012. https://www.nba.com/pacers/montieth/arnie-risen-introduced-indianapolis-new-era-pro-basketball.
24. Gould, Todd. *Pioneers of the Hardwood: Indiana and the Birth of Professional Basketball*, p. 155. Indiana University Press, 1998.
25. Nelson, Murry R. *The National Basketball League: A History, 1935–1949*, pp. 221–222. McFarland, 2009.
26. Stranahan, Bob. "Olympic Champions Pick 'Home.'" *The Indianapolis Star*. May 5, 1949.
27. Reed, William F. "Scandal Branded Him, but His Charm Won People Back." *Sports Illustrated*, November 30, 2007.
28. Swinnen, Andy. "B-17G 'Fancy Nancy III' 42-37856 613th." Remember Our Heroes, n.d. https://www.remember-our-heroes.nl/2276.htm.
29. Byrod, Fred. "Lakers Beat Warriors in NBA Opener, 81–69." *Philadelphia Inquirer*. November 3, 1949.
30. "Jim Pollard, a Star In N.B.A. in 50's; Ex-Laker Was 70." Associated Press. January 25, 1993.
31. Pallette, Philip. *The Game Changer: How Hank Luisetti Revolutionized America's Great Indoor Game*, pp. 385–390. AuthorHouse, 2005.
32. Schumacher, Michael. *Mr. Basketball: George Mikan, the Minneapolis Lakers, and the Birth of the NBA*, p. 94. Bloomsbury USA, 2007.
33. Schumacher, Michael. *Mr. Basketball: George Mikan, the Minneapolis Lakers, and the*

Birth of the NBA, pp. 104–107. Bloomsbury USA, 2007.

34. "75 Cage Aces Chosen by Pro BAA in Draft." United Press. March 22, 1949.

35. "Syracuse Tops Denver Cagers." Associated Press. November 6, 1949.

36. Howlett, Ken. "The Story of Joe Fulks: A Basketball Innovator." A Sea of Blue, August 2, 2010. https://www.aseaofblue.com/2010/8/2/1600997/the-story-of-joe-fulks-an.

37. Byrod, Fred. "Caps Trounce Warriors in Arena, 84–69." *Philadelphia Inquirer*. November 10, 1949.

Chapter 2

1. O'Donnell, John. "Auerbach Succeeds Porter as Blackhawks' Coach." *The Democrat and Leader* (Davenport, IA). November 10, 1949.

2. Taylor, John. *The Rivalry: Bill Russell, Wilt Chamberlain, and the Golden Age of Basketball*, pp. 17–18. Ballantine, 2006.

3. Kessler, Gene. "Pro Cage Costly Venture." *Daily Times* (Chicago, IL). April 7, 1947.

4. Siegel, Morris. "Caps Try to Replace Auerbach; Carnevale Turns Down Offer." *Washington Post*. March 11, 1948.

5. Auerbach, Arnold, and Joe Fitzgerald. *Red Auerbach: An Autobiography*, pp. 73–74. G.P. Putnam's Sons, 1977.

6. Sumner, Jim. *Tales from the Duke Blue Devils Locker Room: A Collection of the Greatest Duke Basketball Stories Ever Told*, p. 19. Sports Publishing, 2016.

7. "Celts, Olympians Win; Lakers, Packers Lose." Associated Press. November 13, 1947.

8. Nelson, Rodger. *The Zollner Piston Story*, pp. 1–15. The Allen County Public Library Foundation, 1995.

9. Cope, Myron. "The Big Z and His Misfiring Pistons." *Sports Illustrated*, December 18, 1967.

10. Katz, Jeff. "Forgotten Man: Bobby McDermott and the Rise of Pro Basketball." Vice, September 5, 2016. https://www.vice.com/en/article/aebkpz/forgotten-man-bobby-mcdermott-and-the-rise-of-pro-basketball.

11. Nelson, Murry R. *The National Basketball League: A History, 1935–1949*, pp. 165–166. McFarland, 2009.

12. "Student Killed, 6 Others Injured." Associated Press. April 30, 1947.

13. Basketball Association of America. "League Minutes." October 3, 1946.

14. Dorr, Dave. "The Big Easy." *St. Louis Post-Dispatch*. December 30, 1990.

15. Schumacher, Michael. *Mr. Basketball: George Mikan, the Minneapolis Lakers, and the Birth of the NBA*, p. 145. Bloomsbury USA, 2007.

16. "Dr. James Naismith's Life." Naismith Basketball Foundation, November 13, 2014. https://naismithbasketballfoundation.com/james-naismith-life/.

17. Naismith, James. "Basket Ball." *The Triangle*, January 15, 1892.

18. "The First Game." Springfield College Archives and Special Collections.

19. Martinez, Courtney. "The First Intercollegiate Basketball Game Was Played on Feb. 9, 1895." NCAA.com, February 9, 2017.

20. "Bowling Green, DePaul Triumph." United Press. February 10, 1946.

21. Peterson, Jim. "Mikan Signed; Plays Tonight." *Minneapolis Morning Tribune*. November 20, 1947.

22. Grundman, Adolph H. *The Golden Age of Amateur Basketball: The AAU Tournament, 1921–1968*, pp. 76–79, 100. University of Nebraska Press, 2004.

23. Kurland, Bob. "Bob Kurland: Olympic Basketball Gold Medalist." Interview by John Erling. Voices of Oklahoma, January 27, 2011. https://www.voicesofoklahoma.com/interviews/kurland-bob.

24. Turkin, Hy. "Aggies Win, 52–44, After Mikan Fouls Out; NYU 3d." *Daily News* (New York, NY). March 30, 1945.

25. Grundman, Adolph H. *The Golden Age of Amateur Basketball: The AAU Tournament, 1921–1968*, pp. 114–117. University of Nebraska Press, 2004.

26. Schumacher, Michael. *Mr. Basketball: George Mikan, the Minneapolis Lakers, and the Birth of the NBA*, pp. 144, 148. Bloomsbury USA, 2007.

27. "Hall of Fame Basketball Player Bob Davies Dies at 70." *Sun Sentinel* (Fort Lauderdale, FL). April 23, 1990.

28. Cook, Kevin. "The Rochester Royals: The Story of Professional Basketball." *Rochester History*, Vol. LVIII, pp. 3–4. Rochester Public Library, 1996.

29. Angelopoulos, Angelo. "Groza Shows Pros a New Pivot Style." *The Indianapolis News*. November 23, 1949.

Chapter 3

1. Hargrave, Howard. "Transfer for Buffalo Club Looms Likely." *The Rock Island Argus*. December 18, 1946.

2. Fasnacht, Andy. "A Local Legend Turns 90: Whitey's Journey to the NBA." LNP. June 27, 2012.

3. Gould, Todd. *Pioneers of the Hardwood: Indiana and the Birth of Professional Basketball*, pp. 170–171. Indiana University Press, 1998.

4. Nelson, Murry R. *The National Basketball League: A History, 1935–1949*, p. 207. McFarland, 2009.

5. Whitmarsh, F.E. *Famous American Athletes of Today*, Vol. XV, p. 38. L.C. Page, 1958.

6. "Redskins Win Overtime Battle, 120–113." *The Sheboygan Press*. November 25, 1949.

7. Reddy, Bill. "Nationals Win by 125–123 in 5th Overtime." *The Post-Standard* (Syracuse, NY). November 25, 1949.

8. "Home Court No Help to Denver." *The Minneapolis Star.* November 26, 1949.
9. "Nuggets Finally Show Sparkle." United Press. November 28, 1946.
10. Nathan, Daniel A. *Baltimore Sports: Stories from Charm City*, p. 116. University of Arkansas Press, 2016.
11. Steadman, John. "Jeannette Paid Dues and More en Route to Hall." *The Sun* (Baltimore, MD). February 9, 1994.
12. "Redskins Win Championship." *The Sheboygan Press.* March 10, 1943.
13. Rosen, Charley. *The First Tip-Off: The Incredible Story of the Birth of the NBA*, p. 126. McGraw-Hill, 2008.
14. Menton, Paul. "Trenton 'Champions.'" *The Evening Sun* (Baltimore, MD). April 16, 1947.
15. Butler, Dylan. "The Butler Did It." *New York Post.* February 12, 2010.
16. Goldstein, Alan. "Bullets Standout Hoffman Dead of Tumor at 73: 1947–48 Rookie of Year Also Starred at Purdue." *The Sun* (Baltimore, MD). November 13, 1998.
17. Byrod, Fred. "Warriors Lose, 66–63, After Leading, 41–20." *Philadelphia Inquirer.* April 14, 1948.
18. Linthicum, Jesse A. "Sunlight on Sports." *The Sun* (Baltimore, MD). November 11, 1948.
19. Goldstein, Alan. "Bullets Standout Hoffman Dead of Tumor at 73: 1947–48 Rookie of Year Also Starred at Purdue." *The Sun* (Baltimore, MD). November 13, 1998.
20. Taragano, Martin. *Basketball Biographies: 434 U.S. Players, Coaches, and Contributors to the Game, 1891–1990*, p. 219. McFarland, 1991.
21. Carlson, Chad. *Making March Madness: The Early Years of the NCAA, NIT, and College Basketball Championships, 1922–1951*, pp. 52, 84. University of Arkansas Press, 2017.
22. Frei, Terry. *March 1939: Before the Madness—The Story of the First NCAA Basketball Tournament Champions*, p. 152. Taylor Trade Publishing, 2014.
23. Carlson, Chad R. "A Tale of Two Tournaments: The Red Cross Games and the Early NCAA-NIT Relationship." *Journal of Intercollegiate Sport*, Vol. 5, no. 2 (2012), pp. 260–280. Human Kinetics.
24. "Pro Hoop Association Opens Play Nov. 1." Associated Press. October 22, 1946.
25. Pope, Edwin. *Football's Greatest Coaches*, pp. 231–238. Taylor Tupper and Love, 1955.
26. Wigmore, John H. *The Illinois Crime Survey*, pp. 1028–1033. Illinois Association for Criminal Justice, 1929.
27. McCormick, Robert R. "Three Bombed; One a Judge." *Chicago Daily Tribune.* February 18, 1928.
28. Barr, Michael. *Cloyce Box: 6'4" and Bulletproof*, p. 196. Texas A&M University Press, 2017.
29. Lewis, Allen. "Warriors Win, 84–71; Fulks Gets 37 Points." *Philadelphia Inquirer.* April 17, 1947.
30. Haugh, David. "Duty Called Whiz Kids." *Chicago Tribune.* April 1, 2005.
31. Cronie, Robert. "New York to Play Stags in Stadium Test." *Chicago Sunday Tribune.* January 11, 1948.
32. Gaff, Glen. "Chicago Takes First 96–82." *Minneapolis Morning Tribune.* November 28, 1949.
33. Gould, Todd. *Pioneers of the Hardwood: Indiana and the Birth of Professional Basketball*, pp. 132–141, 157–158. Indiana University Press, 1998.
34. Rayl, Susan. "The New York Renaissance Professional Black Basketball Team," p. 444. A Thesis in Exercise and Sport Science, Pennsylvania State University, 1996.
35. Gould, Todd. *Pioneers of the Hardwood: Indiana and the Birth of Professional Basketball*, pp. 132–141, 116–117. Indiana University Press, 1998.
36. Glickman, Marty. "When Garden Was the Place for Basketball-Wise." *New York Times.* November 25, 1984.
37. Jackson, Harold, and Jim Haskins. *The House That Jack Built: The Autobiography of a Successful Dreamer, Businessman, and Entertainer*, pp. 65–67. Colossus Books, 2003.
38. Nelson, Murry R. *The National Basketball League: A History, 1935–1949*, p. 234. McFarland & Company, 2009.
39. Gould, Todd. *Pioneers of the Hardwood: Indiana and the Birth of Professional Basketball*, p. 138. Indiana University Press, 1998.
40. Reddy, Bill. "Keeping Posted." *The Post-Standard* (Syracuse, NY). February 26, 1947.
41. Nelson, Murry R. *The National Basketball League: A History, 1935–1949*, p. 234. McFarland & Company, 2009.

Chapter 4

1. Rayl, Susan. "The New York Renaissance Professional Black Basketball Team," pp. 13–24, 33, 42–43, 62. A Thesis in Exercise and Sport Science, Pennsylvania State University, 1996.
2. George, Nelson. *Elevating the Game: Black Men and Basketball*, pp. 35–38. HarperCollins, 1992.
3. McKenna, Dave. "The Syracuse Walking Dream." *Washington City Paper.* May 23, 2008.
4. Rayl, Susan. "The New York Renaissance Professional Black Basketball Team," pp. 452–453. A Thesis in Exercise and Sport Science, Pennsylvania State University, 1996.
5. "Redskins Drop Two Contests." *The Sheboygan Press.* November 28, 1949.
6. Kiesele, Russ. "Otten Voted Most Valuable Player in National League." *Moline Daily Dispatch.* March 25, 1949.
7. Ward, Gene. "Boykoff Scores Record 54 Pts., CCNY Wallops Violets, 91–60." *Daily News* (New York, NY). March 12, 1947.
8. Smith, Russ L. "Hawks Rush Two New Players by Air." *Waterloo Daily Courier.* November 30, 1949.

9. Broeg, Bob. "Bombers Trade Todorovich to Tri-Cities for Mac Otten." *St. Louis Post-Dispatch*. November 28, 1949.

10. Angelopoulos, Angelo. "Olymps Make Minneapolis Pay." *The Indianapolis News*. December 2, 1949.

11. Morrow, Art. "Gardner in Bed, Has Leg Infection." *Philadelphia Inquirer*. November 23, 1949.

12. "Duffey Says Packers to Stay in Anderson." Associated Press. December 6, 1949.

13. Turkin, Hy. "Knicks Overcome Boston, 96–84." *Daily News* (New York, NY). November 27, 1949.

14. Barry, Jack. "Brown Says 'No Holdup' in Contract with Lavelli." *The Boston Daily Globe*. November 18, 1949.

15. Nash, Bruce, and Allan Zullo. *The Basketball Hall of Shame*, p. 23. Pocket Books, 1991.

16. Shevlin, Maurice. "Stags Defeat Washington in Stadium, 75–55." *Chicago Daily Tribune*. December 7, 1949.

17. "Redskins in 77–67 Defeat at Waterloo." *The Sheboygan Press*. December 8, 1949.

18. Hughes, Carl. "Sports Stew—Served Hot." *The Pittsburgh Press*. December 19, 1949.

19. Webster, John. "Warriors Get Livingstone, Send Sadowski to Baltimore." *Philadelphia Inquirer*. December 8, 1949.

20. Rosen, Charley. *The First Tip-Off: The Incredible Story of the Birth of the NBA*, pp. 8–10, 41, 119–123. McGraw-Hill, 2008.

21. Barry, Jack. "Sadowski Refuses to Shoulder Blame for Cage Collapse of Celtics." *The Boston Daily Globe*. April 11, 1948.

22. Angelopoulos, Angelo. "Olymps Take on Old Pro Look, Denver." *The Indianapolis News*. December 9, 1949.

23. Tenny, Ben. "Pistons Whip Lakers; Take to Road to Continue Grind." *The News-Sentinel* (Fort Wayne, IN). December 9, 1949.

24. Schumacher, Michael. *Mr. Basketball: George Mikan, the Minneapolis Lakers, and the Birth of the NBA*, p. 146. Bloomsbury USA, 2007.

25. "Billy Hassett Sold to Lakers." Associated Press. December 8, 1949.

26. Turkin, Hy. "Overtime Shot Knicks Stags, 93–91." *Daily News* (New York, NY). December 11, 1949.

27. Beahon, George. "Royals Capture Donnybrook Over Nats, 69 to 63, to Halt Syracusans' Winning Skein at 12 Games." *Rochester Democrat and Chronicle*. December 11, 1949.

28. Wilson, Diana Eddleman. "The Life and Athletic Achievements of Thomas Dwight Eddleman," pp. 35, 47–50, 57. A Thesis in Physical Education, Eastern Illinois University, 1993.

29. Carlson, Bill. "Role as Regular May Be Harrison Reward." *The Minneapolis Star*. December 12, 1949.

30. Cromie, Robert. "Graboski, 18, Adds Touch of Youth to Stag Line." *Chicago Daily Tribune*. December 20, 1948.

31. Cushing, Elliott. "Royals Acquire Tall Ed Mikan, Stag Pivotman." *Rochester Democrat and Chronicle*. December 11, 1949.

32. Beahon, George. "Royals Rout Minneapolis at Arena, 87–62, to Snare Lead in NBA Central Division." *Rochester Democrat and Chronicle*. December 21, 1949.

33. "Curly May Miss Laker Battle." *The News-Sentinel* (Fort Wayne, IN). December 7, 1949.

34. Angelopoulos, Angelo. "Volker May Face Olymps." *The Indianapolis News*. December 16, 1949.

35. Kiesele, Russ. "Tribe Obtains Boston Pivot Man for Cash." *Moline Daily Dispatch*. December 15, 1949.

Chapter 5

1. Smith, Seymour S. "Bullets Rout Minneapolis Lakers, 87–68, at Coliseum." *The Sun* (Baltimore, MD). December 16, 1949.

2. Holman, Nat. *Scientific Basketball*, pp. 5–10. Incra Publishing Company, 1922.

3. Schumacher, Michael. *Mr. Basketball: George Mikan, the Minneapolis Lakers, and the Birth of the NBA*, pp. 96–97, 151. Bloomsbury USA, 2007.

4. "Team Signs Chaney and Jack Phelan." *The Sheboygan Press*. December 17, 1949.

5. Knight, Kevin. "National Champion & Former NBA Player Joins Us." Produced by Corn Nation. *Of Bangarangs and Daggers*, April 21, 2020. Podcast, 42:00.

6. Vecchione, Joseph. *New York Times Book of Sports Legends: Profiles of 50 of This Century's Greatest Athletes by the Legendary Sportswriters Who Covered Them*, pp. 138–140. Simon & Schuster, 1992.

7. Rosen, Charley. *The First Tip-Off: The Incredible Story of the Birth of the NBA*, p. 13. McGraw-Hill, 2008.

8. Kahn, Roger. "Success and Ned Irish." *Sports Illustrated*, March 27, 1961.

9. Rosen, Charley. *The First Tip-Off: The Incredible Story of the Birth of the NBA*, pp. 16–17. McGraw-Hill, 2008.

10. Kahn, Roger. "Success and Ned Irish." *Sports Illustrated*, March 27, 1961.

11. Rosen, Charley. *The First Tip-Off: The Incredible Story of the Birth of the NBA*, pp. 163–167. McGraw-Hill, 2008.

12. Rosen, Charley. *The Chosen Game: A Jewish Basketball History*, p. 76. University of Nebraska Press, 2017.

13. Franks, Joel S. *Asian American Basketball: A Century of Sport, Community and Culture*, p. 177. McFarland & Company, 2016.

14. Kalinsky, George & Phil Berger. *The New York Knicks: The Official 50th Anniversary Celebration*, p. 4. Macmillan USA, 1996.

15. "Detroit University Protests Pro Grab of Basket Ball Star." Associated Press. February 7, 1947.

16. Kahn, Roger. "Success and Ned Irish." *Sports Illustrated*, March 27, 1961.
17. Schumacher, Michael. *Mr. Basketball: George Mikan, the Minneapolis Lakers, and the Birth of the NBA*, pp. x–xii. Bloomsbury USA, 2007.
18. Young, Dick. "Knicks Down Lakers, 94–84." *Daily News* (New York, NY). December 15, 1949.
19. Kahn, Roger. "Success and Ned Irish." *Sports Illustrated*, March 27, 1961.
20. Smith, Jack. "Vandeweghe Signed for Knick Home Tilts." *Daily News* (New York, NY). October 19, 1949.
21. Angelopoulos, Angelo. "Sub Courageous in Olympians' Defeat." *The Indianapolis News*. December 21, 1949.
22. Kinney, Bill. "Gene Vance Will Join Blackhawks." *The Rock Island Argus*. December 20, 1949.
23. Angelopoulos, Angelo. "Walther to Join Olymps." *The Indianapolis News*. December 21, 1949.
24. Angelopoulos, Angelo. "Olymps Can Be Great When They Want to Win One." *The Indianapolis News*. December 23, 1949.
25. Harwood, Tim. *Ball Hawks: The Arrival and Departure of the NBA in Iowa*, pp. 34–36. University of Iowa Press, 2018.
26. Nelson, Murry R. *The National Basketball League: A History, 1935–1949*, pp. 25, 30, 44, 48, 70. McFarland & Company, 2009.
27. Harwood, Tim. *Ball Hawks: The Arrival and Departure of the NBA in Iowa*, pp. 49, 56–57, 69–73, 79. University of Iowa Press, 2018.
28. Tenny, Ben. "Another Rally Gets 106–95 Piston Wins." *The News-Sentinel* (Fort Wayne, IN). December 19, 1949.
29. Menton, Paul. "Bullets Get Short Rest." *The Evening Sun* (Baltimore, MD). December 23, 1949.
30. Ney, Al. "Down 12 Points With 58 Seconds to Play, Hawks Win in Overtime, 97–93." *Waterloo Courier*. December 26, 1949.
31. Menton, Paul. "Bullets File Game Protest." *The Evening Sun* (Baltimore, MD). December 26, 1949.
32. Reddy, Bill. "Gabor and Seymour Pace Nats Over Anderson in 94–88, Battle." *The Post-Standard* (Syracuse, NY). December 26, 1949.
33. Auerbach, Arnold, and Joe Fitzgerald. *Red Auerbach: An Autobiography*, p. 51. G.P. Putnam's Sons, 1977.
34. McNamara, John. *The Capital of Basketball: A History of DC Area High School Hoops*, pp. 7–9. Georgetown University Press, 2019.
35. Steadman, John. "Opting to Focus on Life's Gifts, Scolari Let Hits Slide Off Back." *The Sun* (Baltimore, MD). March 15, 1998.
36. Pomerantz, Gary M. *The Last Pass: Cousy, Russell, the Celtics, and What Matters in the End*, p. 17. Penguin, 2019.
37. Steadman, John. "Opting to Focus on Life's Gifts, Scolari Let Hits Slide Off Back." *The Sun* (Baltimore, MD). March 15, 1998.
38. Grundman, Adolph H. *The Golden Age of Amateur Basketball: The AAU Tournament, 1921–1968*, p. 72. University of Nebraska Press, 2004.
39. Pomerantz, Gary M. *The Last Pass: Cousy, Russell, the Celtics, and What Matters in the End*, p. 17. Penguin, 2019.
40. Fuchs, Bill. "Syracuse Coach Resents Talk of Easy Schedule." *The Evening Star* (Washington, D.C.). December 29, 1949.
41. Byrod, Fred. "Knicks' Uprising Tops Warriors Five, 79–72." *Philadelphia Inquirer*. December 29, 1949.
42. "Redskins Beat Waterloo in Thriller." *The Sheboygan Press*. December 30, 1949.
43. McClellan, Michael D. "The Bob Brannum Interview." Celtic Nation, December 6, 2018. https://www.celtic-nation.com/blog/2018/12/06/the-bob-brannum-interview/.

Chapter 6

1. Fitzgerald, Tom. "Celts Get Englund, 6-ft.-5 Oshkosh Ace." *The Boston Daily Globe*. December 5, 1949.
2. Angelopoulos, Angelo. "Olymps Get a Bad One Out of System." *The Indianapolis News*. December 7, 1949.
3. Barry, Jack. "'Aid from Englund' Plan Pays Off as Celtics Win." *The Boston Daily Globe*. December 9, 1949.
4. Nelson, Murry. *The Originals: The New York Celtics Invent Modern Basketball*, pp. 57–80, 153. Bowling Green State University Popular Press, 1999.
5. Rosen, Charley. *The First Tip-Off: The Incredible Story of the Birth of the NBA*, p. 37. McGraw-Hill, 2008.
6. Bowie, Bob. "Nugs Drop 11th in Row, 92 to 78." *The Denver Post*. January 2, 1950.
7. "Nuggets Buy Crocker." International News Service. November 10, 1949.
8. Kiesele, Russ. "Tribe Obtains Kirk, Ex-Illini." *Moline Daily Dispatch*. December 31, 1949.
9. Ney, Al. "Charlie Shipp Non-Playing Coach Now." *Waterloo Courier*. January 1, 1950.
10. Carlson, Bill. "It's 'Four to Go' in Lakers Victory Plan." *The Minneapolis Star*. January 2, 1950.
11. Gaff, Glen. "Towery Punch Floors Pollard." *Minneapolis Morning Tribune*. December 29, 1949.
12. Menton, Paul. "Bullets Get Ezersky." *The Evening Sun* (Baltimore, MD). December 31, 1949.
13. "Anderson Five Put on Block." Associated Press. January 5, 1950.
14. Beahon, George. "Controversies Wax on 'Why?' of 3 Straight Royals Losses." *Rochester Democrat and Chronicle*. March 26, 1950.
15. Author interview with Duane Klueh.
16. Partner, Dan. "Win Streak for Nugs." *The Denver Post*. January 6, 1950.
17. "Redskins in 85–82 Victory Over Lakers." *The Sheboygan Press*. January 6, 1950.
18. Schumacher, Michael. *Mr. Basketball:*

George Mikan, the Minneapolis Lakers, and the Birth of the NBA, pp. 8–18. Bloomsbury USA, 2007.

19. Wray, John E. "Bombers Lose Cat-and-Mouse Thriller to Royals, 75-to-73, in Two Overtime Periods." *St. Louis Post-Dispatch.* January 9, 1950.

20. Harwood, Tim. *Ball Hawks: The Arrival and Departure of the NBA in Iowa*, pp. 105–106, 115. University of Iowa Press, 2018.

21. "Cook Scores 44 Points, Sets N.B.A. Record." *The Sheboygan Press.* January 13, 1950.

22. Nelson, Ray. "Easy Ed Trims Mikan, But Bombers Still Lose." *St. Louis Star-Times.* January 13, 1950.

23. Beahon, George. "Royals Down Lakers for 18th Straight Arena Win, 83–77; George Mikan Registers 51 Points to Establish 3 Marks." *Rochester Democrat and Chronicle.* January 16, 1950.

24. Schumacher, Michael. *Mr. Basketball: George Mikan, the Minneapolis Lakers, and the Birth of the NBA*, pp. 93–95, 102–104. Bloomsbury USA, 2007.

25. Carlson, Bill. "Lakers' Tight Defense Turns Back Rochester." *The Minneapolis Star.* January 16, 1950.

26. McCulley, Jim. "Knicks Nose Celtics, 82–80, on Braun's Shot." *Daily News* (New York, NY). January 15, 1950.

27. "Denver Beats 'Skins, 94–80." *The Sheboygan Press.* January 15, 1950.

28. "Redskins Sign Schulz Today." *The Sheboygan Press.* January 16, 1950.

29. "Honoured Members: George Brown." Hockey Hall of Fame, n.d. https://www.hhof.com/HonouredMembers/MemberDetails.html?type=Player&mem=B196101&list=.

30. Rosen, Charley. *The First Tip-Off: The Incredible Story of the Birth of the NBA*, pp. 17–20, 37–41. McGraw-Hill, 2008.

31. Barry, Jack. "Sadowski Refuses to Shoulder Blame for Cage Collapse of Celtics." *The Boston Daily Globe.* April 11, 1948.

32. "Fort Wayne Nips Redskins, 73–72." *The Sheboygan Press.* January 19, 1950.

33. "Packers and Pistons Trade Two for Two." Associated Press. January 19, 1950.

34. Shevlin, Maurice. "Stags Defeat Tri-City, 83–68." *Chicago Daily Tribune.* January 20, 1950.

35. Baumgartner, Stan. "Warriors Nip Lakers, 90–89." *Philadelphia Inquirer.* January 21, 1950.

36. Tenny, Ben. "Pistons Lose and Win Over Week End; Head East for Four Tough Road Games." *The News-Sentinel* (Fort Wayne, IN). January 23, 1950.

37. Reddy, Bill. "Packers Snap Syracuse's Home Winning Streak in Overtime." *The Post-Standard* (Syracuse, NY). January 23, 1950.

38. Thies, Bud. "Bombers Find Celtics Cold, Get Hot to Win, 71–47." *St. Louis Globe-Democrat.* January 23, 1950.

39. Shevlin, Maurice. "Lakers Blast Stags, 80–68; Mikan Gets 40." *Chicago Daily Tribune.* January 25, 1950.

40. "Olympians, Knicks Pass 100 Mark." Associated Press. January 25, 1950.

41. Kiesele, Russ. "From the Press Box." *Moline Daily Dispatch.* January 27, 1950.

42. "Doxie Moore Is Redskins' Coach." *The Sheboygan Press.* June 12, 1946.

43. "Coach and Manager Doxie Moore Signs Two-Year Contract." *The Sheboygan Press.* December 1, 1947.

44. "Eddie Dancker, McDermott, Handle Team During Trip." *The Sheboygan Press.* December 10, 1947.

45. "Board Orders Suspension of Luther Harris." *The Sheboygan Press.* December 16, 1947.

46. "Lambert Claims Darling Still Hasn't Protested Redskins' Use of Harris." Associated Press. December 20, 1947.

47. "Luther Harris Suspended for Rule Violations." *The Sheboygan Press.* December 30, 1947.

48. "Moore Resumes Coaching 'Skins." Associated Press. December 30, 1947.

49. Kramp, Louis J. "Want Officials to Cut Whistling." *The Daily Pantagraph* (Bloomington, IL). March 26, 1943.

Chapter 7

1. Smith, Seymour S. "Ed Sadowski Misses Shot as Game Ends." *The Sun* (Baltimore, MD). January 27, 1950.

2. Reddy, Bill. "Broken Jaw Fails to Halt Gabor During Busy Month." *The Post-Standard* (Syracuse, NY). January 28, 1950.

3. Stark, Douglas. *When Basketball Was Jewish: Voices of Those Who Played the Game*, pp. 180–183. University of Nebraska Press, 2017.

4. Harwood, Tim. *Ball Hawks: The Arrival and Departure of the NBA in Iowa*, pp. 85–88. University of Iowa Press, 2018.

5. Ney, Al. "Hawks Slip, 85–79, Before 4,264 Fans." *Waterloo Courier.* January 30, 1950.

6. Barry, Jack. "Celts Obtain Mahnken, 6–8 Center, for Englund." *The Boston Daily Globe.* January 30, 1950.

7. Byrod, Fred. "Warriors Top Pistons, 87–74." *Philadelphia Inquirer.* January 25, 1950.

8. Gaynor, Brian. "Three Posewitz Brothers Keyed Red Skins' Forerunner Teams." *The Sheboygan Press.* December 26, 2008.

9. Jozwiak, Miller. "From 'Go Home' to 'Welcome Home' for Sheboygan Man." *The Sheboygan Press.* July 10, 2016.

10. Gaynor, Brian. "Sheboygan Welcomed Black Basketball Players Earlier Than Other Cities Did." *The Sheboygan Press.* March 10, 2009.

11. Gaynor, Brian. "Three Posewitz Brothers Keyed Red Skins' Forerunner Teams." *The Sheboygan Press.* December 26, 2008.

12. "Jeanette to Join Redskins Next Tuesday." *The Sheboygan Press.* January 30, 1943.

13. Carlson, Bill. "Mikan Sparkles in 96–81 Rout of New York." *The Minneapolis Star.* February 2, 1950.

14. "Mikan Picked as Greatest Cager." Associated Press. February 1, 1950.
15. Beahon, George. "Royals Oppose Packers in Bid for 19th Home Win." *Rochester Democrat and Chronicle*. January 21, 1950.
16. Beahon, George. "Royals Belt Packers, 95–79, for 19th Straight Arena Win." *Rochester Democrat and Chronicle*. January 22, 1950.
17. "Harrison Proposes NBA Split for Coming Year." Associated Press. February 2, 1950.
18. "Rejects Bid to Split Pro Loop." Associated Press. February 4, 1950.
19. "Joe Lapchick Suggests NBA Split Into Two Divisions." Associated Press. February 26, 1950.
20. "Two NBA Coaches Declare Present Setup Unwieldy." Associated Press. February 26, 1950.
21. O'Donnell, John. "Blackhawks Conquer Warriors." *The Democrat and Leader* (Davenport, IA). February 9, 1950.
22. Kiesele, Russ. "From the Press Box." *Moline Daily Dispatch*. February 25, 1950.
23. Malafronte, Chip. "Podoloff Brothers Possessed Uncanny Business Savvy." *New Haven Register*. June 29, 2012.
24. "History of the American Hockey League." The American Hockey League, n.d. https://theahl.com/history.
25. Goldaper, Sam. "Maurice Podoloff Dead at 95, Was First N.B.A. President." *New York Times*. November 26, 1985.
26. "Podoloff Confident NBA Will Prosper in Coming Years; Foresees Expansion." United Press. February 17, 1950.

Chapter 8

1. "Mikan 'Mr. Basketball of Pros,' Rated All-Time Best." National Enterprise Association. January 13, 1950.
2. Thies, Bud. "Bomber Steam Can't Match Knicks' Fire." *St. Louis Globe-Democrat*. February 3, 1950.
3. Broeg, Bob. "'Team Can Be Bought,' Says Jones." *St. Louis Post-Dispatch*. January 30, 1950.
4. "Emory D. Jones." Associated Press. September 26, 1977.
5. "Sports Roundup." Associated Press. May 20, 1946.
6. Rosen, Charley. *The First Tip-Off: The Incredible Story of the Birth of the NBA*, pp. 142–146. McGraw-Hill, 2008.
7. Mitauer, Harry. "First Contact Made in Deal for Bombers." *St. Louis Globe-Democrat*. February 1, 1950.
8. Cushing, Elliott. "Sports Eye View." *Rochester Democrat and Chronicle*. February 1, 1950.
9. Byrod, Fred. "Warriors Trounce Tri-City, 83–72; Fulks Gets 30; Crossin Sets Record." *Philadelphia Inquirer*. February 4, 1950.
10. "Redskins Face Two Key Tilts." *The Sheboygan Press*. February 7, 1950.
11. Carberry, Jack. "Ft. Wayne Buys Klueh from Nugs." *The Denver Post*. February 6, 1950.
12. Broeg, Bob. "Macauley and Bombers Hoop 'er Up to End Losing Streak." *St. Louis Post-Dispatch*. February 6, 1950.
13. Nelson, Murry R. *The National Basketball League: A History, 1935–1949*, p. 159. McFarland & Company, 2009.
14. Reddy, Bill. "Syracuse Enters National Pro Court League." *The Post-Standard* (Syracuse, NY). July 2, 1946.
15. Gaff, Glen. "Lakers 'Out-Stall' Capitols 71–59." *Minneapolis Morning Tribune*. February 10, 1950.
16. "Redskins Pile Up 104–82 Win Over Tri-Cities." *The Sheboygan Press*. February 10, 1950.
17. Angelopoulos, Angelo. "Packers Deal Olymps Their Worst Beating." *The Indianapolis News*. February 10, 1950.
18. Barry, Jack. "Celts' Question Marks Beat Trade Deadline." *The Boston Daily Globe*. February 11, 1950.
19. Reddy, Bill. "Nats Invade Baltimore; Bids for Player Rejected." *The Post-Standard* (Syracuse, NY). February 11, 1950.
20. "Offer for Fulks Is Turned Down." Associated Press. February 12, 1950.
21. Fuchs, Bill. "Nichols-Otten Trade Puzzling to Caps Fans." *The Evening Star* (Washington, D.C.). February 10, 1950.
22. Tenny, Ben. "Pistons Given Little Time for Rejoicing." *The News-Sentinel* (Fort Wayne, IN). February 13, 1950.
23. O'Donnell, John. "Big Schedule for Blackhawks." *The Democrat and Leader* (Davenport, IA). February 13, 1950.
24. Bowie, Bob. "Nugs Move to Chicago After Repeat Victory." *The Denver Post*. January 2, 1950.
25. Menton, Paul. "Jeannette Has Tough Job in His New Role." *The Evening Sun* (Baltimore, MD). February 14, 1950.
26. Gaff, Glen. "Lakers Shellack Rochester 92–70." *Minneapolis Morning Tribune*. February 16, 1950.
27. Nelson, Ray. "Lakers' Mikan Makes Free Throw in Last Two Seconds and Bombers Lose Thriller, 72–71." *St. Louis Star-Times*. February 17, 1950.
28. Beahon, George. "Royals Enter Home Stretch 13-Tilt Drive." *Rochester Democrat and Chronicle*. February 20, 1950.
29. Ney, Al. "Hawks Win, 76–74, on Goal by Boykoff." *Waterloo Courier*. February 16, 1950.
30. Fuchs, Bill. "Caps Nose Out Indianapolis, 81–79, in Thriller Before 4,409." *The Evening Star* (Washington, D.C.). February 19, 1950.
31. Reddy, Bill. "Nats Nip Olympians, 82–78, 6,704 Fans Pay Tribute to Cervi." *The Post-Standard* (Syracuse, NY). February 20, 1950.
32. Franco, George. "Sailors Paces Nuggets' 89 to 78 Upset of Nats." *The Denver Post*. February 22, 1950.

33. Shevlin, Maurice. "21,666 See Lakers Beat Trotters, 76–60." *Chicago Daily Tribune*. February 22, 1950.
34. Gaff, Glen. "St. Louis Bows in 100–57 Rout." *Minneapolis Morning Tribune*. February 23, 1950.
35. "Boy, 13, Scores All Team's 139 Points." Associated Press. February 3, 1941.
36. Bumpus, Jamie. "Bob Harrison, Hero of 1950 NBA Finals, Links Hard Work, Zeal to Lifetime of Success." *Tennessee Journalist*. February 24, 2010.
37. Mozley, Dana. "Knicks Lead Capitols on 69th Armory Court." *Daily News* (New York, NY). February 23, 1950.
38. Barry, Jack. "Lavelli Stamps Self as Big League Player in Celtics' Win." *The Boston Daily Globe*. February 25, 1950.
39. "Olymps Lose Lead on 5th Loss in Row." Associated Press. February 25, 1950.
40. Beahon, George. "Holzman Leads Royals to 66–64 Win Over Lakers in Tense Arena Battle." *Rochester Democrat and Chronicle*. February 27, 1950.
41. Thies, Bud. "Easy Ed Hot But Bombers' Luck Chills." *St. Louis Globe-Democrat*. February 28, 1950.
42. Ney, Al. "The Sports Alley." *Waterloo Courier*. February 28, 1950.
43. Ney, Al. "Hawks Go, 100–76; Face Syracuse Next." *Waterloo Courier*. February 28, 1950.
44. "Redskins Beaten Over Week End." *The Sheboygan Press*. February 28, 1950.
45. Stann, Francis. "New Coach of Caps to Be Named Soon." *The Evening Star* (Washington, D.C.). February 28, 1950.

Chapter 9

1. Arnold, Ron. "Blackhawks Pummel Denver Nuggets in NBA Contest Here, 97–80." *The Muscatine Journal*. March 2, 1950
2. Byrod, Fred. "Warriors Trip Celtics Before 7897." *Philadelphia Inquirer*. March 2, 1950.
3. Webster, John. "Crossin Rejoins Warrior Squad." *Philadelphia Inquirer*. October 19, 1949.
4. Webster, John. "With Crossin, Mogus Playing Inspired Basketball, Warriors May Have Drive to Reach Playoffs." *Philadelphia Inquirer*. January 27, 1950.
5. Wickstrom, George. "Hawks Shellack Olympians, 96–83." *The Rock Island Argus*. March 4, 1950.
6. Byrod, Fred. "Warriors Win, 66–61, on Rally, Take Fourth." *Philadelphia Inquirer*. March 4, 1950.
7. Smith, Seymour S. "Bullets Top Stags, 77–72." *The Sun* (Baltimore, MD). March 5, 1950.
8. Reddy, Bill. "Nationals Trip Lakers, 84–75, as 9,888 Cheer." *The Post-Standard* (Syracuse, NY). March 6, 1950.
9. Kiesele, Russ. "Brian Bashes Hawks, 88–77." *Moline Daily Dispatch*. March 7, 1950.
10. Angelopoulos, Angelo. "Olymps Keep Chopping and Packers Fall." *The Indianapolis News*. March 8, 1950.
11. Gaff, Glen. "Lakers Toy with 'Skins 90–73." *Minneapolis Morning Tribune*. March 8, 1950.
12. Gaff, Glen. "Lakers Win 68–65; Trail by 12 in Last Period." *Minneapolis Morning Tribune*. March 9, 1950.
13. Stann, Francis. "Caps Down Bullets, Need One Victory to Clinch Third Place." *The Evening Star* (Washington, D.C.). March 9, 1950.
14. Turkin, Hy. "Simmons Is Ready for Knick-Cap Tilt." *Daily News* (New York, NY). March 21, 1950.
15. Turkin, Hy. "Knicks Capture 80–78 Thriller." *Daily News* (New York, NY). March 9, 1950.
16. Ney, Al. "Post Largest Margin; Olympians Next." *Waterloo Courier*. March 9, 1950.
17. Stann, Francis. "McKinney, Caps' New Coach, to See Little Action as Player." *The Evening Star* (Washington, D.C.). March 10, 1950.
18. Ruby, Earl. "'Terrible-Tempered Mr. Bones' Is a Fun-Loving Cage Clown Selling Pro Game at Capital." *The Courier Journal* (Louisville, KY). February 29, 1948.
19. Tenny, Ben. "Next Week End, Two Games Will Tell How Pistons Finish; They Split Two." *The News-Sentinel* (Fort Wayne, IN). March 13, 1950.
20. "Packers Nudge Knicks, 91–89." Associated Press. March 12, 1950.
21. Smith, Seymour S. "Bullets Down Boston, 79–75, to Strengthen Hold on Fourth Place." *The Sun* (Baltimore, MD). March 12, 1950.
22. Gaff, Glen. "Lakers Whip Knicks 87–66." *Minneapolis Morning Tribune*. March 13, 1950.
23. Angelopoulos, Angelo. "Grim Olymps Regain Tie for 1st by Beating Nats." *The Indianapolis News*. March 15, 1950.
24. Barry, Jack. "Bombers Finish Celtics' Playoff Hopes, 86 to 76." *The Boston Daily Globe*. March 15, 1950.
25. Byrod, Fred. "Warriors Top Packers in Overtime, 83–80." *Philadelphia Inquirer*. March 16, 1950.
26. Gaff, Glen. "Lakers Dent Bullets 96–62." *Minneapolis Morning Tribune*. March 16, 1950.
27. Young, Dick. "Knicks Shade Celtics, 88–84." *Daily News* (New York, NY). March 16, 1950.
28. "Redskins Lose 88–75 Clash with Syracuse; Face Chicago Monday." *The Sheboygan Press*. March 17, 1950.
29. "Olymps Appear 'In' as Western Champions." Associated Press. March 17, 1950.
30. Fleischman, Bill. "Bombers Stop Bullets; 22 Points for Easy Ed." *St. Louis Star-Times*. March 17, 1950.
31. Barry, Jack. "700 (New Low) See Celtics Lose Finals in Two Overtimes, 98–96." *The Boston Daily Globe*. March 18, 1950.
32. Fitzgerald, Tom. "'I'm Not Tough Enough for Pro Ball'—Julian." *The Boston Daily Globe*. March 23, 1950.

33. "St. Louis Bombers Lace Chicago Stags, 85 to 69." Associated Press. March 18, 1950.

34. Byrod, Fred. "Warriors Win, 85–59, to Clinch Tie for 4th." *Philadelphia Inquirer*. March 18, 1950.

35. Poisall, Bob. "Olympians Set Scoring Record in 108 to 73 Win Here." *The Owensboro Messenger*. March 19, 1950.

36. Grundman, Adolph H. *The Golden Age of Amateur Basketball: The AAU Tournament, 1921–1968*, pp. 27–41, 57–62. University of Nebraska Press, 2004.

37. Ney, Al. "Payak Goal at Final Horn Wins, 79–77." *Waterloo Courier*. March 20, 1950.

38. Thies, Bud. "Bombers Drop Finale to Stags, Easy Ed Shines." *St. Louis Globe-Democrat*. March 20, 1950.

39. Tenny, Ben. "Pistons, Stags Play Tonight for 3rd Post." *The News-Sentinel* (Fort Wayne, IN). March 20, 1950.

40. Beahon, George. "Hot Royals Humble Baltimore Bullets, 97–66; Face Lakers Here Tomorrow in Division Tie." *Rochester Democrat and Chronicle*. March 20, 1950.

41. Green, Ronald. "Basketball Worst Pro Sport, Says Hoffman." *The Charlotte News*. March 25, 1950.

Chapter 10

1. Tenny, Ben. "Pistons, in Third Spot, Await Royals or Lakers." *The News-Sentinel* (Fort Wayne, IN). March 21, 1950.

2. Beahon, George. "Jaros' Set Shot with 3 Seconds Remaining Gives Lakers Tingling 78–76 Win Over Royals." *Rochester Democrat and Chronicle*. March 22, 1950.

3. Fuchs, Bill. "Caps, Tough in Defeat, Face Worried Knicks Tonight." *The Evening Star* (Washington, D.C.). March 22, 1950.

4. Haven, Orville. "Late Anderson Drive Dumps Blackhawks, 89–77." *Anderson Herald*. March 22, 1950.

5. Angelopoulos, Angelo. "Olymps Stagger In." *The Indianapolis News*. March 22, 1950.

6. Andrews, Jack. "Nationals Thump Warriors, 93–76, in Opening Playoff Game." *The Post-Standard* (Syracuse, NY). March 23, 1950.

7. Mozley, Dana. "Knicks Eliminate Caps in NBA Playoff, 103–83." *Daily News* (New York, NY). March 23, 1950.

8. Carlson, Bill. "Lakers Tired? Stags Can Use Two Days Rest, Too." *The Minneapolis Star*. March 23, 1950.

9. Beahon, George. "Zollners Beat Royals, 90–84, as Late Rally Falls Short; Visitors' Big Men Dominate." *Rochester Democrat and Chronicle*. March 24, 1950.

10. Byrod, Fred. "Warrior Five Eliminated by Nats, 59–53." *Philadelphia Inquirer*. March 24, 1950.

11. "Redskins Win, Even Series." *The Sheboygan Press*. March 24, 1950.

12. Herman, Dick. "Hawks and Packers to Settle Playoff Argument at Anderson." *The Daily Times* (Davenport, IA). March 24, 1950.

13. Luther, Fred. "Anderson Finishes Off Hawks with 94–71 Rout." *Moline Daily Dispatch*. March 25, 1950.

14. Tenny, Ben. "Bring on Those Lakers! That's Pistons' Cry After Disposing of Royals' Squad." *The News-Sentinel* (Fort Wayne, IN). March 25, 1950.

15. Angelopoulos, Angelo. "Olymps Fashion One for Memory Book." *The Indianapolis News*. March 27, 1950.

16. Carlson, Bill. "Lakers Beat Chicago 75–67." *The Minneapolis Star*. March 26, 1950.

17. Reddy, Bill. "Nationals Edge Knicks in Extra Period, 91–83." *The Post-Standard* (Syracuse, NY). March 27, 1950.

18. Gaff, Glen. "Lakers Rip Ft. Wayne." *Minneapolis Morning Tribune*. March 28, 1950.

19. Angelopoulos, Angelo. "Never-Yield Olymps Give Fans an Unbelievable Rally." *The Indianapolis News*. March 29, 1950.

20. Tenny, Ben. "That Man Mikan, His Mates End Piston Hopes." *The News-Sentinel* (Fort Wayne, IN). March 29, 1950.

21. Turkin, Hy. "Knicks Lock Nat Series at 1–1 with 80–76 Win." *Daily News* (New York, NY). March 31, 1950.

22. "Packers Even Series with Olympians." Associated Press. March 31, 1950.

23. Angelopoulos, Angelo. "Olymps Find Selves Too Tired to Pull Off Another Miracle." *The Indianapolis News*. April 3, 1950.

24. Reddy, Bill. "Nats Defeat Knicks in Final, 91–80." *The Post-Standard* (Syracuse, NY). April 3, 1950.

25. Gaff, Glen. "Lakers Overwhelm Stalling Anderson 75–50." *Minneapolis Morning Tribune*. April 6, 1950.

26. "Doxie Moore Seeks Purdue Job." Associated Press. April 7, 1950.

27. Hargrave, Howard. "Auerbach Considered for post at Maryland." *The Rock Island Argus*. April 6, 1950.

28. Carlson, Bill. "Lakers' Three Ms Oust Anderson." *The Minneapolis Star*. April 7, 1950.

29. Vargas, Ramon A. *Fight, Grin & Squarely Play the Game: The 1945 Loyola New Orleans Basketball Championship & Legacy*, chap. 7. The History Press, 2013.

Chapter 11

1. "Syracuse Bandits Carry Off Safe, Possibly $15,000." United Press. April 7, 1950.

2. "Syracuse Police Kill Man and Wound Two in Ambush." *The Post-Standard* (Syracuse, NY). May 12, 1950.

3. Reddy, Bill. "Lakers Nip Nats in Last Second, 68–66." *The Post-Standard* (Syracuse, NY). April 9, 1950.

4. Reddy, Bill. "Harrison Almost Didn't Play;

Couldn't Find Jersey." *The Post-Standard* (Syracuse, NY). April 9, 1950.

5. Reddy, Bill. "Nats Even NBA Series with Lakers." *The Post-Standard* (Syracuse, NY). April 10, 1950.

6. Cushing, Elliott. "Sports Eye View." *Rochester Democrat and Chronicle*. March 19, 1950.

7. Morrison, Robert. "Future of Bombers Up in the Air but Decision to Be Made Soon." *St. Louis Post-Dispatch*. March 20, 1950.

8. Kinney, Bill. "Along the Sport Trail." *The Rock Island Argus*. April 1, 1950.

9. Broeg, Bob. "End Appears Near for Bombers; Decision After League Meeting Monday." *St. Louis Post-Dispatch*. April 21, 1950.

10. Hendrickson, Joe. "Hot Info on NBA Pruning." *Minneapolis Morning Tribune*. April 15, 1950.

11. "Plans Being Drafted for Affiliated Loop in Pro Cage Play." Associated Press. April 15, 1950.

12. "Anderson Packers Quit; Pro League May Trim Members." Associated Press. April 11, 1950.

13. "Sports Roundup." Associated Press. March 6, 1950.

14. Jurgens, Jerry. "Red Auerbach Turns in Resignation as Coach of Blackhawks." *The Daily Times* (Davenport, IA). April 12, 1950.

15. Gaff, Glen. "Lakers, Syracuse Resume Tonight." *Minneapolis Morning Tribune*. April 14, 1950.

16. Carlson, Bill. "Syracuse Cripples Likely to be Ready Sunday." *The Minneapolis Star*. April 15, 1950.

17. "Hot Info on NBA Pruning." *Minneapolis Morning Tribune*. April 15, 1950.

18. "Redskins Seek to Organize New, Independent League." *The Sheboygan Press*. April 17, 1950.

19. Gaff, Glen. "Lakers Whip Syracuse for 3-1 Lead." *Minneapolis Morning Tribune*. April 17, 1950.

20. "Sheboygan May Start New Loop." Associated Press. April 17, 1950.

21. Menton, Paul. "Bullets Bid for Bombers." *The Evening Sun* (Baltimore, MD). April 18, 1950.

22. Burnes, Robert L. "The Benchwarmer." *St. Louis Globe-Democrat*. April 21, 1950.

23. Gaff, Glen. "'We'll Run 'Em Again,' Says Nats' Cervi." *Minneapolis Morning Tribune*. April 20, 1950.

24. Reddy, Bill. "Nationals Trounce Lakers, 83 to 76." *The Post-Standard* (Syracuse, NY). April 21, 1950.

25. "Auerbach Resigns Coaching Position with Hawk Quintet." Associated Press. April 13, 1950.

26. Flachsbart, Harold. "Bombers Ask Permission to Sell Players." *St. Louis Post-Dispatch*. April 23, 1950.

27. Gaff, Glen. "Lakers Gird for Nats Here." *Minneapolis Morning Tribune*. April 22, 1950.

28. Gaff, Glen. "Lakers Win, 110-95, for Third Title." *Minneapolis Morning Tribune*. April 24, 1950.

29. Hendrickson, Joe. "'Worst Officiating'—Cervi; 'Pressure Fired Tempers'—Pollard." *Minneapolis Morning Tribune*. April 24, 1950.

Chapter 12

1. Nason, Jerry. "Brown Turns Tough; N.B.A. Must Aid Celtics or They'll Quit League." *The Boston Daily Globe*. April 24, 1950.

2. "League Pays $30,000 for Bomber Players and Suspends Franchise." Associated Press. April 25, 1950.

3. "Indianapolis to Repeat Proposal Made by Packers." Associated Press. April 15, 1950.

4. "Redskins Push Conditions for Entry in NBA." Associated Press. April 18, 1950.

5. "Denver, Sheboygan, Waterloo Quit NBA; Form Rival League." Associated Press. April 26, 1950.

6. "NBA Revamps With 12-Team Organization." United Press. April 25, 1950.

7. Cromie, Robert. "N.B.A. Castoffs to Form Basket League." *Chicago Daily Tribune*. April 25, 1950.

8. "Denver Cagers, Waterloo Also Are Expelled." United Press. April 25, 1950.

9. Ney, Al. "Hawks, Sheboygan, Denver, Milwaukee or Oshkosh Set; to Seek Six More Teams." *Waterloo Courier*. April 25, 1950.

10. Mozley, Dana. "Knicks' Lapchick Lauds '50 College Hoop Crop." *Daily News* (New York, NY). March 19, 1950.

11. Gaff, Glen. "Lakers Get Hutton, Lose Haskins." *Minneapolis Morning Tribune*. May 25, 1950.

12. Thomas, Ron. *They Cleared the Lane: The NBA's Black Pioneers*, pp. 109, 113-118. University of Nebraska Press, 2004

13. Gould, Todd. *Pioneers of the Hardwood: Indiana and the Birth of Professional Basketball*, p. 177. Indiana University Press, 1998.

14. Sullivan, George. "Remember…" *The Boston Daily Globe*. April 3, 1977.

15. Ney, Al. "Hawks, Sheboygan, Denver, Milwaukee or Oshkosh Set; to Seek Six More Teams." *Waterloo Courier*. April 25, 1950.

16. Stann, Francis. "Lloyd and Hunter Sign Contracts with Caps." *The Evening Star* (Washington, D.C.). May 7, 1950.

17. "Washington Capitols Sign Center Don Otten." Associated Press. October 17, 1950.

18. Ralby, Herb. "Auerbach, New Coach, Says All Celts on Block." *The Boston Daily Globe*. April 28, 1950.

19. "Former Gopher Cage Coach to Tri-City." United Press. May 3, 1950.

20. "Cooper and Dahler to Play Pro Ball." Associated Press. April 25, 1950.

21. Ney, Al. "Pops Harrison to be General Manager Here." *Waterloo Courier*. May 7, 1950.

22. Ney, Al. "Cage Hawks Sign Top NBA Draft Choice." *Waterloo Courier*. May 10, 1950.

23. Shevlin, Maurice. "Six Teams Form New Pro League." *Chicago Sunday Tribune*. May 14, 1950.

24. "New League Is Expected to Have 10 Teams." *The Sheboygan Press.* May 13, 1950.
25. Thies, Bud. "Podoloff Declares War on New Pro Basketball League." *St. Louis Globe-Democrat.* May 17, 1950.
26. Kinney, Bill. "Along the Sport Trail." *The Rock Island Argus.* May 24, 1950.
27. "New Anderson Club Signs Komenich, Black Despite NBA." Associated Press. May 24, 1950.
28. Thomas, Ron. *They Cleared the Lane: The NBA's Black Pioneers*, p. 125. University of Nebraska Press, 2004
29. "Hall of Fame to Induct XU's 'Sweetwater' Clifton." Xavier University of Louisiana Athletics. August 7, 2014, https://xulagold.com/honors/hall-of-fame/nat-sweetwater-clifton/2.
30. Burns, Joe. "Sweetwater Plays Prodigal, to Return Here With Mets." *The Dayton Herald.* January 24, 1947.
31. "Globetrotters Sign Clifton for $10,000." United Press. July 31, 1948.
32. Smith, Sam. "'Sweetwater' Keeps Rollin'" *Chicago Tribune.* June 9, 1985.
33. Holmes, Tommy. "Pro Cage Knicks Make Title Move." *Brooklyn Eagle.* May 25, 1950.
34. Araton, Harvey. "He Was a Knicks Pioneer, and He Has Proof." *The New York Times.* February 18, 2012.
35. "Mehen, Boykoff, Sailors Sign to Play in N.B.A." Associated Press. May 26, 1950.
36. "Sports Roundup." Associated Press. June 2, 1950.
37. Smith, Red. "4 Negro Stars Due Tryout With Bullets." *The Evening Sun* (Baltimore, MD). May 31, 1950.
38. "St. Louis' Cage Bid Rejected." Associated Press. June 5, 1950.
39. "Dayton, Toledo in Pro Field." United Press. June 4, 1950.
40. Cushing, Elliott. "Sports Eye View." *Rochester Democrat and Chronicle.* June 11, 1950.
41. "Abe Saperstein Acquires Stags in $50,000 Deal." Associated Press. June 20, 1950.
42. Thomas, Damion L. *Globetrotting: African American Athletes and Cold War Politics*, pp. 53–60. University of Illinois Press, 2012.
43. Lofstrom, R.A. "Right and Left in Sports." *The St. Cloud Daily Times and the Daily Journal-Press.* April 21, 1937.
44. Green, Ben. *Spinning the Globe: The Rise, Fall, and Return to Greatness of the Harlem Globetrotters*, pp. 3–5, 32–50. Amistad Press, 2006.
45. Strickler, George. "Renaissance to Battle Oshkosh for Pro Crown." *Chicago Daily Tribune.* March 28, 1939.
46. Smith, Wilfrid. "Bruins Win in Overtime; Rens Lose to Harlem." *Chicago Daily Tribune.* March 19, 1940.
47. Kelley, Jack. "Trotters and Tatum Rip Mercuries, 78–58." *Tulsa Daily World.* February 16, 1953.
48. Ward, Arch. "Trotters Top Lakers with Rally, 61–59." *Chicago Daily Tribune.* February 20, 1948.
49. "Trotters, Stars End Tour." Associated Press. April 20, 1950.
50. Ward, Arch. "In the Wake of the News." *Chicago Daily Tribune.* April 24, 1950.
51. Smith, Wilfrid. "Stags May Move from Stadium to Coliseum." *Chicago Daily Tribune.* July 2, 1950.
52. Hargrave, Howard. "Fifth Quarter." *The Rock Island Argus.* June 8, 1950.
53. "Grand Rapids Get 'Pro' Cage Berth." Associated Press. June 22, 1950.
54. Nelson, Murry R. *The National Basketball League: A History, 1935–1949*, p. 96, 143. McFarland & Company, 2009.
55. "Grand Rapids Get 'Pro' Cage Berth." Associated Press. June 22, 1950.
56. Ney, Al. "The Sports Alley." *Waterloo Courier.* June 30, 1950.
57. Collett, Ritter. "Journal of Sports." *Journal Herald* (Dayton, OH). June 30, 1950.
58. "New Cage League May Have to Fold." Associated Press. June 30, 1950.
59. "Three Cities Considered as NPBL Sites." Associated Press. June 30, 1950.
60. Ahern, John. "Celtics Sign Duquesne's Negro Star." *The Boston Daily Globe.* June 30, 1950.
61. Ney, Al. "Court Denies Ban on Talks with Cagers." *Waterloo Courier.* July 18, 1950.
62. Ralby, Herb. "Brown, Pieri Buy Celtics Franchise from Garden." *The Boston Daily Globe.* July 31, 1950.
63. "Ten-Club Circuit Vetoed by NPBL." United Press. August 3, 1950.
64. Ney, Al. "The Sports Alley." *Waterloo Courier.* August 8, 1950.
65. Ruby, Earl. "Top 'Toppers Adopt Louisville, Hope to Copy Olympians Set-Up; Need Manager, Coach, and Backers." *The Courier Journal* (Louisville, KY). August 10, 1950.
66. "Stags Change Name to Chicago Bruins." United Press. August 15, 1950.
67. "Kansas City Added to NPBL." Associated Press. September 2, 1950.
68. Cromie, Robert. "Bruins Fold as Saperstein Drops Plans." *Chicago Daily Tribune.* September 26, 1950.
69. United Nations. Security Council. *Complaint of Aggression upon the Republic of Korea.* June 27, 1950. 83, S/1511.
70. McCulley, Jim. "Braun in Service." *Daily News* (New York, NY). September 28, 1950.

Bibliography

"Abe Saperstein Acquires Stags in $50,000 Deal," Associated Press. June 20, 1950.
Ahern, John. "Celtics Sign Duquesne's Negro Star," *Boston Daily Globe*. June 30, 1950.
"Anderson Five Put on Block," Associated Press. January 5, 1950.
"Anderson Packers Quit; Pro League May Trim Members," Associated Press. April 11, 1950.
Andrews, Jack. "Nationals Thump Warriors, 93–76, in Opening Playoff Game," *The Post-Standard* (Syracuse, NY). March 23, 1950.
Angelopoulos, Angelo. "Grim Olymps Regain Tie for 1st by Beating Nats," *Indianapolis News*. March 15, 1950.
_____. "Groza Shows Pros a New Pivot Style," *Indianapolis News*. November 23, 1949.
_____. "Never-Yield Olymps Give Fans an Unbelievable Rally," *Indianapolis News*. March 29, 1950.
_____. "Olymps Can Be Great When They Want to Win One," *Indianapolis News*. December 23, 1949.
_____. "Olymps Fashion One for Memory Book," *Indianapolis News*. March 27, 1950.
_____. "Olymps Find Selves Too Tired to Pull Off Another Miracle," *Indianapolis News*. April 3, 1950.
_____. "Olymps Get a Bad One Out of System," *Indianapolis News*. December 7, 1949.
_____. "Olymps Keep Chopping and Packers Fall," *Indianapolis News*. March 8, 1950.
_____. "Olymps Make Minneapolis Pay," *Indianapolis News*. December 2, 1949.
_____. "Olymps Stagger In," *Indianapolis News*. March 22, 1950.
_____. "Olymps Take on Old Pro Look, Denver," *Indianapolis News*. December 9, 1949.
_____. "Packers Deal Olymps Their Worst Beating," *Indianapolis News*. February 10, 1950.
_____. "Sub Courageous in Olympians' Defeat," *Indianapolis News*. December 21, 1949.
_____. "Volker May Face Olymps," *Indianapolis News*. December 16, 1949.
_____. "Walther to Join Olymps," *Indianapolis News*. December 21, 1949.
Araton, Harvey. "He Was a Knicks Pioneer, and He Has Proof," *New York Times*. February 18, 2012.
Arnold, Ron. "Blackhawks Pummel Denver Nuggets in NBA Contest Here, 97–80," *Muscatine Journal*. March 2, 1950
Auerbach, Arnold, and Joe Fitzgerald. *Red Auerbach: An Autobiography*. G.P. Putnam's Sons, 1977.
"Auerbach Resigns Coaching Position with Hawk Quintet," Associated Press. April 13, 1950.
Barr, Michael. *Cloyce Box: 6'4" and Bulletproof*. Texas A&M University Press, 2017.
Barry, Jack. "'Aid from Englund' Plan Pays Off as Celtics Win," *Boston Daily Globe*. December 9, 1949.
_____. "Bombers Finish Celtics' Playoff Hopes, 86 to 76," *Boston Daily Globe*. March 15, 1950.
_____. "Brown Says 'No Holdup' in Contract with Lavelli," *Boston Daily Globe*. November 18, 1949.
_____. "Celts Obtain Mahnken, 6-8 Center, for Englund," *Boston Daily Globe*. January 30, 1950.
_____. "Celts' Question Marks Beat Trade Deadline," *Boston Daily Globe*. February 11, 1950.
_____. "Lavelli Stamps Self as Big League Player in Celtics' Win," *Boston Daily Globe*. February 25, 1950.
_____. "Sadowski Refuses to Shoulder Blame for Cage Collapse of Celtics," *Boston Daily Globe*. April 11, 1948.
_____. "700 (New Low) See Celtics Lose Finals in Two Overtimes, 98–96," *Boston Daily Globe*. March 18, 1950.
Basketball Association of America. "League Minutes," October 3, 1946.
Baumgartner, Stan. "Warriors Nip Lakers, 90–89," *Philadelphia Inquirer*. January 21, 1950.
Beahon, George. "Controversies Wax on 'Why?' of 3 Straight Royals Losses," *Rochester Democrat and Chronicle*. March 26, 1950.
_____. "Holzman Leads Royals to 66-64 Win Over Lakers in Tense Arena Battle," *Rochester Democrat and Chronicle*. February 27, 1950.
_____. "Hot Royals Humble Baltimore Bullets, 97–66; Face Lakers Here Tomorrow in Division Tie," *Rochester Democrat and Chronicle*. March 20, 1950.
_____. "Jaros' Set Shot with 3 Seconds Remaining Gives Lakers Tingling 78–76 Win Over Royals," *Rochester Democrat and Chronicle*. March 22, 1950.
_____. "Royals Belt Packers, 95–79, for 19th Straight Arena Win," *Rochester Democrat and Chronicle*. January 22, 1950.
_____. "Royals Capture Donnybrook Over Nats, 69 to 63, to Halt Syracusans' Winning Skein at 12 Games," *Rochester Democrat and Chronicle*. December 11, 1949.
_____. "Royals Down Lakers for 18th Straight Arena Win, 83–77; George Mikan Registers 51 Points to Establish 3 Marks," *Rochester Democrat and Chronicle*. January 16, 1950.

———. "Royals Enter Home Stretch 13-Tilt Drive," *Rochester Democrat and Chronicle*. February 20, 1950.
———. "Royals Oppose Packers in Bid for 19th Home Win," *Rochester Democrat and Chronicle*. January 21, 1950.
———. "Royals Rout Minneapolis at Arena, 87–62, to Snare Lead in NBA Central Division," *Rochester Democrat and Chronicle*. December 21, 1949.
———. "Zollners Beat Royals, 90–84, as Late Rally Falls Short; Visitors' Big Men Dominate," *Rochester Democrat and Chronicle*. March 24, 1950.
"Billy Hassett Sold to Lakers," Associated Press. December 8, 1949.
"Board Orders Suspension of Luther Harris," *Sheboygan Press*. December 16, 1947.
Bowie, Bob. "Nugs Drop 11th in Row, 92 to 78," *Denver Post*. January 2, 1950.
———. "Nugs Move to Chicago After Repeat Victory," *Denver Post*. January 2, 1950.
"Bowling Green, DePaul Triumph," United Press. February 10, 1946.
"Boy, 13, Scores All Team's 139 Points," Associated Press. February 3, 1941.
Broeg, Bob. "Bombers Trade Todorovich to Tri-Cities for Mac Otten," *St. Louis Post-Dispatch*. November 28, 1949.
———. "End Appears Near for Bombers; Decision After League Meeting Monday," *St. Louis Post-Dispatch*. April 21, 1950.
———. "Macauley and Bombers Hoop 'Er Up to End Losing Streak," *St. Louis Post-Dispatch*. February 6, 1950.
———. "'Team Can Be Bought,' Says Jones," *St. Louis Post-Dispatch*. January 30, 1950.
Bumpus, Jamie. "Bob Harrison, Hero of 1950 NBA Finals, Links Hard Work, Zeal to Lifetime of Success," *Tennessee Journalist*. February 24, 2010.
Burnes, Robert L. "The Benchwarmer," *St. Louis Globe-Democrat*. April 21, 1950.
Burns, Joe. "Sweetwater Plays Prodigal, to Return Here with Mets," *Dayton Herald*. January 24, 1947.
Butler, Dylan. "The Butler Did It," *New York Post*. February 12, 2010.
Byrod, Fred. "Caps Trounce Warriors in Arena, 84–69," *Philadelphia Inquirer*. November 10, 1949.
———. "Knicks' Uprising Tops Warriors Five, 79–72," *Philadelphia Inquirer*. December 29, 1949.
———. "Lakers Beat Warriors in NBA Opener, 81–69," *Philadelphia Inquirer*. November 3, 1949.
———. "Warrior Five Eliminated by Nats, 59–53," *Philadelphia Inquirer*. March 24, 1950.
———. "Warriors Lose, 66–63, After Leading, 41–20," *Philadelphia Inquirer*. April 14, 1948.
———. "Warriors Top Packers in Overtime, 83–80," *Philadelphia Inquirer*. March 16, 1950.
———. "Warriors Top Pistons, 87–74," *Philadelphia Inquirer*. January 25, 1950.
———. "Warriors Trip Celtics Before 7897," *Philadelphia Inquirer*. March 2, 1950.
———. "Warriors Trounce Tri-City, 83–72; Fulks Gets 30; Crossin Sets Record," *Philadelphia Inquirer*. February 4, 1950.
———. "Warriors Win, 66–61, on Rally, Take Fourth," *Philadelphia Inquirer*. March 4, 1950.
———. "Warriors Win, 85–59, to Clinch Tie for 4th," *Philadelphia Inquirer*. March 18, 1950.
"Cage Loop Meets," United Press. August 11, 1949.
Carberry, Jack. "Ft. Wayne Buys Klueh from Nugs," *Denver Post*. February 6, 1950.
Carlson, Bill. "It's 'Four to Go' in Lakers Victory Plan," *Minneapolis Star*. January 2, 1950.
———. "Lakers Beat Chicago 75–67," *Minneapolis Star*. March 26, 1950.
———. "Lakers' Three Ms Oust Anderson," *Minneapolis Star*. April 7, 1950.
———. "Lakers' Tight Defense Turns Back Rochester," *Minneapolis Star*. January 16, 1950.
———. "Lakers Tired? Stags Can Use Two Days Rest, Too," *Minneapolis Star*. March 23, 1950.
———. "Mikan Sparkles in 96–81 Rout of New York," *Minneapolis Star*. February 2, 1950.
———. "Role as Regular May Be Harrison Reward," *Minneapolis Star*. December 12, 1949.
———. "Syracuse Cripples Likely to be Ready Sunday," *Minneapolis Star*. April 15, 1950.
Carlson, Chad. *Making March Madness: The Early Years of the NCAA, NIT, and College Basketball Championships, 1922–1951*. University of Arkansas Press, 2017.
———. "A Tale of Two Tournaments: The Red Cross Games and the Early NCAA-NIT Relationship," *Journal of Intercollegiate Sport*, Vol. 5, no. 2 (2012). Human Kinetics.
"Celts, Olympians Win; Lakers, Packers Lose," Associated Press. November 13, 1947.
"Coach and Manager Doxie Moore Signs Two-Year Contract," *Sheboygan Press*. December 1, 1947.
Collett, Ritter. "Journal of Sports," *Journal Herald* (Dayton, OH). June 30, 1950.
Cook, Kevin. "The Rochester Royals: The Story of Professional Basketball." *Rochester History*, Vol. LVIII. Rochester Public Library, 1996.
"Cook Scores 44 Points, Sets N.B.A. Record," *Sheboygan Press*. January 13, 1950.
"Cooper and Dahler to Play Pro Ball," Associated Press. April 25, 1950.
Cope, Myron. "The Big Z and His Misfiring Pistons," *Sports Illustrated*, December 18, 1967.
Cromie, Robert. "Bruins Fold as Saperstein Drops Plans," *Chicago Daily Tribune*. September 26, 1950.
———. "Graboski, 18, Adds Touch of Youth to Stag Line," *Chicago Daily Tribune*. December 20, 1948.
———. "N.B.A. Castoffs to Form Basket League," *Chicago Daily Tribune*. April 25, 1950.
———. "New York to Play Stags in Stadium Test," *Chicago Sunday Tribune*. January 11, 1948.

Bibliography

"Curly May Miss Laker Battle," *News-Sentinel* (Fort Wayne, IN). December 7, 1949.
Cushing, Elliott. "Royals Acquire Tall Ed Mikan, Stag Pivotman," *Rochester Democrat and Chronicle*. December 11, 1949.
_____. "Sports Eye View," *Rochester Democrat and Chronicle*. March 19, 1950.
_____. "Sports Eye View," *Rochester Democrat and Chronicle*. June 11, 1950.
"Dayton, Toledo in Pro Field," United Press. June 4, 1950.
"Denver Beats 'Skins, 94–80," *Sheboygan Press*. January 15, 1950.
"Denver Cagers, Waterloo Also Are Expelled," United Press. April 25, 1950.
"Denver, Sheboygan, Waterloo Quit NBA; Form Rival League," Associated Press. April 26, 1950.
"Detroit University Protests Pro Grab of Basket Ball Star," Associated Press. February 7, 1947.
"Dr. James Naismith's Life," Naismith Basketball Foundation, November 13, 2014. https://naismithbasketballfoundation.com/james-naismith-life/.
Dorr, Dave. "The Big Easy," *St. Louis Post-Dispatch*. December 30, 1990.
"Doxie Moore Is Redskins' Coach," *Sheboygan Press*. June 12, 1946.
"Doxie Moore Seeks Purdue Job," Associated Press. April 7, 1950.
"Duffey Says Packers to Stay in Anderson," Associated Press. December 6, 1949.
"Eddie Dancker, McDermott, Handle Team During Trip," *Sheboygan Press*. December 10, 1947.
"Eddleman Tallies 48 Points as Blackhawks Stop Ft. Wayne," *Daily Times* (Davenport, IA). December 18, 1950.
"Emory D. Jones," Associated Press. September 26, 1977.
Fasnacht, Andy. "A Local Legend Turns 90: Whitey's Journey to the NBA," *LNP*. June 27, 2012.
"The First Game," Springfield College Archives and Special Collections.
Fitzgerald, Tom. "Celts Get Englund, 6-ft.-5 Oshkosh Ace," *Boston Daily Globe*. December 5, 1949.
_____. "'I'm Not Tough Enough for Pro Ball'—Julian," *Boston Daily Globe*. March 23, 1950.
Flachsbart, Harold. "Bombers Ask Permission to Sell Players," *St. Louis Post-Dispatch*. April 23, 1950.
Fleischman, Bill. "Bombers Stop Bullets; 22 Points for Easy Ed," *St. Louis Star-Times*. March 17, 1950.
"Former Gopher Cage Coach to Tri-City," United Press. May 3, 1950.
"Fort Wayne Nips Redskins, 73–72," *Sheboygan Press*. January 19, 1950.
Franco, George. "Sailors Paces Nuggets' 89 to 78 Upset of Nats," *Denver Post*. February 22, 1950.
Franks, Joel S. *Asian American Basketball: A Century of Sport, Community and Culture*. McFarland, 2016.
Frei, Terry. *March 1939: Before the Madness—The Story of the First NCAA Basketball Tournament Champions*. Taylor Trade, 2014.
Fuchs, Bill. "Caps Nose Out Indianapolis, 81–79, in Thriller Before 4,409," *Evening Star* (Washington, D.C.). February 19, 1950.
_____. "Caps, Tough in Defeat, Face Worried Knicks Tonight," *Evening Star* (Washington, D.C.). March 22, 1950.
_____. "Nichols-Otten Trade Puzzling to Caps Fans," *Evening Star* (Washington, D.C.). February 10, 1950.
_____. "Syracuse Coach Resents Talk of Easy Schedule," *Evening Star* (Washington, D.C.). December 29, 1949.
Gaff, Glen. "Chicago Takes First 96–82," *Minneapolis Morning Tribune*. November 28, 1949.
_____. "Lakers 'Out-Stall' Capitols 71–59," *Minneapolis Morning Tribune*. February 10, 1950.
_____. "Lakers Dent Bullets 96–62," *Minneapolis Morning Tribune*. March 16, 1950.
_____. "Lakers Get Hutton, Lose Haskins," *Minneapolis Morning Tribune*. May 25, 1950.
_____. "Lakers Gird for Nats Here," *Minneapolis Morning Tribune*. April 22, 1950.
_____. "Lakers Overwhelm Stalling Anderson 75–50," *Minneapolis Morning Tribune*. April 6, 1950.
_____. "Lakers Rip Ft. Wayne," *Minneapolis Morning Tribune*. March 28, 1950.
_____. "Lakers Shellack Rochester 92–70," *Minneapolis Morning Tribune*. February 16, 1950.
_____. "Lakers Toy with 'Skins 90–73," *Minneapolis Morning Tribune*. March 8, 1950.
_____. "Lakers Whip Knicks 87–66," *Minneapolis Morning Tribune*. March 13, 1950.
_____. "Lakers Whip Syracuse for 3–1 Lead," *Minneapolis Morning Tribune*. April 17, 1950.
_____. "Lakers Win 68–65; Trail by 12 in Last Period," *Minneapolis Morning Tribune*. March 9, 1950.
_____. "Lakers Win, 110–95, for Third Title," *Minneapolis Morning Tribune*. April 24, 1950.
_____. "Lakers, Syracuse Resume Tonight," *Minneapolis Morning Tribune*. April 14, 1950.
_____. "St. Louis Bows in 100–57 Rout," *Minneapolis Morning Tribune*. February 23, 1950.
_____. "Towery Punch Floors Pollard," *Minneapolis Morning Tribune*. December 29, 1949.
_____. "'We'll Run 'Em Again,' Says Nats' Cervi," *Minneapolis Morning Tribune*. April 20, 1950.
Gaynor, Brian. "Three Posewitz Brothers Keyed Red Skins' Forerunner Teams," *Sheboygan Press*. December 26, 2008.
George, Nelson. *Elevating the Game: Black Men and Basketball*. HarperCollins, 1992.
Glickman, Marty. "When Garden Was the Place for Basketball-Wise," *New York Times*. November 25, 1984.
"Globetrotters Sign Clifton for $10,000," United Press. July 31, 1948.
Goldaper, Sam. "Maurice Podoloff Dead at 95, Was First N.B.A. President," *New York Times*. November 26, 1985.

Goldstein, Alan. "Bullets Standout Hoffman Dead of Tumor at 73: 1947–48 Rookie of Year Also Starred at Purdue," *Sun* (Baltimore, MD). November 13, 1998.
Gould, Todd. *Pioneers of the Hardwood: Indiana and the Birth of Professional Basketball.* Indiana University Press, 1998.
"Grand Rapids Get 'Pro' Cage Berth," Associated Press. June 22, 1950.
Green, Ben. *Spinning the Globe: The Rise, Fall, and Return to Greatness of the Harlem Globetrotters.* Amistad Press, 2006.
Green, Ronald. "Basketball Worst Pro Sport, Says Hoffman," *Charlotte News.* March 25, 1950.
Grundman, Adolph H. *The Golden Age of Amateur Basketball: The AAU Tournament, 1921–1968.* University of Nebraska Press, 2004.
Hahn, Alan. *New York Knicks: The Complete Illustrated History.* MVP Books, 2012.
"Hall of Fame Basketball Player Bob Davies Dies at 70," *Sun Sentinel* (Fort Lauderdale, FL). April 23, 1990.
"Hall of Fame to Induct XU's 'Sweetwater' Clifton," Xavier University of Louisiana Athletics. August 7, 2014, https://xulagold.com/honors/hall-of-fame/nat-sweetwater-clifton/2.
Hargrave, Howard. "Auerbach Considered for Post at Maryland," *Rock Island Argus.* April 6, 1950.
———. "Fifth Quarter," *Rock Island Argus.* June 8, 1950.
———. "Transfer for Buffalo Club Looms Likely," *Rock Island Argus.* December 18, 1946.
"Harrison Proposes NBA Split for Coming Year," Associated Press. February 2, 1950.
Harwood, Tim. *Ball Hawks: The Arrival and Departure of the NBA in Iowa.* University of Iowa Press, 2018.
Haugh, David. "Duty Called Whiz Kids," *Chicago Tribune.* April 1, 2005.
Haven, Orville. "Late Anderson Drive Dumps Blackhawks, 89–77," *Anderson Herald.* March 22, 1950.
Hendrickson, Joe. "Hot Info on NBA Pruning," *Minneapolis Morning Tribune.* April 15, 1950.
Herman, Dick. "Hawks and Packers to Settle Playoff Argument at Anderson," *Daily Times* (Davenport, IA). March 24, 1950.
"History of the American Hockey League," The American Hockey League, n.d. https://theahl.com/history.
Holman, Nat. *Scientific Basketball.* Incra Publishing Company, 1922.
Holmes, Tommy. "Pro Cage Knicks Make Title Move," *Brooklyn Eagle.* May 25, 1950.
"Home Court No Help to Denver," *Minneapolis Star.* November 26, 1949.
"Honoured Members: George Brown," Hockey Hall of Fame, n.d. https://www.hhof.com/HonouredMembers/MemberDetails.html?type=Player&mem=B196101&list=.
Howlett, Ken. "The Story of Joe Fulks: A Basketball Innovator," A Sea of Blue, August 2, 2010. https://www.aseaofblue.com/2010/8/2/1600997/the-story-of-joe-fulks-an.
Hughes, Carl. "Sports Stew—Served Hot," *Pittsburgh Press.* December 19, 1949.
"Indianapolis to Repeat Proposal Made by Packers," Associated Press. April 15, 1950.
Jackson, Harold, and Jim Haskins. *The House that Jack Built: The Autobiography of a Successful Dreamer, Businessman, and Entertainer.* Colossus Books, 2003.
"Jeanette to Join Redskins Next Tuesday," *Sheboygan Press.* January 30, 1943.
"Jim Pollard, a Star in N.B.A. in 50's; Ex-Laker Was 70," Associated Press. January 25, 1993.
"Joe Lapchick Suggests NBA Split into Two Divisions," Associated Press. February 26, 1950.
Johnson, Claude. *The Black Fives: The Epic Story of Basketball's Forgotten Era.* Abrams Press, 2022.
Jozwiak, Miller. "From 'Go Home' to 'Welcome Home' for Sheboygan Man," *Sheboygan Press.* July 10, 2016.
Jurgens, Jerry. "Red Auerbach Turns in Resignation as Coach of Blackhawks," *Daily Times* (Davenport, IA). April 12, 1950.
Kahn, Roger. "Success and Ned Irish," *Sports Illustrated,* March 27, 1961.
Kalinsky, George, and Phil Berger. *The New York Knicks: The Official 50th Anniversary Celebration.* Macmillan, 1996.
"Kansas City Added to NPBL," Associated Press. September 2, 1950.
Katz, Jeff. "Forgotten Man: Bobby McDermott and the Rise of Pro Basketball," Vice, September 5, 2016. https://www.vice.com/en/article/aebkpz/forgotten-man-bobby-mcdermott-and-the-rise-of-pro-basketball.
Kelley, Jack. "Trotters and Tatum Rip Mercuries, 78–58," *Tulsa Daily World.* February 16, 1953.
Kessler, Gene. "Pro Cage Costly Venture," *Daily Times* (Chicago, IL). April 7, 1947.
Kiesele, Russ. "Brian Bashes Hawks, 88–77," *Moline Daily Dispatch.* March 7, 1950.
———. "From the Press Box," *Moline Daily Dispatch.* January 27, 1950.
———. "From the Press Box," *Moline Daily Dispatch.* February 25, 1950.
———. "Otten Voted Most Valuable Player in National League," *Moline Daily Dispatch.* March 25, 1949.
———. "Tribe Obtains Boston Pivot Man for Cash," *Moline Daily Dispatch.* December 15, 1949.
———. "Tribe Obtains Kirk, Ex-Illini," *Moline Daily Dispatch.* December 31, 1949.
Kinney, Bill. "Along the Sport Trail," *Rock Island Argus.* April 1, 1950.
———. "Along the Sport Trail," *Rock Island Argus.* May 24, 1950.
———. "Gene Vance Will Join Blackhawks," *Rock Island Argus.* December 20, 1949.
Knight, Kevin. "National Champion & Former NBA Player Joins Us," Produced by Corn Nation. *Of Bangarangs and Daggers,* April 21, 2020. Podcast, 42:00.
Kramp, Louis J. "Want Officials to Cut Whistling," *Daily Pantagraph* (Bloomington, IL). March 26, 1943.

Kurland, Bob. "Bob Kurland: Olympic Basketball Gold Medalist," Interview by John Erling. Voices of Oklahoma, January 27, 2011. https://www.voicesofoklahoma.com/interviews/kurland-bob
"Lambert Claims Darling Still Hasn't Protested Redskins' Use of Harris," Associated Press. December 20, 1947.
"League Pays $30,000 for Bomber Players and Suspends Franchise," Associated Press. April 25, 1950.
Lewis, Allen. "Warriors Win, 84–71; Fulks Gets 37 Points," *Philadelphia Inquirer*. April 17, 1947.
Linthicum, Jesse A. "Sunlight on Sports," *Sun* (Baltimore, MD). November 11, 1948.
Lofstrom, R.A. "Right and Left in Sports," *St. Cloud Daily Times and Daily Journal-Press*. April 21, 1937.
Luther, Fred. "Anderson Finishes Off Hawks with 94–71 Rout," *Moline Daily Dispatch*. March 25, 1950.
"Luther Harris Suspended for Rule Violations," *Sheboygan Press*. December 30, 1947.
Malafronte, Chip. "Podoloff Brothers Possessed Uncanny Business Savvy," *New Haven Register*. June 29, 2012.
Martinez, Courtney. "The First Intercollegiate Basketball Game Was Played on Feb. 9, 1895," NCAA.com, February 9, 2017.
McClellan, Michael D. "The Arnie Risen Interview," Celtic Nation, December 9, 2018. https://www.celtic-nation.com/blog/2018/12/09/the-arnie-risen-interview/.
———. "The Bob Brannum Interview," Celtic Nation, December 6, 2018. https://www.celtic-nation.com/blog/2018/12/06/the-bob-brannum-interview/.
McCormick, Robert R. "Three Bombed; One a Judge," *Chicago Daily Tribune*. February 18, 1928.
McCulley, Jim. "Braun in Service," *Daily News* (New York, NY). September 28, 1950.
———. "Knicks Nose Celtics, 82–80, on Braun's Shot," *Daily News* (New York, NY). January 15, 1950.
McKenna, Dave. "The Syracuse Walking Dream," *Washington City Paper*. May 23, 2008.
McNamara, John. *The Capital of Basketball: A History of DC Area High School Hoops*. Georgetown University Press, 2019.
"Mehen, Boykoff, Sailors Sign to Play in N.B.A," Associated Press. May 26, 1950.
Menton, Paul. "Bullets Bid for Bombers," *Evening Sun* (Baltimore, MD). April 18, 1950.
———. "Bullets File Game Protest," *Evening Sun* (Baltimore, MD). December 26, 1949.
———. "Bullets Get Ezersky," *Evening Sun* (Baltimore, MD). December 31, 1949.
———. "Bullets Get Short Rest," *Evening Sun* (Baltimore, MD). December 23, 1949.
———. "Jeannette Has Tough Job in His New Role," *Evening Sun* (Baltimore, MD). February 14, 1950.
———. "Trenton 'Champions,'" *Evening Sun* (Baltimore, MD). April 16, 1947.
"Mikan 'Mr. Basketball of Pros,' Rated All-Time Best," National Enterprise Association. January 13, 1950.
"Mikan Picked as Greatest Cager," Associated Press. February 1, 1950.
Mitauer, Harry. "First Contact Made in Deal for Bombers," *St. Louis Globe-Democrat*. February 1, 1950.
Montieth, Mark. "Arnie Risen Introduced Indianapolis to New Era in Pro Basketball," NBA.com, September 14, 2012. https://www.nba.com/pacers/montieth/arnie-risen-introduced-indianapolis-new-era-pro-basketball.
"Moore Resumes Coaching 'Skins," Associated Press. December 30, 1947.
Morrison, Robert. "Future of Bombers Up in the Air but Decision to Be Made Soon," *St. Louis Post-Dispatch*. March 20, 1950.
Morrow, Art. "Gardner in Bed, Has Leg Infection," *Philadelphia Inquirer*. November 23, 1949.
Mozley, Dana. "BAA, NBL Join in 18-Club Loop," *Daily News* (New York, NY). August 4, 1949.
———. "Knicks Eliminate Caps in NBA Playoff, 103–83," *Daily News* (New York, NY). March 23, 1950.
———. "Knicks' Lapchick Lauds '50 College Hoop Crop," *Daily News* (New York, NY). March 19, 1950.
———. "Knicks Lead Capitols on 69th Armory Court," *Daily News* (New York, NY). February 23, 1950.
Naismith, James. "Basket Ball," *Triangle*. January 15, 1892.
Nash, Bruce, and Allan Zullo. *The Basketball Hall of Shame*. Pocket Books, 1991.
Nason, Jerry. "Brown Turns Tough; N.B.A. Must Aid Celtics or They'll Quit League," *Boston Daily Globe*. April 24, 1950.
Nathan, Daniel A. *Baltimore Sports: Stories from Charm City*. University of Arkansas Press, 2016.
"NBA Revamps with 12-Team Organization," United Press. April 25, 1950.
Nelson, Murry. *The National Basketball League: A History, 1935–1949*. McFarland, 2009.
———. *The Originals: The New York Celtics Invent Modern Basketball*. Bowling Green State University Popular Press, 1999.
Nelson, Ray. "Easy Ed Trims Mikan, But Bombers Still Lose," *St. Louis Star-Times*. January 13, 1950.
———. "Lakers' Mikan Makes Free Throw in Last Two Seconds and Bombers Lose Thriller, 72–71," *St. Louis Star-Times*. February 17, 1950.
Nelson, Rodger. *The Zollner Piston Story*. The Allen County Public Library Foundation, 1995.
"New Anderson Club Signs Komenich, Black Despite NBA," Associated Press. May 24, 1950.
"New Cage League May Have to Fold," Associated Press. June 30, 1950.
"New League is Expected to Have 10 Teams," *Sheboygan Press*. May 13, 1950.
Ney, Al. "Cage Hawks Sign Top NBA Draft Choice," *Waterloo Courier*. May 10, 1950.
———. "Charlie Shipp Non-Playing Coach Now," *Waterloo Courier*. January 1, 1950.

———. "Court Denies Ban on Talks with Cagers," *Waterloo Courier*. July 18, 1950.
———. "Down 12 Points with 58 Seconds to Play, Hawks Win in Overtime, 97–93," *Waterloo Courier*. December 26, 1949.
———. "Hawks Go, 100–76; Face Syracuse Next," *Waterloo Courier*. February 28, 1950.
———. "Hawks Slip, 85–79, Before 4,264 Fans," *Waterloo Courier*. January 30, 1950.
———. "Hawks Win, 76–74, on Goal by Boykoff," *Waterloo Courier*. February 16, 1950.
———. "Hawks, Sheboygan, Denver, Milwaukee or Oshkosh Set; to Seek Six More Teams," *Waterloo Courier*. April 25, 1950.
———. "Payak Goal at Final Horn Wins, 79–77," *Waterloo Courier*. March 20, 1950.
———. "Pops Harrison to be General Manager Here," *Waterloo Courier*. May 7, 1950.
———. "Post Largest Margin; Olympians Next," *Waterloo Courier*. March 9, 1950.
———. "The Sports Alley," *Waterloo Courier*. August 8, 1950.
———. "The Sports Alley," *Waterloo Courier*. February 28, 1950.
———. "The Sports Alley," *Waterloo Courier*. June 30, 1950.
"Nuggets Buy Crocker," International News Service. November 10, 1949.
"Nuggets Finally Show Sparkle," United Press. November 28, 1946.
O'Donnell, John. "Auerbach Succeeds Porter as Blackhawks' Coach," *Democrat and Leader* (Davenport, IA). November 10, 1949.
———. "Big Schedule for Blackhawks," *Democrat and Leader* (Davenport, IA). February 13, 1950.
———. "Blackhawks Conquer Warriors," *Democrat and Leader* (Davenport, IA). February 9, 1950.
———. "Denver Nugget Team Stopped Before 3,450," *Democrat and Leader* (Davenport, IA). August 30, 1949.
"Offer for Fulks Is Turned Down," Associated Press. February 12, 1950.
"Olympians Clip Denver, Knicks Edge Past Stags," Associated Press. November 2, 1949.
"Olympians, Knicks Pass 100 Mark," Associated Press. January 25, 1950.
"Olymps Appear 'In' as Western Champions," Associated Press. March 17, 1950.
"Olymps Lose Lead on 5th Loss in Row," Associated Press. February 25, 1950.
"Oshkosh All Stars Reach End of Line, Franchise Forfeited," *Oshkosh Daily Northwestern*. September 9, 1949.
"Packers and Pistons Trade Two for Two," Associated Press. January 19, 1950.
"Packers Even Series with Olympians," Associated Press. March 31, 1950.
"Packers Nudge Knicks, 91–89," Associated Press. March 12, 1950.
Pallette, Philip. *The Game Changer: How Hank Luisetti Revolutionized America's Great Indoor Game*. AuthorHouse, 2005.
Partner, Dan. "Win Streak for Nugs," *Denver Post*. January 6, 1950.
Peterson, Jim. "Mikan Signed; Plays Tonight," *Minneapolis Morning Tribune*. November 20, 1947.
"Plans Being Drafted for Affiliated Loop in Pro Cage Play," Associated Press. April 15, 1950.
"Podoloff Confident NBA Will Prosper in Coming Years; Foresees Expansion," United Press. February 17, 1950.
Poisall, Bob. "Olympians Set Scoring Record in 108 to 73 Win Here," *Owensboro Messenger*. March 19, 1950.
Pomerantz, Gary M. *The Last Pass: Cousy, Russell, the Celtics, and What Matters in the End*. Penguin, 2019.
Pope, Edwin. *Football's Greatest Coaches*. Taylor Tupper and Love, 1955.
"Pro Court Loop Splits Up Into Two Divisions," Associated Press. August 11, 1949.
"Pro Hoop Association Opens Play Nov. 1," Associated Press. October 22, 1946.
Ralby, Herb. "Auerbach, New Coach, Says All Celts on Block," *Boston Daily Globe*. April 28, 1950.
———. "Brown, Pieri Buy Celtics Franchise from Garden," *Boston Daily Globe*. July 31, 1950.
Rayl, Susan. "The New York Renaissance Professional Black Basketball Team." Thesis. Pennsylvania State University, 1996.
Reddy, Bill. "Broken Jaw Fails to Halt Gabor During Busy Month," *Post-Standard* (Syracuse, NY). January 28, 1950.
———. "Gabor and Seymour Pace Nats Over Anderson in 94–88, Battle," *Post-Standard* (Syracuse, NY). December 26, 1949.
———. "Gabor to Play Pro Basketball with Syracuse," *Post-Standard* (Syracuse, NY). July 14, 1948.
———. "Harrison Almost Didn't Play; Couldn't Find Jersey," *Post-Standard* (Syracuse, NY). April 9, 1950.
———. "Keeping Posted," *Post-Standard* (Syracuse, NY). February 13, 1952.
———. "Keeping Posted," *Post-Standard* (Syracuse, NY). February 26, 1947.
———. "Lakers Nip Nats in Last Second, 68–66," *Post-Standard* (Syracuse, NY). April 9, 1950.
———. "Nationals Edge Knicks in Extra Period, 91–83," *Post-Standard* (Syracuse, NY). March 27, 1950.
———. "Nationals Trip Lakers, 84–75, as 9,888 Cheer," *Post-Standard* (Syracuse, NY). March 6, 1950.
———. "Nationals Trounce Lakers, 83 to 76," *Post-Standard* (Syracuse, NY). April 21, 1950.
———. "Nationals Win by 125–123 in 5th Overtime," *Post-Standard* (Syracuse, NY). November 25, 1949.
———. "Nats Defeat Knicks in Final, 91–80," *Post-Standard* (Syracuse, NY). April 3, 1950.
———. "Nats Even NBA Series with Lakers," *Post-Standard* (Syracuse, NY). April 10, 1950.

Bibliography

———. "Nats Invade Baltimore; Bids for Player Rejected," *Post-Standard* (Syracuse, NY). February 11, 1950.
———. "Nats Nip Olympians, 82–78, 6,704 Fans Pay Tribute to Cervi," *Post-Standard* (Syracuse, NY). February 20, 1950.
———. "Packers Snap Syracuse's Home Winning Streak in Overtime," *Post-Standard* (Syracuse, NY). January 23, 1950.
———. "Syracuse Enters National Pro Court League," *Post-Standard* (Syracuse, NY). July 2, 1946.
"Redskins Beat Waterloo in Thriller," *Sheboygan Press*. December 30, 1949.
"Redskins Beaten Over Week End," *Sheboygan Press*. February 28, 1950.
"Redskins Drop Two Contests," *Sheboygan Press*. November 28, 1949.
"Redskins Face Two Key Tilts," *Sheboygan Press*. February 7, 1950.
"Redskins in 85–82 Victory Over Lakers," *Sheboygan Press*. January 6, 1950.
"Redskins in 77–67 Defeat at Waterloo," *Sheboygan Press*. December 8, 1949.
"Redskins Lose 88–75 Clash with Syracuse; Face Chicago Monday," *Sheboygan Press*. March 17, 1950.
"Redskins Pile Up 104–82 Win Over Tri-Cities," *Sheboygan Press*. February 10, 1950.
"Redskins Push Conditions for Entry in NBA," Associated Press. April 18, 1950.
"Redskins Seek to Organize New, Independent League," *Sheboygan Press*. April 17, 1950.
"Redskins Sign Schulz Today," *Sheboygan Press*. January 16, 1950.
"Redskins Win Championship," *Sheboygan Press*. March 10, 1943.
"Redskins Win, Even Series," *Sheboygan Press*. March 24, 1950.
"Redskins Win Overtime Battle, 120–113," *Sheboygan Press*. November 25, 1949.
Reed, William F. "Scandal Branded Him, but His Charm Won People Back," *Sports Illustrated,* November 30, 2007.
"Rejects Bid to Split Pro Loop," Associated Press. February 4, 1950.
Rosen, Charley. *The Chosen Game: A Jewish Basketball History.* University of Nebraska Press, 2017.
———. *The First Tip-Off: The Incredible Story of the Birth of the NBA*. McGraw-Hill, 2008.
———. *Sugar: Micheal Ray Richardson, Eighties Excess, and the NBA.* University of Nebraska Press, 2018.
Ruby, Earl. "'Terrible-Tempered Mr. Bones' Is a Fun-Loving Cage Clown Selling Pro Game at Capital," *Courier Journal* (Louisville, KY). February 29, 1948.
———. "Top 'Toppers Adopt Louisville, Hope to Copy Olympians Set-Up; Need Manager, Coach, and Backers," *Courier Journal* (Louisville, KY). August 10, 1950.
"St. Louis Bombers Lace Chicago Stags, 85 to 69," Associated Press. March 18, 1950.
"St. Louis' Cage Bid Rejected," Associated Press. June 5, 1950.
Schumacher, Michael. *Mr. Basketball: George Mikan, the Minneapolis Lakers, and the Birth of the NBA.* Bloomsbury USA, 2007.
"75 Cage Aces Chosen by Pro BAA in Draft," United Press. March 22, 1949.
"Sheboygan May Start New Loop," Associated Press. April 17, 1950.
"Sheboygan Welcomed Black Basketball Players Earlier Than Other Cities Did," *Sheboygan Press*. March 10, 2009.
Shevlin, Maurice. "Lakers Blast Stags, 80–68; Mikan Gets 40," *Chicago Daily Tribune*. January 25, 1950.
———. "National League Withdraws from Basketball Group," *Rochester Democrat and Chronicle*. April 9, 1947.
———. "Six Teams Form New Pro League," *Chicago Sunday Tribune*. May 14, 1950.
———. "Stags Defeat Tri-City, 83–68," *Chicago Daily Tribune*. January 20, 1950.
———. "Stags Defeat Washington in Stadium, 75–55," *Chicago Daily Tribune*. December 7, 1949.
———. "21,666 See Lakers Beat Trotters, 76–60," *Chicago Daily Tribune*. February 22, 1950.
Siegel, Morris. "Caps Try to Replace Auerbach; Carnevale Turns Down Offer," *Washington Post*. March 11, 1948.
Smith, Jack. "Vandeweghe Signed for Knick Home Tilts," *Daily News* (New York, NY). October 19, 1949.
Smith, Red. "4 Negro Stars Due Tryout with Bullets," *Evening Sun* (Baltimore, MD). May 31, 1950.
Smith, Russ L. "Hawks Rush Two New Players by Air," *Waterloo Daily Courier*. November 30, 1949.
———. "NBA Realigns Into Three Divisions; Opens Oct. 29," *Waterloo Daily Courier*. October 10, 1949.
Smith, Sam. "'Sweetwater' Keeps Rollin,'" *Chicago Tribune*. June 9, 1985.
Smith, S. "Bullets Down Boston, 79–75, to Strengthen Hold on Fourth Place," *Sun* (Baltimore, MD). March 12, 1950.
———. "Bullets Rout Minneapolis Lakers, 87–68, at Coliseum," *Sun* (Baltimore, MD). December 16, 1949.
———. "Bullets Top Stags, 77–72," *Sun* (Baltimore, MD). March 5, 1950.
———. "Ed Sadowski Misses Shot as Game Ends," *Sun* (Baltimore, MD). January 27, 1950.
Smith, Wilfrid. "Bruins Win in Overtime; Rens Lose to Harlem," *Chicago Daily Tribune*. March 19, 1940.
———. "Stags May Move from Stadium to Coliseum," *Chicago Daily Tribune*. July 2, 1950.
"Sports Roundup," Associated Press. June 2, 1950.
———. Associated Press. March 6, 1950.
———. Associated Press. May 20, 1946.
"Stags Change Name to Chicago Bruins," United Press. August 15, 1950.

Stann, Francis. "Caps Down Bullets, Need One Victory to Clinch Third Place," *Evening Star* (Washington, D.C.). March 9, 1950.
———. "Lloyd and Hunter Sign Contracts with Caps," *Evening Star* (Washington, D.C.). May 7, 1950.
———. "McKinney, Caps' New Coach, to See Little Action as Player," *Evening Star* (Washington, D.C.). March 10, 1950.
———. "New Coach of Caps to be Named Soon," *Evening Star* (Washington, D.C.). February 28, 1950.
Stark, Douglas. *When Basketball Was Jewish: Voices of Those Who Played the Game.* University of Nebraska Press, 2017.
Steadman, John. "Jeannette Paid Dues and More En Route to Hall," *Sun* (Baltimore, MD). February 9, 1994.
———. "Opting to Focus on Life's Gifts, Scolari Let Hits Slide Off Back," *Sun* (Baltimore, MD). March 15, 1998.
Stranahan, Bob. "Olympic Champions Pick 'Home,'" *Indianapolis Star.* May 5, 1949.
Strickler, George. "Renaissance to Battle Oshkosh for Pro Crown," *Chicago Daily Tribune.* March 28, 1939.
"Student Killed, 6 Others Injured," Associated Press. April 30, 1947.
Sullivan, George. "Remember…" *Boston Daily Globe.* April 3, 1977.
Sumner, Jim. *Tales from the Duke Blue Devils Locker Room: A Collection of the Greatest Duke Basketball Stories Ever Told.* Sports Publishing, 2016.
Swinnen, Andy. "B-17G 'Fancy Nancy III' 42–37856 613th," Remember Our Heroes, n.d. https://www.remember-our-heroes.nl/2276.htm.
"Syracuse Bandits Carry Off Safe, Possibly $15,000," United Press. April 7, 1950.
"Syracuse Police Kill Man and Wound Two in Ambush," *Post-Standard* (Syracuse, NY). May 12, 1950.
"Syracuse Tops Denver Cagers," Associated Press. November 6, 1949.
Taragano, Martin. *Basketball Biographies: 434 U.S. Players, Coaches, and Contributors to the Game, 1891–1990.* McFarland, 1991.
Taylor, John. *The Rivalry: Bill Russell, Wilt Chamberlain, and the Golden Age of Basketball.* Ballantine, 2006.
"Team Signs Chaney and Jack Phelan," *Sheboygan Press.* December 17, 1949.
"Ten-Club Circuit Vetoed by NPBL," United Press. August 3, 1950.
Tenny, Ben. "Another Rally Gets 106–95 Piston Wins," *News-Sentinel* (Fort Wayne, IN). December 19, 1949.
———. "Bring on Those Lakers! That's Pistons' Cry After Disposing of Royals' Squad," *News-Sentinel* (Fort Wayne, IN). March 25, 1950.
———. "Next Week End, Two Games Will Tell How Pistons Finish; They Split Two," *News-Sentinel* (Fort Wayne, IN). March 13, 1950.
———. "Pistons Given Little Time for Rejoicing," *News-Sentinel* (Fort Wayne, IN). February 13, 1950.
———. "Pistons Lose and Win Over Week End; Head East for Four Tough Road Games," *News-Sentinel* (Fort Wayne, IN). January 23, 1950.
———. "Pistons Whip Lakers; Take to Road to Continue Grind," *News-Sentinel* (Fort Wayne, IN). December 9, 1949.
———. "Pistons, in Third Spot, Await Royals or Lakers," *News-Sentinel* (Fort Wayne, IN). March 21, 1950.
———. "Pistons, Stags Play Tonight for 3rd Post," *News-Sentinel* (Fort Wayne, IN). March 20, 1950.
———. "That Man Mikan, His Mates End Piston Hopes," *News-Sentinel* (Fort Wayne, IN). March 29, 1950.
Thies, Bud. "Bomber Steam Can't Match Knicks' Fire," *St. Louis Globe-Democrat.* February 3, 1950.
———. "Bombers Drop Finale to Stags, Easy Ed Shines," *St. Louis Globe-Democrat.* March 20, 1950.
———. "Bombers Find Celtics Cold, Get Hot to Win, 71–47," *St. Louis Globe-Democrat.* January 23, 1950.
———. "Easy Ed Hot But Bombers' Luck Chills," *St. Louis Globe-Democrat.* February 28, 1950.
———. "Podoloff Declares War on New Pro Basketball League," *St. Louis Globe-Democrat.* May 17, 1950.
Thomas, Damion L. *Globetrotting: African American Athletes and Cold War Politics.* University of Illinois Press, 2012.
Thomas, Ron. *They Cleared the Lane: The NBA's Black Pioneers.* University of Nebraska Press, 2004.
"Three Cities Considered as NPBL Sites," Associated Press. June 30, 1950.
Triptow, Richard F. *The Dynasty That Never Was: Chicago's First Professional Basketball Champions.* Richard F. Triptow, 1997.
"Trotters, Stars End Tour," Associated Press. April 20, 1950.
Turkin, Hy. "Aggies Win, 52–44, After Mikan Fouls Out; NYU 3d," *Daily News* (New York, NY). March 30, 1945.
———. "Knicks Capture 80–78 Thriller," *Daily News* (New York, NY). March 9, 1950.
———. "Knicks Lock Nat Series at 1–1 with 80–76 Win," *Daily News* (New York, NY). March 31, 1950.
———. "Knicks Overcome Boston, 96–84," *Daily News* (New York, NY). November 27, 1949.
———. "Overtime Shot Knicks Stags, 93–91," *Daily News* (New York, NY). December 11, 1949.
———. "Simmons Is Ready for Knick-Cap Tilt," *Daily News* (New York, NY). March 21, 1950.
"Two NBA Coaches Declare Present Setup Unwieldy," Associated Press. February 26, 1950.
United Nations. Security Council. *Complaint of Aggression upon the Republic of Korea.* June 27, 1950. 83, S/1511.
Vargas, Ramon A. Fight, Grin & Squarely Play the Game: *The 1945 Loyola New Orleans Basketball Championship & Legacy.* The History Press, 2013.

Vecchione, Joseph. *New York Times Book of Sports Legends: Profiles of 50 of This Century's Greatest Athletes by the Legendary Sportswriters Who Covered Them.* Simon & Schuster, 1992.

Ward, Arch. "In the Wake of the News," *Chicago Daily Tribune.* April 24, 1950.

———. "Trotters Top Lakers with Rally, 61–59," *Chicago Daily Tribune.* February 20, 1948.

Ward, Gene. "Boykoff Scores Record 54 Pts., CCNY Wallops Violets, 91–60," *Daily News* (New York, NY). March 12, 1947.

"Washington Capitols Sign Center Don Otten," Associated Press. October 17, 1950.

Webster, John. "Crossin Rejoins Warrior Squad," *Philadelphia Inquirer.* October 19, 1949.

———. "Warriors Get Livingstone, Send Sadowski to Baltimore," *Philadelphia Inquirer.* December 8, 1949.

———. "With Crossin, Mogus Playing Inspired Basketball, Warriors May Have Drive to Reach Playoffs," *Philadelphia Inquirer.* January 27, 1950.

Whitmarsh, F.E. *Famous American Athletes of Today,* Vol. XV. L.C. Page, 1958.

Wickstrom, George. "Hawks Shellack Olympians, 96–83," *Rock Island Argus.* March 4, 1950.

Wigmore, John H. *The Illinois Crime Survey.* Illinois Association for Criminal Justice, 1929.

Wilson, Diana Eddleman. "The Life and Athletic Achievements of Thomas Dwight Eddleman." Thesis. Eastern Illinois University, 1993.

"'Worst Officiating'—Cervi; 'Pressure Fired Tempers'—Pollard," *Minneapolis Morning Tribune.* April 24, 1950.

Wray, John E. "Bombers Lose Cat-and-Mouse Thriller to Royals, 75-to-73, in Two Overtime Periods," *St. Louis Post-Dispatch.* January 9, 1950.

Young, Dick. "Knicks Down Lakers, 94–84," *Daily News* (New York, NY). December 15, 1949.

———. "Knicks Shade Celtics, 88–84," *Daily News* (New York, NY). March 16, 1950.

Index

Adams, Boots 33
Akron Firestones 9, 14, 93, 115
Akron Goodyears 14, 93, 204
Allmen, Stanley 133
Alpha Physical Culture Club 61
Amateur Athletic Union 15, 19, 20, 26, 32–35, 51, 56, 71, 98–99, 125, 150–153, 155, 189–191, 196, 198
American Basketball League (1925–31) 25, 63–64, 102, 120–121, 207
American Basketball League (1933–53) 23, 26, 44–45, 56, 58, 72, 105, 113, 121, 154, 205–206
American Hockey League 86, 98, 129–130, 207
American League of Philadelphia 120
Anderson Packers 3, 7–8, 11, 15, 24–25, 27–28, 36, 41–44, 54–57, 66–67, 69, 74, 76, 92, 94, 97, 103–106, 109, 113–119, 123, 125, 127–128, 133–134, 137, 139, 143–145, 147–148, 150, 152, 154, 156, 158–159, 162–164, 166, 168–172, 175–179, 185, 187–188, 191–192, 195–196, 207, 208
anti-Semitism 4–6, 87, 120, 128
Arizin, Paul 152, 187, 192, 195, 204
Armstrong, Curly 26–28, 55, 80, 108, 113, 119, 137, 165
Auerbach, Red 21, 23–24, 52, 71, 77, 97–99, 122, 134–135, 144, 158, 162, 170, 177, 182, 194, 207

Baltimore Bullets 3, 6, 28, 42, 44–47, 54–55, 72, 74, 76, 78, 80–83, 89–90, 92, 95, 97, 101, 104–105, 111, 113, 118–119, 126–128, 135–136, 138–139, 142–143, 146–150, 153–155, 176–177, 180, 186–188, 190–193, 198, 206
Baltimore Clippers 44

Banks, Davey 120
Barker, Cliff 15, 17, 75, 90, 97, 110, 114, 148, 150, 159, 162, 168
Barksdale, Don 189–191, 196, 198
Barnhorst, Leo 78, 114, 204
barnstorming 7, 55, 57–58, 64–65, 120–121, 124, 198–200
Basketball Association of America 3–6, 8–9, 11–13, 15–16, 18–19, 21–25, 27–29, 33, 36–37, 41–42, 44–47, 49, 51–54, 56–58, 60, 66, 68–74, 76, 78, 81, 85–91, 96–99, 101–102, 106, 112–113, 119, 121, 126, 128–132, 134–135, 138, 142–143, 149–150, 154–155, 174–175, 177, 183–185, 188–189, 193, 195, 204, 207
Beard, Ralph 15–17, 28, 76, 90–91, 110, 115, 140, 145, 150, 155, 159, 164, 166, 168–169
Becker, Moe 5–6
Beckman, Johnny 102
Beiersdorfer, Jim 182–183
Bell, Puggy 64
Bennett, Carl 10–11, 25–27, 66, 108, 172–173, 191
Berce, Gene 3
Berger, Ben 19, 110–111, 128, 189
Biasatti, Hank 73
Biasone, Danny 41–42, 108, 133, 172
Birch, Paul 5–6
Bishop, Ralph 151–152
Black, Charlie 28, 56, 74, 79, 113–114, 119, 137, 145, 168–171, 192, 196
Black, Hughie 120
black pre-integration basketball 7, 58–59, 61–66, 199–204
Bleach, Larry 202
Bluitt, Ben 198
Bobb, Nelson 143
Bodie, Gary 23
Bornheimer, Jake 115, 143
Boryla, Vince 75, 84, 89–90, 125–126, 158, 160, 164, 168–169, 190
Boston Celtics 3, 6, 11, 21, 28, 46, 54, 67, 69–70, 73–74, 77, 81, 84, 87, 95, 97, 101–102, 104–105, 108, 111–113, 115, 119–120, 122–123, 128, 131, 133–134, 136, 139, 142–144, 146–149, 152, 154, 170, 175–177, 185–188, 190–195, 198, 206–207
Boswell, Sonny 57, 202
Boven, Don 83, 94–95, 97, 108
Boykoff, Harry 33, 39, 42, 67, 76, 85, 87, 94–95, 108, 137, 140, 198
Brannum, Bob 21, 43, 83, 100, 111, 140, 159, 162, 164, 187, 206
Brannum, Clarence 100
Braun, Carl 12–13, 17, 75, 84, 88–90, 111, 118, 126, 136, 139, 146–148, 154–155, 157–158, 160, 164–165, 168–169, 209
Brazil, Lloyd 88
Brian, Frank 36, 56, 66–67, 69, 76, 104, 106, 113–115, 119, 131, 134, 145, 147–148, 154–155, 158–159, 162, 168–171, 192
Brinkman, Magnus 116–117, 125, 179–180, 186–188, 195–196, 199, 205, 207
Bro, Ed 122
Brookfield, Price 92
Brooklyn Eagles 202
Brooklyn Visitation 26–27
Brown, Bob 12, 21, 106, 137
Brown, Hillery 57
Brown, Walter 70, 81, 86, 101–102, 112–113, 149, 175, 185–186, 193–195, 198, 206
Brown Paper Mill 150
Browne, Jimmy 54
Brownstein, Phil 53–54, 78–79, 91, 114, 161, 164
Budko, Walt 104
Buehler, Ken 124–125
Bunker Hill Sailors 53
Burmaster, Jack 43, 100, 111, 123, 147, 159, 164, 206

233

Index

Bushnell, Asa 129
Byers, Lefty 93
Byrnes, Tommy 84, 95, 105, 118, 136, 146

Calhoun, Bill 75, 106, 126–127, 140, 153, 161, 190
Calumet Buccaneers 57, 60, 66, 94, 179, 205
Camp Grant Warriors 53
Carlson, Don 75, 138–139, 165, 182–184, 194
Carnevale, Ben 24
Carpenter, Bob 80, 94, 101, 119, 137, 161, 163
Carpenter, Gordon 34–35
Carr, Joe 120
Cervi, Al 27–28, 37–38, 41–42, 75–76, 99, 103, 108, 118, 133, 137, 141, 148, 155, 159–162, 165, 168–169, 172–174, 178–185, 204
Chalfen, Morris 19, 110–111
Chase, William 32
Cherry Point Leathernecks 23
Chicago Bruins 9, 207
Chicago Crusaders 124, 201
Chicago Gears 9–10, 12, 15, 27, 41, 58, 65, 83, 181, 205
Chicago Reds 201
Chicago Stags 3, 5–6, 12–13, 16, 19, 23–24, 36, 40, 46–47, 49–54, 68, 71, 74–75, 78–79, 83, 87–92, 97, 99, 104, 108, 112, 114–116, 126, 128, 133–138, 140, 142–143, 147, 149, 153–154, 156–157, 161, 164, 176–177, 184, 186–188, 190, 192–193, 196, 198–199, 204, 207–208
Chicago Studebakers 9, 57, 125
Chollet, Leroy 162, 165, 171
Cleveland Chase Brass 57
Cleveland Rebels 5, 73–74, 116, 129
Cleveland Rosenblums 64, 84
Cleveland Transfers 27, 133
Clifton, Nathaniel 193, 196–198, 204, 206
Closs, Bill 56, 66–67, 97, 119, 145, 148, 162–163, 169, 171, 191
Coast Guard Sealions 19
Cohalan, Neil 4, 87
Coleman, Jack 79, 106, 126–127, 136, 161, 163
College All-Stars 32, 204
Colvin, Tex 151
Commonwealth Big Five 62
Connors, Kevin 112
Cook, Bobby 21, 72, 83, 100, 107, 109–111, 116, 123, 131–132, 134, 140, 145, 147, 159, 164
Cooper, Chuck 189, 193–195, 198, 206
Cooper, John Miller 22

Cooper, Tarzan 7, 63–64, 202
Cope, Bob 93
Corley, Ray 43–44, 76, 141, 159–160
Cotton, Jack 106
Cousy, Bob 152, 193–194, 204
Cramer, Frank 48
Crocker, Dillard 44, 80, 103, 106, 111, 135, 137, 140, 142
Cronk, Howard 55
Crossin, Chink 115, 143, 147, 160
Crowe, George 59
Cumberland, Duke 57
Curran, Fran 94, 106, 108, 136, 157, 163

Dallmar, Howie 143
Dambrot, Irwin 152, 193
Dancker, Ed 45, 116–117, 124–125
Darden, Jim 76, 80, 102–103, 106
Dardi Dandies 99
Darling, Lon 6–7, 11, 117, 188, 207
Davies, Bob 4, 11, 36–38, 41, 68, 75, 78–79, 96, 100, 105, 108, 126, 135–136, 140, 145, 150, 153, 155, 157, 161, 163, 202, 204
Davis, Hal 140, 152, 186
Dayton Dive Bombers 58, 202
Dayton London Bobbies 93
Dayton Metropolitans 197
Dayton NPBL franchise 199, 204–206, 208
Deal, Snake 22
Dean, Everett 18
Dehnert, Dutch 102, 116
Denver Chevrolets 35
Denver Nuggets 3–4, 7–8, 12–13, 18, 21, 40–41, 44, 54, 56, 60, 67, 77, 80–81, 91, 95, 97, 101–102, 104, 106, 109–111, 114, 123, 125–126, 128, 133, 135, 137–138, 140, 142–143, 145–148, 150–154, 176–178, 186–188, 190, 195–196, 198, 205, 207–208
Detroit Eagles 45, 64, 72, 202
Detroit Falcons 53, 96
Detroit Gems 20–21, 59, 110, 133, 197
Detroit Hed-Aids 9
Detroit Kings 57, 60
Deutsch, Art 165
DeZonie, Hank 59
dispersal draft 11, 21, 53, 111, 185, 188–189, 191–192
Dolhon, Joe 47, 95, 105, 118, 146
Doll, Bob 29, 101, 112, 122, 139, 148–149
Dolly King Five 58
Donato, Billy 107

Donlon, John 184
Donovan, Harry 126, 157
Douglas, Bob 57, 61–64, 66, 124, 201
Dowell, Bob 151
draft (BAA) 11–13, 16, 21, 28–29, 42, 68–70, 72, 79–80, 86–87, 89, 108, 127, 139
draft (NBA) 149, 152, 174–175, 185, 187–189, 191–195, 198, 204
Duffey, Ike 11–12, 15, 55–57, 59, 66, 69, 105, 113–114, 116–117, 128–129, 133, 175–177, 185, 195
Duffy Florals of Chicago 9, 202
Duncan, Andy 106, 111, 140
Dyer, Bill 46, 72, 105, 135

East Liverpool Potters 148
Eastern Basketball League 120–121
Eddleman, Dike 3, 43, 77–78, 103, 125, 142, 144, 158, 163, 206
Edwards, Leroy 7, 92–94
Embry, Jake 135
Endacott, Paul 33
Englund, Gene 94, 101, 112, 122, 134, 141, 144, 158, 170
Ezersky, John 81, 105, 148

Fabulous Five (University of Kentucky) 15–17, 33, 35, 68, 78, 100, 150
Farber, Saul 54
Farrow, Bill 59
Feerick, Bob 23–24, 70–71, 95, 97, 99, 133, 135, 139, 141, 147, 158, 160
Feigenbaum, George 105
Ferrin, Arnie 75, 78, 138–139, 164, 167, 173, 178–179, 184
Ferris, Leo 11, 15, 40–42, 57–58, 70, 76, 133–134, 179–180
first basketball game 30
Fischer, Leo 25, 133
Fitzgerald, Mike 24, 81, 103, 122, 134, 206
Fleet Marine Force Leathernecks 22
Fleishman, Jerry 121, 143
Forbes, Frank 62–63
Ford, Gerald 10
Fort Wayne Caseys 25
Fort Wayne General Electrics 14, 26, 93
Fort Wayne Harvesters 25, 202
Fort Wayne Pistons 3, 5–6, 8–12, 24–28, 33, 36, 45, 47, 55, 58, 65–68, 72–75, 79–80, 90, 93–95, 97, 101, 104, 108, 113–116, 119, 125–126, 128, 133, 135, 137–138, 140, 142, 144–145, 147, 153–154, 156–157, 161, 163–166,

Index

172, 174–176, 184, 186–188, 191–193, 196
Fortenberry, Joe 33–34
Foster, Bob 134
Foust, Larry 193, 208
Fulks, Joe 4, 18, 21–23, 46, 52–54, 68, 74, 78, 90–91, 104, 119, 125, 131–132, 134, 136, 142–143, 146–149, 154, 159–162
Furey, Jim 102

Gabor, Billy 42, 76, 97, 118, 133, 137, 141, 160, 165, 168–169, 172–174, 177–184
Gallatin, Harry 12–13, 84, 88–90, 125–126, 146, 148, 158, 160, 165, 168
Gardner, Vern 68, 78, 115, 142–143, 159–160, 162
Garland, Dave 106
Gates, Frank 56, 113, 145, 169, 192
Gates, Pop 58–59, 64
George, Andy 92, 94
George, Pinkie 92, 94, 193
Gerard, Gerry 24
Gibson, Dee 3, 103, 125, 144, 207
Gibson, Ward 95, 97
Gilmur, Chuck 24, 52, 99, 157, 160
Gladieux, Virgil 11
Glamack, George 15, 94, 100, 204–205
Goldberg, Sid 57, 105
Gotthoffer, Shikey 121
Gottlieb, Eddie 22, 66, 119–121, 128, 131, 134, 136, 142–143, 146, 161, 184, 191
Gottlieb, Leo 4
Graboski, Joe 54, 71, 79, 91, 114, 134
Graf, Moose 124
Grand Rapids Hornets 179, 188, 204–208
Grant, Bud 139, 153, 173–174, 182–184, 194
Great Depression 14, 17, 22, 64, 197
Great Lakes Bluejackets 100
Groza, Alex 15–18, 21, 28–29, 35–36, 38–39, 42, 68, 74, 78, 90–91, 96–97, 100, 104, 106, 109–110, 114, 125, 133–134, 137, 139–140, 143, 145, 148, 150, 154–155, 159, 162, 164, 166, 168–169, 190
Gruenig, Ace 151–152
Gulick, Dr. Luther 30
Guokas, Al 80, 102, 106, 133
Guokas, Matt, Sr. 102

Halas, George 9, 120, 207
Halbert, Chuck 24, 51–53, 74, 99, 157–158, 194

Hale, Bruce 90, 110, 114, 137, 140, 199, 205
Hamilton, C.D.P., Jr. 29, 130, 133, 182, 185
Hamilton, Dale 94
Hannum, Alex 133, 141, 144, 159–161, 165, 168, 173–174, 177–181, 183
Haraway, William 150–152
Hargis, John 36, 44, 56, 66, 69, 119, 134, 145, 158–159, 163, 166, 169–171, 192
Harlem Globetrotters 7, 55, 57, 64, 66, 71, 102, 114, 124, 131, 138, 189, 193, 195, 197–204, 206
Harlem Yankees 206
Harper, Dick 197
Harris, Bob 21, 80, 119, 137, 156, 161, 165
Harris, Luther 116–117
Harrison, Bob 75, 78, 115, 139, 146, 171, 173, 184
Harrison, Les 15, 37, 41, 58, 126–129, 161, 163, 179
Harrison, Pops 177–178, 194–195, 206
Hart, Major 61
Hartford Hurricanes 105
Hartman, Sid 19, 21, 83, 110–111
Hassett, Billy 12, 43, 75, 91, 103, 144, 184
Hatchett, Bucky 189, 198
Hawkins, Marshall 18, 90–91, 110, 114
Hayman, Lew 73
Haynes, Marques 138, 197, 202–203
Healey Motors 151
Heft, Arnold 168
Henderson, Dr. Edwin B. 61, 98
Henry, Bill 71, 133, 135, 144, 158, 162
Hermsen, Kleggie 24, 45, 47, 54, 71, 78–79, 114, 135, 153, 164, 194, 196, 208
Hertzberg, Sonny 4, 21, 69, 81, 87, 111, 149
Hilgemann, Jim 26
Hillhouse, Art 121
Hinkle, Tony 170
Hoffman, Paul 28, 46–47, 90, 95, 104–105, 118, 154
Holland, Joe 16, 90, 110, 114, 159, 164, 168–169
Holman, Nat 82, 102, 125
Holzman, Red 23, 37–39, 87, 106, 136, 140, 145, 156–157
Hudson, Roosie 57
Hunter, Harold 193–194
Hutton, Joe 82
Hyatt, Chuck 125

Iba, Hank 33, 150
Imig, Ed 124
Indianapolis Kautskys 9–11, 13–15, 27, 36, 41, 55–56, 110, 124, 195, 205
Indianapolis Olympians 3, 7–8, 12–13, 16–18, 28–29, 39–41, 54, 68–69, 74–76, 80, 90–91, 95, 97, 101, 104, 106, 109, 114–116, 119, 123, 125, 128, 131, 133–135, 137, 139–141, 143–145, 147–148, 150, 154, 156, 159, 162–164, 166, 168–169, 175–176, 185–188, 190, 192–193, 199, 205, 207
integration 9, 57–60, 66, 87, 139, 189–191, 193–198
invention of basketball 30–32
Iowa Pre-Flight Seahawks 53, 116
Irish, Ned 4, 13, 42, 49, 84–89, 112, 125–126, 175, 180, 185, 188–189, 191, 196
Isaacs, John 7, 64

Jackson, Inman 201–202
Jacobs, Glenn 150–151
James, Gene 148
Jaros, Tony 138–140, 146, 157, 161, 184, 194
Jeannette, Buddy 27, 45–47, 95, 103–105, 118, 125, 135–136, 146, 153–155, 180, 202
Jenkins, Fats 63, 197
Johnson, Arnie 75, 106, 126, 161, 163
Johnson, Ralph 69, 113, 119, 137, 153, 156, 174
Jones, Emory 29, 130–131, 175–176, 182, 185
Jones, Wah Wah 15–17, 28, 90, 95, 97, 110, 115, 137, 159, 162, 164, 166, 168–169
Jorgensen, Noble 28–29, 39, 42–43, 72, 83, 90, 92, 100, 104, 123, 145–146, 159, 164, 178, 206
Judaism 4–6, 42, 52, 87, 120–121, 201
Julian, Doggie 21, 69, 74, 81, 111–113, 122, 134, 149, 194

Kaftan, George 21, 70, 81, 101, 111–112, 134, 136, 147
Kaighn, Raymond 30, 32
Kansas City Hi-Spots 188, 208
Kaplowitz, Ralph 53
Kase, Max 86, 112
Kaselman, Cy 121
Katkaveck, Leo 118, 133, 160
Kautsky, Frank 10, 14–15
Kautz, Wibs 9
Keaney, Frank 113
Kennedy, Pat 112, 182

Index

Keogan, George 107
Kerner, Ben 23–24, 40, 89, 128–129, 170, 175–180, 185–186, 194, 206
Kerris, Jack 89, 119, 137, 163
Kiendl, Ted 100
Kimbrough, Babe 18, 91, 110, 185–186
King, Dolly 58–59, 64
King, Willie 59
Kinney, Bob 69, 81, 111, 123, 147
Kirk, Walt 44, 103, 125, 144, 206
Klier, Leo 80, 137
Klueh, Duane 102–103, 106, 133, 137
Knorek, Lee 88
Komenich, Milo 10, 27, 69, 113–114, 119, 127, 134, 145, 166, 168–171, 189, 192, 196
Korean War 208–209
Kubiak, Leo 67, 76, 94–95, 99, 195
Kudelka, Frank 78, 114
Kundla, John 21, 36, 74–75, 82–83, 85, 138, 170, 173, 177, 181–182, 184, 194
Kurland, Bob 32–35, 68, 75, 190

Lambert, Ward 11, 117
Lancaster Red Roses 40
Lapchick, Joe 64, 73, 84–85, 102, 126, 128, 134, 146, 160, 165, 168, 172, 189, 198
Lautenbach, Walt 100
Lautenschlager, Rube 124–125
Lautman, Inky 121
Lavelli, Tony 70, 139, 143, 147–149, 204
Lavoy, Bob 193
Lee Tires 51
Leede, Ed 81, 111, 139, 149
L'Estrange, Jerry 186–187
Levane, Fuzzy 44, 76, 141, 165, 168, 174, 180
Lewis, Fred 116–117
Lewis, Grady 33, 96, 131, 148–149
Lifschultz Fast Freighters 151
Liston, Emil 48
Litwack, Harry 121
Livingstone, Ron 72, 74, 97, 142–143, 146
Lloyd, Earl 193–194, 206
Loeffler, Ken 96, 99, 101, 130–131
Loendi Big Five 62–63
Lofgran, Don 193
Logan, Johnny 12, 29–30, 96, 130, 134, 153, 175–176, 192, 194–195
Louisville Aluminites 207–208
Lowery, Emmett 170

Luisetti, Hank 18–20, 58, 83, 98–99, 125, 204
Lumpp, Ray 126, 146, 190

Macauley, Ed 29, 34, 39, 68, 96, 130–131, 133–134, 136, 140, 142, 145, 148–149, 153–154, 165, 174–176, 178, 180, 189, 191, 194–195
Macknowski, Johnny 43, 141, 165, 168–169, 174, 177–184
MacMillan, Dave 194
Mahnken, John 37, 122–123, 170
Major League Baseball 6, 46, 53, 59, 130
Malanowicz, Eddie 37
Mann, Jack 124
Marsau, Chris 94, 179–180, 186–188
Marshall, George Preston 120
Martin, Bill 33
Martin, Slater 74–75, 115, 139, 166–167, 170–171, 173, 179–180, 183–184
Maughan, Ace 96, 134, 153, 192
McCracken, Jack 150–153
McDermott, Bobby 10–11, 23, 26–27, 41, 45, 65, 67, 72, 82–83, 89, 94, 104, 116–117, 184, 205
McGuire, Dick 12–13, 75, 78, 84–85, 89, 114, 126, 148, 155, 157–158, 160, 164–165, 168–169
McIntyre, Jim 32
McKinney, Bones 6, 23–24, 70–71, 97, 99, 139, 146–147, 160
McLendon, John 194
McMullen, Malcolm 97, 110, 166
McNamee, Joe 193
Meehan, Chick 59
Mehen, Dick 67, 76, 94–95, 122, 137, 155, 187, 198, 206
Mendenhall, Murray 55–56, 66–67, 108, 113, 161
Mendenhall, Murray, Jr. 56
Metropolitan Basketball League 121
Meyer, Ray 107
Miasek, Stan 53–54, 78–79, 91, 134
Midwest Basketball Conference 7, 9, 14, 26, 92–93, 202
Mikan, Ed 79, 91, 106, 136, 161, 163
Mikan, George 4, 9–11, 13, 15, 18–19, 21, 24, 28, 32–36, 38, 43, 54, 65–66, 68, 71–72, 74–75, 78–79, 82–84, 89–91, 104, 106–111, 113, 115–116, 119, 125, 127, 133, 135–136, 138–141, 144, 146, 148–149, 153–155, 157, 161, 163–167, 170–171, 173–174, 177–184, 194–195, 197–198, 202–203
Mikkelsen, Vern 29–30, 32, 35–36, 68, 74–75, 82, 109, 111, 115, 138–140, 144, 146, 148, 157, 161, 165–166, 170–171, 173–174, 177–182, 184, 196
Millikan, Bud 182
Mills, Douglas 53
Minneapolis Lakers 3, 6, 8, 11, 18–19, 21, 24–25, 29–30, 35–36, 44, 47, 54, 66, 68–69, 71, 74–75, 78–79, 82, 90–91, 95, 97, 101, 104–111, 114–116, 119, 125–126, 128, 133–136, 138–141, 143–146, 148, 150, 153–154, 156–157, 161, 164–174, 176–184, 186–189, 191–193, 196–199, 202–204
Minneapolis Sparklers 58
Minor, Dave 189, 198
Misaka, Wat 87
Mogus, Leo 15, 73, 142–143, 147, 161
Monde, Leon 62–63
Moore, Doxie 56, 59, 113, 116–117, 123, 166, 169–173, 177, 188, 195–196, 198–199, 204–206
Morris, Max 83, 100, 107, 111, 123, 134, 140, 162, 164, 206
Morstadt, Ray 93
Myers, Bob 105

Naismith, the Rev. Dr. James 30–32, 48–50, 151, 153
National Basketball League 3–15, 19, 21, 25–27, 33, 36–46, 55–60, 65–68, 72, 74–77, 83, 89, 91–94, 96, 101, 105–106, 110–112, 115–117, 122–125, 127–129, 133–134, 138, 150, 152, 155, 175, 177, 184, 186–188, 195–197, 202–205, 207
National College Basketball Tournament 48
National Football League 9, 57, 64–65, 78, 85, 120, 187, 189, 201
National Hockey League 112, 129, 157
National Invitational Tournament 34, 48–49, 58, 68, 84–85
National Professional Basketball League 186–188, 195–196, 198–199, 204–208
Navy Zoomers 34
NBA Finals 8, 91, 128, 156, 168–169, 171–185
NBA Playoffs 8, 67, 76–78, 90–91, 96–97, 99, 101, 104, 111, 113, 115–116, 119, 123, 126, 128, 131, 133–136, 138, 140–142,

145–150, 152–154, 156–185, 189
NCAA Tournament 21, 26–27, 48–49, 87, 149, 204
Negratti, Al 37
Negro league baseball 62
New Orleans Hurricanes 76
New York All-Stars 61
New York Knicks 3–6, 12–13, 19, 21, 28, 39–40, 42, 45–47, 52–53, 69–70, 73–75, 78–79, 82–89, 91, 101, 104–105, 111–112, 114–116, 118–119, 122–123, 125–126, 128, 130–131, 134–136, 138–139, 142–143, 146–149, 152, 154, 156–158, 160, 162, 164–165, 167–169, 171–172, 175–176, 180, 186–189, 191–193, 196–199, 206, 209
New York Renaissance 7, 14, 55, 57–66, 120–121, 123–124, 197, 201–202
Nichols, Jack 24, 39, 71, 79, 99, 111, 134–135, 143–144, 158–159, 162, 178
Niemiera, Richie 113–115, 145, 166, 192
Norfolk NTS Bluejackets 23
Norlander, John 23, 97, 99, 133, 139, 147
Nostrand, George 3, 73, 81, 91, 114, 153
Noszka, Stan 6
Novak, Mike 9, 41, 116, 125, 146
Nucatola, John 179, 183

Oakland Bittners 19, 35, 189–191, 196, 198
O'Brien, John 102
O'Connell, Dermie 111, 123, 192
O'Donnell, Andy 118
O'Keefe, Dick 22, 99, 160
Oklahoma City Parks 33
Oldham, John 74, 80, 137, 161, 163
Olsen, Harold 14, 47–49, 52–54, 71, 78
Olympian Athletic League 61
Olympic Games 15–17, 33–34, 48, 78, 84, 190–191
Omaha NPBL franchise 188, 199, 205, 207–208
Original Celtics 7, 14, 27, 63–64, 82, 84, 120–121
O'Shea, Kevin 193
Oshkosh All-Stars 7–8, 10–11, 18, 25, 27, 56–58, 64, 71, 80, 92–94, 99–101, 116–117, 122, 124–125, 129, 141, 188, 195, 202, 207
Oshkosh Stars 101
Otten, Don 11, 32–33, 40, 42–43, 58, 77–78, 91, 125, 134–135, 137, 141, 144, 157–158, 160, 194, 197, 207
Otten, Mac 43, 68, 96, 192
Owens, Jim 43, 103, 145, 158–159, 169, 192

Pacific Coast League 123
Pan American Games 196
Parham, Easy 96, 192
Passon, Chick 120
Passon, Harry 120–121
Patrick, Stan 94–95, 107–108, 132, 164
Payak, Johnny 99, 152, 195
Pelkington, Jake 27, 45
Perkins, Warren 43, 91, 125, 144, 158
Peterson, Ed 133, 141, 144, 159, 165, 173–174
Peyton, Tony 57
Phelan, Jack 83–84, 100
Philadelphia Sphas 4, 6, 120–121
Philadelphia Warriors 3, 6, 18, 21–23, 46, 52–53, 66, 68–69, 72, 74, 78, 81, 84, 88, 90–92, 95, 97, 99, 101, 104, 111, 113, 115, 118–119, 121–122, 124, 128, 131–136, 139, 142–143, 146–150, 152–156, 159–162, 175–176, 186–188, 191–192, 195–196
Phillip, Andy 53–54, 78, 96, 114, 126, 134, 155–156, 164, 208
Phillips Oilers 15, 33–35, 51, 75, 151–153, 190–191, 196
Pieri, Lou 206–207
Pittsburgh Ironmen 5–6, 28–29, 87
Pittsburgh Raiders 55, 133
Podoloff, Maurice 3–4, 11–12, 45–46, 56, 70, 73, 86, 88–89, 105, 128–129, 175–180, 186, 188, 195–196, 198–199, 204, 206
Pollard, Jim 18–21, 36, 54, 68, 74, 82, 104–105, 107, 109–111, 115, 136, 138–140, 146, 155, 157, 161, 164–167, 170, 172–174, 178–184, 190, 202
Posewitz, Tony 124
Posey, Cumberland 62–63
Potter, Roger 23, 122, 144, 205
Pressley, Babe 202–203
Price, Bernie 57, 202
Professional Basketball League of America 9–12, 19, 21, 29, 56–57, 76, 83, 92, 111
Providence Steamrollers 12–13, 21, 73, 105–106, 131, 207
Pugh, Les 105
Pullins, Runt 199
Purnhage, Perk 108, 122
Putman, Don 96, 192

racism 58, 63–65, 87, 171, 190–191, 199–200
Rash, Joe 135, 180, 185
Ratkovicz, George 133, 137, 139, 141, 144, 159–161, 165, 168–169, 172–174, 180–181, 183–184
Ray, Don 77, 144, 162, 207
Rehfeldt, Don 175, 187–188, 193, 195, 204
Reiser, Chick 46–47, 71, 99, 103, 133, 137, 160
Renick, Cab 34–35
Rhodes, Lenny 198
Ricks, Pappy 63
Riebe, Mel 5, 27
Risen, Arnie 4, 10, 14–15, 36, 39, 42, 49, 68, 75, 79, 91, 106, 113, 126–127, 135–136, 140–141, 144–145, 157, 161, 163, 205
Ritter, Goebel 126, 168
Roberts, Bill 96, 192
Roberts, Glenn 22
Robinson, Ermer 138, 202–203
Robinson, Jackie (amateur basketball player) 190
Robinson, Jackie (professional baseball player) 59, 200
Rocha, Red 29, 68, 96, 134, 136, 148, 153, 176, 189, 191
Rochester Royals 3, 6, 8, 10–12, 15, 27, 36–42, 44–45, 56, 58, 65, 68, 75–76, 79, 87, 90–91, 94, 97, 104–106, 108, 110–111, 113–114, 116, 118–119, 124, 126–128, 133, 135–137, 140, 144–145, 147, 149–150, 153–154, 156–157, 161, 163, 176, 186–188, 190, 192–193, 196, 199, 202, 204–205
Rolfe, Red 130
Rollins, Kenny 15–16, 114, 207
Rosenblum, Max 120
Roth, Carl 124–125
Royer, Bobby 21
Rucker, John 198
Rupp, Adolph 14, 17, 22, 100, 109–110, 190
Russell, Honey 46, 73, 113, 194

Sadowski, Ed 27, 68, 72–74, 90, 95, 104, 113, 154–155, 202
Sailors, Kenny 21–22, 27, 44, 53, 69, 76, 80, 102, 106, 111, 114, 135, 137, 142, 145, 152, 155, 187, 198
St. Christopher Club 61
St. Louis Bombers 3, 6, 12, 29–30, 36, 39, 68, 74, 81, 84, 88, 96–97, 99, 101, 104, 108–109, 115, 119, 123, 128, 130–134, 136, 138, 140, 142, 145–149, 153–154, 174–180, 182, 185, 188–189, 191–192, 195, 198–199, 208

Index

St. Mary's Pre-Flight 19
St. Paul Lights 188, 196, 207–208
Saitch, Eyre 123
Salesian Boys Club of San Francisco 98
San Francisco Dons 19
San Francisco Olympic Club 151
Saperstein, Abe 66, 102, 195, 197–204, 207–208
Saul, Pep 161
Sbarbaro, John 50–51, 54, 91, 134, 138, 193
Schaefer, Herman 26–27, 55, 74–75, 138–139, 157, 161
Schatzman, Marv 105
Schaus, Fred 28, 74, 79, 137, 147, 155–156, 161, 163, 165–166
Schayes, Adolph 42–43, 66, 75–76, 87, 97, 110, 118, 133, 137, 139, 141, 144, 152, 154–155, 159–160, 162, 164–165, 168–169, 172–174, 177–184
Schectman, Ossie 3–4, 6, 58, 121
Schmidt, Ernest 150–151
Schnittker, Dick 187–188, 193
Schoon, Milt 72, 100, 109, 111, 147
Schultz, Howie 55–56, 59, 66–67, 69, 113, 116, 119, 137, 156, 161, 165–166, 196
Schulz, Dick 46–47, 73, 103, 111, 113, 116
Schwartz, Butch 121
Scolari, Fred 4, 6, 20, 23, 97–99, 111, 139, 142, 147, 149, 157–158, 160
Seattle Athletics 123
See, Wayne 94–95
Seltz, Rollie 44, 55–56, 192
Seminoff, Jim 149
Senesky, George 69, 115, 142–143, 148–149, 162
service league basketball 19, 22–23, 34, 37, 53, 77, 98, 100, 116, 142–143
Seymour, Paul 44, 76, 97, 118, 141, 162, 169, 172–173, 178–184
Shaeffer, Carl 110, 114, 137, 168
Shannon, Howie 21, 69, 111, 139
Share, Chuck 152, 174–175, 186, 188–189, 193–195, 198
Sharkey, Steve 116
Sheboygan Redskins 3, 7, 9, 11–12, 21, 27–29, 37, 39, 41–45, 54, 57, 67–69, 72, 74, 81, 83–84, 93, 97, 100, 103–104, 106, 108–109, 111, 113, 115–118, 122–125, 128, 131, 133–135, 140, 146–148, 154, 156, 159, 162–164, 166, 175–180, 186–188, 195–196, 202, 205–208

Sheeks, Paul 14, 184
Shelton, Everett 151–152
Shipp, Charley 27, 92–95, 97, 103, 108, 155, 177
Sidat-Singh, Wilmeth 64–65
Simmons, Connie 46–47, 75, 79, 84, 90, 116, 126, 146–147, 157–158, 160, 164, 168, 189
Smart Set Athletic Club 61
Smawley, Belus 30, 96, 130, 133, 140, 153, 175–176, 192
Smiley, Jack 67–68, 83, 108, 152, 195
Smith, Willie 7, 57, 64
Sobek, George 100, 132–133, 147, 159, 164
Soell, Bob 131, 175–176, 179, 182
Sokody, Paul 124
South Side Germans 194
Southern Kansas Stage Lines 151
Spartan Field Club 41
Spears, Odie 54, 78–79, 114, 134, 161, 164, 207–208
Spector, Art 149
Stagg, Amos Alonzo 49–50
Stanczak, Ed 44, 55, 134, 145, 162, 166, 171, 192
Stebbins, James 31
Stewart, Flucie 170
street ball 13, 46
Strong, Ted 57, 201–202
Stump, Gene 75
Stutz, Stan 4, 44–45
Suesens, Kenny 42, 100, 117, 123, 132, 159
Sutphin, Al 112, 129
Syracuse Nationals 3, 7–8, 21, 24, 27–28, 40–44, 54, 56–57, 59, 69, 74–76, 84, 87, 91–92, 97, 99, 104, 108–109, 115–116, 118, 125–126, 128, 133–135, 137–141, 144, 148, 150, 152, 154–156, 159–162, 164–165, 167–169, 171–174, 176–184, 186–188, 190, 192–193
Syracuse Reds 202

Tanenbaum, Sid 47
Tatum, Goose 138, 197, 202–203
Taube, Mel 170
Taylor, Chuck 77
Taylor, Harry 194
territorial pick 29–30, 152, 174–175, 185, 192, 195
Thornton, Walter 57
Todorovich, Mike 68, 77–78, 103, 106, 122, 125, 135, 142, 144, 158, 162
Toledo Jeeps 11, 57, 66–67, 76, 94, 100, 105
Toledo NPBL franchise 188, 199, 204, 208

Toledo White Chevrolets 9, 57, 195
Toomay, Jack 21, 80, 106, 147
Torgoff, Irv 6, 121
Toronto Huskies 3, 45, 73
Tough, Bob 95, 108
Towery, Carlisle 26–28, 95, 104–105, 143, 146
Trenton Tigers 45, 121
Tri-Cities Blackhawks 3–4, 7, 9, 11–12, 23–24, 40–44, 54–55, 57–59, 66–68, 75–78, 81, 83, 89, 91–92, 97, 99, 101, 103–106, 109, 111, 114, 116–119, 122–123, 125, 128, 131, 133–135, 138, 142–145, 150, 152, 154, 156, 158–159, 162–163, 170, 175–178, 182, 185–188, 191–195, 197, 205–207
Tri-Council Caseys 120
Troy Trojans 184
Tucker, Gerald 33
Tyrrell, Peter A. 121

Uline, Mike 24, 97–98, 135, 141
Ulm, Bob 19
U.S Men's National Basketball Team 15–17, 33–35, 48, 78, 84, 151, 190, 196
U.S. Tires 92

van Breda Kolff, Bill 126
Vance, Gene 91, 103, 125, 140, 144, 152, 158
Vandeweghe, Ernie 84, 89, 125–126, 146, 148, 157, 160, 169
Volker, Floyd 80, 103, 106, 137
Von Nieda, Whitey 3, 40, 43, 91, 103, 118, 144

Wager, Clint 161
Wagner, Danny 43
Walk, Paul 15
Walker, Brady 81, 112, 122, 149
Walther, Paul 75, 91, 145, 164, 166
Walthour, Rabbit 206
Wanzer, Bobby 38–39, 75, 79, 83, 105, 126–127, 136, 145, 153, 157, 161, 163
Ward, Norris 10
Washington Bears 58–59, 64–66
Washington Capitols 3, 6, 13, 21–24, 39, 46–47, 52, 68, 70–72, 78–79, 86, 95, 97–99, 103–104, 108, 111, 115–116, 118, 122, 128, 131, 133–135, 137, 139, 141–142, 146–147, 149, 153–154, 156–158, 160, 176, 183, 186–188, 190, 192–194, 199, 206–207
Waterloo Hawks 3, 7, 54, 56,

Index

67–69, 72, 76–77, 83, 87, 91–92, 94–95, 97, 99–101, 103–104, 108, 111, 114, 116, 119, 122, 125, 128, 131–133, 137, 140, 143, 146–147, 152, 154, 175–180, 186–188, 193, 195–196, 198, 205–208
Waterloo Pro-Hawks 29, 92
Waterloo Rockets 108
Wendt, Bill 107
Wertis, Ray 73
White, Maurice 9–10, 57
Whiting Ciesars 202
Whitty, Johnny 184
Whiz Kids (University of Illinois) 53, 67, 78, 91
Wichita Henrys 150

Wier, Murray 11–12, 103, 122, 125, 142, 144, 152, 177–178, 206
Wilcutt, D.C. 192
Wilkes-Barre Barons 205
Wilmington Blue Bombers 72
Winter, Max 35, 139
Wirtz, Arthur 129
Wisconsin State League 101
Wolfe, Red 121
Wooden, Johnny 14, 92, 116, 170
World Professional Basketball Tournament 7, 25, 55, 58–59, 64, 66, 72, 197, 202
World War II 9, 12, 14, 17, 19, 21–23, 26–28, 33–34, 37, 40, 45–46, 49, 51, 53, 58, 65, 67, 71, 77, 85–86, 89, 92, 98, 100, 105, 110, 116, 124–125, 138, 142–143, 152, 197, 204
Wright Kittyhawks 37, 77

Yardley, George 193
Young Men's Christian Association 30, 32, 48–49
Youngstown Bears 5, 59

Zaslofsky, Max 4, 24, 52–54, 75, 78, 85, 87, 91, 114, 134, 140, 147, 154–155, 164, 208
Ziegenfuss, George 19
Zollner, Fred 25–26, 28, 185
Zummach, Frank 124

www.ingramcontent.com/pod-product-compliance
Lightning Source LLC
Chambersburg PA
CBHW060340010526
44117CB00017B/2907